# Life Stories

## Exploring Issues in Educational History Through Biography

# Life Stories

## Exploring Issues in Educational History Through Biography

**Edited by**

**Linda C. Morice and Laurel Puchner**
***Southern Illinois University Edwardsville***

IAP

**Information Age Publishing, Inc.**
Charlotte, North Carolina • www.infoagepub.com

**Library of Congress Cataloging-in-Publication Data**

CIP data for this book can be found on the Library of Congress website
http://www.loc.gov/index.html

**Paperback:** 978-1-62396-490-0
**Hardcover:** 978-1-62396-491-7
**E-Book:** 978-1-62396-492-4



Printed in the United States of America

# CONTENTS

# PREFACE

**Linda C. Morice and Laurel Puchner**

*Life Stories: Exploring Issues in Educational History Through Biography* grew out of the 2012 conference of the International Society for Educational Biography (ISEB) in St. Louis, MO. At the meeting, ISEB Executive Committee members discussed ways of commemorating the 30th anniversary of an organization with a rich history. ISEB was founded in 1983 at Iowa State University when L. Glenn Smith invited colleagues to participate in an educational biography conference. Smith proposed publishing the conference proceedings in a new journal called *Vitae Scholasticae: The Bulletin of Educational Biography*. Over the years, *Vitae Scholasticae* evolved from a bulletin to a refereed journal published once a year, to a biannual journal with a blind peer review process. Today *Vitae* features a variety of methodological approaches to studying educators' lives, and its editorial advisory board includes scholars from North America, Europe, and Australia. Given the staying power of ISEB and its journal, members of the executive committee felt the 30th anniversary could best be marked by an edited book with selected articles from *Vitae*.

As editors of *Vitae Scholasticae*, we looked for articles that clustered around important questions in the lives of educators. We found them in the writing of educational historians whose published essays in *Vitae* merit the attention of scholars and practitioners alike. Perhaps most important, the articles we chose for *Life Stories* illustrate the important contributions that biographers and historians can make to each other's work.

We thank the ISEB for providing, over a period of 3 decades, what former president Lucy E. Bailey calls "generative spaces to explore diverse

*Life Stories: Exploring Issues in Educational History Through Biography*
pp. vii–viii

interactions among lives and education that have expanded the contours of educational research."[1] In particular, we thank members who submitted manuscripts to *Vitae* and who reviewed submissions to aid us in the selection process and provide helpful feedback to both established and emerging scholars. Finally, we thank the authors of the 13 essays in this volume for their exemplary scholarship. We hope the essays in this anniversary publication will encourage more people to "expand the contours" of an interesting field of research.

## NOTE

1. Lucy E. Bailey, "Auto/biography in Educational Contexts," *Vitae Scholasticae 30*(1), 5.

# INTRODUCTION

**Linda C. Morice and Laurel Puchner**

Barbara Finkelstein wrote that for the educational historian, biographical studies are not just individual chronicles.

> Taken together ... [t]hey provide a documentary context within which to judge the relative power of material and ideological circumstances, the meaning of education policy, the utility of schooling, the definition of literacy and the relationship between teaching and learning and policy and practice."[1]

It is with this recognition that we present 13 essays, each of which offers perspective on at least one of four key questions that have long drawn scholarly attention: What should schools teach? Who gets to decide? How should educators adapt to a changing world to provide opportunity for all students? How should educators' experiences be interpreted for future audiences?

*Life Stories: Exploring Issues in Educational History Through Biography* commemorates the thirtieth anniversary of the International Society for Educational Biography and of its journal, *Vitae Scholasticae.* As editors of the journal, we have been privileged to work with scholars who research and write about people who shape the future by teaching others. The essays, all of which have appeared in *Vitae Scholasticae*, are set in a variety of educational environments that span 174 years. The essays appear as individual chapters and are organized into four parts.

Part I, "The Scope and Nature of Education," addresses the "what" of teaching, a subject of discussion in the United States from colonial times

*Life Stories: Exploring Issues in Educational History Through Biography*
pp. ix–xiv

to the present.[2] Part I presents three contexts in which historical figures addressed what schools should teach. Chapter 1 explores the scope and nature of Black education, a subject well documented by Anderson,[3] Lewis,[4] Norrell,[5] and Smock,[6] particularly in their presentations of the views of Booker T. Washington and W.E.B. DuBois. However, Carol B. Conaway shows that during the Antebellum period—long before Washington and DuBois aired their famous differences—Frederick Douglass and Mary Ann Shadd Cary disagreed on the relative merits of job training versus an intellectual education for Black students. Finkelstein stressed the importance of understanding the "material and ideological circumstances" under which biographical figures acted, and Conaway illustrates these circumstances for Douglass and Shadd Cary, and eventually Washington and DuBois. In Chapter 2, Bart Dredge further contextualizes the idea of education-as-training by studying schools for children of White mill workers in South Carolina. Many educational historians have explored efforts to promote what Finkelstein calls "the utility of schooling"[7] as, for example, in Herbert M. Kliebard's discussion of vocational education in the seminal work, *The Struggle for the American Curriculum, 1893–1958*.[8] However, Dredge's description of Lawrence Peter Hollis and the way the mill used schools in the Parker District provides an alarming and detailed example of schools serving a purely corporate agenda. The final chapter in Part 1 supports an expansive view of education by illustrating how a policy of academic freedom helped to mitigate against expressions of racial hostility during Black poet Langston Hughes' Depression-era visit to the University of North Carolina. In this chapter, authors Bart Dredge and Cayce Tabor give readers a context for what Finkelstein calls "the meaning of educational policy" as well as "the relationship between teaching and learning and policy and practice."[9]

Part II explores what Finkelstein calls "relative power" and the contexts in which it is used to advance an educational agenda.[10] According to historian Joel Spring, the U.S. education system has long been characterized by the interplay of bureaucrats, interest groups, elected officials, and knowledge brokers who try to promote their own self-interests; this interaction occurs in a climate of expectation in which individuals and groups look to schools to help meet their needs and goals.[11] In Part II, the types of political forces observed by Spring are contextualized in three historical examples of advancement of an educational agenda. In Chapter 4, Jared R. Stallones introduces readers to two Texas school leaders during the late nineteenth and early twentieth centuries. Laurine C. Anderson (Principal of Prairie Normal Institute) and Edward L. Blackshear (Superintendent of Colored Schools in Austin) discovered that they needed to become skilled politicians to procure adequate funding for their Black students. Although they regarded themselves as educators rather than politicians, the circumstances in which the two men found themselves required them to play both roles. In Chapter 5, Edward A. Janak presents John Eldred Swearingen, who lost his sight at age 13. Although his disability made him a member of a marginalized group, Swearingen gained agency through his election as South Carolina's State Superintendent of Education. He went on to advance educational opportunity for children in the state, regardless of disability, race, or socioeconomic status. Chapter 6, "Correspondence Study and the 'Crime of the Century': Helen Williams, Nathan Leopold, and the Stateville Correspondence School," presents unlikely figures who advanced an educational agenda from inside the walls of an Illinois state prison. Von Pittman details how convicted murderer Nathan Leopold worked through officials in the Illinois penal system and with a little-known administrator at the State University of Iowa Bureau of Correspondence Study to create a statewide secondary education program for incarcerated adults whom Illinois had previously ignored. As the *de facto* director of the Stateville Correspondence School (knowledge of which was kept from the press), Leopold not only realized an educational vision but improved the quality of his prison life by achieving personal goals such as having sweet rolls delivered to his cell each morning and having access to an office with a washroom and shower.

Part III deals with the question, "How should educators adapt to a changing world to provide opportunity for all students?" Finkelstein contended that biography provides an opportunity to envision new educational possibilities as well as to observe the nature of social change.[12] While she pointed to the biography of reformer Horace Mann as one example, educational historians have created other lenses through which to study promulgators of new ideas, as in Sam F. Stack's biography of progressive educator Elsie Ripley Clapp[13] and Kate Rousmaniere's biography of teacher leader Margaret Haley.[14] In Chapter 7 of this volume, John F. Wakefield portrays the life of educational leader John Milton Gregory to illustrate how the new idea of democratic education spread throughout the United States during the nineteenth century. Democratic education was promoted by evangelical millennialists like Gregory, but eventually his views became outdated because he was unable to adapt to a changing world in which public education was progressive but not religious. In the next chapter, Andrea Walton describes how scientist and reformer Christine Ladd-Franklin tried to break down gender barriers in higher education. During her life (1847–1930), Ladd-Franklin set an example of a distinguished lecturer and excellent scholar, an effort she hoped would stir the consciences of Columbia University men and allow the advancement of women on campus and in the academy. Another strategy for a woman educational reformer is seen in Chapter 9, as Lynne Tretheway details the work of Australian Lucy Spence Morice

(1859–1951). Trethewey discusses Morice's use of informal social ties, as well as progressive professional networks, to effect reforms through citizen education and collective, non-party political activism. Part III ends with "George S. Counts: Leading Social Reconstructionist." Author Bruce Romanish looks at the life of an educational luminary who, in the depths of the Great Depression, wrote *Dare the School Build a New Social Order?* The chapter gives context to Counts' work as a social reconstructionist and leading scholar at Teachers College at Columbia University.

Part IV addresses the question, "How should educators' experiences be interpreted for future audiences?" In discussing this issue, Finkelstein contended that biography can contribute to educational history by correcting "a persistent fallacy in historical reasoning." She wrote that historians have a "tendency to promulgate interpretive schemes or sense-making myths" that reveal historical developments and social change while deemphasizing "both human agency and historical processes."[15] Finkelstein argued, "No matter how grand or elegant or how evocative or compelling their schemes, grand historical interpretations never become complex enough to integrate the whole of history."[16] In Chapter 11, A. J. Angulo contends with the issue of historical interpretation by examining the relationship between biography and history, juxtaposed against the life story of scientist William Barton Rogers (1804–1882), the conceptual founder of Massachusetts Institute of Technology. Angulo urges biographers and historians to be mindful of the relationships that exist between their respective fields. Biographers should understand the need to read the historical scholarship relating to a particular life, and historians should know that sweeping scholarly claims don't always align to the lives of individuals. In Chapter 12, Kay Whitehead illustrates the problem of fitting educators' lives into broad categories or interpretations. Whitehead discusses the difficulty of assigning a national identity that encompasses the national and international prominence of Lillian de Lissa, principal of the Gipsy Hill Training College in England. De Lissa was born in colonial New South Wales which, by the time her career began, made her a citizen of the newly federated Australia. She was a British subject by virtue of Australia's membership in the British Empire, and traveled extensively in Europe and the United States. She lived in England for 50 years until her death in 1967. Whitehead shows that de Lissa's national identity was never fixed; rather, it was constructed in context. Finally, in Chapter 13, Lucy E. Bailey discusses the challenges of accurately portraying the life of a single historical figure in "Necessary Betrayals: Reflections on Biographical Work with a Racist Ancestor." Bailey reminds readers that biographies are not always heroic narratives. She cautions that the biographical genre "welcomes subjects cast in a romantic glow.... Yet our connections to the past are constructed, complex, and fraught with darkness as well as light."[17]

We hope these essays, taken together, will demonstrate the important contributions biography can make to educational history. Whether the subject is what to teach, who makes educational decisions, how schools change, or how educators' lives are interpreted, biography can serve as a powerful lens for educational historians. In Finkelstein's words, "Biography is to history what a telescope is to the stars."[18] May *Life Stories* provide insights that will stimulate your scholarly work in ways that will benefit both biography and educational history!

## NOTES

1. Barbara Finkelstein, "Revealing Human Agency: The Uses of Biography in the Study of Educational History," in Craig Kridel, ed., *Writing Educational Biography: Explorations in Qualitative Research* (New York: Garland Publishing, 1998), 59.
2. Joel Spring, *The American School, A Global Context: From the Puritans to the Obama Administration.* (New York: McGraw-Hill, 2011).
3. James D. Anderson, *The Education of Blacks in the South, 1860–1935.* (Chapel Hill: University of North Carolina Press, 1988).
4. David Levering Lewis, *W.E. B. DuBois: Biography of a Race, 1868–1919* (New York: Owl Books, 1994): David Levering Lewis, *W. E. B. DuBois: The Fight for Equality and the American Century, 1919–1963.* (New York: Owl Books, 2001).
5. Robert J. Norrell, *Up From History, the Life of Booker T. Washington* (Cambridge: Belknap Press, 2011).
6. Raymond W. Smock, *Booker T. Washington: Black Leadership in the Age of Jim Crow.* (Chicago: Ivan R. Dee, 2009).
7. Finkelstein, 59.
8. Herbert M. Kliebard, *The Struggle for the American Curriculum, 1893–1958.* (New York: Routledge, 1986).
9. Finkelstein, 59.
10. Finkelstein, 59.
11. Joel Spring, *Political Agendas for Education: From the Religious Right to the Green Party,* 2nd ed. (Mahwah, N. J.: Lawrence Erlbaum Associates, 2002; Joel Spring, *Conflicts of Interests: The Politics of American Education.* (New York: Longman, 1988).
12. Finkelstein, 46.
13. Sam F. Stack, *Elsie Ripley Clapp (1879–1965): Her Life and the Community School* (New York: Peter Lang, 2004).
14. Kate Rousmaniere, *Citizen Teacher: The Life and Leadership of Margaret Haley* (Albany: SUNY Press, 205).
15. Finkelstein, 58.
16. Finkelstein, 59.

17. Lucy E.Bailey, "Necessary Betrayals: Reflections on Biographical Work on a Racist Ancestory," *Vitae Scholasticae, 26* (1): 113.
18. Finkelstein, 45.

# PART I

## THE SCOPE AND NATURE OF EDUCATION

CHAPTER 1

# RACIALLY INTEGRATED EDUCATION

## The Antebellum Thought of Mary Ann Shadd Cary and Frederick Douglass

**Carol B. Conaway**

Approximately 100 years before the landmark case *Brown versus Board of Education of Topeka* (1954), in which the U.S. Supreme Court ruled that segregated schools were unconstitutional, two Black activist-journalists, Mary Ann Shadd Cary and Frederick Douglass, published articles advocating racially integrated education. While they agreed that such schools constituted the ideal educational setting for Black students, they disagreed on the type of education these students should acquire. Their differing ideas were shaped by the complex relationships of gender, race, and class in antebellum African American and Afro Canadian communities. Their views of these relationships are reflected in the curricula they proposed for racially integrated schools. This essay explores the contours and complexities of their lives and their thoughts on Black education as revealed between 1852 and 1857 in their abolitionist newspapers, the *Provincial Freeman* and *Frederick Douglass' Paper.*[1]

*Life Stories: Exploring Issues in Educational History Through Biography*
pp. 3–21

Shadd Cary, editor of the *Provincial Freeman* (1854–1861), published her newspaper in what is now the province of Ontario, Canada. Douglass published his from 1851 to 1860 in Rochester, New York. The *Provincial Freeman* was the first newspaper Shadd Cary owned and edited, though many of her letters to the editor, as well as a small pamphlet, had been published in the newspapers of Douglass and other African Americans. Douglass had significant journalistic experience before founding the *Frederick Douglasss' Paper.* From 1847 to 1851, he published a Black abolitionist weekly called the *North Star.* Shadd Cary and Douglass well understood the power of the press in developing an awareness of the issues and in fostering debates and social progress for Black people on both sides of the Canadian-American border.

Most Black male and female activists spoke and wrote about the responsibility of their race to raise itself from poverty to prosperity and to move from slavery and its devastating consequences to middle-class status and its entitlements. Black community leaders stressed that education, strong moral values, honest labor, thrift, and so forth would change the myths that Whites had about Blacks' inferiority. Essentially, this meant the ascent from ignorance to literacy. Shadd Cary and Douglass were also strong advocates for the advancement of Black people through self-help, which largely meant changing Blacks' social and economic status through education. They agreed that racially integrated education would promote racial uplift, but why did they disagree on school curricula? The response to that question is apparent when their differing biographies are considered in conjunction with the sexism, racism, and classism that confronted both individuals.

## THE FORMATIVE YEARS OF SHADD CARY

Mary Ann Camberton Shadd Cary (1823–1893) was an African American/ Afro Canadian woman born into a multiple-race, middle class family in Wilmington, Delaware. The Shadds were staunch abolitionists, and their home was a *stop* on the Underground Railroad. Shadd Cary, despite her light skin color and class, was denied an education in Delaware because of her race and gender. Seeing no way to educate their eldest daughter in Delaware, the Shadds moved to West Chester, Pennsylvania, near Philadelphia, when Shadd Cary was ten years old. At the time Black children were not admitted to West Chester's 11 public schools, but Shadd Cary was given a private education for six years by Quakers at Miss Phoebe Darlington's school.[2] According to biographer and historian Jane Rhodes, she very likely received instruction in religion and philosophy, literature, writing, basic mathematics, Latin and French, the mechanical arts, and the values of the Society of Friends.[3] When her formal education ended, Shadd Cary left the Philadelphia area to teach in a school for Black children in Delaware, and later taught in schools in Black areas of Pennsylvania, New Jersey, and New York City.

Throughout her childhood and adolescence, Shadd Cary also received a great deal of political education from her parents, particularly her father, Abraham Shadd. The Shadds were members of the Philadelphia-area Black elite—a circle that later helped to support Shadd Cary with fundraising events for her newspaper. Abraham Shadd was a widely respected and influential Black community leader. He attended numerous antislavery meetings and conventions during the 1840s, and often took his daughter with him. While there, he urged Shadd Cary to speak publicly regarding Black liberation and to voice her criticisms of Black leaders.[4] Very few women attended these events, and those who did were mostly silent. Shadd Cary took the floor to publicly debate men or deliver impassioned speeches on the failure of Black leadership to inspire middle-class Blacks to imitate the positive traits of middle-class Whites.[5]

Toward the end of the 1840s, Shadd and his daughter turned their attention to the emigrationist movement. Black emigrationists, the majority of whom were separatists in the 1840s, argued that the only way for Blacks to liberate themselves fully was to leave "the racist Yankee republic" and settle in another country in North America, Latin America, the Caribbean, or Africa.[6] Increasingly pessimistic about any possibility of Black liberation and racial integration in the United States, the Shadd family thought that emigration to Canada represented the best opportunity for Blacks. English was Canada's primary spoken language. Canada's climate resembled that of the northern United States, and the country offered rich farmland and virginal forests. Most importantly, Blacks had been free in Canada since 1833, when slavery was abolished across the British Commonwealth.

Initially, there was much African American resistance to emigration. However, the passage of the federal Fugitive Slave Law of 1850 in the United States changed their opposition. The new legislation stipulated that runaway slaves, if caught, had to be returned to their owners. The chilling implication of the Fugitive Slave Law was that even free Black persons in the North might be subject to arrest and extradition to the South.[7] Realizing that the very public Shadds were likely to be arrested and sent to the South, Shadd Cary and her brother crossed the border into Canada in 1852. Other family members followed later.

As a recently arrived émigré, Shadd Cary sought introductions to the Black leadership. At one social event, she met Henry Bibb and his wife, Mary. The Bibbs were abolitionist activists and the editors of a Black newspaper called the *Voice of the Fugitive*. Impressed by Shadd Cary, they invited her to teach school in Windsor, Canada. She accepted their offer and began teaching in a very small school for the children of Black refugees from the American South.

Shortly thereafter, the American Missionary Society (AMA) offered Shadd Cary the opportunity to open her own school in Chatham, Canada West. Soon after she had settled there, however, she began an intense ideological campaign against the Bibbs, the AMA, and the Refugee Home Society (RHS). The RHS was a group comprising the Bibbs and other members of the Black Canadian male establishment who advocated and/or provided charity for fugitives from the United States. Shadd Cary contended that the AMA focused the sights of Blacks on heaven and overlooked the reality of their lives on earth. She accused the RHS of fostering the mentality of *begging* (her term for accepting charity) when it provided poor refugees with food, clothing, and shelter after their arrival from America. In letters to the Bibbs' newspaper, the *Voice of the Fugitive*, Shadd Cary accused both the AMA and the RHS of catering to the slave mentality developed by those who were owned by White Christians. She argued that these organizations should be demanding that the new arrivals become independent as quickly as possible. She believed that White citizens would never respect or accept former slaves if they were living on charity.

Shadd Cary deemed the Black separatists' campaign for racially segregated education and settlements in Canada West far worse than advocating the acceptance of charity. As opponents of integrated education, Henry Bibb and other separatists argued that Black, racially exclusive education in all-Black Canadian settlements was the best antislavery weapon Blacks could wield. They believed that Black success with no help or interference from Whites would provide indisputable evidence of Black self-reliance and achievement for skeptical Whites, including those who were members of the Colonizationist Movement. Colonizationist Movement members such as Harriet Beecher Stowe (author of *Uncle Tom's Cabin*) wanted to repatriate Blacks to Liberia.[8]

As an assimilationist, Shadd Cary promulgated the opposite position. She argued vehemently that Blacks could overcome the arguments of White racists only through self-help and rapid assimilation into White Canadian society.[9] She believed that Blacks and Whites would benefit from being exposed to each other, because only exposure would guarantee each race's appreciation of and respect for the other. As Shirley J. Yee (1997) notes, "[Shadd Cary] denounced racial separatism in any form, which challenged both segregationist practices in the larger society and Black nationalist views about how the Black community should be constructed."[10]

The Bibbs, in turn, considered Shadd Cary a public disgrace and a nuisance for her attacks on the Black male establishment. She had transgressed gender boundaries by stepping into a male-dominated public sphere.[11] The Black male establishment and even some Black women denounced Shadd Cary for conduct considered *improper* for a Black woman and member of the Black elite, because she had a particular set of ideas and assumptions that were middle-class, reformist, and Christian.[12]

When Shadd Cary realized that the Bibbs' *Voice of the Fugitive* was censoring her letters to the editor, if they published them at all, she decided to found her own newspaper. She closed her school at the end of December, 1852. In March of the next year, she announced in a prospectus that she and her highly respected associates, the Reverend Samuel Ringgold Ward and Alexander McArthur, would publish the *Provincial Freeman*. The first issue of her weekly broadsheet was published in March 1854.[13] While the publication was primarily an abolitionist newspaper, it also dealt with issues such as temperance, immigration, the conditions of slaves, and current events. Shadd Cary acknowledged herself only as "publishing agent," but the Afro Canadian and African American communities knew that she was the newspaper's editor, which failed to improve her standing in either community.

With regard to her activism on behalf of integration, Shadd Cary worked assiduously to insert herself into the male world of political leadership. Shirley J. Yee interprets Shadd Cary's vision of *integration* as being two-fold: encompassing both racial and gender integration. Her concept of integration was as much about her securing a place for herself in the movement as it was about finding a safe haven for fugitive Blacks.[14] By and large, it was easier to find a new geographical location for Blacks than it was for her to be accepted as an equal by the Black male leadership of Canada West.

Shadd Cary was able to engage in the Black male public conversation regarding integrated or segregated education, because she was a liminal figure in the male-dominated Afro Canadian society.[15] Female self-assertion lay outside the boundaries of appropriate behavior for a Black woman in the 1850s, but Shadd Cary was not consciously self-limited or socially limited by traditional gender roles. She ignored social boundaries and she no longer cared about power and privilege, role, status, law, or institutions. Groomed for leadership since her early childhood, Shadd Cary assumed a dominant position in the community. She stood on principle and courageously pursued life as an activist working solely for the good of the community. Her father's tutelage and influence, her private schooling, the world of ideas, a strong moral conviction, and a cosmopolitan view were evident in Shadd Cary's activism. In her utopian world view, men and women, Black and White, were equals who recognized the humanity of the other.

## THE FORMATIVE YEARS OF DOUGLASS

The biography of Frederick Douglass (1813–1895) stands in marked contrast to that of Shadd Cary. He was born a slave in Talbot County, Maryland. His mother, whom he described as "quite dark,"[16] was a slave on another plantation. Douglass saw her only four or five times before she died when he was seven years old. It was rumored that his father was the White plantation owner. Douglass lived in a cabin with his maternal grandmother (also a slave) on the outskirts of the plantation.

Douglass was taught to read by the mistress of one of his *families* and he learned how to write by working in a shipyard, copying letters, and tricking literate people into teaching him. Douglass wrote in his 1845 autobiography that "my copy-book was the board fence, brick wall, and pavement; my pen and ink was a lump of chalk."[17] He worked at literacy until he could forge his master's handwriting. In his autobiography, Douglass described his epiphany after a violent altercation with his sadistic last master:

> It was the turning-point in my career as a slave. It rekindled the few expiring embers of freedom, and revived within me a sense of my own manhood. It recalled the departed self-confidence, and inspired me again [to vow that those who] succeed in whipping me, must also succeed in killing me.[18]

In 1838, Douglass succeeded in his second escape attempt, and made his way to New York.[19]

Although he was literate, racial discrimination prevented him from finding employment that required literacy. His first job was stowing a sloop with a load of oil. When he attempted to find a second job caulking, he was confronted with the racial prejudice of White caulkers, who refused to work with him. Seeing no future for himself in New York, Douglass moved to New Bedford, Massachusetts, where a sympathetic White man hired him to perform a less menial job.[20]

Soon after his arrival in New Bedford, he began to read William Lloyd Garrison's abolitionist newspaper, the *Liberator*. It quickly became his "meat and drink."[21] Influenced by Garrison's stands on "the principles, measures, and spirit of the anti-slavery reform," he took up the abolitionist cause, pleading the case of those who were still enslaved.[22] Douglass addressed antislavery meetings and was hired as a lecturer by Garrisonian abolitionists. In May of 1845, he published his first autobiography, *Narra-*

*tive of the Life of Frederick Douglass, an American Slave.*[23] From 1845 to 1847, he traveled in Great Britain as an abolitionist lecturer. Establishing his family in Rochester, New York, he published the first issue of his weekly newspaper, the *North Star,* in 1848. According to his own account, he broke with White Garrisonian abolitionists between May and June of 1851, and revamped his newspaper into a vehicle for the Liberty Party, calling it *Frederick Douglass' Paper.*

Douglass strongly advocated racial integration in every aspect of American life, including education. Like other Black leaders, he believed that education was the linchpin of racial uplift and equality. However, Douglass also was realistic about the power of White racism in the United States and elsewhere. What good would even the finest education be, if racism continued to deny Blacks their rightful place in any occupation, professional or vocational? Although Douglass respected all forms of labor, he regarded menial labor—another form of slavery—as a state from which one should escape as soon as possible.[24]

## THE ROOTS OF SHADD CARY AND DOUGLASSS' EDUCATIONAL VIEWS

Shadd Cary and Douglass' theories of racially integrated education were rooted in their gender, race, and class differences, which affected their worldviews, experiences, and thought in different ways. While both Shadd Cary and Douglass experienced White racism, Shadd Cary was born into a family that was free. She did not know the sting of the lash and the sound of the whip. White Quakers educated Shadd Cary and partially shaped who she was; Douglass was taught to read by the mistress of the family that enslaved him. Although Shadd Cary was of mixed race, her gender, class, and education made it possible for her to be employed as a teacher—a job generally reserved for Whites. Douglass was forced to accept menial employment because of his race, sex, former slave status, and class. Shadd Cary was lauded by her family and her elite circle for aspiring to have White mores, values, and behaviors, while Douglass struggled to overcome his former status as a slave. Shadd Cary's light skin color may have led her to believe that any Black person could achieve what she had accomplished. Douglass' darker hue may have made it easier for him to understand the difficulties of dark-skinned Blacks, who were discriminated against by both Whites and light-skinned Blacks.

Sexism was as crucial an oppression as racism and classism in the antebellum years. Because Shadd Cary was female, the Black leadership of Canada harshly criticized her for her participation in the public sphere. But African Americans praised Douglass' leadership because he was acting within his gender role as a Black male community leader. Shadd Cary's memory of the sexism that, in part, prevented her from obtaining an education in Delaware influenced her feminist position on the necessity of education for girls and women. As a male, Douglass encountered no such prejudice.

## ANALYSIS OF SHADD CARY'S AND DOUGLASS' BACKGROUNDS

A common thread among African Americans and Afro Canadians in the antebellum years was their strong desire to dispel the pernicious mythologies about Black inferiority, bestiality, and hypersexuality. On both sides of the border, most Black people aspired to improve the status of their race by any means possible, but especially through education. Shadd Cary and Douglass agreed that the route to equality and assimilation lay in Black education. In this respect, Afro Canadians were better positioned than African Americans in the struggle for education prohibited by Whites, because Afro Canadians were citizens of their adopted country.

Shadd Cary's education served as her model for the intellectual curriculum she advocated. However, her model curriculum was best suited for—and only available to—the Black middle- and upper-middle classes of the 1850s. Former slaves were not well regarded by some of the Black elite unless they aspired to the Protestant ethic. This meant that Shadd Cary's theory was classist. However, her personal experiences with racism and gender discrimination at an early age in Delaware, and her struggle to overcome both, surely led her to believe that racism and sexism could be eradicated with intellectual education comprising literature, languages, arts, and sciences. She thought that if *she* could succeed, so could others. What Shadd Cary failed to consider was her class privilege, including not having to fight for survival. Her model curriculum assumed that Blacks had assimilated successfully and were preparing to enter the professions.

Douglass' curricular theories were far more inclusive than those of Shadd Cary. As his plans for the American Industrial School demonstrate, Douglass was an egalitarian of the first order. The school was to admit any student, regardless of complexional distinction, class, or gender. Douglass' egalitarianism was rooted in his past. His memories of his former enslavement and early days of freedom influenced his later thought on the education Blacks needed for their survival. Thus, Douglass' theory of what a good Black education should comprise was not only the literature, languages, arts, and sciences that Shadd Cary proposed, but also a vocation such as agriculture, cooking, sewing, and other such occupations so that students would always be able to earn a living, even if racial discrimination barred them from the professions. His was a curriculum based upon honing the intellect and learning how to survive in a racist society.

## DOUGLASS' AND SHADD CARY'S NEWSPAPER DISCOURSE ON THE EDUCATION OF BLACKS

Douglass thought that African Americans' status as slaves was due to both White and Black ignorance, and that education—whether integrated or segregated—was central to the progress of Black people. In a speech made on August 10, 1852, at the successful Black settlement in Buxton, Canada West, he emphasized the relationship between ignorance and slavery:

> Ignorance is another evil of, and indispensable to slavery. Knowledge enlightens and expands the mind, elevates the thoughts, and makes the slave dissatisfied with his condition and to pant after liberty. Hence, in all the slaveholding States, the most stringent laws are enacted, the violation of which entails the severest punishment, to forbid the slave, either to read or to write, aye, to forbid even to learn the nature and existence of that God who breathed into him the breath of life.[25]

Douglass extolled the pleasures and pursuits of the trained mind such as participation in literary societies. He strongly believed that human dignity lay in the cultivation of the intellect and understanding of one's ethical and spiritual obligations.[26]

Shadd Cary concurred with Douglass regarding ignorance and thought that the remedy for it lay in integrated education and assimilation. Writing about affairs in the state of Kentucky in her editorial, "White and Black Slavery," she argued:

> It is essential that the [Black] youth [of Kentucky] should all be educated.... Slavery prevents this being done. What do the few wealth[y] planters in the State care for the education of the masses? Nothing at all. Their sons at college, their daughters at boarding school, [wealthy whites] control the legislation of the State, and take care to see, that taxes for educational purposes, do not, bear too hardly upon them. They seek to monopolize the intelligence, as they monopolize the wealth of the State.[27]

Shadd Cary surmised that Whites, especially Southern plantation owners, would not support education for the Black masses, primarily because education put the entire slavocracy at risk. In providing this pointed rationale for the ignorance of the Black masses, Shadd Cary buttressed her pessimism with her belief that the prospect of slave liberation and Black assimilation in the United States was delusional. Although some Black separatists such as Martin Delany and Henry Highland Garnet were convinced that it would be only a matter of time before the United States annexed Canada and re-institutionalized slavery there, Shadd Cary believed that Canada would remain the bastion of Black freedom and equality in North America.[28]

Douglass held a more cautious view of what lay ahead for both free and enslaved Black people. He recalled the prejudice that he had suffered before being accepted as a literate person, and surmised that Black people would need two types of education: intellectual and vocational. Whether obtained clandestinely in slave cabins and Black churches or openly in free public schools, African Americans, he believed, had the goal of achieving some level of literacy. Ultimately, Douglass hoped that integrated rather than segregated education would lead to assimilation. He considered segregated institutions of any kind to be detrimental to human progress. However, Douglass recognized that separate Black institutions might be necessary in view of the ferocity of entrenched White racism. As Douglass wrote in his article, "Equal School Rights":

> The subject of exclusive organizations among our people is one, in which we have long been interested. As a general thing, we consider them detrimental to our interests, having a tendency to foment the spirit of proscription where it does not. But we can easily conceive of certain exigencies, in which they may be absolutely necessary to our well being. We would not have our people support a colored school, or colored church, in these places, where they can procure admission into schools and churches, in which there are not complexional distinctions, where they will be in the possession of the same rights and privileges, that others enjoy. This is our private opinion, publicly expressed.[29]

His acknowledgement that segregated institutions such as schools and churches might continue to be segregated is evidence of Douglass' fears for the future of Blacks in the United States.

Shadd Cary, on the other hand, seemed to ignore the increasing racism in the provisionally racially integrated society of Canada. She believed that Blacks alone were responsible for surmounting whatever challenges lay before them in obtaining an education. In a *Provincial Freeman* editorial (no title) published on January 20, 1854, Shadd Cary praised the virtues of former slave William Wells Brown, who had given a series of lectures "embracing other topics than the anti-slavery subject" in Philadelphia. Commenting on Brown's lecture on "The Humble Origin of Great Men," she wrote that he "spoke of the beauties of several noted places in London and Paris. ['Humble Origin'] was well-chosen, as it was calculated to inspire the colored people with energy, and cause them to surmount difficulties to educate themselves." Shadd Cary thought that Brown was an excellent example of her philosophy of self-education: Blacks would have to lift themselves up by their bootstraps and educate themselves and their children, despite racism.

Douglass also believed that Blacks were compelled to be responsible for procuring their education. As he stated in his editorial, "This Age": "The colored man must no longer depend upon his White friends for intellectual resources with his hat in his hand, and head towards the earth....it is time that intellectual effort be sustained by the people of color themselves."[30] But while Douglass alluded to the importance of an intellectual education, he adamantly espoused a type of education that he thought was more practical for Blacks of the 1850s. As he wrote in his article, "The Industrial School":

> As to a mere knowledge of books, I have no faith in it. I do not say that I undervalue education, for I think that every child should be kept in school till twelve or fourteen years old, at least. But a mere knowledge of books, without a trade of some kind is useless, as the colored people are situated now.[31]

To survive in the dominant society, Douglass believed that African Americans required an education that stressed vocational skills as well as intellectual development.

Shadd Cary's newspaper rhetoric suggests that a rudimentary *intellectual* education was not sufficient for racial uplift. As she stated in her response to a Letter to the Editor:

> All labor is respectable, yet we must not be content to be a class of common laborers; we have fair portion of these already. What we want, and what we must have, is a fair proportion of other classes among us. Some fitted for School Teachers, Lawyers, Doctors, Merchants, &c. We must educate ourselves and educate our children.[32]

Shadd Cary's position on the necessity for a purely liberal arts education did not waver in the 1850s. If anything, she was even more insistent that Afro Canadians obtain an intellectual education as quickly as possible, leaving behind menial skills. On May 6, 1854, Shadd Cary published a reader's Letter to the Editor that stated, "We must devote a portion of our time to mental cultures; we must become a reading people."[33] Shadd Cary responded thusly:

> We must dip or pry into the fine arts and sciences; we must become painters, sculptors, architects; in short, scientific and it must be by our own exertions. When we have ended our collegiate course, we are not truly wise, but must become so by research afterwards.[34]

Although Douglass was a staunch feminist and advocated the education of Black girls and women, Shadd Cary was an even more committed proponent of Black female education. As she wrote in her article "Miscellaneous" concerning the education of Black girls: "Whatever your position in society, educate your daughter for some business in her life, educate her according to your means and condition, according to her tastes, and capacity."[35] This statement suggests that Shadd Cary was hearkening back to her own education, both formal and informal, as a young girl and adolescent. Shadd Cary may have attributed her temerity and activism to her unusual education, which was not available to most girls. As she continued in "Miscellaneous":

> The "sphere of woman," which has always reduced far below the hemisphere which all accord her as a right, includes the whole range of teaching—in letters, in science, in music, and drawing, and whatever else is learned in our schools. [Women's mission] surely is to teach.[36]

In other words, educated women were the key to the future of Black advancement.

One of Shadd Cary's most impassioned editorials, "Female Education," was inspired by her zeal for educating girls:

> Oh, it is a burning shame that our women are not educated to a greater vigor of body and mind! If the world were mine, and I could educate by one sex, it should be the girls. I could make a greater and better world of the next generation by educating girls of this.... Strengthen the woman-heart, and you strengthen the world. Give me a nation of noble women, and I will give you a noble nation. Cultivate the woman-mind if you would cultivate the race.[37]

The above statements reflect more than Shadd Cary's upbringing and her strong identification with her father's teachings. They also reflect the indignities she had suffered as a female activist, whose case for gender equality was tried constantly in Black communities on both sides of the Canadian-American border.

Shadd Cary enthusiastically envisioned a future that included not only women's education, but also the integration of Blacks and Whites in the same classroom. Her faith in her integrationist theory is exemplified in her editorial, "The Future of the Colored Canadians."[38] "The Future" begins with her exceptionally optimistic assumption that racism was merely a product of ignorance, and that the coeducation of Blacks and Whites would remove racism from Canadian society. She argued that the missing factor in the equality equation was a quality liberal arts education in racially integrated schools. Shadd Cary envisioned a learning environment in which Blacks and Whites would reveal their best qualities, and from that intimacy grow to appreciate one another. Without such an environment, she believed, Blacks and Whites were indeed laying the groundwork for a separatist future. As she wrote in "The Future of the Colored Canadians":

> The position of the colored people in Canada will ultimately be the same as that of their white fellow citizens. A perfect equality among the people of different nations in this country is the will of God.... Our position in and relations to the country will help to bring about such a result. The increasing influence of our piety, our intelligence, and wealth, will fix the fact irrevocably. Our children will as certainly seek and find their level, which will be the white boys and girls of their generation, as water finds its level and wind its equilibrium![39]

Shadd Cary hoped that the contemporary Black adult population would acquire a certain amount of wealth from agriculture, and that they would use that wealth to fund their children's education. This would make it possible for the next generation to eventually become educated professionals.

Douglass contended that menial occupations might be necessary for Blacks to survive in the racist culture of the United States. African Americans performed almost all of the menial work in American society at that time, because that was what they were permitted to do. Douglass therefore maintained that Blacks must receive a vocational education in addition to a classical education, just to stay alive and free.

Acting on this belief, Douglass took steps to establish the American Industrial School, a school that would be open to all, regardless of race. The American Industrial School was to be financed by the Black community and located 100 miles from Erie, Pennsylvania, an area that had been hospitable to Blacks and that was rural enough for training in agriculture, animal husbandry, etc. Douglass announced his plans for the school in a speech he gave to a group of Black leaders in the spring of 1854 in Rochester, New York:

> The American Industrial School is to be established by the colored people of this country as soon as they can raise $30,000 to do it with. It is to be based on a farm of not less than two hundred acres, one hundred and fifty of them sacredly reserved for Agriculture; males and females to be equally employed as teachers and received as pupils; no distinctions of exclusions to be made on account of color; the school is to be managed by fifteen trustees, six of them appointed by the Committee on education of the National Council and nine chosen by the stockholders.[40]

Douglass described the proposed curriculum in his article, and stipulated quite clearly what he expected the American Industrial School to accomplish:

> 1. For every branch of Literature taught, there shall be one branch of handicraft also taught in the school.
> 2. Each pupil shall occupy one half of his time, when at school, in work at some handicraft or on the farm.
> 3. The handicrafts shall be such that their products will be articles salable for money's worth at a market within easy access from the school ... If it can be established on the principles here set forth, the colored people of this country will have a better seminary than the whites have.[41]

Shadd Cary assumed that slavery had taught Blacks everything about farming, but Douglass knew that the slaves had not acquired the critical skills for owning and managing their own farms. Slave owners, as a rule, did not educate Blacks formally in agriculture or animal husbandry. If Blacks were ever to profit from performing menial tasks, they had to acquire excellent skills and exceed the expectations of their White employers. Competent teachers of any race were necessary if Blacks were to be more than cooks and barbers. As Douglass wrote in his article,

> The colored race has been severely and to some extent justly arraigned for their general addiction to servile employment; but this reproach must be tempered by the fact that while they can easily find instructors in cooking, shaving, grooming, coat brushing, etc., it is generally difficult for a black man to find any competent person who will tack [sic] him how to build or paint houses, forge or weld iron, print or bind books or even make their own clothes and shoes. Let us help them to have a chance to learn the more honored handicrafts, and then if they will stick to scouring knives and blacking boots, we'll help denounce them for it to the best of our ability.[42]

Douglass thought that Blacks would not be taken seriously or make a definitive physical and intellectual statement until Whites accepted the fact that Blacks could educate themselves—and Whites, as well. He was convinced that the establishment of the American Industrial School would prove that Blacks were capable of spending money wisely, and that they were willing to invest in their self-help efforts without the assistance of even the most sympathetic Whites.

Shadd Cary and Douglass agreed that Black literacy rates were woefully small in both Canada and the United States. According to Douglass, however, there existed a small cadre of educated Blacks in the United States, who were living proof of the importance of honing the intellect and cutting away the chains:

> Once it was a curiosity to see the Negro read; and a book was formerly written to prove that it was not a sin to baptize a Negro but now we behold the sable brow redolent with intellect, and uplifted under the inspiring influence of the highest and noblest thoughts. Need he mention the Garnets, the Cromwells, the Smiths, the Wards, and a host of others, who are not considered unworthy to pace the platform with the most learned and eloquent Divines of the day.
>
> We have among us, Doctors of Law and Medicine, Editors, Ministers and Lawyers, and in every way we are progressing, though comparatively slow, owing to the great prejudice existing in the public mind against our color.[43]

As Shadd Cary stated, "What intellectually we most need, and the absence of which we most feel, is the knowledge of the White man."[44]

## CONCLUSION

Both Shadd Cary and Douglass were advocates of racially integrated education; but their differing ideas about curriculum were shaped by the complex relationships of gender, race, and class in antebellum African American and Afro Canadian communities. Shadd Cary's emphasis on intellectual education pertained primarily to the Black elite of the 1850s (i.e., those middle- and upper-middle-class Blacks who already were poised to take advantage of an intellectual education comprising the humanities rather than vocational education). Her theory was not at all conducive to the needs of most Black people in the lower and enslaved classes. As such, her theory was elitist and racist. It may be argued that Shadd Cary thought those Blacks who emigrated to Canada had the wherewithal to become members of the fledgling Afro Canadian middle class quickly—as her statements on *begging*, self-education, feminism, and racial integration demonstrate. However, she must have been aware that most of the refugees were nowhere near to having the qualities and resources necessary to achieve middle-class status when they crossed the border into Canada. Shadd Cary's class and race privilege, in addition to her unadulterated optimism, exaggerated her sense of the possible. She did not address the issue of basic survival. As her newspaper articles reveal, Shadd Cary was communicating with those who were ready for, or who already had attained, middle- or upper-middle-class status—not those who were struggling to survive.

Douglass' theory about the curriculum for racially integrated schools and what the short-term and long-term future held for African Americans and Afro Canadians was sensitive to the plight and status of all Blacks. He well understood that former slaves like him faced a future of struggling against more White racism once they were free, and his theory of the appropriate curriculum drew upon his personal experiences as a slave and as a free Black man. It was only his faith in America's fundamental principles of liberty and equality that made him believe Blacks would need to learn a trade only for the short term; he thought America's future was promising for African Americans. Once Blacks were able to survive and thrive, intellectual education would be their sole goal. In other words, *survival* is the word that best describes his curriculum.

While these debates were waged among the Black elite, the Black masses were struggling to survive from day to day. Even in Canada, the Afro Canadian community had the challenge of taming the wilderness and establishing settlements. It is informative that Black separatists in both countries did not want integrated schools or communities.[45] One reason for this self-segregation was that Blacks did not want to be educated with the people who had enslaved them. Neither Shadd Cary nor Douglass accepted the separatists' arguments, although Douglass understood that segregated institutions might be necessary for some time to come because of institutionalized racism. Shadd Cary did not find arguments for segregated schools or segregated Canadian settlements at all acceptable, no matter what the reason. She espoused a racially integrated Canada where even intermarriage would aid assimilation.

Neither Shadd Cary nor Douglass lived to experience the horror of *Plessy versus Ferguson* (1896), the decision by the U.S. Supreme Court that the racist institution of *separate but equal* was constitutional. That decision was not overturned until *Brown* in 1954. When considering the cases of Shadd Cary and Douglass, one might be reminded of the differing educational thought of post-bellum theorists W.E.B. DuBois and Booker T. Washington. Although DuBois' and Washington's debates do not exactly parallel those of Shadd Cary and Douglass, there are enough motifs in common that we can understand the very roots from which the theories of DuBois and Washington stem. The history of antebellum Black education in America and Canada and its influence on the twentieth and twenty-first centuries cannot be underestimated.

## NOTES

1. Although plagiarism by newspaper journalists was very common from the 1850s onward, Mary Ann Shadd Cary and Frederick Douglass so often cited the sources of their editorial and articles that it is very likely that the editorials and articles discussed in this article were their original works.

See Robert Macfarlane's study of nineteenth century plagiarism in literature: *Original Copy: Plagiarism and Originality in Nineteenth-Century Literature*. New York: Oxford University Press, 2007. Macfarlane argues that "ideas surrounding the theory and practice of originality were unmistakably reshaped during the second half of the nineteenth century" (p. 14). There were intense debates among intellectuals as to what was the constitution of original works which had been *borrowed* from unattributed sources.

2. Jane Rhodes, *Mary Ann Shadd Cary: The Black Press and Protest in the Nineteenth Century* (Bloomington, IN: University of Indiana Press, 1998), 17. According to Jane Rhodes, Abraham Shadd "reported that one day school and one Sabbath school served the small Black population of West Chester in 1837." My conclusion is that Shadd Cary's Quaker teachers at Phoebe Darlington's school were probably White.
3. Rhodes also notes that the Society of Friends inculcated the principle of taking "the moral high ground" in political and social issues at an early age in their students (*Mary Ann Shadd Cary: The Black Press and Protest in the Nineteenth Century*, 1998, 17). Shadd Cary's life showed the influence of her early training.
4. Rhodes, *Mary Ann Shadd Cary*, 17, 19.
5. Ibid., 22. Rhodes, throughout her biography of Shadd Cary, points to instances in which Shadd Cary excoriated middle-class Black people for wasting money on finery in an attempt to imitate Whites' rituals. She abhorred gaudy displays in funeral processions and believed Blacks should imitate Whites in progressive ways such as practicing thrift and seeking an education.
6. C. Peter Ripley, Mary Alice Herrle, and Paul A. Cimbala, *The Black Abolitionist Papers, II: Canada, 1830–1865* (Chapel Hill: University of North Carolina Press, 1986), 6. According to C. Peter Ripley et al., Canada's reputation among Blacks as being a haven for them was based upon three conditions: "the absence of slavery, protection from extradition, and the civil rights Canada offered to all its citizens regardless of color."
7. Rhodes, *Mary Ann Shadd Cary: The Black Press and Protest in the Nineteenth Century*. Ripley et al. estimate that three thousand free Blacks crossed the border into Canada in the fall of 1850 (*The Black Abolitionist Papers Volume II: Canada, 1830–1865*).
8. Those who most supported the position that Blacks should be repatriated to West Africa were the majority of White members of the Colonization Movement. The colonizationists held that Blacks who already were free, and those to be freed from slavery in the future, should be repatriated to countries in West Africa, particularly Liberia. Two prominent abolitionists who were colonizationists and who supported the goals of the movement were Harriet Beecher Stowe and William Lloyd Garrison. The movement provoked fierce debates within the Black abolitionist movement, because assimilationist leaders such as Douglass believed that the destiny of North American Blacks lay in remaining in the United States.
9. Rhodes, *Mary Ann Shadd Cary: The Black Press and Protest in the Nineteenth Century*.

10. Shirley J. Yee, "Finding a Place: Mary Ann Shadd Cary and the Dilemmas of Black Migration to Canada, 1850–1870," *Frontiers: A Journal of Women's Studies* 18 (1997): 2.
11. See Frankie Hutton, *The Early Black Press in America, 1827–1860* (Westport, CT: Greenwood Press, 1993), on the Black male establishment's control of the press.
12. Yee, *Frontiers: A Journal of Women's Studies*, 3.
13. Rhodes, *Mary Ann Shadd Cary: The Black Press and Protest in the Nineteenth Century.*
14. Yee, *Frontiers: A Journal of Women's Studies*, 1.
15. See Victor Turner, "Liminal to Liminoid, in Play, Flow, and Ritual: An Essay in Comparative Symbology," *Rice University Studies* 60 (1974): 53–92, about his theory of liminality. See also Carla Peterson, *Doers of the Word: African American Women Speakers and Writers in the North (1830–1880)* (New York: Oxford University Press, 1995), about her theory regarding Shadd Cary's liminality.
16. Frederick Douglass, *Narrative of the Life of Frederick Douglass, an American Slave* (New York: Penguin Books, 1982), 13.
17. Ibid., 37.
18. Ibid., 54.
19. New York was hardly a bastion of Black liberation when Douglass sought refuge there. The state was rife with institutionalized racism, especially in rural areas.
20. Douglass, *Narrative of the Life of Frederick Douglass, an American Slave*, 80.
21. Ibid., 80.
22. Ibid., 80.
23. Douglass' 1845 biographical narrative was the first of three such narratives published during Douglass' lifetime.
24. Gayle McKeen, "Whose Rights? Whose Responsibility? Self-Help in African American Thought," *Polity*, 34(2002): 418.
25. "Speech of Frederick Douglass from *Frederick Douglass' Paper*," *Chatham Western Planet*, August 18, 1854.
26. John W. Blassingame, ed., *The Frederick Douglass Papers*, Series One: Speeches, Debate, and Interviews, Vol. 2, 1847–54 (New Haven: Yale University Press, 1982). Douglass favored intellectual labor for Black people over labor of the arms or legs. He derived a great deal of pleasure and political acumen from reading. See also Gayle McKeen, "Whose Rights? Whose Responsibility? Self-Help in African American Thought," *Polity*, 34(2002): 409–432, for further discussion of Douglass' bias toward the cultivation of the mind rather than the performance of menial labor.
27. *Provincial Freeman*, December 29, 1855.
28. Rhodes, *Mary Ann Shadd Cary: The Black Press and Protest in the Nineteenth Century*, x.
29. *Frederick Douglass' Paper*, April 13, 1855. Free Northern Blacks had to contest school racial segregation laws in places such as Boston and New York.
30. Ibid.

31. "The Industrial School," *Frederick Douglass' Paper*, May 19, 1854. Douglass gave the speech in the spring of 1854. The *New York Tribune* (date unknown) published the speech. Douglass saw this account of his speech and reported it in *Frederick Douglass' Paper*. At the end of the article, he noted that the source was the *New York Times*.
32. "Mr. Editor: Education, Wealth, Numbers," Letter to the Editor, *Provincial Freeman*, April 22, 1854.
33. Ibid.
34. Ibid.
35. *Provincial Freeman*, November 4, 1854.
36. Ibid.
37. *Provincial Freeman*, June 7, 1856.
38. "The Future of the Colored Canadians," *Provincial Freeman*, October 20, 1855.
39. Ibid.
40. Douglass later published his speech in the *Frederick Douglass' Paper* (May 19, 1854).
41. Ibid.
42. Ibid.
43. Ibid.
44. Rhodes, *Mary Ann Shadd Cary: The Black Press and Protest in the Nineteenth Century*, 21.
45. Carter Godwin Woodson, *Education of the Negro Prior to 1861: A History of the Education of the Colored People of the United States from the Beginning of Slavery to the Civil War* (New York and London: G. P. Putnam's Sons, 1915).

CHAPTER 2

# COMPANY SCHOOLING IN THE NEW SOUTH

## Lawrence Peter Hollis and the Parker Mill Schools in South Carolina

**Bart Dredge**

### INTRODUCTION

Early in 1922, a number of cotton textile executives from Greenville, South Carolina, petitioned the State Assembly to establish the Parker District, in part a consolidation of company-owned schools that would create the largest such district in the history of the state. Passed on February 17, 1922, Special Act 369 combined nine large mill villages including Woodside, Mills Mill, Monaghan, Poe, West Greenville, Judson, Dunean, Union Bleachery, and American Spinning (Sampson Mill).[1] The new District also included the suburbs of City View and Sans Souci, both "areas of deterioration between the city and the mill communities."[2] At the time, over 7,000 students attended company-owned grade schools in the District, yet no high school awaited those children who had successfully completed their elementary grades. The District had been named for Thomas F. Parker (1861–1926), a local textile entrepreneur and cousin of another

*Life Stories: Exploring Issues in Educational History Through Biography*
pp. 23–43

significant textile leader, Lewis W. Parker (1865–1916).[3] Both believed that mill schools should teach habits of industry and principles of workplace efficiency as forms of moral uplift among workers, because "anything which tends to degrade or lower the employees as a class meets our earnest and persistent disapprobation."[4]

While other forms of welfare such as churches and recreational activities were important in the new District, it was in its schools that Parker was soon to make educational history. Recognizing that success in the mill schools would require effective management, Thomas F. Parker turned to his trusted assistant, Lawrence Peter "Pete" Hollis, whom he had hired in 1905 to manage expanding mill welfare programs intended to "improve the ethical, mental, social and physical standards of the mill village community."[5] Now, with Hollis fully acclimated to the special concerns of the textile industry, Parker in 1916 called on him to serve as Superintendent of the 14 schools scattered among the mill villages, eventually including the new high school. The appointment turned out to be a brilliant decision, and Pete Hollis quickly became synonymous with company schools throughout the textile South.

Born on November 29, 1883, in Chester, South Carolina, Hollis worked on the family farm and enjoyed only the episodic moments of formal education that were possible in part-time schools typically in session only during the two months of "lay-by time" every summer between "cotton hoeing and cotton picking."[6] Even when available, classes were not separated by grades, and study consisted of little more than rote memorization in preparation for when the principal would "hear your lesson." While this left Hollis woefully unprepared for college, much of his later success in the Parker District resulted from his repudiation of the still common method of rote learning and recitation.[7]

As a teenager, Hollis took a college entrance exam and "got nowhere with it," leaving officials to suggest that he return home and come back when better prepared. Afraid that he would disappoint those back home who had earlier celebrated his leaving for college, and knowing that such a failure would leave him "ruined socially," Hollis arranged to meet with the president of South Carolina College (now the University of South Carolina), who eventually agreed to accept him on a probationary status. Hollis persevered and eventually graduated, although regretting for the remainder of his life that he had not gone home to prepare for the rigors of college work. Only an average student, Hollis nevertheless distinguished himself by becoming a student leader, eventually accepting the presidency of the "Clarisophic Literary Society," then the "highest honor in the school," winning the Roddy Medal for debate in 1904, and serving as president of the college YMCA.[8] Hollis graduated from the college with a B.A. degree in 1905.

It was through his work with the college YMCA that Hollis met I. E. Unger, a former Christian missionary and current welfare secretary for Thomas F. Parker at the Monaghan (Mill) YMCA in Greenville.[9] Through his contacts with Unger, Hollis came to Parker's attention and soon accepted an appointment as assistant welfare secretary for the mill communities near Greenville. Shortly thereafter, Hollis took over full responsibilities for the mill welfare plans, and later explained the rapid promotion as the result of Unger's lack of ease among the thousands of Southern mill hands. Evidently Unger did not "speak the same language we spoke here in the cotton mills," and had even married a woman who "said things that she thought"—a problem because some of those things "did not take well with the people." In any case, Hollis rose quickly and soon controlled the welfare activities offered to mill hands.[10]

Hollis began his work in the mills at $40.00 per week and quickly brought professional knowledge and skills to the earlier hodge-podge of ineffective welfare methods in a mill community that at the time boasted "207 homes and 125 cows," as well as a boarding house for an additional 50 mill hands.[11] As part of his work, Hollis took over a greater role in mill village education when appointed head of the Victor-Monaghan elementary schools in 1916.[12] From the beginning Hollis earned the favor of mill workers and company officials alike and long remembered his first days as a time when the mill hands "arose up [sic] and demanded that I be made the [welfare] secretary of the YMCA." While this may represent a bit of selective memory, his success came from a combination of technical skills and personal savvy, as well as extraordinary energy and a "little ability to work with people."[13] To help him better understand the mill people and their lives, Hollis lived in the Monaghan village along with the mill superintendent, an overseer, and five teachers from the company school.[14] And, to further improve his knowledge, he frequently traveled to national conferences where he learned the details of YMCA welfare work as it came to be practiced in a number of industrial settings.[15]

One early goal tackled by Pete Hollis was the elimination of the costly tendency among mill operatives to move about among the mills, never staying long enough in one place to become members of the community. With the support of Parker, Hollis first began to address the unpleasant and unattractive living conditions faced by residents in most mill villages. He had the small backyards between the company homes plowed for gardens and provided the necessary seeds and fertilizer. From Georgia he purchased "carloads of cows and pigs" and distributed them among the mill hands, believing, "if a man had a fat hog in the summertime down South here, he couldn't move that hog very well, and he couldn't kill it because the meat would spoil."[16] He would stay in place. On another occasion, Hollis traveled to New York and returned with a "motion picture man and four actors" who produced a film intended to discourage mill hands from packing up in one village and moving to another. One memorable scene showed movers carelessly dropping and destroying a valuable organ,—a not-so-subtle message that it was "foolish to move around" if the mill hands might "lose all they had" if they tried to do so. By Hollis' own account, the experimental movie was "quite a success."[17]

Hollis also ordered bathtubs for families who chose to purchase one, and for the others provided showers at the company YMCA. He organized regular celebrations for the Fourth of July, and Christmas parties that featured fruit baskets for the mill children.[18] Finally, to help recruit new workers to the District mills Hollis outfitted one of the nicer mill homes as a "show house" to help lure potential workers. Located in a particularly pleasant setting, and featuring a sewing machine, sofa, rugs, and a prominently displayed family Bible, the house was a routine stop for the mountain families considering the move to the Piedmont textile communities.[19] Hollis also tried to connect mill families to the company towns through the printed word. For example, in late 1923 he published a District newspaper called "The Joymaker" that featured local events and gossip and, when it failed for lack of subscribers, Hollis began the more popular *Parker Progress*, a village weekly that billed itself as the "official organ of the Parker District." The first issue of 16 pages appeared on March 6, 1925, and sold for five cents, promising on its masthead that it would be the official newspaper for "all the PEOPLE of that populous, progressive group of mill villages and suburbs [emphasis in original]."[20]

Although the Parker District was a model for company-owned schools at the elementary level, by the early 1920s Thomas F. Parker had come to understand the importance of expanding educational opportunities beyond the lower grades. As a result, his plans for the new Parker High School developed rapidly, with a laying of the cornerstone on April 5, 1923. The celebration began with "full Masonic rites" and a long procession through village streets with music provided by the Parker District band. Over 1,000 spectators accompanied the mill chorus with "Welcome Sweet Springtime" and later listened to the keynote address, "The Ideal of the School," by Furman University professor Francis Pendleton Gaines. Recognizing the historical importance of the new mill high school, many cheered as Gaines described the school as the "gateway of youth; the fortress of democracy; and a temple of the spirit."[21] At the end of the ceremonies, the presiding officials buried into the cornerstone a copper time capsule that held, among other things, a sheaf of local news reports on the creation of the school, a copy of the legislative act that created the District, a map of the Southern textile region, cotton items produced by local mill hands, and a photograph of Lawrence Peter Hollis, our subject here.[22]

Upon its completion in October, 1924, the new school boasted a main classroom building, and an annex with library, conference room, "materials bureau" and cafeteria.[23] Students enjoyed a large gymnasium with two basketball courts, a football field and quarter-mile track, six bowling lanes, horseshoe pits and volleyball courts, steel bleachers seating five thousand spectators, and a large field house. Later the school expanded to include a new "Vocational Building" with welding and machine shops, sewing and other textile equipment, a drafting department, and spaces for cosmetology and commercial studies.[24] Seventeen students graduated from the first class in 1924, and the school quickly became the centerpiece of the District. By the end of its first decade, 33 teachers taught nearly 900 high school students per year, while another 6,500 students attended an elementary school associated with one of the Parker mill villages.[25]

## PARKER CURRICULUM

While Pete Hollis may have reluctantly accepted the appointment with the Parker District, and then only after other candidates had "visited the district, took a look at the ancient buildings, read the figures in the meager budget, and declined the offer," he nevertheless soon embraced the work.[26] From the beginning, his plan for mill children included physical health and recreation, the inculcation of strong spiritual values, the appreciation of aesthetic beauty, and most importantly, the acceptance of authority and the ability to "adjust to the problems of life."[27] Having once told a student reporter that "We do not believe that head training is any more important than training of hands, heart and health, which includes character training," Hollis launched an educational program clearly intended to serve the mill companies that provided the schools.[28] As reported in the trade magazine *Textile World*, Hollis infused into his school district "an impulse which, for want of a better term, we shall call industrial consciousness."[29] Even today, the prominent two-story textile training facility on Parker High School grounds remains the visible representation of the historical relationship between mill companies and the education they provided cotton mill children. The textile production process would soon be taught to those planning to enter the mills, and any discussion of Pete Hollis' contribution to textile education must begin with this narrow focus. After all, as David Clark, the controversial editor of the *Southern Textile Bulletin* and the South's greatest defender of textile interests once noted, the "mills know that ninety per cent of the children in the mill village will be mill operatives and the object of the mill school is to educate them and make them better citizens and more proficient in their life work."[30]

While the Parker High School was not the only mill school to include a training mill facility—the Saxon Mill in North Carolina created a "Textile Industrial Institute" of six buildings and a "handsome little model mill" for the training of mill hands—the size and scope of the Parker experiment stands alone.[31] From the beginning, Pete Hollis prepared Parker District children to work on equipment "they had never seen nor heard of before," because he understood that while some children would escape the textile industry, most would not, and he was obliged to prepare them for work in the area mills.[32] Hollis based his educational philosophy on the belief that "the child learns by doing," and that he or she would be happier "if the program includes the things which affect him at present." At Parker, students could "learn what they live," and the school offered an education that would "make sense to these sons and daughters of the mill workers"[33] The program took mill children beyond material offered in "regular text books," and led them to appreciative preparation for their work in the mills.[34] As Greenville *News* reporter Don West noted, "book learning" was not "unduly stressed" in the Parker schools that instead focused on "fitting the student" for a trade required by the textile industry.[35] At Parker, the "Hollis system of education starts with children, not with textbooks," and the curriculum centers on the belief that "students learn better by doing than by rote."[36]

While some condemned a "dictatorial" training that might "ruin the future of those children," Hollis nevertheless insisted on a curricular emphasis on "cooperative work, social attitudes, character development, and so forth," rather than academic knowledge.[37] In his study of the Parker High School curriculum in 1936, Tippett noted that school officials devoted some effort toward "skills of reading, writing and arithmetic," but that the central focus was on the "qualities of co-operation, initiative, resourcefulness, respect for self and social order, creativeness, practice of desirable characteristics, open-mindedness, and acceptance of responsibilities."[38] All of these traits were important to the textile employers who would hire these children and they were never far from the center of Pete Hollis' curricular plans. As one observer confirmed, the students who attended the Parker District schools were the children of mill hands and, for the most part, "education has been adopted to meet their particular needs."[39] A Parker education served textile employers as students learned the habits of work, the correct attitudes on the job, and the development of workplace co-operation and sociability. As the vice-president of Judson Mills once noted, the Parker High School was a benefit for mill hands that needed to be "happy in their homes and contented with their work and wages."[40]

Gil Rowland of the Greenville *News*, and a Parker High School teacher from 1931 to 1945, confirmed the picture of a curriculum firmly in Pete Hollis' hands. He recalled that Hollis thought it impractical to teach mill children "traditional college-preparatory courses," as most could be expected to spend their "working lives" in the "mill district," so the centerpiece of the school was an "application of vocational training" of value only to those who pursued jobs "needed by the mill community."[41] Throughout his career, Hollis successfully nurtured the relationship between the schools and the mill officials who supported them, and frequently offered public statements of appreciation for the contributions textile employers made to the schools. He was thankful, for example, that the mill foreman and overseers assisted in the development of "our course of study," and that the mills regularly donated supplies to keep the campus "machines running," and allowed students to "work with their regular employees so that they may get mutual experience on the job."[42]

A 1925 editorial in the Greenville *Journal* agreed with Hollis and noted that in the Parker District the "importance of local industries is stressed" and that connecting work to school created "pride in the occupation of the father" and inculcated the important value of giving fair service to one's employer.[43] As Hollis once taught, all the luxury items in the world failed to be as rewarding as the "thrill which comes from doing a good job."[44] In fact, Hollis often taught students that "whether you plow or whether you cook or whether you build a wall or whether you make cloth, all of these things may be just as beautiful as a picture which an artist would paint."[45] As John Gillespie, a teacher at Parker High School from 1956 to 1986 recalled, Hollis believed students should rise to their fullest potential—even if that meant only being the "best mill operative one could be."[46]

To facilitate the training for textile work that he had in mind, the Parker High School boasted a two-story building that "duplicates an actual cotton mill," in which students learned the "carding, spinning, twisting, quilling, and weaving" functions of a typical cotton mill.[47] Area mills donated the equipment needed to have "raw cotton transformed into woven cloth," and when new equipment emerged, Parker officials saw to it that the students had access to the same equipment.[48] Parker students could also focus on "home economics, carpentry, machine shop, mechanical drawing and textile courses in weaving, in loom fixing, cloth analysis and designing," as well as textile machinery repair, and those who studied in the campus textile facilities soon manufactured finished products such as towels, curtains, and blankets that they sold to other students and their parents.[49]

In addition to textile training, other opportunities were available as well, especially for female students. For example, the cafeteria doubled as a workroom for Home Economics classes that allowed girls to "get their hands in the dough."[50] The female students also learned to walk properly, dress and apply cosmetics, and behave on dates, while many took advantage of "special courses" in clothing design, ready-to-wear garment selection, and the best methods of "laundering, patching and darning." Additional training exposed students to the "preparation and service of wholesome meals," nursing, first aid, and home care of the sick. Despite these additional opportunities, however, it was the "textile division" that dominated the high school curriculum. Training in loom fixing, carding, weaving, designing, card grinding, roving frame fixing, spinning frame fixing, and cloth inspection prepared most Parker students only for work in a textile industry that expected a return on their investments in mill village schools.[51]

It is important to note, though, that in addition to vocational skills, Pete Hollis worked to encourage certain values of citizenship among the students. To that end, in 1931 he initiated a complicated system of student government, complete with a written constitution and an adversarial judicial system. Before long the student government included not only a school president and other executive officials, but a student senate and house of representatives, student court with prosecutors, defense attorneys and judges, and student juries charged with adjudicating minor disputes and assessing responsibility for the violation of various campus rules. [52] While citizenship training is a common and laudable goal in any school, in this context Hollis hoped to teach a brand of citizenship that featured "dependability, punctuality, vocational competence and cooperation"—a definition sure to please most of the mill officials who were to employ Parker graduates.[53]

While most of the training for mill work and life occurred in the high school, the Parker District elementary schools also offered a steady diet of explicit and implicit instruction that focused on textile manufacturing. In the "social science" offerings, for example, teachers stressed the interdependence among various components of society, highlighting foremost the social utility of cotton production and textile manufacturing. Students in the first grade learned that "farmers raise lots of cotton to sell," and "buy things for the farm with the money;" second graders discovered that "merchants sell cotton cloth," made from "cotton raised by the farmer;" third grade teachers taught that the "Dutch manufacture cotton cloth;" and fourth grade children examined farm states that sell wheat and corn to the South in direct exchange for "cotton and cotton goods." Later, fifth grade students learned that the United States exchanges "cotton goods for wool, silk, and linen from Australia, Japan, and Belgium."[54]

It was especially in the fifth grade that the educational focus on the textile industry became more comprehensive, including the science classes in which students were required to identify the various insects that might threaten cotton crops, and others learned to test the comparative strength of cotton and wool fibers. Even music students practiced and performed songs with lyrics that recalled the mills, including "The Spinning Song," and "Spin, Maiden, Spin," or the musical ode "To the Little Silkworm." One public presentation featured students dramatizing a "cotton plantation scene," complete with performances of the life histories of Eli Whitney and early textile industrialist Samuel Slater—as well as student reenactments of the life of a cotton plant from raw fiber to finished fabric.[55] Finally, on one occasion a Poe Mill elementary class constructed a 30-foot square miniature city. "Parkerville" was lighted by street lamps and featured scale replicas of a fire station, post office, and hotel. Most notable on the model, of course, was the cotton mill.[56] It should be noted that the connection between mill education and textile employment also found expression in printed materials as well. The South Carolina supervisor of mill schools, William Banks, complained in 1923 that many textbooks used in other state schools were "unsuited to mill schools." For example, mathematics problems that required the "measuring acres of ground, computing size and value of piles of wood," were fine for other students, but the "mill child" required practical problems. He should be learning how to "measure cloth, to compute the number of strands in a yard of cloth," and other tasks of immediate use to the textile manufacturer.[57]

Finally, the textile education that dominated the Parker District curriculum was not something about which one might only speculate. In "The Objectives of Parker High School, 1964–1965," Pete Hollis and other textile officials made clear their intention to "meet the major occupational needs of the industrial community, which is primarily textiles, by offering a three-year course in textiles and other subjects" that would also serve local industry.[58] Likewise, in a 1925 letter to mill village residents Hollis noted that it was the "policy of the board of trustees" to developed the "first practical trade school in the South right here in the Parker District" so that the children of mill hands could "prepare for a useful occupation."[59] It should be kept in mind as well that the District charter called for five unelected trustees selected from among textile executives of the District mills, and as such the dominance of the textile industry was clear.[60] The Parker trustees had the power to levy taxes, select textbooks, and determine the curriculum of all District schools, and it remains no surprise that they developed a curriculum that best served their own interests.[61]

## TEACHER TRAINING

The mill education required by the area companies called for a cadre of teachers who could engage in the "desired training in vocational and textile work."[62] As might be expected, Pete Hollis personally selected the "teaching corps" in terms of their understanding and willing acceptance of his view of education, and when he found teachers who were unsure of themselves or his project, he quickly trained them himself. During the first decades of the Parker District, hiring teachers with no college education or professional certification, Hollis developed the "Parker Institute"—an extensive in-service training plan for mill teachers.[63] As part of the training, Hollis imported speakers from other "teacher-training institutions" to present new theories and practices to the Parker teaching staff. For example, Dr. Thomas Alexander of Teachers College, Columbia University, helped initiate a series of "standard tests" for use by teachers who wanted to gain insights into the talents of their individual students. Alexander visited the Parker District on several occasions in its early years, first arriving in 1927 to help Pete Hollis establish his version of "progressive education" on the campus of the high school.[64] At other times, Hollis sent individual teachers for extra training, as in 1924 when he sent "Professor" D. W. McSwain, the head of the Parker textile department, to New York and the Boston Training School to study advanced methods of vocational training[65]

Of more immediate significance, Hollis also taught teachers to translate "general theory into specific practice," through annual training sessions at a mountain camp owned by the Victor-Monaghan Mills—later expanding the training in 1935 at another mountain retreat at Tamassee, South Carolina, which was owned by the Daughters of the American Revolution.[66] For Hollis, it was important for new teachers to develop a clear sense of "how Parker District differs from other communities," and the training sessions could help Hollis assess just how "loyal, without any pay, our teachers are."[67] Later, when no longer able to use the new camp at Tamassee, Hollis arranged a donation of a 100-acre spot at Blythe Shoals in the South Carolina foothills. Soon called "Camp Parker" (and later "Camp Hollis"), the mountain location quickly became a favorite for teacher training and other District events including an annual "Band Camp" for members of the Parker High School Band and Orchestra.[68] One tangible result of the Parker training was a series of booklets produced during the summer sessions and later shared across the District, on such topics as poetry, health, industrial arts, and physical education, and later a set of "spellers" appeared along with 12 sets of second grade readers.[69] These books also joined the over 5,000 books already devoted to teacher training and held in the library at Camp Parker.[70]

Despite the apparent success of summer training, Hollis remained concerned about the lack of professionalism among Parker teachers, and knew that the entire system was vulnerable to criticism on those grounds. To remedy this problem, in 1931 Hollis arranged for 26 Parker teachers to travel by bus for six weeks of formal training at the Teachers College at

Columbia University, and later provided funds for similar travel to other locations in Florida, Georgia, Ohio, and North Carolina.[71] On another occasion, 21 teachers traveled to Peabody College for additional summer training, and small groups of teachers also visited experimental programs in Seattle, Nashville, Chicago, and elsewhere.[72] Another such trip found ten Parker High School teachers in Columbus, Ohio visiting a new "demonstration school" developed at Ohio State University.[73] Finally, to supplement the travel away from campus and follow up on lessons already learned, Hollis invited outside speakers to visit the District, including one such invitation in 1941 to Dr. Daniel R. Prescott, then director of child development studies at the University of Chicago.[74] No matter the method, Hollis invested extraordinary time, energy and resources to ensure the best possible teaching staff. Hiring teachers from outside the normal pool of competent and credentialed teachers, Hollis could not otherwise have been successful in pursuing his particular educational vision.

## NIGHT SCHOOL

In addition to offering industrial training for students in the various schools of the Parker District, including the high school, Hollis joined other Southern mill officials promoting night classes as a prerequisite for internal advancement, and stressed practical subjects such as "textile mathematics and the credo of paternalism."[75] For example, at one point Hollis organized a "Textile Club" that helped mill hands study leadership, personality improvement and adjustment, and the "specific duties of the foreman."[76] He also offered instruction to nearly 600 adult students each year through a variety of "trade extension" classes that met for four hours per week, including in 1932 an array of opportunities that included 14 courses in loom fixing, two in cloth design, four in card grinding and fixing, two classes in frame fixing, and one in weaving.[77]

## PEOPLE'S COLLEGE

A more ambitious experiment began in October, 1929, when Hollis developed, "The People's College." With classes held at times convenient for the housewife, courses included interior decorating, cooking, rug making, dancing, music, and dressmaking—all intended to help "the average family appreciate and make a better life."[78] Operating under Hollis' slogan, "All Sorts of Classes for All Sorts of People," the "People's College" sought to develop "more cooperative attitudes" among mill hands and soon became an important feature of Parker District life.[79] Meeting on Tuesday and Thursday nights, each session featured an end-of-term assembly for the performance of demonstrations, plays, "chalk sketches," movies, and slide presentations—most concerning some aspect of the textile industry.[80] Beyond a dollar tuition that was due at registration, students paid no additional fees, a high school diploma was not required for enrollment, and there were no examinations, tests, or reports. Well over 1,000 people registered for the first sessions, and over time nearly 3,000 workers took courses in the "People's College," studying a wide array of topics including singing in a choir, butchering various cuts of meat, and the "art of setting a table"—in the process developing "more cooperative attitudes" toward their employers.[81]

## PATHFINDER

Another major educational innovation that Pete Hollis brought to the Parker District came with the commissioning of a "truck library" in October, 1922. The first "bookmobile" in South Carolina, the truck delivered carefully chosen books to mill workers and their children throughout the District.[82] On the first day of operation, the truck "drove up to the Poe Mill" and workers checked out books at the rate of one a minute for the three hours the truck remained in place.[83] Outfitted specifically for this task, the truck had glass doors that made book selection easy, and in its first six months the truck distributed over 30,000 books to District residents.[84] The library truck received early international attention when featured in the *Christian Science Monitor* and described as a "Library on Wheels" that was a "highly economical" means of serving a large number of people. Moreover, the truck carried with it a "certain air of romance" for the adults and children who "had the advantage of the mill schools," but had never before had books "come their way."[85]

The library project, later called the "Pathfinder" after a naming contest that awarded a ten-dollar gold coin to the winner, received financial support from the "generous help" of Thomas F. Parker and Pete Hollis, as well as District mill students who sold ribbons for 50 cents each to support the mobile library. An additional $1,800 was raised from contributions from mill parents through the Parker District PTA.[86] The "Pathfinder" was first staffed by the "chauffer and librarian," Nell Barmore, a graduate of Randolph-Macon College for Women and the Carnegie Library School of Atlanta. Barmore was by all accounts a competent librarian and, as an extra bonus for this particular job, there was "very little that Miss Barmore did not know about an automobile."[87] The "Pathfinder" program was so successful that by September, 1925, Hollis pressed a second truck into service, and Miss Margaret Moseley from Monaghan—a member of the first graduating class at Parker High School—became the second "Pathfinder" librarian.[88] The library program lasted for well over ten years, and eventually boasted nearly 18,614 adults and 84,164 children as "registered borrowers."[89]

Most Parker residents seemed to prefer "love," or "adventure," or popular "out-of-doors" books, and by 1925 novels were so popular that the Pathfinder staff began carrying two copies of each.[90] Beyond limited access to pleasure reading, however, an early news article announced to mill residents that they would soon be able to check out books of more practical educational value, including books on the history of cotton growing, and the weaving and spinning of cotton cloth.[91] As Lyons noted in 1937, a mill manager "know[s] what reading matter is good for the child-like minds" of his workers and he "selects it." This seems to have been the case here, at least in terms of the vocational offerings made available by the "Pathfinder" staff.[92] Nevertheless, mill schools typically owned few books, but one could often find eager students "in the yard around the library truck, which was undoubtedly a major component of the educational program in the District."[93]

## PARKER SCHOOL OF THE AIR

In 1933, Pete Hollis reaffirmed the value of company education when, to acquaint local adults with the activities in the District schools, he began a weekly broadcast from local radio station W.F.B.C. The "Parker's Half-Hour" broadcast 30 minute programs on such topics as "Home Economics Night," "Alumni Night," "Using the library," and "Vocational Activities." Other programs, including "What Makes a Good Teacher?" and "Are We Training Boys and Girls in Character?" targeted parents and others who Hollis believed needed to further appreciate the work done in the District schools.[94] The radio program enjoyed an immediate audience of over 6,000 listeners, but to broaden the audience even further in 1934 Hollis used funds from the Parker PTA to supply radios for each of the District schools. Once the radios were in place, Hollis foreshadowed later projects by supplementing classroom teaching with the radio programs, requiring teachers to discuss with their students the issues raised during the Thursday morning broadcasts.[95] Finally, with similar educational goals in mind, Hollis had a large truck constructed that became the Parker "school mobile," announcing its arrival through a huge loudspeaker intended to "attract the attention of housewives." Home Economics teachers assigned from Parker High School to the truck taught mill families short courses on up-to-date methods of baking biscuits, making dresses, and vacuuming floors.[96] There were also demonstrations of electric stoves, sewing machines, modern refrigerators and other appliances, and in 1935, the "school mobile" joined with the South Carolina Board of

Health in a regional campaign against pellagra, explaining through moving exhibits the importance of a balanced diet.[97]

## MATERNITY SHELTER

A final example of the educational efforts initiated in the Parker District by Pete Hollis reveals his concern for the health and well-being of the mill children and families under his charge. In 1928, Hollis used $1,000 to buy and outfit a small frame house near Parker High School to "do something for the mothers who are going to have child birth [sic]." Hollis later recalled that "We called it the maternity shelter, and we took nobody but people who didn't have money."[98] Patients were not billed for the services, and the local mills provided the necessary clothing, towels and sheets.

Hollis saw the Maternity Shelter as providing a safe and healthy environment for child birth.[99] Assisted by Emily Passmore Nesbitt, a Red Cross nurse and community worker employed for a time by the Parker District, he appointed teenage girls who resided in the Parker District to offer rudimentary medical advice, care for babies and their mothers, and provide follow-up services for as long as two years following a birth. These girls also conducted weekly clinics in individual mill homes, and working under the auspices of the high school, lent "much weight to the preparation for parenthood."[100] Also, after acquiring parental permission to do so, the girls assisted during child birth, and after 20 hours of service became "Health Couriers" who traveled among the mill homes "preaching" the importance of proper screen windows and sufficient and healthy family diets, while also reporting any illnesses or other problems they thought might be of interest to mill officials.[101] As a later part of the work of the Maternity Shelter, Parker High School students also organized a "Health Club" in the school, and club members wore specially made uniforms as they held monthly classes for District girls and women.[102]

By one account in 1935, the high school girls who ran the Shelter conducted over 10,000 individual services in its first ten years of existence, including pre-natal clinics, tuberculin tests, adult hygiene classes, health-related home visits and over 370 births.[103] Hollis also later claimed that there had been over 3,000 births "in that little old shelter."[104] The "Maternity Clinic" operated at least until 1951, although before that time it had been moved to one of the rooms in the school gymnasium and its services had been dramatically reduced.[105]

## DENTAL/MEDICAL

Again addressing health problems to provide better conditions for textile education and mill village life, Hollis in 1925 hired Dr. W. T. McFall as a full-time dentist to work with District children.[106] If nothing else, Hollis understood that "sick people do not show up regularly for work."[107] Whatever the motivation, by early 1925 McFall could report that, among other services, he had performed over 2,000 "operations"; with many of these procedures conducted in his mobile dental clinic.[108] In June 1925, he also announced that he had given 25 lectures in school "chapels," 19 presentations before PTA gatherings, 16 lectures to grade school classes, 43 oral hygiene and tooth brushing drills, 3 presentations to public health nurses, 21 home visits, and 19 charity dental calls. Among other specific dental treatments, he treated 1,620 patients in 13 schools, and completed 1,068 amalgam fillings, 654 cement fillings, 837 extractions, and more. While this seems an impressive accomplishment in a short time, McFall also reported that approximately 97% of all children in the Parker District suffered from significant "dental defects." [109]

While laudable, the dental program risked humiliating the very people it served. For example, under Dr. McFall the District required children to keep a "Health Booklet" that asked them for private details of personal hygiene, including the frequency of the brushing of teeth, the presence of clean linen in the home, and the bathing habits of themselves and their parents. They were also required to report on their consumption of milk, leafy vegetables, and fruit, their daily consumption of coffee or tea and, undoubtedly most disturbing, the timing of their most recent bowel movements.[110] While some parents and students undoubtedly felt uncomfortable with these requests, McFall offered ongoing encouragement in a column called "Tooth Tales" that he wrote for the *Parker Progress*.[111] Finally, another health-related program arranged by Pete Hollis during the spring of 1924 was a visit by "Professor Happy," who led student health- related discussions called "Feeding and Washing the Human Structure." Professor Happy was actually Clifford Goldsmith of Child Health Associates of New York, brought in by Hollis to improve the overall health among mill hands.[112] Goldsmith had published a short guidebook from which he taught children with bits of homespun advice such as "sleep with the windows open and the mouth shut," and "have horse sense and eat oatmeal," as well as the insight that "thin soup never made anyone fat."[113]

## CONCLUSION

In 1951, Parker High School consolidated with the state school system, and shortly after began to lose its distinctive identity. Most teachers remained loyal and stayed with the school, and Pete Hollis maintained an office in the high school for several years, earning a stipend from District mill executives for his services as an anti-union consultant.[114] Late in 1970, Pete Hollis met with a reporter from the Greenville *News*, and recalled his experiences, remaining unapologetic about the narrowly defined industrial focus of the school curriculum. With evident pride he noted that, "We were starting from scratch, so we didn't have to conform to educator's [sic] prejudice. We were going to have a school that started off with pupils, working from what the needs and interests of the people are." To that end, Hollis remembered that the Parker District offered classes in "textile, machine shop, carpentry, auto mechanics, typewriting, and cosmetology, and that this gave students "an opportunity to make a good living from the things we taught them in school."[115] The final class of Parker High School students graduated on June 6, 1985.[116]

Hollis retired in March, 1952, and was succeeded at Parker High School by J. H. Anderson who had served as Assistant Superintendent since 1924.[117] By the time of his retirement, Hollis had received two honorary degrees from Furman University and his alma mater, the University of South Carolina. He served as the President of the Association of Retired Teachers in South Carolina, and following retirement invested two years organizing South Carolina school boards after the Greenville County school consolidation that drew Parker High School into the state system.[118] He had earlier served as president of the South Carolina Education Association in 1928, and had been appointed in 1939 to the legislative commission of the National Education Association.[119] Pete Hollis died in 1978 at the age of 95, having during his long life married twice, once to a teacher retired from the Parker schools. He had four children and later enjoyed eight grandchildren and 15 great grandchildren who affectionately knew him as "Daddy Pete."[120] Among other honors, Hollis had been named as one of America's top 100 educators by "Look" magazine in 1949, and today there is a new full-sized statue of Hollis in Greenville, South Carolina, erected in honor of his contributions to the Parker District schools.[121] The statue is prominently situated on a corner of the newly designated Pete Hollis Memorial Highway—on the outer edge of the Parker District to which he had devoted his life.[122]

## NOTES

1. A. V. Huff, *Greenville: History of the City and County in the South Carolina Piedmont*, (Columbia: University of South Carolina Press, 1995), 296; Ellison M. Smith, "Effectively combining academics and practical education: How the Parker Junior-Senior High School meets the needs of girls and boys and is promoting the welfare of the District's people, institutions and industries," *The Greenville Journal* 4 (October 1925):6-7. Act 369 was unsuc-

cessfully challenged in court on the grounds that it gave corporations the right to levy taxes. See *Walker v. Bennett*, 125 S.C. 389, 118 S. E. 779 (1923).

2. Joy Kay Bates Saxton, "A history of Parker High School of Greenville, South Carolina," (MS thesis, Furman University, 1965): 22–23; Azile Milling Fletcher, "Parker High School's graduates look at its curriculum." (MA thesis, Furman University, 1940): 4, 7.
3. Judith Bainbridge, "Closing of Parker is the end of an era," Greenville *News* (October 7, 2003); Allen Tullos, *Habits of Industry: White Culture and the Transformation of the Carolina Piedmont* (Chapel Hill: University of North Carolina Press, 1989): 181.
4. Lewis Parker, "Compulsory Education: The Solution of Child Labor Problem," *Annals of the American Academy of Political and Social Science* 32 (1908): 40–56, 49.
5. Thomas F. Parker "The true greatness of South Carolina," Address delivered to the Federation of Women's Clubs of South Carolina, (Columbia, South Carolina, May 1908): 6.
6. Hollis describes his early memories in his unpublished autobiographical account, Hughes Library, n.d., p. 1.
7. Hollis, 3.
8. Ibid., 4.
9. Mary G. Ariail and Nancy J. Smith, *Weaver of Dreams: A History of the Parker District*, (Greenville, South Carolina: R. L. Bryan Publishers, 1977): 24; Judith T. Bainbridge, *Greenville Communities*, Unpublished essays separately numbered, at the South Carolina Room, Hughes Library, (Greenville, South Carolina, 1999).
10. Hollis, 4.
11. Bainbridge, n.p.; Hollis, 7.
12. Huff, 296; Ariail and Smith, 24; Samuel F. Stack, "A critical analysis of welfare capitalism as educational ideology (Parker School District)," (PhD diss., University of South Carolina, 1990): 78.
13. Hollis, 4.
14. Bainbridge, n.p.
15. Hollis, 5.
16. Recalled in Hollis, 5.
17. Hollis, 5.
18. Bainbridge, n.p.; See also *Joymaker* 1 (April 14, 1924): 3.
19. Bainbridge, 1999, n.p.
20. The remaining copies of the *Parker Progress* can be found on microfilm in the South Carolina Room, Hughes Library, Greenville, South Carolina. See *Parker Progress* (March 6, 1925); Ariail and Smith, 73; Huff, 297.
21. Quoted in James Arthur Dunlap, III, "Changing symbols of success: Economic development in twentieth century Greenville, South Carolina," (PhD diss., University of South Carolina, 1994): 86; see also the Greenville *News* (April 19, 1924), copy in the Parker Scrapbook Collection, Volume 1, p. 14, Hughes Library, Greenville, South Carolina. The Parker Scrapbooks are a series of eight over-sized scrapbooks that contain well over 3,000

clippings from various sources pertaining to the history of the Parker District and its schools.

22. *Joymaker* 1 (April 4, 1924); also Parker Scrapbook 1, 10.
23. Greenville *News* (November 11, 1924): 7.
24. William G. Dwyer, *Technique in administration for improving the high school curriculum: A report of a "Type C Project,"* (EdD thesis, Teachers College, Columbia University, 1951): 25; William Hays Simpson, *Life in Mill Communities*, (Clinton, South Carolina: Presbyterian College Press, 1941): 43–44.
25. Dunlap, 91; Ira Claude Davis, "The educational program of the Parker School District," (EdM thesis, Duke University, 1935): 21.
26. George Kent, "Mill town miracle," *School and Society* 54 (1941):81–85, 82.
27. Stack, 5.
28. Parker Scrapbook, 1, 86.
29. Editorial quoted in Huff, 298.
30. David Clark, "Education of Mill Children," *Southern Textile Bulletin* 15 (April 4, 1918): 14.
31. Marjorie Potwin, *Cotton Mill People of the Piedmont: A Study in Social Change*, (Chapel Hill: University of North Carolina Press, 1927; reprinted New York: AMS Press, 1968): 84–85.
32. Hollis, 4, 7; Jim McAllister, *L. P. Hollis: A Man Ahead of His Time: An Interview*, (Greenville, South Carolina: Greenville County Foundation, 1975): 8.
33. Dwyer, 26.
34. Davis, 16.
35. Quoted in Tullos, 181; Huff, 277–279, *Parker Progress* (October 15, 1926): 6.
36. Unidentified clipping, n.d., Hollis papers, Strom Thurmond Archives, Clemson University, Mss161.
37. Orlando Ramirez Pena, "A study of the ways in which the Parker School cares for individual differences," (MA thesis, Furman University, 1938): 34, 53.
38. James F. Tippett, *Schools for Growing Democracy*, (New York: Ginn and Company, 1936): 312.
39. Parker Scrapbook, 8, 41.
40. Pena, 28; Mahon quoted in the Greenville *Journal* (October 1925): 9.
41. Rowland quoted in Stack, 112.
42. See Davis, 48–49.
43. Sadie Coggans, "Schools to fit the individual, not individuals to fit the schools: Work of Parker schools is not limited to the three R's but is on a broad scale intended to help all pupils, to advance then as they merit and to aid right living," Greenville *Journal* 4 (October, 1925): 14–15.
44. Quoted in Toby Harper Moore, "The unmaking of a cotton mill world: Place, politics and the dismantling of the South's mill village system." (PhD diss., University of Iowa, 1999): 83; Huff, 298; Tullos, 180–181.
45. Hollis, 13.
46. Stack,117.
47. Tippett, 236.
48. Dwyer, 34.

49. Davis, 46; Ariail and Smith, 47.
50. Saxton, 27; Gil Rowland, "Good afternoon, this is Gil Rowland," Greenville *News-Piedmont* (July 16, 1964): 4.
51. Pena, 40–42.
52. Bainbridge, 2003, n.p.; Dwyer, 32.
53. Hollis quoted in Samuel F. Stack, "Lawrence Peter Hollis: A charismatic leader in education," *Vitae Scholasticae* 8 (1989):323–328, 327.
54. Tippett, 269–271.
55. Ibid., 157–159.
56. Parker Scrapbook, 3, 43.
57. Annual Report, *Annual Report of the State Superintendent of Education,* (Columbia *South Carolina, 1923*): 114–130; cited in Moore, 82.
58. Saxton, 1965, Appendix E, Objective #3.
59. Letter entitled "Dear Parker Patrons," *Parker Progress* (May 29, 1925): 1.
60. To get a sense of the dominance of textile interests in the Parker District, one must only consider the make-up of the original board of trustees which included Richard W. Arrington, Superintendent at Union Bleachery; Clifford N. Wallace, Cost Accountant at the Dunean Mill; Edward Hutchings, a merchandise broker and president of the Textile Bank; J. Frank White, a local real estate broker and owner of various businesses on Woodside Avenue in the middle of the Parker District; and Thomas M. Bennett, an official at Brandon Mills. See Dunlap, 84, fn. 20.
61. B.L. Parkinson, "The Parker School District," *South Carolina Education* 5 (1925): 7–9. South Carolina Law 5547(3) Special Tax, gave the Parker District the "power to levy and collect" taxes on "all real and personal property" in the District. See Saxton, 63.
62. Parker District Faculty, *Parker High School Serves Its People: A Report Prepared by the Parker District High School Faculty, With the Assistance of the Staff of the Southern Association Study,* (Greenville, South Carolina: Parker District Schools, 1942): 1.
63. Parkinson, 7–9.
64. Tippett, 118; Parker Scrapbook, 8, 96.
65. Parker Scrapbook, 1, 14.
66. James S. Tippett, "A venture in teacher education," *Childhood Education* 15 (1939): 413–416, 413.
67. Hollis, 11; Dwyer, 30.
68. Dwyer, 27.
69. One such manual was *The Teacher's Handbook in Natural Science for the Elementary Schools*, 1929; the other was *A Social Studies Handbook for Teachers*, 1933. Both were published privately by the Parker School District.
70. Parker Scrapbook, 4, 14.
71. Tippett, 1936, 26–28; Davis, 14; Dwyer, 27; also Parker Scrapbook, 4, 5–6.
72. Parker Scrapbook, 1, 68.
73. Ibid., 8, 39.
74. Ibid., 8, 89.
75. Harry Boyte, "The textile industry: Keel of Southern industrialization," *Radical America* 6 (1972): 4–49, 25; Harriet Herring, *Welfare Work in Mill*

*Villages: The Story of Extra-Mill Activities in North Carolina*, (Chapel Hill: University of North Carolina Press, 1929): 77.

76. Dwyer, 35–36.
77. Davis, 97–98; Tippett, 1936, 238–239.
78. Dwyer, 36; Mendel S. Fletcher, "Parker Peoples College," *South Carolina Education* 12 (1930): 13–14, 13.
79. Ariail and Smith, 35; Fletcher, 13; Greenville *News* (January 3, 1932): 1.
80. Fletcher, 1930, 14.
81. Ariail and Smith, 35; Fletcher, 13; Kent, 83.
82. Ariail and Smith, 27; Judson W. Chapman, "The Parker District is half of Greater Greenville: And the halves are everlastingly and steadfastly united, for their mutual good—What this vast district is, who its people are, and what they are doing," *The Greenville Journal* 4 (October, 1925):3, 24.
83. *Joymaker* 1 (October 19, 1923): 1; Greenville *News* (October 2, 1923): 3.
84. *Joymaker* 1 (December 14, 1923): 1.
85. Anonymous, "Library on Wheels," *Christian Science Monitor* (October 15, 1924): n.p.
86. *Joymaker* 1 (October 19, 1923): 1.
87. Anonymous, n.p.
88. Parker Scrapbook, 1, 23.
89. Fletcher, 1940, 13.
90. For a brief discussion of the schedule and the popularity of novels on the Pathfinder, see "Parker Progress" (March 13, 1925): 5,7.
91. *Joymaker* 1 (November 16, 1923): 4.
92. Ralph M. Lyon, *The Basis for Constructing Curricular Materials in Adult Education for Carolina Cotton Mill Workers*, (New York: Teachers College, Columbia University, 1937): 57.
93. Coggans, 15.
94. Parker Scrapbook, 6, 8.
95. Davis, 114–115; Parker Scrapbook, 6, 18.
96. Davis, 104–105.
97. Tippett, 1936, 309–310.
98. See Hollis, 9; McAllister, 1; Davis, 106. Additional funding came from Junior Charities, the American Legion Auxillary, the St. Paul Mission Association, and the Palmetto Club. See Parker Scrapbook, 6, 4 and 8.
99. Hollis, 10.
100. Dwyer, 85; Parker Scrapbook, 4, 47; Parker Scrapbook, 1, 87.
101. Kent, 82–83.
102. Hollis, 10.
103. Cited in rudimentary chart form in Davis, 1935, 107.
104. Hollis, 10.
105. Dwyer, 25.
106. Greenville *News* (October, 27, 1923): 1.
107. Robert Elliott Veto, "Looms and weavers, schools and teachers: Schooling in North Carolina mill towns, 1910–1940," (DA diss., Carnage Mellon University, 1989): 86.
108. *Parker Progress* (March 13, 1925): 5.

109. Walter T. McFall, "Mouth hygiene program, Parker School District," *South Carolina Education* 7 (1926):138–139.
110. McFall, 138. The Parker High School motto was, interestingly, "Head, Heart, Hand, and Health." See Ariail and Smith, 51.
111. *Parker Progress* (January 7, 1927): 8.
112. Joymaker 1 (March 26, 1924): 1.
113. Clifford Goldsmith, *The Wisdom of Professor Happy by the Professor Himself*, (New York: American Child Health Association, 1923).
114. Stack, 1990, 116.
115. Greenville *News* (October 26, 1970): 1.
116. Dunlap, 77, 135;Greenville *News* (May 19, 1985): 1.
117. Saxton, 44–45.
118. Hollis, 12.
119. Parker Scrapbook, Volume 8, 24.
120. Hollis, 6, 13.
121. Bainbridge, 2003, n.p.
122. Greenville *Journal* (August 5, 2005): 52–53.

CHAPTER 3

# DREAMS DEFERRED

## White Reaction to Langston Hughes' Depression-Era Educational Tour of the South

**Bart Dredge and Cayce Tabor**

On November 11, 1931, newly elected University of North Carolina president Frank Porter Graham offered as his inaugural address "The University Today," in part staking out a position on academic freedom he would find himself defending for years. To Graham, university faculty enjoyed and required the freedom to control the curriculum and establish scholarly standards, while teaching and speaking freely as "scholars and seekers for the truth." Along with university administrators, professors could express their views about issues of importance while "fearing no special interest."

Academic freedom also implied the right of university citizens to reject the "prejudices of section, race, or creeds," and the right to remain open to the "plight of unorganized and inarticulate peoples" in a world in which "high pressure lobbies" could and did impose their will on the general life of the state. A university community should be free to hear anyone speaking for the "unvoiced millions" and even the "hated minorities"—and no criticism of that freedom should tempt the university

*Life Stories: Exploring Issues in Educational History Through Biography*
pp. 45–63

to prohibit speech or publications that were the resources of "a free university, a free religion, and a free state." No matter its challenges, academic freedom was gathering momentum and through it democracy, "sometimes sleeping but never dead," would continually reassert intellectual integrity and individual moral autonomy. Widely heralded for this expansive view of intellectual and institutional freedom, within days of his inauguration President Graham faced his first major challenge with the arrival of the poet Langston Hughes on the Chapel Hill campus.[1]

Langston Hughes (1902–1967) was arguably the premier American poet, social activist, novelist and playwright associated with the Harlem Renaissance. Born in Joplin, Missouri, Hughes spent most of his youth in Lawrence, Kansas, later leaving to attend Columbia University, which drew him to the Harlem that was to be such a major focus of his life and work. While successful at Columbia, Hughes nevertheless left for a period of odd jobs and world travel, returning eventually to attend and finish his studies at Lincoln University, the historically Black institution in Pennsylvania. Hughes was an extraordinarily prolific writer of 12 volumes of poetry, several plays, novels, and other works that frequently "exposed the contradictions" of racial and class subordination.[2] Perhaps as a result, Hughes quickly developed a self-image of many hues, including a belief that he could serve as a "people's poet" who could reeducate himself and his audiences by lifting the theory of Black art closer into alignment with the lived difficulties experienced by millions.[3]

Perhaps the best expression of this sense of self and mission began in 1931 when Hughes wrote to the presidents of Southern Black colleges to inquire whether they would pay him to appear on their campuses. Receiving numerous positive responses, he applied to the Rosenwald Fund, later receiving a $1,000 grant. He then bought a Ford that he could not drive, and recruited Radcliffe Lucas, a former classmate at Lincoln University to join him for his tour of Southern schools.[4] The two began the tour on November 2$^{nd}$, stopping first at Dowington Industrial and Agricultural School for Boys, and then at Morgan College in Baltimore, Virginia Union in Richmond, the Hampton Institute, and Virginia State College where it is likely Hughes studied a portrait of John Mercer Langston, the first president of the college and a distant relative. Hughes was well received early in his tour, especially when his audiences got over their surprise that he was "short, slight and not particularly African."[5] Yet, soon after leaving Virginia he headed into the "troubled Jim Crow South of ever-present danger for Negroes."[6] Hughes' first stop in the South was at the University of North Carolina, the only White school he visited, perhaps thinking that a presentation at Chapel Hill would help publicize his tour, at least "if he wasn't killed first."[7] He had earlier written to Sociology Professor Guy Johnson, then teaching a course on Black culture, who invited Hughes to campus, but apologized that "most of us white folks" were "too hypocritical or too crowded" to put him up for the night.[8]

Born Black, Hughes was "stuck in the mud from the beginning," with Jim Crow grabbing him "by the heels" whenever he tried to "float in the clouds," and as a "social poet" he had experienced his own "skirmishes" with censorship.[9] In a way, the tour of the South was a direct challenge to Jim Crow as Hughes believed that his form of literary education could create "spiritual freedom" in the South.[10] Perhaps at no other time would that freedom mean as much to Hughes, and to the South, as his tour followed so closely the tragic events of the now infamous prosecution of the Scottsboro Boys. Arrested in March 1931 while traveling from Chattanooga to Memphis, the nine young Black males were charged with having raped two White girls also traveling on the rails in search of jobs. In a series of hurried trials with little attention to due process, all except one of the boys was found guilty of rape and sentenced to death, the common sentence at the time in Alabama for young Black males thought to have transgressed the racial divide. The complete story of the injustice at Scottsboro has been frequently and well told, so does not need to be repeated here, but it should be stressed that it was in the shadow of this case that Hughes began his educational sojourn into the American South.[11] In the "Negro Artist and the Racial Mountain," Hughes saw the "common people" as the proper muse for the Black poet. Yet, while he directed his poetry at Blacks and other "low down folks" who struggle through life, he wanted as well to transform the "ugly face of the Southland," and this would require him to reach White audiences as well.[12] Perhaps by exposure to his Black intelligence and artistic flexibility, even White Southerners might come to help accelerate social and racial change.[13] Such a mission might well offend some, of course, and Hughes expected as much. He wrote that, "If White people are pleased, we are glad. If they are not, it doesn't matter." Likewise, "if colored people are pleased, we are pleased. If they are not, their displeasure doesn't matter either." He understood that like all who educate, writers and poets "build our temples for tomorrow," and stand "on top of the mountain, free within ourselves"—a freedom he demanded for himself and his audiences as well.[14]

During the same week as his much-publicized visit to Chapel Hill, Hughes also published two contributions to a new literary magazine that had already begun to draw attention to itself at the University and beyond. Edited by two former UNC students, Milton Abernethy and Anthony Buttitta, *Contempo: A Review of Books and Personalities* joined other culturally radical magazines during the early 1930s including *Dial*, *Hound and Horn*, and the *New Masses*.[15] The editorial policy encouraged literary controversy, including the two issues devoted to the Scottsboro case. The journal published political and literary essays, book reviews, short stories, poetry, and excerpts from works in progress by such writers as Sherwood Anderson, Malcolm Cowley, Countee Cullen and Upton Sinclair. Editors Abernethy and Buttitta also opened the Intimate Bookshop situated directly across from campus in an area most traveled to this day by students.[16] Certainly aided by the intellectual energy produced by *Contempo*, the bookstore quickly became an off-campus center of intellectual and educational life. One astute observer, in fact, later described the Intimate Bookshop as "an oasis in the Sahara of the Bozart," another the "guts of the town's intellectual life," and a third "North Carolina's Algonquin, its Greenwich Village, its Bloomberg, [and] its City Lights."[17] The bookstore quickly became a haven for those who absorbed the radical politics that "mingled with the bookstore's dust," a reputation decidedly gilded by *Contempo's* aggressive critique of Jim Crow and its tragic expression in Scottsboro.[18] No writer, however, generated as much controversy in the pages of the magazine as Langston Hughes with two short publications that dramatically altered his experience in Chapel Hill.

Certain to generate substantial hostility in a region dominated by the cotton textile industry, Hughes first directed "Southern Gentlemen, White Prostitutes, Mill-Owners and Negroes" to those most likely to be offended by its every word. Hughes claimed that if any of the nine Scottsboro boys were executed, the South should be ashamed of itself, and all should learn to "what absurd farces an Alabama court can descend." For the honor of "Southern gentlemen (if there ever were any)," the South should rise and demand the freedom of the "dumb young Blacks, so indiscreet as to travel, unwittingly, on the same freight train with two white prostitutes." Also, why not let Alabama mill owners pay "decent wages" so their women won't need to be prostitutes; and why not provide schools for Alabama Blacks so that the "mulatto children of Southern gentlemen (I reckon they're gentlemen)" won't be so dumb again? Otherwise, let "Dixie justice (blind and syphilitic as it may be)" takes its course and let Alabama's men "amuse themselves" by burning the eight young Blacks to death in the state's electric chair.[19] As would be expected by anyone familiar with the history of the textile industry in the South, this essay inflamed countless people, especially offered as it was by a Northern Black who, like the Scottsboro boys themselves, clearly failed to understand his proper place in the prevailing racial hierarchy.

Perhaps worse, appearing on the same page as the Scottsboro essay Hughes published "Christ in Alabama"—a poem that could only have provoked the wrath of Southern Christians.[20]

"Christ in Alabama"
Christ is a Nigger,
Beaten and Black—
O, bare your back.
Mary is His Mother—
Mammy of the South,
Silence your mouth.
God's His Father—
White Master above,
Grant us your love.
Most holy bastard
Of the bleeding mouth;
Nigger Christ
*On the cross of the South.*[21]

The trope of Christ as a suffering Black man, of course, was not original with Hughes. W. E. B. Du Bois had used the same image in his 1924 novel, *Darkwater*; and other examples of a lynched Black Savior appeared in Countee Cullen's "Christ Recrucified," in 1922, and Walter White's, *The Fire in the Flint* in 1924.[22] Hughes later wrote that "Christ in Alabama" inspired more criticism than the "Southern Gentlemen" essay, describing it as an "ironic poem" encouraged by the thought of how Christ, with no human father, would be accepted were "He born in the South of a negro mother." With its "malign caricature of racist justice" Hughes' poem was calculated to generate an angry response from all Southerners. The inflammatory first line of "Christ in Alabama" specifies Christ as a "dark-skinned man," against traditional portrayals of the "pale Savior." [23] Perhaps for that reason, one critic suggested, "Christ in Alabama" was a "modern poem we have wanted to forget." The three stanzas insist that Christ bare his back, Mary silence her mouth and God grant His love, and turn the false accusation of rape back on the dominant culture of White power and privilege. The actual violence in Alabama was not a crime committed by nine young Blacks, but the historical violence White men had long visited upon Black women.[24] Implicit is a condemnation of modern Christians who "gather like Pontius Pilate's Romans" to murder Christ again. The victim is the product of the rape of a Black woman by a White man, who then represses his paternity by murdering his own son. This "omnipresent and universally denied trinity" serves as the backdrop for the South's repeated crucifixion scenes—"Nigger Christ/On the Cross of the South." In every Southern town there is a Calvary on which hangs the "bleeding, ritualized product of denial and repression."[25] The earlier essay, coupled with the poem, "Christ in Alabama" and the invitation to Hughes to speak to White students at Chapel Hill, ignited a public controversy that dragged on for months among elite and popular commentators alike.

Among the most vociferous critics among those who condemned Hughes was the racist demagogue and trade journal editor David Clark of Charlotte who first paid attention to Langston Hughes and *Contempo* on November 26, 1931. Editorializing in his privately owned *Southern Textile Bulletin,* Clark reprinted the "scurrilous and blasphemous articles" by Hughes and pointed out that in most of the South such a man would be "fortunate to escape bodily harm." Yet, it appeared that a negro communist could go to Chapel Hill after calling Christ a bastard, and declaring that there were no Southern gentlemen, and still have "students sit at his feet."[26] It should be noted that Clark's hint about "bodily harm" was consistent with views held long before Langston Hughes visited Chapel Hill. In 1922, for example, Clark had written that perhaps the Ku Klux Klan could be called upon to ensure the "purity of the blood" of mill workers against outside agitators from the North. Now it was clear that Hughes, one of those agitators, had "spit in the faces" of Southern Whites.[27]

Even as late as January 1932, Clark criticized UNC for remaining silent about the insulting and blasphemous "negro author, Langston Hughes." In fact, the "negro communist" had been honored by those who praised him in an "exceedingly complimentary" student editorial.[28] After hoping the "insults of this negro" had affected only a few, Clark lamented that the student newspaper, the *Daily Tar Heel,* had found his writings the "expression of a clear and sincere spirit."[29] Continuing for months, Clark took every occasion to remind his readers that UNC had earlier brought to campus "the negro, Langston Hughes"—and here one begins to see the corrosive effect of such repetition—after he had insulted the South and had written sacrilegious poetry.[30] Such unending commentary finally led UNC student body president Mayne Albright to respond. In May 1932, Albright condemned the continuing attacks against academic freedom. Framed as an answer to Clark's charges that "radicalism finds nourishment" on the UNC campus, Albright insisted that there were no professors on campus who taught "communism, atheism, free love or the doctrine of other subversive forces." Moreover, no campus visitors or speakers sustained such doctrines, perhaps especially Langston Hughes who offered students a "respectful, restrained and humorous story of his life and work."[31] Clark persisted, however, even suggesting that UNC officials allowed Hughes access to the campus to avoid a "call-down" from the American Association of University Professors, known to be "allied with" the American Civil Liberties Union and a host of "other subversive forces."[32] Even two years after the controversy had finally died down, Clark returned to Hughes—that "paid worker for communism" whose "alleged poetry" was nothing more than a means for "furthering the cause of communism."[33]

Other elite commentators responded to the Hughes affair as well. In a lengthy exchange of letters, Kemp Lewis of the Erwin Cotton Mills in Durham agreed with Clark that the *Daily Tar Heel* sometimes published "wild statements" about which he did not approve, and undoubtedly some UNC students were "highly irregular" in their religious views or shared radical thoughts. Still, one could not expel them all. More importantly, the University was "much disgusted" by Hughes, but the controversy would have passed quietly had Clark himself not published inflammatory editorials that undoubtedly pleased the *Contempo* editors and prolonged the life of the publication.[34] Perhaps worse, the "rather intemperate" editorials Clark offered were potentially "hurtful" to textile interests, never mind the University as well.[35] Others, however, failed to find any problem with Clark's assessment of the Hughes situation in Chapel Hill, including John Wilkins who wrote that Clark had been "perfectly right" about the teaching of "atheism-communism [sic] and socialism" on the UNC campus. Evidently students and professors alike failed to recognize that the Church was mankind's "best civilizer," and that one could not destroy the teachings of the "child born in Bethlehem." Only "small ignorant people" run down everything that "breathes of the Church," and they were widely understood to be the "stumbling blocks on the highways of life." As for reading the "negro Langston Hughes," Wilkins asked, why not read Tennyson, the Bard of Avon, and the English classics? If nothing else, those who enjoy "real literature" should not waste time with "modern trash," produced by "high intellectuals" forgotten in short order and soon adrift in the "Ocean of Lost Authors." It could not be clearer that the University had made a huge mistake when encouraging "Atheism, Socialism, Communism and the Negro Langston Hughes."[36]

Kemp Lewis later wrote to UNC President Frank Graham that the publications by Hughes made "the blood of every Southerner boil," and "propaganda sheets" like *Contempo* struck at the very "foundations of our civilization and our social relationships" in the region.[37] He wrote later still that he was "intensely worried" about the Hughes incident. David Clark had written editorials that "could not but irritate," but they had to resist striking out at him by approving "the *Contempo* attitude," or by praising Hughes. If nothing else, some parents had evidently decided to enroll their sons in other colleges because UNC had invited to campus such "undesirable citizens" as Langston Hughes. There were, again, certain fundamental ideals and doctrines in our "Southern civilization" that demanded protection.[38] Another important correspondent, attorney Kemp D. Battle of Rocky Mount, wrote to UNC executive secretary to the president, Robert House, that while he had "due regard for free speech," he wondered if loyalty to that principle required the university to provide campus support and facilities for "blasphemous" speeches.[39] House later responded that although both its editors had once been UNC students, *Contempo* was not under University jurisdiction. Clearly, though, they had "made a mess" of the freedom of inquiry so perhaps "we have failed." Besides, while on campus Hughes had behaved in such a "gentlemanly manner" it was unfortunate that *Contempo* had carried the two "horrible examples of bad taste" at the same time. Obviously, House concluded, this was what one could expect from "half-baked, uneducated, and wholly reprehensible adolescents."[40]

Soon after Hughes' campus appearance, textile industry executive J. Harper Erwin, Jr., of Durham wrote to Frank Graham on behalf of Greenville, South Carolina attorney James D. Poag, also a UNC alumnus. Having read Hughes' contributions to *Contempo*, Poag reprimanded Graham for allowing "communists and others of that stripe" to do their "preaching" at the university. To Poag, Graham should avoid a repetition of such events and insisted that claiming too little advance information about the Hughes presentation would appease no one.[41] Graham later conceded that many in Chapel Hill had condemned *Contempo* for its intellectual irresponsibility, as well as Hughes for his audacity. Still, such problems were the price that the University pays for its freedom, although in this case the price was admittedly very high. Nevertheless, Graham would not, as some had suggested, prohibit "representative Negroes" from speaking to students, as a better understanding between the races tended to be the result.[42]

One day later, Thomas P. Graham of the Charlotte-based Crompton & Knowles Loom Works also wrote to President Graham that the entire state had been "stirred" because the "infamous negro" had been allowed to speak on campus. He had recently developed a closer understanding of God and Christianity, and thus found any teaching contrary to Jesus distasteful, and when a "blasphemous negro" speaks at the University he found it difficult to put words to paper. He had been loyal to UNC for decades, but if something did not change, he would support another university—preferably one with the "nerve and power" to stand in the "fear of God." President Graham must immediately deny campus access to "predators" like Hughes and weed out all professors who engage in "Communistic or Anti-Christian teachings." He wanted to continue helping UNC in teaching "Christian Ideals and Character," but his assistance was contingent upon removing the "disgrace and dishonor" brought to Chapel Hill by this "blasphemous and Anti-Christian negro."[43]

In another denunciation of Hughes and his writings, Anderson, South Carolina publisher Wilton E. Hall asked Governor O. Max Gardner on December 8, 1930 to "take a hand in the management" of *Contempo*. Publisher of the *Anderson Daily Mail* and the *Daily Independent* and a former United States Senator, Hall asked the governor whether a "White Democrat" could ever sanction the blasphemy and slurs against White mill women, or abide imputations that Southern justice was both blind and diseased. Had the governor ever seen the "red flag of Communism" so defiantly waved in the "face of Southern Democracy" as in this case? Something must be done about writings that left so many Southerners "busted open with rage" and Hall insisted that Governor Gardner at least close down *Contempo* for having given space for Hughes to express his venom.[44] Interestingly, even Upton Sinclair weighed in briefly on the Hall complaint, writing that the Governor of North Carolina should not "take over" the magazine, as there were undoubtedly enough "dull publications" in the state already.[45] At minimum, a final critic added, no university should offer encouragement to anyone capable of writing such an "outrageous, unfair and unscrupulous denunciation of the South."[46]

Amid the countless other duties of a newly appointed university president, Frank Graham also found time to comment on the Hughes controversy. He acknowledged that the essay and poem appearing in *Contempo* had grievously offended the religious sensibilities and racial prejudices of many. While he would refuse to censor anyone's "interpretation of life and its conflicts," he was equally adamant that journal editors themselves bore a "moral responsibility" to express a decent regard for honest religious convictions and improved race relations. The intellectual irresponsibility demonstrated by *Contempo* was antithetical to the educational approach of any modern university, but perhaps especially one leading a section of the country so deeply plagued by the delicate problems of race and religion.[47] Frank Graham wrote to Kemp Lewis that the irresponsible "antics of sensationalism and exhibitionism" of the *Contempo* staff had energized David Clark. They gave Clark just what he needed to "impute the University," and in exchange received the recognition they had "craved" and had been generally denied at Chapel Hill. As for Langston Hughes and his campus visit, Graham reminded Lewis that a representative Negro leader appeared on campus every year. Professor Guy Johnson was likely "horrified at the misuse of his purpose" by the editors of *Contempo*, but Graham insisted that Johnson remained "entirely innocent" of any blame in the growing controversy. As president, Graham could have simply closed the door on Hughes, but "not for the world" would he have done so. If others insisted on reprimanding anyone on campus, he would readily accept that rebuke even though he had nothing but contempt for "the language and the spirit" expressed in the Hughes poem and essay. Graham added that he would "take his punishment and not squeal," although he found it odd to be attacked by the editors of *Contempo* at one end and by the *Southern Textile Bulletin* at the other. Nevertheless, no matter the source of the denunciation, he would "bend to neither."[48] In fact, when Clark and others later demanded the dismissals of Guy Johnson and other professors for having invited Hughes to campus, Graham pointedly told the Board of Trustees, "I am responsible for what happens on this campus. You fire me."[49] Inevitably, on this and other principled positions he was to take in the future, Graham avoided an escalation perhaps desired by those who preferred to see him display "the martyr pose."[50]

To be sure, President Graham was not the only campus voice to weigh in on the Hughes controversy. The *Daily Tar Heel* offered its unalloyed support of Hughes and the University, insisting that the campus presentation had been an excellent "biographical, poetical, and philosophical disquisition," that concentrated not only on those Blacks who were "delimited" in their opportunities, but all in Depression-era America who were finding opportunities denied them and discovering that their only choice was to "submit or to struggle or perhaps die."[51] Later, aware of the relentless criticism lodged against Hughes and UNC by David Clark, the student newspaper wrote that Clark had once again "cast his horrified gaze" toward Chapel Hill and with his "trusty slingshot," gathered a "goodly supply of spitballs" as weapons in his campaign to destroy the "mythical Goliath of communism at Carolina." Having aroused himself to a "spasm of vitriolic activity" by Langston Hughes, it was clear to everyone that Clark was little more than a "ham actor" who loved the spotlight. Still, with Clark mischaracterizing academic freedom and intellectual experimentation as "socialistic policies," the University had no choice but to defend itself.[52]

Often during lingering controversies elite opinion eventually wends its way down into popular consciousness, and the Hughes affair offered no exception. While some congratulated *Contempo* and its writers for their courage in having stood against the "decaying throne of the Southern Bourbons," most were livid at UNC for inviting Hughes to speak on campus, and at *Contempo* for having published his criticism of the Scottsboro case.[53] For example, during Hughes' campus presentation, local police officers congregated around Gerrard Hall as Hughes felt the tension of race that is "peculiar to the South." While no trouble erupted, many were inclined to run Hughes out of town, including one of the police bodyguards who remarked that: "Sure he should be run out! It's bad enough to call Christ a bastard. But when he calls him a *Nigger* [sic], he's gone too far."[54] In other cases unsigned newspaper editorials focused on Hughes, as when the *Charlotte Observer* found the campus visit and his writings "utterly inexcusable" as he was clearly a "negro Communist and defamer of the South."[55] Likewise, the *Gastonia Daily Gazette* condemned Hughes and his writings as "common, filthy, obnoxious, putrid, rancid, nauseating, rotten, vile, and stinking"—opprobrium so offensive that Sinclair

Lewis wrote that such "charming praise" had led him to subscribe to the magazine.[56] When reports of these reactions reached the North, his mother begged Hughes to abandon his plans to visit the Scottsboro boys at Kilby prison, and asked her local church to pray for her son, while his friend Elmer Carter wrote of his fears of the "hot-headed cracker types" in the South who might injure any Black man who violated the prevailing social etiquette of White supremacy.[57]

Another critic posed a more serious threat to Hughes and the University of North Carolina by his ability to organize the anger of others into political action. In September 1932 the *Chapel Hill Weekly* reported that L. A. Tatum, a retired cotton mill executive from Belmont, North Carolina, had delivered to Governor O. Max Gardner an address entitled, "The Anti-Religious Invasion of Higher Education." In the form of a petition signed by over 250 state citizens, Tatum and his signatories had extracted from recent accounts and some college textbooks "pornographic paragraphs" that, in his view, proved that UNC was teaching "free love" and encouraging students to delve into "sexual filth." The local paper noted that while the University might on occasion produce intellectual offspring who are "veritable monsters to hard common sense," that did not justify Tatum's attacks. If listened to at the highest levels, Tatum would reduce UNC to a "timid association of boss-ridden pedagogues." Undoubtedly Tatum, who reduced his own prejudices to an anti-intellectual petition, and David Clark who advertised the South as a "paradise of low-priced labor," had damaged the region far more than any visitor like Langston Hughes could ever accomplish in a classroom with UNC students.[58]

Tatum asked the governor to join him and others as they prepared for battle in an effort to "rout the bureaucratic army" that had perverted the universities so much as to raise a "stench that is reaching to high heaven."[59] To ensure gubernatorial assistance in his campaign, Tatum suggested that the governor might himself be "the anointed of Israel"—Moses destined to lead North Carolina out of the intellectual and spiritual wilderness.[60] The petition itself "bristled with the pernicious outpourings" of Freud, Langston Hughes, and Bertrand Russell, and drew special attention to the "utterly inexcusable" presentation by Langston Hughes, again the "negro communist and defamer of the South."[61] About Hughes, Tatum insisted that the state of North Carolina had to make a clear choice as it could not serve "both Christ and Lenin."[63] As might be expected, the Tatum petition generated significant heat. The *Raleigh News & Observer*, for example, argued that if the state universities submitted to the petition, "they do not deserve to exist." Education could admit none of the limits proscribed by the "aroused brethren," as they had written what amounted to a "death warrant" for the University. To be sure, UNC had often provoked resentment among those who preferred to see professors and students confined to the "groove of tradition," but now hundreds of citizens had organized to demand that the governor spare the state from the "predatory acts" of these "so-called modern educators." As was often true, these reactionary censors relied almost exclusively on the "time-worn cry that the wind is blowing in Moscow" and thus remained ill-equipped to understand modern education.[64] Despite the energy Tatum devoted to his cause, and the support he seemed to have engendered among some, the governor ignored the petition.

Finally, in some ways one is more disturbed by a public reaction to the Hughes controversy expressed in letters often sent to the same newspapers that had excited the issue on their editorial pages. The overwhelming majority of such public commentary was negative in tone, spiteful in posture, and unreservedly critical of the University and the poet, and all who failed to see the threat that his mere presence, leaving aside his writings and speeches, posed to fundamentally important Southern values. Not all critics, however, agreed. For example, Albert Snider condemned the Tatum petition and other attacks against UNC as a menace that threatened "another Waterloo" between the "forces of light and the forces of darkness." In another statement, he warned the North Carolina governor and University trustees to "not dare lay your hand[s] upon the faculty" over this issue. To do so "means war" of perhaps "a thousand years." After all, Tatum and his supporters were no better than "puny petitioners" intent upon requiring intelligent young Southerners to don Tatum's own "Black cap of ignorance." Likewise, the *Charlotte Observer* later published an unsigned letter noting that it might be nice to constitute a "Committee of One Hundred, all bundled into one," like the Tatum petitioners, or to live as David Clark—a "one-man Spanish Inquisition" destroying others for "heretical beliefs"—but one prayed such days are past. After all, fair-minded Southerners recognize that they live "side by side, saints, sinners and all." Finally, to Wilton Cathey from Gastonia the Hughes dispute reminded him of Dayton, Tennessee and the "self-appointed censors" who had left the town forever branded as a "synonym for crystallized ignorance."[65] The University and Langston Hughes were not entirely alone.

Most public commentary, however, was different, ranging from the hortatory in purpose to the horrific in tone. One critic, for example, wrote that only a "hopeless moron," would teach students that Jesus Christ was a "Black bastard." Everyone, perhaps even including the "collegiate moron," should agree that "pink-parlor socialists" as well as the "homeopathic social perverts" in universities bore direct responsibility for the generation of students who had "wrecked Russia." Unless willing to accept the same fate, the South could not accept the presence of more "notorious characters" like Langston Hughes who "defiantly expectorate" in the face of those decent people whose children went to college to learn the ideals of social and racial purity. Annie Ashcraft, also from Charlotte, agreed. She complained that too many college professors desired to be among the "intelligentsia and the intellectual high-brows" rather than among the "narrow-minded, the conservative and provincial," even becoming so broad-minded that they encouraged "a negro" to smear "that name that is above every name." Yet, she did not condemn the "negro"—only those Whites who bowed before his "irreverence and blasphemy." Even more pointedly, S. S. Dunlap saw the Langston Hughes episode as new only in its "degree of boldness." Such was to be expected from those who enjoyed the "powers of darkness" and haunted modern schools with a commitment to "overthrow the truth." Inevitably, exposing students to Langston Hughes and others of his kind would yield the "bitter fruit of our previous sowing."[66]

J. E. L. Winecoff from Montreat, North Carolina supported the Tatum petition as having been written by men competent to judge "what is good and what is bad, what is moral and what is immoral, what is wholesome and what is harmful." This was crucial as the average Southern student was incapable of thinking for himself, especially when confronted by professors determined to exploit their "pet or wild theories," highlight the "lower impulses or animal nature" of visiting speakers, and encourage social decay among their innocent students. If Chapel Hill was to continue as a "real blessing" to the South, students must enjoy protection from the "wrong character, or the wrong moral or mental slant," and no character was worse for the students than that demonstrated by Langston Hughes; at the same time, M. Bullock of Lumberton focused on the insidious "self-indifference" and profound "mediocrity and degeneracy" often masked on college campuses as "tolerance" for radical ideas. He was angered by the absence of the "righteous indignation" that should have ignited a "state of rebellion" over the "blasphemous, unholy, degenerate remarks" offered by Hughes during his tour of Southern universities. Educators shared a moral obligation to protect their students from "degenerate infidels" like the Harlem poet and other "low-down rascals." Yet, campus leaders had remained silent. Perhaps, Bullock warned, such "stark emptiness of life without morals" would someday bring on a "civil war"—a tragedy seemingly encouraged by the "cowards and ambitious demagogues" teaching and preaching in Southern universities. Finally, Walter C. Guy simply wrote to the *Charlotte Observer* that he feared that the young would be led into the "jaws of the vilest type of Communism" by university teachers and their invited comrades such as Langston Hughes.[67]

Reflecting in 1934 on his tour of Southern schools, Hughes denounced the "cowards from the colleges," too often led by "weak professors and well-paid presidents" willingly submitting to Southern White supremacy. Many of the faculty and administrators in historically Black colleges produced among their students "spineless Uncle Toms" who, if informed at all, were full of "mental and moral evasions."[68] Hughes, however, was not alone in expressing this dismay. As early as 1930, addressing graduates at Howard University, W. E. B. Du Bois chastised faculty and students alike: "Our college man today is, on the average, a man untouched by real culture....We have in our colleges a growing mass of stupidity and indifference."[69] In another instance, President Lafayette Harris of Philander Smith College in Arkansas castigated his students for their estrangement from most Southern Blacks, and condemned the "fatalistic and nonchalant" attitude of too many college-educated Blacks who "know nothing of their less fortunate fellows and care less."[70] The unwillingness to confront racial injustice on the part of young Blacks and their educational mentors continued to disturb Hughes as he came to recognize that "the old abolitionist spirit" from which many Negro colleges had evolved had turned "strangely conservative" about contemporary problems, including the horrors at Scottsboro.[71]

Following his trip to Chapel Hill and the violent response among Whites to his short poem and essay condemning the Scottsboro injustices, papers all over the South covered the excitement at Chapel Hill, and yet, still troubled by the Scottsboro injustice, Hughes followed through on his plan to visit the defendants on death row at the infamous Kilby prison in Alabama. He later recalled his reaction: "For a moment the fear comes: even for me, a Sunday morning visitor, the doors might never open again.... And I'm only a Nigger poet."[72] To Hughes his poems sounded "futile and stupid in the face of death," but the boys themselves listened quietly and then came to the bars to shake his hand. Touched by their reaction, and angrier than before about the grotesque injustice portrayed in the Scottsboro affair, Hughes traveled to the Tuskegee Institute and even there found only silence about the "unspeakable" Scottsboro, again a difficult lesson for someone who had "never known such uncompromising prejudices."[73] Years after his tour of the South, Hughes remembered again his educational visit to Chapel Hill and the storm that greeted his contributions to *Contempo*. As he left Chapel Hill, he went deeper into Dixie "with poetry as a passport," stopping to speak to overflow Black audiences who knew he had "walked into the lion's den, and come out like Daniel, unscathed."[74] Yet, it was clear that his expedition taught him something of value as well. UNC students and faculty alike had treated him with courtesy as they distanced themselves from the hateful "anti-Negro elements" in the state. It was at the University of North Carolina, surrounded by the ever-deafening chords of anti-intellectual posturing, simmering racial fears, and defensive White supremacy, that Hughes discovered "how hard it is to be a White liberal in the South."[75]

## NOTES

1. Reprinted in John Ehle, *Dr. Frank: Life with Frank Porter Graham*, (Chapel Hill: Franklin Street Books, 1993): Appendix F, 275–276, 275; Also UNC *Alumni Review* 29 (December 1931): 110.
2. Langston Hughes and Arna Bontemps, *The Poetry of the Negro, 1746–1949*, (New York: Doubleday, 1949); and Nicholas Coles and Janet Zandy, *Working Class Literature: An Anthology*, (New York: Oxford University Press, 2006), 370.
3. For general treatment of Hughes and his work during the early period, see Arnold Rampersad, *The Life of Langston Hughes: Volume I: 1902–1941: I, Too, Sing America*, (New York: Oxford University Press, 2002); and Faith Berry, *Before and Beyond Harlem: A Biography of Langston Hughes*, (New York: Citadel, 1992, reprint).
4. Langston Hughes, *I Wonder as I Wander: An Autobiographical Journey*, (New York: Hill and Wang, 1956), 72–73. For more on the Julius Rosenwald Fund, see J. Scott McCormick, "The Julius Rosenwald Fund," *Journal of Negro Education* 3 (October 1934): 605–626; A. Gilbert Belles, "The College Faculty, the Negro Scholar, and the Julius Rosenwald Fund," Journal of Negro History 54 (October 1969): 383–392.
5. Rampersad, 223–224.
6. Rampersad, 223. See also Mary Beth Culp, "Religion in the Poetry of Langston Hughes," *Phylon* 48 (3rd Quarter, 1987): 240–245.
7. Rampersad, 226.
8. Rampersad, 224; Guy Johnson to Langston Hughes, October 27, 1931, in the Guy Benton Johnson papers #03826, (hereinafter Johnson papers), Southern Historical Collection, Wilson Library, University of North Carolina at Chapel Hill.
9. Langston Hughes, "My Adventures as a Social Poet," *Phylon* (3rd Qtr. 1947): 205–206.
10. Anthony Dawahare, "Langston Hughes's Radical Poetry and the `End of Race'," *MELUS* 23 (Autumn 1998): 21–41.
11. See, for example, Dan T. Carter, *Scottsboro: A Tragedy of the American South*, (Baton Rouge: Louisiana State University Press, 2007); and James A. Miller, *Remembering Scottsboro: Legacy of an Infamous Trial*, (Princeton: Princeton University Press, 2009).
12. Langston Hughes, "The Negro Artist and the Racial Mountain," *The Nation* (June 23, 1926): 692; generally see Maryemma Graham, "The Practice of a Social Art," 213–235 in Henry Louis Gates and K. A. Appiah (eds.), *Langston Hughes: Critical Perspectives Past and Present*, (New York: Amistad, 1993): 213; Michael Thurston, "Black Christ, Red Flag: Langston Hughes on Scottsboro," *College Literature* 22 (October 1995): 30–49. Langs-

ton Hughes, "To Negro Writers," 139–141, Henry Hart (ed)., *American Writers Congress* (New York: International Publishers, 1935), 140.

13. Arnold Rampersad, Introduction, 34–40 in Alain Locke (ed.), *The New Negro*, (New York: Athenaeum, 1992), xvi.
14. Hughes, "Negro Artist," 694.
15. *Daily Tar Heel*, (April 28, 1931): 1. See this discussed in Colquitt, Clare, "'Contempo' Magazine: Asylum for Aggrieved Authors," *Library Chronicle of the University of Texas at Austin* 27 (1984): 19–45, 22.
16. *Contempo: A Review of Ideas and Personalities* (June 1931): 3.
17. Quoted in Glenda Elizabeth Gilmore, *Defying Dixie: The Radical Roots of Civil Rights, 1919–1950*, (New York: W. W. Norton, 2009), 206. The image derives from H. L. Mencken, "The Sahara of the Bozart," in Mencken, *Prejudices: A Selection*, (Baltimore: Johns Hopkins University Press, 1996), 69–81.
18. Junius Irving Scales and Richard Nickson, *Cause at Heart: A Former Communist Remembers*, (Athens: University of Georgia Press, 1987), 45–46, 63; Gilmore, *Defying Dixie*, 207.
19. Hughes, "Southern Gentlemen, White Prostitutes, Mill-Owners and Negroes," *Contempo* 1 (December 1, 1931): 1.
20. Langston Hughes to Milton Abernethy, October 23, 1931, *Contempo* Records, #04408 (hereinafter *Contempo* Records), Southern Historical Collection, Wilson Library, University of North Carolina at Chapel Hill.
21. Italics in the original. See Langston Hughes, "Christ in Alabama," *Contempo* 1 (December 1, 1931), 1.
22. W. E. B. Du Bois, *Darkwater: Voices from Within the Veil*, (New York: Washington Square Press), 2004; Walter White, *The Fire in the Flint: A Young Doctor's Tragic Confrontation with the Segregated South*, (Athens: University of Georgia Press, 1996).
23. Thurston, "Black Christ," 31–33; see Langston Hughes, "Cowards from the Colleges," *Crisis* 41 (1934): 227.
24. Cary Nelson, *Revolutionary Memory: Recovering the Poetry of the American Left*," (New York: Routledge, 2003): 70–75. See this also discussed in Thurston, "Black Christ," 34.
25. Nelson, 70–71; On these points see also, William J. Maxwell, *New Negro, Old Left: African American Writing and Communism Between the Wars*, (New York: Columbia University Press, 1999).
26. Clark, "Lower and Lower," *Southern Textile Bulletin*, (December 3, 1931): 18. Clark, "Communist Paper at Chapel Hill," *Southern Textile Bulletin*, (November 26, 1931).
27. Also see Clark, "Two Examples of Student Journalism," *Southern Textile Bulletin*, (November 26, 1931): 11. For more on Clark's views on race, see Bart Dredge, "Defending White Supremacy: David Clark and the *Southern Textile Bulletin*, 1911 to 1955," *North Carolina Historical Review* 89 (January 2012): 1–34.
28. Clark, "New England Operatives Not Wanted," *Southern Textile Bulletin*, (July 6, 1922): 18; and Clark, "How Strange?" *Southern Textile Bulletin*, (December 31, 1931): 19.

29. David Clark, "A Discreditable Evasion," *Southern Textile Bulletin*, (January 28, 1932): 19.
30. Clark, "Lower and Lower," *Southern Textile Bulletin*, (December 3, 1931): 18. As might have been expected, Clark was also angered when the *Daily Tar Heel* referred to Langston Hughes as "Mr. Hughes." See Clark, "Greensboro Daily News Evades Publication," *Southern Textile Bulletin*, (December 17, 1931): 19.
31. See, for example, Clark, "Norman Thomas Again," *Southern Textile Bulletin*, (April 14, 1932): 18.
32. "Students Defend Graham's Policy," "Answer Criticism Alleging Abuse of Free Speech Privilege at University," *Raleigh News and Observer*, (May 30, 1932), copy in Frank Porter Graham papers, 1908–1972, #01819 (hereinafter Graham papers), Southern Historical Collection, Wilson Library, University of North Carolina at Chapel Hill.
33. David Clark, "Institution, Itself, All Right; Not with Some of the Things Going On," letter to the editor, *Charlotte Observer*, (April 29, 1932).
34. David Clark, "No Ghost Hunter," letter to the editor, *Charlotte Observer*, (October 4, 1933).
35. Kemp P. Lewis to David Clark, February 19, 1932, Graham papers. It should be noted that space allows for only a sampling of both popular and elite reactions to the Langston Hughes campus visit and his writings in *Contempo*.
36. Kemp P. Lewis to John M. Booker, January 5, 1932, Graham papers.
37. "Mr. Clark's Answer," John Grimball Wilkins, letter to the editor, *Charlotte Observer*, (October 3, 1932).
38. Kemp P. Lewis to Frank P. Graham, November 28, 1931, Graham papers. At the bottom of this letter was a scribbled note: "Mr. Lewis phoned and said disregard this letter."
39. Kemp P. Lewis to Frank P. Graham, December 7, 1931, Graham papers.
40. Kemp D. Battle to Robert B. House, December 1931 [sic], Graham papers.
41. Robert B. House to Kemp D. Battle, December 17, 1931, Graham papers.
42. James D Poag quotes from J. Harper Erwin, Jr., to Frank P. Graham, December 6, 1931, Graham papers.
43. Frank P. Graham to J. Harper Erwin, Jr., December 24, 1931, Graham papers.
44. Thomas P. Graham to Frank P. Graham, December 18, 1931; Graham Papers. Another correspondent, attorney James A. Gray of Winston-Salem, later inquired whether there might be federal restrictions on postal delivery of magazines like *Contempo* because even though the University had no ties to the offensive magazine, most continued to see "Chapel Hill" and "University" as synonymous. See James A. Gray to Frank P. Graham, December 29, 1931, Graham papers.
45. "Governor Gardner Declines to Give `Nut-Paper' a Kick," *Greensboro Daily News*, (December 8, 1931). See also "Officials Say University Not Connected with Paper," and "Magazine at Chapel Hill is Attacked by Publisher," *Greensboro Daily News*, (December 8, 1931).
46. Upton Sinclair to Abernethy, December 16, 1931, *Contempo* Records.

47. Tom Glascow to Frank P. Graham, January 25, 1932, Graham papers.
48. Frank P. Graham to Milton Abernethy, December 10, 1931, Graham papers.
49. Frank P. Graham to Kemp P. Lewis, December 15, 1931, Graham papers.
50. This comment appears in a number of locations, including Warren Ashby, *Frank Porter Graham: A Southern Liberal,* (Winston-Salem: John F. Blair, Publisher, 1980); see also Guion Griffis Johnson, May 28, 1974, interview F-0029-3, Southern Oral History Program Collection (#4007), Southern Historical Collection, Wilson Library, University of North Carolina at Chapel Hill.
51. See this point in Virginius Dabney, "Reds in Dixie," *Sewanee Review* 42 (October-December, 1934): 415–422.
52. "The Free," *Daily Tar Heel,* (November 24, 1931).
53. "David and Goliath," *Daily Tar Heel,* (December 2, 1931). "Oh Tell Us Pretty Maiden," *Daily Tar Heel,* (April 21, 1932).
54. See, for example, David Doren to Abernethy, December 11, 1931, *Contempo* Records.
55. Hughes, "Adventure," 208. See also Langston Hughes, *I Wonder,* 46; and Faith Berry, 135.
56. "Liberalism," *Charlotte Observer,* (April 21, 1932). The very next day the *Charlotte Observer* had to offer a partial retraction when it noted that Chapel Hill readers were surprised to learn that Hughes had read his poem, "Christ in Alabama" while on the UNC campus. Hughes had not read his poem. See "Deny Poem Recited at N.C. University," Privately Owned Magazine at Chapel Hill Printed Article to Which Editorial Exception Was Taken," *Charlotte Observer,* (April 22, 1932).
57. Sinclair Lewis to Abernethy, December 14, 1931; See this description used later in an advertisement in *Contempo,* 1 (January 1, 1932): 4.
58. Thurston, "Black Christ," 36; Thurston relies upon Rampersad, 225, who quotes Carrie Clarke to Langston Hughes, December 11, 1931, and Elmer A. Carter to Langston Hughes, January 8, 1932.
59. The cover of the petition implored: "In Heaven's Name, Governor, Save Our State from Further Predatory Acts by These So-Called Modern Educators Against `Things of the Spirit'." See, "Tatum Spanked by the Press," *Chapel Hill Weekly,* (September 16, 1932). The concern for sexual and social filth appears frequently in commentary about Hughes and others, including in Robert Madry, "Submits Emphatic Denial of Allegations of Falsity," letter to the editor, *Charlotte Observer,* (September 18, 1932).
60. "Read by L. A. Tatum," *Greensboro Daily News,* (August 9, 1932).
61. The list of signatories included mayor Charles Lambeth, of Charlotte, Bishop J. Kenneth Pfohl of Winston-Salem, publisher Col. Wade H. Harris of the *Charlotte Observer,* and businessmen J. D. Efird and W. H. Belk. Most importantly, the roster "abounds with the signatures of the textile barons." See "Chief Crusader Tatum Found to be a Roman Catholic — Crusaders Persuaded Devils Need Casting Out But They Will Not Let Mr. Tatum Be Chief Caster-Out," *Greensboro Daily News,* (September 12, 1932).

62. "Read by L. A. Tatum," *Greensboro Daily News*, (August 9, 1932). See also "Presentation of Petition Fails to Arouse Village," *Greensboro Daily News*, (August 9, 1932).
63. *Raleigh News & Observer*, (September 8, 1932); "State University Target in Attack," "Professor English Bagby Singled Out in Protest Made to Governor," *Raleigh News & Observer*, (September 9, 1932); also "Ask Governor to Purge University," and "Petitioners Assert that Freud and Other Liberalists are Emphasized," *Asheville Advocate*, (September 9, 1932).
64. "Carolina Reaction," *Raleigh News & Observer*, (August 14, 1932).
65. Albert Monroe Snider of Hoffman, North Carolina, "Concerning the Petition," letter to the editor, *Charlotte Observer*, (September 10, 1932); also see Snider, "An Oration Against Modern Educators," letter to the editor, *Charlotte Observer*, (September 13, 1932). Also see Anonymous, "Would Square Clark and Hughes," letter to the editor, *Charlotte Observer*, (October 2, 1932); and Wilton Cathey, "Confidence in Frank Graham," letter to the editor, *Charlotte Observer*, (September 18, 1932).
66. Arthur Talmadge Abernethy, "A Discussion from the Standpoint of the People," letter to the editor, *Charlotte Observer*, (September 18, 1932); also Annie Bickett Ashcraft, "Intellectual High-Browing," letter to the editor, *Charlotte Observer*, (April 27, 1932); and S. S. Dunlap, "Liberalism," letter to the editor, *Charlotte Observer*, (April 28, 1932).
67. J. E. L. Winecoff, letter to the editor, *Charlotte Observer*, (September 17, 1932). M. Bullock, "University Criticism," letter to the editor, *Charlotte Observer*, (May 3, 1932). "Advising Clark: Students Will Take Care of the So-Called Atheists in the Schools," Walter C. Guy from Durham, North Carolina, in the Open Forum section of the *Charlotte Observer*, (October 4, 1932).
68. Langston Hughes, "Cowards," 226–228.
69. Quoted in V. P. Franklin, "Whatever Happened to the College-Bred Negro?" *History of Education Quarterly* 24 (Fall 1984): 461–468.
70. See Lafayette Harris, "Problems before the College Negro," *Crisis* 44 (August 1937): 234–236. On this issue generally, see James D. Anderson, *The Education of Blacks in the South, 1860–1935*, (Chapel Hill: University of North Carolina Press, 1988), especially 276–278. Note that Hughes later published a small booklet, *Scottsboro Limited*, that included his one-act play, "Scottsboro, Ltd.," "Justice," and two short poems, "The Town of Scottsboro," and "Christ in Alabama," contributing the proceeds to the International Labor Defense to help fund the Scottsboro appeals. See Hughes, *Scottsboro Limited*, (New York: Golden Stair, 1932). The one-act play appeared earlier in the *New Masses* 7 (November, 1931): 18–21. Also See Thurston, 40; Rampersad, 217.
71. Hughes, *I Wonder*, 73.
72. Ibid., 90.
73. Quoted in Rampersad, 231–232.
74. Hughes, *I Wonder*, 77.
75. Langston Hughes, "Adventures," 208.

# PART II

## ADVANCING AN EDUCATIONAL AGENDA

CHAPTER 4

# EDUCATION AND POLITICS IN TEXAS

## The Legacies of Laurine C. Anderson and Edward L. Blackshear

**Jared Stallones**

In 1896, Laurine C. Anderson and Edward L. Blackshear swapped the two most influential positions in Texas Black education. Blackshear left his post as Superintendent of Colored Schools in Austin, the state capital, to lead Prairie View Normal Institute, Texas' only state-supported institution of higher learning for African Americans. Anderson, recently fired as Principal of Prairie View, moved to Austin to take the position Blackshear had vacated. The two men could not have been more outwardly different. Anderson was a slight, scholarly Republican educated for the ministry and adept at the details of administration, while Blackshear was a husky, outgoing Democrat as much at home at political rallies as in the classroom. Despite appearances and political affiliations, though, the two men had much in common. Besides serving in the same posts over a number of years, the two shared a struggle for resources to further Black education in Texas in the face of an increasingly dominant and rigid White power structure, and they held a common commitment to improving the lot of African American Texans through education.

*Life Stories: Exploring Issues in Educational History Through Biography*
pp. 67–83

The most thorough analysis of the work of these two men appears in George R. Woolfolk's dated but insightful history, *Prairie View: A Study in Public Conscience, 1878–1946*. In that book, Woolfolk sometimes casts these two Prairie View principals as innocents in a world of power politics beyond their grasp. This paper provides a more nuanced view. Using a variety of archival resources, contemporary accounts, and secondary sources, this piece portrays the two men as shrewd politicians who used the fads and fears of the dominant White political and educational establishments to the advantage of African American education. It begins with a brief overview of the state of public higher education for Black Texans following the Civil War. Then, Laurine Anderson is profiled and his political struggles are outlined followed by a description of his demise as principal of Prairie View. Anderson was succeeded in that post by Edward Blackshear, and so the account picks up with Blackshear's elevation to the principalship and describes his political activities and ultimate demise. Throughout the battles for control of the curriculum in the schools and majorities in the statehouse that typified late nineteenth century Texas, Anderson and Blackshear continually played one side against another to gain a bigger share of the educational pie for Black Texans.

## BEGINNINGS OF PUBLIC HIGHER EDUCATION FOR BLACK TEXANS

In the years after the Civil War, the unpopular Reconstruction governments of Texas sought to build a centralized system of free schools where none had existed before, but an uncooperative population and occasional violence undermined their efforts. By the time Texans met to write their "own" constitution in 1875, the schools were in shambles. The U.S. Commissioner of Education described Texas as, "… the darkest field, educationally, in the United States."[1] With an eye toward correcting the situation, the delegates to the Constitutional Convention provided for the equal, if not integrated, education of all races. Article VII, Section 7 of the Constitution read, "Separate schools shall be provided for the white and colored children, and impartial provisions shall be made for both." On August 14, 1876, the Legislature passed an act, "to establish an Agricultural and Mechanical College of Texas, for the benefit of Colored Youths and to make appropriations therefor," in part to meet federal Morrill Act funding requirements.[2] The college would be a branch of the nearby White A&M College, and under its supervision.

March 11, 1878 was opening day of the new Alta Vista Agricultural College for Colored Youth, but it proved to be a disappointment. L.W. Minor was the on-site Principal, and he prepared for 20 students. Only eight students enrolled. Thomas S. Gathright, A&M's White President, attributed the low enrollment to the fact that "there is no demand for higher education among the blacks,"[3] even though Alta Vista attracted more students than the White college enrolled at its opening. The A&M Board declared the Black school a failure and discontinued classes in late 1878.

Closing the only state-supported institution of higher learning for Blacks in Texas was not a permanent option. Both the Texas Constitution and the Morrill Act required its continued operation in some form or another. At the same time, Texas suffered from an acute shortage of teachers for its Black common schools due to explosive enrollments in those schools.[4] The private colleges in Texas could not keep up with the demand for Black teachers.

To help meet the need for Black teachers, Governor Oran M. Roberts prompted the 16th Texas Legislature to reorganize Alta Vista as the Prairie View Normal Institute for Blacks. Six thousand dollars a year was appropriated from the Permanent University Fund for the new school, to be matched by the Peabody Education Fund. Thus, on April 19, 1879, Prairie View became the first public institution for teacher education in Texas. It remained under the supervision of the White A&M College at College Station. With the appointment in October of Ernest H. Anderson as Principal and his brother Laurine as his assistant, Prairie View was ready to begin its new life as a center for Black teacher education.

The term opened that fall with 16 students. Admission to the school was to be by competitive examination, but early admissions standards were necessarily lax, owing to the uneven quality of education in the lower schools. For this reason, although the Board had authorized a one-year course including arithmetic, grammar, geography, and Texas history, all at about the seventh grade level, the course of study was remedial.[5] Still, the school was a success. By the end of the term, enrollment grew to 60, and additional students were turned away for lack of space. Apparently, Gathright was mistaken in his opinion that Black Texans had little interest in higher education.

## ENTER LAURINE C. ANDERSON

Born in Memphis in 1853, Laurine Cecil Anderson was among the first students to attend the public free schools for African American children in that city. He went on to Fisk University and studied for the Methodist ministry. He taught with Booker T. Washington at Tuskegee Institute for a time, and then followed his brother to Texas. His first position was as principal of a school in Brenham, but he soon made the short move to Prairie View in eastern central Texas. From the somewhat sheltered position of assistant to his brother there, Anderson launched into a number of political crusades.

His first foray into the politics of education involved the perennial issue of a college for African American Texans provided in the Texas Constitution. Article VII, Section 14 mandates a "College or Branch University for the instruction of the colored youths of the State." Questions of where, how, and when to establish it were bones of contention between the Black community and White politicians until 1946, but these questions were just the fodder for debate. The underlying issue was whether and to what degree Black Texans would continue to wield political power in Texas after Reconstruction.

## L.C. ANDERSON AND THE POLITICS OF EDUCATION

When the 16th Legislature recreated Prairie View as a normal school without discontinuing its connection to the Agricultural and Mechanical College, it confused the issue of the school's legal status. There was some question as to whether Prairie View could be simultaneously a Morrill Act college and also the constitutionally mandated "College or Branch University for the instruction of the colored youths of the State."[6] A normal school could hardly be called a university, but if Prairie View did not provide higher education for Texas Blacks, then Morrill Act funds for A&M would be jeopardized.

In the spring of 1881, Governor Roberts asked the 17th Legislature to clarify the school's identity. The Legislature decided that Prairie View, as a branch university, was eligible for participation in Permanent University Fund monies, and appropriated $8,000 for the biennium. The independently elected State Comptroller, William M. Brown, disagreed, however, and refused to pay Prairie View bills from the Fund. By early 1882, the school was insolvent. Roberts published an open letter in several newspapers eliciting sympathy for the school. Donations from individuals throughout Texas paid the bills for a few months, but a long-term arrangement was needed.

Governor Roberts asked the A&M Board for help. At its February 9 meeting, the Board voted to use accrued Morrill Fund interest, "not being needed to pay the Professors and officers of the Agricultural and Mechanical College"[7] in Prairie View's behalf. This solved the immediate problem, but Prairie View's legal status needed clear definition.

Roberts called a special session of the Legislature that summer in which it voted to pay Prairie View's debts from general revenues and schedule a statewide election to choose a site for the Black university. The governor invited communities to nominate themselves for a place on the

November election ballot. Prairie View nominated itself and L.C. Anderson promoted its cause in letters to newspapers around the state. In one, he argued that, "A high duty rest [sic] upon the state to furnish facilities for the education of the colored youths of Texas that they may be better prepared for the duties of citizenship."[8] With this statement, Anderson sounded a cry that would be of great use to the cause of Black education in its struggle with the White establishment: the role of education in producing the "right" kind of Black citizens for Texas. The election was held November 2, 1882, and despite Anderson's efforts Austin was chosen as the site for the Black university, but the penurious Legislature neglected to act. Prairie View remained the sole state-supported institution for higher learning for Black Texans.

Anderson soon found another vehicle for his political impulses. In 1884, he joined an elite group of Black educators in the formation of the Colored Teachers State Association of Texas at Prairie View. Anderson was chosen as its first president and served in that capacity until 1889. Although one of its chroniclers has claimed that, "The colored Association has never participated in the activities of the State Legislature,"[9] it was from the start as much a political organization as an educational one. Its leaders felt that the political education of its members was a primary duty, and to that end, "Often various candidates for local, state, and national offices would attend the meetings of the Association for the purpose of campaigning. Sometimes members of the Association would speak to the assembly in behalf of certain candidates."[10] This activity became such a dominant part of the meetings that in 1899 the Association had to prohibit candidates from campaigning at its annual meeting.

That same year L.C. Anderson gained greater prominence in educational circles when he became Principal of Prairie View after Ernest Anderson died on October 29, 1885. Now L.C. Anderson stood simultaneously at the head of Texas' only state-supported institution of higher learning for African Americans and its most prestigious Black teachers' organization. In this dual role, he soon found himself in the eye of a political storm concerning the direction of Black education in Texas.

## THE POLITICS OF CURRICULUM

Texas was on the verge of plunging into a decades-long struggle over control of the curriculum in its schools. The contest pitted proponents of a traditional classical/liberal education, those favoring the new manual training, and the agriculturalists against one another. Advocates for manual training saw useful skills as the key to gainful employment in an industrializing state. Black leaders were concerned that their young men were being squeezed out of traditional apprenticeships due to racial bigotry, and that career training in schools was their only option. White industrialists sought able factory hands. The agriculturalists feared losing their supply of farm labor if schools emphasized other career choices too effectively. Backers of a classical/liberal school curriculum believed that such an education was the path to social mobility and racial equality. The curriculum battles that these forces waged throughout this period were felt at every level of schooling and politics in both the White and Black communities. Anderson and his successor at Prairie View would learn to exploit these struggles to extract resources from the dominant White political and educational establishments to benefit Black education in Texas.

As the nineteenth century drew to a close, America was an increasingly urban, industrial society, and its education system struggled to meet changing demands. There was growing pressure on schools to prepare students for careers in industry. Businessmen like Andrew Carnegie decried the traditional curriculum as,

> to waste energies upon obtaining a knowledge of such languages as Greek and Latin, which are of no more practical use to them than Choctaw.... They have in no sense received instruction. On the contrary, what they have obtained has served to imbue them with false ideas and to give them a distaste for practical life."[11]

Many educators concurred. The Superintendent of the New Orleans schools told a National Education Association gathering, "We are living in a practical, money-making age.... The big thing today is the reward, the dollar, and it is paid for practice and not for the theory and training behind the practice."[12]

Some favored an industrial curriculum for the Black schools of Texas, as well. Many in the community saw that traditional apprenticeships were increasingly difficult for young Black men to find and turned to the schools for training. Anderson agreed that some industrial education was necessary, but not at the expense of classical-liberal studies. In a newspaper article arguing his point, he wrote, "This question of labor is the disturbing one of the present and is destined to still further complicate politics, unless it is met and solved in the schoolroom ... this can be accomplished without materially changing the literary instruction given."[13]

White Texans also found reasons to support industrial education for Black students. To some it was a matter of conscience, "[I have] always felt that it was our duty, claiming to be the superior race, and having control of the government, to do all in our power that promised beneficial and practical results, to educate and elevate our colored citizens."[14] Some saw it as an economic necessity: "The people of Texas depend on Negroes and Mexicans for practically all agricultural and manufacturing labor. On account of the ignorance of the laborers they require constant supervision and in many cases lack the ability to obey orders. This great ignorance necessarily means an increase in the cost of production."[15] Better schooling was the answer.

Others opposed industrial education for Black Texans. This was a time of growing resentment toward Blacks and attempts to draw strict color lines in political and economic life throughout the South. Blacks were often denied membership in labor unions, pushing them out of the industrial trades. At the same time, White workers were moving into such traditionally Black domains as domestic service. Paul B. Barringer of the University of Virginia expressed the fears of some Whites when he asked the Southern Educational Association meeting in Richmond, "Shall we, having by great effort gotten rid of the Negro as a political menace, deliberately proceed to equip the Negro of the future as an economic menace? Shall we, knowing his primitive racial needs, arm him and pit him against the poor Whites of the South?"[16]

The version that finally impacted Prairie View originated with the Russian educator Victor Della Vos. His blend of manual, literary, and moral education in both theoretical and practical instruction was adopted by General Samuel C. Armstrong at the Hampton Normal and Agricultural Institute in Virginia and by Booker T. Washington at Tuskegee Institute, where Anderson had worked. It dovetailed neatly with the emphasis on character education described in Prairie View literature, "Plainly a system is required which shall be at once constructive of mental and moral worth and destructive of the vices characteristic of the slave."[17]

Industrial education was formally initiated at Prairie View in 1888, with the creation of an Agricultural and Mechanical Department. Receipt of Morrill Act funds had always implied that the curriculum would include at least some agricultural and industrial components. Professor Randolph, a Hampton Institute graduate, led instruction in woodworking, printing, and mechanics. In addition, a Ladies Industrial Department was established under the leadership of Prairie View alumna Sallie Ewell to teach home economics.

The critics of industrial education for Blacks need not have worried about Prairie View becoming an industrial training center. The industrial course was not even listed in the college catalogue until 1893, and Anderson's unique twist on the curriculum oriented it toward producing teachers of industrial arts, not merely artisans themselves. Besides, industrial education at Prairie View was already being undermined by the agricultural populists.

Agricultural education had been Prairie View's original mission and the initial lack of student interest did not deter those who saw Prairie View as a training school for farmers from pressing to institute their vision. When Prairie View launched its Industrial Department, it started an Agricultural Department as well. A graduate of Tuskegee Institute was put in charge; the agricultural course of study blended classroom instruction in farming methods and general academic subjects with fieldwork. The agriculturalists gained momentum in the 1890s, and funding questions were again a catalyst for curriculum change.

The Texas Grange lobbied Governors Roberts and Lawrence S. Ross to end instruction in the classical subjects at the land-grant schools in Texas. The Grange saw money spent on these as a violation of the intent of the Morrill Acts, although Justin Morrill himself argued that his intention was for Morrill Act money to fund liberal studies as well as industrial and agricultural training. Bowing to the pressure, Prairie View dropped Latin from the course of study, and a growing senior college program was discontinued. In a typically paternalistic statement, the A&M Board declared, "We believe that it is not higher education, but practical education that the Negro race needs for its development."[18] Texas A&M also succumbed to the political pressure, and ultimately dropped courses in Greek and French, made Latin and Spanish elective courses, and instituted compulsory labor on school farms.

## THE POLITICS OF EDUCATION FUNDING

As the struggle for political power between Republicans and Democrats heated up, Prairie View found itself increasingly at the center of political controversy. Some Black Republicans saw education issues as a means to stop the erosion of their political influence, and the second Morrill Act offered a vehicle. Texas Republican Party Chairman Norris Wright Cuney led an effort in 1890 to lobby the federal government to rescind Morrill funds for A&M on the basis that Texas practiced systematic discrimination in its funding for Black schools. There was some truth to the accusation. Throughout this period of Democratic state administrations, there was considerable inequality between Black and White schools in Texas in terms of teacher salaries, county tuitions charged,[19] school buildings,[20] and school libraries. Governor Ross denied the accusation. He claimed that reductions in school spending for the years 1885–89 had been the result of an accounting error and that "white and colored children suffered equally" from its effects.[21] Responding to charges that funding inequities were politically motivated, Ross pointed out that most Black teachers and some state education officials were Republicans, despite the availability of White Democrats to fill the posts. He concluded by reasoning that, "The Democrat loves his money as well as other people. How is it he pays so liberally to elevate and care for the Negroes always found voting against him? Certainly there is only one explanation, and it is that the Democrats of Texas have agreed that the Negro shall enjoy equal rights before the law...cost what it may."[22] Whether or not Ross' eloquence was the deciding factor, his version held sway, and U.S. Secretary of the Interior John W. Noble consented to release the Morrill Act funds to Texas.

The animosity between Black Republicans and White Democrats continued. Governor Ross divided the Morrill money 2/3 to A&M and 1/3 to Prairie View, but when the 22nd Legislature convened in the spring of 1891, it reallocated the funds 3/4 to A&M and only 1/4 to Prairie View. Later, Black Republicans won a hollow victory when they prevailed on the Legislature to set aside unappropriated public lands for the endowment of the yet-to-be-constructed Black university. The Texas Supreme Court overturned the endowment, ruling that there was no unappropriated public land left.

## L.C. ANDERSON'S DEMISE

The end of Anderson's tenure at Prairie View pointed up the vulnerability of the Prairie View principal. The immediate cause was a minor incident, but one of a type that was becoming all too frequent in an increasingly intolerant Texas. In an A&M Board meeting held at Prairie View in 1896, Board member D.A. Paulus made disparaging remarks about Black rights, one of Anderson's passionate causes. Anderson blew up at him and was fired on the spot. Many felt that since Anderson's performance as an administrator at Prairie View had been above reproach he was purposely baited in order to give cause to replace him. T.W. McCall expressed the sentiment of many when he wrote in the *Galveston News*, "Why such a broad and progressive man as he [Anderson] is retired from the executive head of such a broad interest is yet to be shown to an inquisitive and dissatisfied public...it is demoralizing to our free institution and discouraging to true merit and manly courage when they are pushed aside for political preference."[23] The firing looked even more blatantly political when Anderson was replaced with a Democrat, Edward L. Blackshear. But with Blackshear, the White political establishment got an even more outspoken and effective politician than L.C. Anderson had been, and one who shared with Anderson the commitment to education as a means of advancing the cause of African Americans in Texas.

## ENTER EDWARD L. BLACKSHEAR

Edward Blackshear was born into slavery in Montgomery, Alabama on September 8, 1862. He learned to read and write alongside his master's children and attended the first public school for African Americans in Montgomery and an American Mission Society school. In 1875, at the age of 13, he entered Tabor College in Iowa. There he earned his Bachelor of Arts degree in 1881, and later the L.L.D. He came to Texas to teach in 1882. In 1892, he became supervisor of all the Black schools in Austin. This high profile position brought him to the attention of Governor Hogg, who appointed him Principal of Prairie View in 1896.

Blackshear showed himself to be adept at political maneuvering in his first Prairie View commencement. He invited the Black educator best known to and most respected by Whites, Booker T. Washington, to address the convocation. Washington spoke on June 4, 1897 to an overflow crowd of Blacks and Whites. Blackshear had shrewdly invited a number of important politicians and educators to share in the event. Texas House Speaker L. Travis Dashiell joined Washington on the stage, along with the other prominent White leaders in education and politics. In the flush of good will following Washington's address, the President of the A&M Board told the crowd that the Board endorsed Washington's every word. Dashiell, too, praised Washington and Prairie View. On the heels of the Speaker's endorsement, Blackshear pressed the A&M Board for an expanded course of classical-liberal studies.

Typically, White leaders favored the gradual growth of a classical university at Prairie View. The Democrats, at their State Convention in August 1896, claimed, "The Prairie View Normal School should be enlarged, making provision for industrial features and gradually converting it into a university for the colored people."[24] Board Chairman W.R. Cavitt had laid out the plans as early as 1884. He asked, "But why not make Prairie View Normal School the nucleus of all the educational interest of the colored people in the State? First, and appropriately first, it is the training school of teachers. Such industrial features may next be added as the demand arises, until full instruction is reached in Agricultural and Mechanic Arts, and finally, when people are ready for them, colleges for classical and literary education and the learned professions may be established."[25] Some Black leaders agreed. In 1896, Colored Teachers State Association President M.H. Broyles called for a course of college study to be instituted at Prairie View.

However, others held out for the Black university promised in the Texas Constitution. Blackshear disagreed with this strategy. In a piece written for the *Texas School Journal* he argued that, ". . . if this were done, it would be the last of the 'University,' but of course, we do not dare express this as the general opinion . . .We are not in any way hostile to Prairie View . . ., but we believe that we should have a university on a broader scale equipped with first-class facilities."[26] But the *Journal* was a publication for all Texas educators, so Blackshear was giving a wide audience the impression that his view was the "general opinion." Moreover, the *Journal* had already carried an editorial call for political action on behalf of a separate "colored university." The Republican Party made a separate university a rallying cry, calling in its platforms of 1884, 1892, 1894, and 1896 for "extending to our colored youths the opportunities of a university education" apart from Prairie View.[27]

Despite this support, Principal Blackshear had to take the politically pragmatic approach. After assessing the forces arrayed against him, he shelved his dream of a separate university. Instead, he turned his energies to gradually building Prairie View's curriculum. In 1896, the school was reorganized into academic departments. There were separate departments for Science, Math, Pedagogy, History and English, and Music, as well as a Mechanical Department, Agricultural Department, and Girls' Industrial Department. In 1899, the Legislature renamed the school Prairie View State Normal and Industrial College. More classical elements were also added to the curriculum.

In his *Biennial Report* that same year, Blackshear called for a four-year Normal course followed by a three-year course taught at the college level. He admitted that his chief aim was, "the improvement of the teaching profession and the offering of an opportunity for higher education for those desiring it until the State deemed it necessary and practicable to establish a branch of the University for negroes ordained by the State Constitution."[28] He added some teeth to his request by subtly appealing to the White establishment's fears of a radicalized African American population. He wrote,

> As there is probably no single agency in the state doing more than this institution to bring about that proper understanding and relationship between the races, which harmonized with Southern sentiment and tradition and which in turn is so essential to the peace, happiness, prosperity, and progress of both races in the South, there seems to be wisdom and propriety in an enlargement of the school to meet the growing needs educationally and industrially of the Negro race in Texas.[29]

The Legislature responded by appropriating money in 1901 for the "maintenance of a four-year college course of classical and scientific studies" at Prairie View.[30] The A&M Board, though, authorized only a two-year course. Although this gave classical/liberal studies a foothold at Prairie View, Blackshear was not satisfied.

The winds of public opinion soon revived the question of industrial training for African American Texans. Blackshear adapted his approach to meet the new challenge. In fact, he was so convincing in this about face that he had to address the Colored Teachers Association in 1901 to, "correct the general misimpression that he was against intellectual education for the race. He committed himself to an industrial, Christian, and higher education for his race."[31] His writings from this period seem to be directed at White as well as African American audiences and treat political as much as educational topics. In a 1902 treatise entitled "What is the Negro Teacher Doing in the Matter of Uplifting his Race" he agonized over the political implications of the teacher's role. He called the African American teacher, "a herald of civilization to the youth of his people ... the colored teacher, too, has always been conservative and has been the wise advisor of his people.... Perhaps if only the Christian missionary teachers had come and the political missionaries had remained at home, all might have been better."[32]

In 1904, Blackshear ascended to the presidency of the Colored Teachers State Association. From this prominent post he could freely exercise his political skills, but he was not alone. The 1904 Annual Meeting was a hotbed of political maneuvering and debate on issues both large and small, whether they had to do with education or not. The Resolutions Committee on which Blackshear served urged principals to hold parents' meetings "to awaken the parents as regards the duties of their children ... that the cultivation of moral sentiment and development of citizenship have the chief concerns of education."[33] To this end, the committee called for systematic instruction in ethics and civics for African American students. Blackshear and Anderson served together that year on the Association's Advisory Council. In planning strategy for the upcoming legislative session they advised, "we do not think it wise at this time to have two committees before the Legislature at the same session working for different objects."[34] It also issued a strong statement decrying "any discrimination on the part of labor unions or otherwise against free employment of capable Negroes in mechanical pursuits, and especially do we deplore the practices of White-capping, mob violence, peonage and like practices ... which tend to drive Negroes from [their] natal districts."[35]

The crowning piece of political rhetoric at the 1904 meeting, though, was Blackshear's presidential address. It was a rambling and remarkable compilation of his thought up to that point on the African American community's need for self-reliance, the role of the teacher in the progress of his people, and race relations. It also contained subtle, but dire warnings to those in the White establishment who would deny educational opportunity to Black students. He began by advising that, "The colored people must more and more improve to the full advantages afforded by the public free schools. . . They must not, however, depend entirely on the State for in many communities the term allowed by the State appropriations is too short to permit reasonable progress on the part of the pupils."[36] This was in keeping with his Advisory Council's call for Black communities to tax themselves to support their schools.

Blackshear went on to praise the Black teacher, but lamented that, "Better qualified teachers is a crying need of the negroes of Texas.... Good teachers are still rare."[37] Then he added a charge to the "wise teacher" that was at once impassioned and embittered. He said,

> He should teach [his people] how to so shape their business dealings with the Anglo-Saxon people about them as to steer clear of racial invitation.... In short the colored teacher should be a peacemaker and he can do this without becoming what negroes, both during slavery and since, have opprobriously termed "a white folks nigger."[38]

In his speech, Blackshear could not pass up the opportunity to argue once more for a separate university for African American Texans, but this time his thesis carried more than a hint of menace for the White establishment. It began with a call to cede Prairie View to the agriculturalists and the advocates of industrial training by incorporating it fully into the A&M system. Then, Blackshear reasoned,

> the field would be clear for the subsequent fulfillment of the pledge in the Constitution of Texas to establish a university, or school, of liberal learning for the negro youth of Texas, where those who are to be the teachers and leaders of the life and thought of their race can receive the broad, deep and genuine culture essential to conservative and sane leadership. It is half educated, rattle-brained leaders who must lead if there are no better, that foment discord, create issues, and rush in headlong where angels fear to tread.[39]

The message to the political leaders was clear; they must either provide the promised university and enjoy harmony between the races, or risk the Black community passing from "conservative and sane leadership" to the type of rabble-rousing, northern-educated activists that struck fear in the hearts of Southern Democrats.

But Blackshear was not done. He outlined his theory of friction between the races. The cause was, he explained, "the greater flexibility of the negro mind and its greater capacity for adaptation on the one hand and the relative fixity of the Anglo-Saxon mind and inflexibility of its organized will on the other."[40] Lawless outbreaks arise, Blackshear noted, when innocent Blacks are oppressed and cheated by Whites. Then he concluded with yet another veiled threat: "When these racial outbreaks arise, the innocent are as apt ... to suffer as the guilty."[41]

## THE DEMISE OF BLACKSHEAR AND THE DECLINE OF BLACK POLITICAL POWER

In many ways this speech was the climax of Blackshear's political activities. He continued to be an effective administrator and educator at Prairie View, and to articulate its mission of providing higher education for Blacks in the face of depredations by curriculum ideologues, but it was increasingly a defensive battle. Prairie View's first Bachelor of Arts degrees were granted in 1904. They were also the last that would issue from there for decades. The Colored Teachers State Association, with the active support of Blackshear, Anderson, and others, continued to call for Texas to make good its Constitutional pledge of a university for Black Texans, but the calls fell increasingly on deaf ears. The political influence of Republicans and the electoral power of African Americans in Texas were rapidly slipping away. Beginning with the institution of the poll tax in 1902, the voting rights of African American Texans were eroded and eventually extinguished during this era.

The end of Edward Blackshear's tenure as principal of Prairie View resulted from his involvement in a political battle that had little to do with education. Prohibition had been a growing source of factional strife in Texas since the failure of the first constitutional amendment to ban alcohol in 1887. In 1910, a prohibitionist Legislature was elected and quickly scheduled another constitutional vote for June 22, 1911. Determined not to suffer another statewide defeat, the prohibition forces invited all interested parties to join their cause, regardless of race or party. Many Black leaders saw this as a chance to prop open the door of electoral participation that had been all but closed to them.

Despite all the efforts of prohibitionists Black and White, the amendment failed. Blackshear and other African Americans who had stood with prohibitionist Thomas Ball in the amendment fight campaigned for Ball in the 1914 Democratic Party primary. Ball lost that election and James P. Ferguson became governor. He then exacted political revenge. In supporting an appropriation for Prairie View, Ferguson told members of the A&M Board, "I want to serve notice on you right now that E.L. Blackshear at the head of the institution has got to go."[42] The Board asked Blackshear to account for his political activities and seemed satisfied with his response, but Ferguson continued to apply pressure. Blackshear was forced to resign in early 1915.

## FINAL YEARS AND LEGACIES

The dismissal of these men from their posts at Prairie View did not end their contributions to education in Texas. Edward L. Blackshear moved to Fort Worth and then Houston to lead schools there, then back to Prairie View to head a multi-state agricultural extension service for Black farmers. He passed away at Prairie View on December 12, 1919 and was buried nearby. In 1936, one of the oldest Black elementary schools in Austin was named in his honor.

Laurine C. Anderson had a long and distinguished career in the Austin schools after his service at Prairie View. He served as superintendent of the Black schools there from 1896 until 1929 when ill health forced his retirement. He stayed on as Latin instructor at E.H. Anderson High School, named for his brother, until his death on January 8, 1938. Within two days of his passing the name of Austin's Black high school was changed to L.C. Anderson High School. During his tenure in Austin, he presided over a growing program of secondary education for Blacks, the beginnings of a night school for adults, and one of the first manual training programs for Black students in Texas.

It is unlikely that either of these men would want to be remembered as political operators. They thought of themselves first and foremost as educators and leaders of their people. But the times in which they lived required that an effective advocate for Black education be skilled in politics as well, even the politics of race. Race remains a major issue in American society. The movie *Crash* masterfully manipulates White majority fears of Blacks and Hispanics for dramatic effect and Yale law professor Stephen L. Carter plays on those fears in his story "the Most Dangerous Children in America."[43]

Some educators have followed Anderson and Blackshear in using the fears of the majority culture to appropriate resources for schools. Across the country, urban minority children sitting in neat rows and wearing school uniforms, just like their affluent suburban counterparts, has become the picture of "success" for the school choice movement, and has fueled its growth. Today, millions of students, often children from impoverished urban minority communities, are educated in these alternative formats drawing funding from the public school system. The strategy of playing the race card in education works today just as it has in the past.

## NOTES

1. U.S. Bureau of Education, *Report*. (Washington, D.C., 1871), 14.

2. H. P. Gammel, *The Laws of Texas*, 1822–1897 Vol. VIII (Austin: The Gammel Book Company, 1898), 237.
3. *Reports of the Agricultural and Mechanical College of Texas, Alta Vista College for Colored Youths*, December 1878, Thomas S. Gathright, President (Galveston: News Steam Book and Job Printing Establishment, 1878).
4. U.S. Commissioner of Education *Report* (Washington, D.C., 1877), 231, 410–11.
5. Annie Mae Vaught White, "The Development of the Program of Studies of the Prairie View State Normal and Industrial College" (master's thesis, University of Texas at Austin, 1938), 5.
6. Texas Constitution (1876), art. 7, sec. 14.
7. *Report of the Board of Directors of the State Agricultural and Mechanical College* of the State of Texas, Located in Brazos County, March 28, 1882. (Austin: State Printing Office, D. and D. Institution, 1882).
8. *Houston Daily Post*, 21 September 1882.
9. Junior Nathaniel Nelum, "A Study of the First Seventy Years of the Colored Teachers State Association of Texas" (EdD diss., University of Texas at Austin, 1955), 293.
10. Interview with Mary G. Campbell, Tyler, Texas, 11 December 1954. In Nelum, 28.
11. Andrew Carnegie, *The Empire of Business* (New York: 1902), 79.
12. National Education Association, *Proceedings*, 1914, 264.
13. *Rockdale Reporter* (Rockdale, Texas), 17 January 1889.
14. A. J. Peeler, *Message* Accompanying the Report of the Board of the A. and M. College of the State of Texas, 1879–1880. (Galveston: News, Book and Job Office, 1881), 46–48.
15. Hazel Platt, "Negro Education in Texas" (master's thesis, University of Texas at Austin, 1917), 5.
16. George Woolfolk, *Prairie View: A Study in Public Conscience, 1878–1946*. (New York: Pageant Press, 1962), 114.
17. *Report of the Prairie View Normal School*, December 9, 1882 (Austin: E.W. Swindells State Printer, 1883).
18. *Biennial Report* of the Prairie View Normal and Industrial College, Prairie View, Texas, for the two years Beginning September 1, 1904 and Ending August 31, 1906, (Austin: Von Boeckmann and Schutze, State Printers, 1906).
19. Texas State Board of Education, *Report*, 1880/82, 4, 249–250.
20. State Board, 1888/1890, 22, 50.
21. L.S. Ross, *The Education of the Colored Race* (Austin, 1890), 1.
22. Ibid., 3.
23. *Galveston News*, 11 July 1896.
24. Ernest W. Winkler, *Platforms of Political Parties in Texas* (Austin: The University of Texas, 1916), 388.
25. *Biennial Report*, 1884.
26. *Annual Report*, 398.
27. Winkler, 427.
28. *Biennial Report*, 1899.

29. *Biennial Report*, 1902.
30. Texas *Acts* (1901) Chapter 30, Section 1, 35.
31. *Proceedings* of the 17th Annual Meeting of the Colored Teachers State Association and Principals' Division, San Antonio, Texas, 1901. Marshall: Wiley Print, n.d., 9.
32. Edward L. Blackshear, in *Twentieth Century Literature or A Cyclopedia of Thought on the Vital Topics Relating to the American Negro by One Hundred of America's Greatest Negroes*. Atlanta: J.L. Nichols & Co., 1902, 335.
33. *Proceedings* of the 20th Annual Meeting of the Colored Teachers State Association and Principals' Division, Marshall, Texas, 1904. Marshall: Wiley Print, 1902, 11.
34. Ibid., 24.
35. Ibid., 31.
36. Ibid., 32.
37. Ibid., 37.
38. Ibid., 38.
39. Ibid., 35.
40. Ibid., 35–36.
41. Ibid.
42. J. R. Lee, letter to M. M. Rogers, 9 February 1915; M. M. Rogers, letter to J. R. Lee, 11 February 1915, cited in Woolfolk, 159.
43. Stephen L. Carter, *The Culture of Disbelief: How American Law and Politics Trivialize Religious Devotion*. New York: Basic Books, 1993, 205.

CHAPTER 5

# ADVENTITIOUSLY BLIND, ADVANTAGEOUSLY POLITICAL

## John Eldred Swearingen and Social Definitions of Disability in Progressive-Era South Carolina

**Edward A. Janak**

John Eldred Swearingen was elected South Carolina State Superintendent of Education for the first time in 1907. Throughout the 14 years he held office, Swearingen made great strides in improving the state's education for all students, regardless of race, ethnicity, or income. In accomplishing his goals, he conflicted with textbook vendors, state legislators, the Governor, the General Education Board, and even the Ku Klux Klan. Swearingen willingly battled local, state, and national officials in his drive to increase state funding, pass a compulsory education bill, implement the Smith-Hughes Act, and resist the Cardinal Principles report.[1] Swearingen did more for the hitherto undereducated populations in South Carolina—children of the mills and African American students—than any superintendent before, and many after. As biographer James Dreyfuss noted, "Swearingen ultimately believed, in the broadest sense, that educa-

*Life Stories: Exploring Issues in Educational History Through Biography*
pp. 85–105

tion should be equitably provided, funded, and available to all citizens, regardless of class, race, or gender."[2] Also, Swearingen was adventitiously blind, born sighted but developing blindness later in life. He became one of the "mettlesome souls" that "broke out of these confining molds" of what the blind were thought to be capable, who "made places for themselves in the world at large."[3]

Born in 1875 during Reconstruction—or, more specifically, South Carolina's resistance to Reconstruction—Swearingen was very much a product of his time. While his society tried to instill that those who were "different," either in race or ability, were inferior, he acted to reject what he had been taught about his capabilities, particularly as a man who was blind.[4] Swearingen knew what it was like to be seen as "different" and have society categorize him, making his actions to benefit underrepresented voices fully understandable. In her memoirs, Swearingen's wife, Mary Hough Swearingen, related a story about her husband that occurred during their 1918 honeymoon. She recalled they were en route from Greenville, South Carolina, to New York City when

> On the train [she] asked the porter to see whether Mr. Swearingen needed any help in the dressing room. He unhesitatingly consented to do so, but in a few moments he came up the aisle chuckling. "Lady," he said, "that man don't need nothing! He's in yonder shavin' himself with a long straight razor, and everybody is a gaping at him. They can hardly use their own little safety razors—but not him. Lordy, miss, that's a man!"[5]

The story is both summative and metaphoric of Swearingen's life. While Swearingen did not live constantly attempting to prove his ability, social definitions of disability did influence his actions, both proactively and reactively.

It may be useful to remember life writer James Garraty's three-tiered typology of biographical subjects, sorted by the writer's "over-all view of the importance of individual intelligence and character in determining the course of events." First were subjects who are "significant only because the times in which they live make them so"; second, subjects who are "forceful individuals" that have "change[d] the trend of events"; and third, subjects who are not controlled by themselves or their times, but rather an outside force such as luck, chance, or destiny.[6] Within this typology, this work seeks to show that Swearingen's life evidences most definitely the second type: a forceful figure who worked to change the society in which he lived. Swearingen was unafraid to take on any and all challengers to his vision of what the schools of South Carolina should be.

## CONTEXT: SWEARINGEN'S LIFE AND TIMES

In the midst of the political and educational turmoil of Reconstruction, John Eldred Swearingen was born January 9, 1875 near the town of Trenton in Edgefield County, South Carolina. His parents were John Cloud Swearingen, a Confederate veteran and Red Shirt Rider, and Anna Tillman Swearingen, sister of U.S. Senator Benjamin "Pitchfork Ben" Tillman. Swearingen was immediately a product of society and family who upheld traditional notions of what it meant to be a man—service to country and defense of one's way of life. His father had a distinguished career in the Confederacy; John Cloud was among the first troops to leave Edgefield County, fighting as an officer in the 22nd South Carolina Infantry unit of the CSA. Despite sustaining injuries at both Gettysburg and Lookout Mountain, John Cloud Swearingen remained on active duty until War's end.[7] Anna Tillman was widely recognized for her exceptional intellect. She was a skilled musician, needle worker, homemaker, and planter's wife, and hosted a private day school for her children and those of her neighbors. An avid reader, she loved poetry and literary classics; this love of reading and desire for learning passed down to their son.

Swearingen's youth was like that of any other White, sighted boy in the rural South; however, it would change drastically once he entered his teen years. One of the rites of passage in Southern "boy culture" was learning to hunt. Swearingen received his first shotgun, against his mother's wishes, for his thirteenth birthday. Like many children with a new toy, Swearingen carried it constantly. Less than a week after receiving his gift, he went out on a firewood hauling expedition with some of the field hands. He saw a dove and shot it, but in his excitement to retrieve his kill, the trigger of the second barrel of his gun snagged and tripped on a branch, discharging the birdshot. The shot entered at his right little finger and exited at the base of the thumb, shattering every bone in the hand before settling into his forehead, face and eyes, blinding him.[8]

Swearingen's entire family—brother George, sister Sophie, and both parents—hoped and prayed for his eyesight to return. His mother, ever the educator, refused to accept her son as helpless and began a strict re-education program for him. She started by having him re-learn simple household chores such as lighting stove fires, bringing in firewood, and fetching water for the garden. She advanced his training to include proper table manners, the techniques of which Swearingen later used as a teacher of the blind. Eventually, she taught what would be called a "wellness program" in modern vernacular, encouraging him to learn physical activities such as basic exercises, acrobatics, wrestling, and horseback riding.[9]

As Swearingen re-mastered household duties and activities, his mother continued reading to him and had him recite lessons in the belief that his eyesight would eventually return. While this home schooling was typical of the era, it also reflected contemporary suspicions about the direction of education. Although he did attend a traditional school, Swearingen was still exposed to a huge variety of social structures that would reinforce social norms regarding the treatment of people who are "other," such as the disabled or of another race. However, because of his blindness, Swearingen did not have these patterns (or those setting adolescent normative values surrounding race and sex) set in him via his teenage play; this likely is one reason among many that explains the progressive social attitudes held by Swearingen throughout his career.

In spite of their likely reservations about public education at the time, Swearingen's family chose not to home school him for the entirety of his academic preparation. Initially, the family sent him to an institution in Macon, Georgia, to work with a Dr. Calhoun from Atlanta who specialized in vision recovery; however, that placement was short lived as Dr. Calhoun informed the family there was no hope of Swearingen's vision returning. With his family finally accepting that his blindness was permanent, in 1899, he began attending the South Carolina School for the Deaf and Blind at Cedar Spring.[10] In testament to his mother's preparations, he quickly worked his way through the school's standard curriculum, making his teachers design a series of independent study projects to keep him challenged. He learned, for example, to fluently play multiple musical instruments and performed on the organ at the school's graduation ceremonies. As further proof that his mother came to accept her son's lack of vision, Anna Tillman became one of two people of all his friends, family, and colleagues to learn the point print (the precursor to Braille) method of writing; as such, she became his best friend and guide for years to come.[11]

Swearingen was fortunate; schools such as Cedar Springs were at that time a relatively recent phenomenon. Mainstream society often equated those who had lost their vision with those who had mental disabilities. However, thanks to pioneers such as Samuel Gridley Howe, that perception was beginning to change. In the mid-1800s, Howe led a campaign to "redefine blindness by stressing that the blind were essentially no different from the sighted: they were merely people who could not see." Howe was wont to ask "what is blindness," answering his own question by explaining it as a condition that

> deprives a man of the perception of light, and limits the freedom of his locomotion, but which touches not his life, which impairs not his health,

which dwarfs not his mind, which affects not his soul, and which cuts him off from none of the high and essential sources of human happiness.[12]

Had Swearingen been born even a handful of decades previous, his experiences certainly would have been remarkably different. However, by the beginning of the twentieth century, people with disabilities—particularly those who were blind—were making inroads into the mainstream. For example, by the time Swearingen concluded his studies at Cedar Springs, there were two journals catering to an unsighted audience: *The Problem*, published in Leavenworth, Kansas, which was a publication of the American Blind People's Higher Education and General Improvement Association, ran from 1900 to 1903; and *The Outlook for the Blind*, started in 1907 by the same group now titled the American Association of Workers for the Blind, which would remain in print almost until the U.S. intervention into World War II in 1941.[13]

This was also the period during which Helen Keller was making headlines. From 1887, the time that Keller met Anne Sullivan, to 1896, when Mark Twain raised funds on her behalf, to 1907, when Keller wrote a series of articles in the popular magazine *Ladies' Home Journal*, Keller had rapidly entered the national consciousness. Keller and her teacher became a fixture on the vaudeville circuit through 1924, literally and figuratively setting the stage for people with disabilities.[14] Taking the matter into the realm of the arts, Helen Menken, a New York City-based actress, brought her production of Shakespeare's Merchant of Venice to Columbia, South Carolina, in 1922. This was unique, for the production was performed by Menken and a company of six other actors entirely in sign language—not a word was spoken during the entire performance.[15]

It wasn't just in the North or just people who were deaf making progress in societal attitudes; in the South, there was a sea change in attitudes of the general public regarding people with disabilities in the time of Swearingen's childhood. Due to the enormous physical toll taken on the men of the South by the U.S. Civil War, seeing men with the full gamut of visible disabilities was common. Indeed, on one level, Confederate veterans in the South were the first disability activists. As reminded by historian Catherine Kudlik, at this time being a disabled man was a badge of honor, not a stigma, because they "sustained their injuries in the patriotic and sacrificial act of serving their country, thereby investing their disability with an honorable quality." While this attitude didn't always carry over to civilians (who were perceived as receiving welfare as opposed to earning benefits), it very likely influenced Swearingen to want to serve his state even more.[16]

Due to such temporal-social circumstances, the beliefs of his mother and his entire family, and the efforts of educators such as Howe and public figures such as Keller paving the road, Swearingen was confident enough in himself to want to pursue further education; upon his graduation from Cedar Springs, in 1895 Swearingen applied to South Carolina College (now the University of South Carolina). Providing a significant taste of discrimination against the disabled, Swearingen was rejected because of his blindness. Obviously, the trustees of the University were of the mindset, now proven incorrect but unfortunately pervasive through the twentieth century in the United States, that the blind were incapable of functioning in larger society. One 1951 study on blindness, which took a perspective representative of the times, explained the premise using the metaphor of a canary: to the author, the blind were like a caged canary "singing lustily in the hall." While kept in the home, it "responds intelligently to its caged condition." However, according to Thomas Cutsforth,

> [t]he deficiencies of the canary would become apparent as soon as it was released from its cage and compelled to shift for itself in the much larger and more complex situation in which the wild birds represent the normal. The caged canary is *functionally feeble-minded* as compared with the free bird who is able to perceive relationships that are not in the former's world.[17]

The college trustees wanted to keep Swearingen safe in his "cage," either at home in Edgefield or at Cedar Spring. They clearly did not share Cutsforth's opinion, however, that college life was "an ideal situation for social adjustment" for a young adult who was blind. Cutsforth argues that due to a variety of reasons, including the safe and insular physical environment of many college campuses, students who are blind that enter college place "themselves in one of the most favorable environments open to young blind graduates."[18] Swearingen, however, had to formally appeal to the president and board of trustees, who granted him provisional admission. While modern universities provide provisions for people who are differently abled, such was not the case at the turn of the twentieth century. Swearingen had to provide his own guide and readers for his textbooks. Moreover, should Swearingen have fallen behind in his studies, any sign that he could not keep up with the other students would have resulted in his being asked to withdraw from the college.[19]

In many cases, once a person with a disability is presented with the social stigma associated with it, their self-esteem is affected. As explained by Myron Eisenberg, even if the person with disabilities "rejects the label," very often their "awareness of the reactions of others will contribute to changing the social interactions of which he is part."[20] This is true for Swearingen; however, rather than allow such social stigma to become a self-fulfilling prophecy of academic failure, instead it steeled his resolve to not only succeed, but become the most academically successful student on campus.

Much to the surprise of everyone except Swearingen, he excelled in his coursework, doublestarring in all but three courses.[21] By 1891, Swearingen earned a reputation as the most intelligent student on campus. It was in college that Swearingen further developed his competitive spirit: Swearingen strongly desired to prove his worth in the academic arena—the only one perceived to be open to a blind student at the time.[22] By the time Swearingen graduated from college, he had amazed his fellow students with his feats. He could walk unassisted anywhere on campus with no difficulty and could identify all 200 students on campus by voice. As recalled by Swearingen's son, John Jr.,[23] college friends of his father's visited their house years after Swearingen had retired from public life. "As I was growing up, I observed many of them come by and shake hands with him, and say that 'I learned more from you than I ever learned from any one of our professors'." When he graduated June 17, 1899, Swearingen was the top graduate in the college and had completed the penultimate goal: making the record books. His records of academic achievement remained unbroken into the 1950s. [24]

It took Swearingen little time to apply his own hard labor and careful planning to a successful career path; upon graduation, Swearingen returned to the Cedar Springs Institute as a teacher. During the first few years following graduation, he wanted to pursue a career in the field of law. Since he did not have the money for graduate school, in 1903 he applied for a Rhodes scholarship to pursue a degree in law starting at Oxford University and ending at Columbia University. To this end, he secured effusive letters of recommendation from almost every professor he had at the college and he mustered the political clout of his uncle, United States Senator Ben Tillman. In spite of these efforts, the Rhodes committee refused the scholarship, likely due to Swearingen's blindness. "Here again," explains wife Mary, "the authorities in charge probably doubted the wisdom of admitting a blind applicant, and his efforts were fruitless."[25]

Throughout his life, Swearingen maintained a sense of decorum and propriety; the fact that he had lost his sight did nothing to change this. People who attempted to relax those standards due to his lack of sight did not remain in his acquaintance long—no matter how close the relationship. Before meeting his wife Mary, Swearingen "found a certain young lady very congenial, and he called on her very often." After one short visit with her, Swearingen asked his driver how he liked the looks of the young lady in question and what color dress she was wearing. When the hackman replied she was wearing a kimono-style dressing robe and wasn't dressed, "[t]hat was the end of the budding romance. He never went back; he never forgot it." In fact, upon meeting the young lady at a social gathering many years later, Swearingen asked aloud "if she still wears that kimono in the presence of gentlemen."[26]

In spite of being very successful in the classroom by all accounts, his career as a teacher did not last. Soon after becoming a teacher in 1899, Swearingen became principal of the blind department, earning a reputation as a tough, compassionate instructor and leader. By the 1907–08 school year, Swearingen rose to become superintendent of Cedar Springs, even learning sign language, holding the hands of the deaf students with whom he was communicating to read their signs. However, he did not serve long in this position either. In 1908, he opted out of education and into a career that combined his love of politics, service, South Carolina, and education with his sense of duty and pride: he decided to run for State Superintendent of Education. While Southern honor and duty was most frequently expressed through military service—something Swearingen desired to do, but could not—serving the state through support of its schools offered an alternative way to gain civic identity. If he couldn't carry a musket and bayonet to serve his state on the battlefield, he could carry his beliefs and efforts to serve his state in its capitol.

## CAREER: SWEARINGEN AND THE SCHOOLS OF SOUTH CAROLINA

Political campaigning during this period was difficult. Commenting on the oddities of the process, Mary Swearingen remembered that it was "a grueling practice which may not be peculiar to South Carolina, but which is certainly peculiar."[27] Making this travel even more uncomfortable were the coal-burning trains, with their discomforts of coal smoke and hot cinders in the cars. Candidates publicly debated throughout the intense heat of summer in every county in South Carolina. But, in an apparent slight to his ability, both of Swearingen's opponents disregarded him, an act which brought out his competitive nature. After listening to one of his competitors deliver the same speech at every whistle stop, Swearingen used his remarkable memory for humorous end. At the next stop, at which Swearingen was slated to deliver his address first, Swearingen rose and recited his competitor's oration verbatim—leaving the man quite literally speechless.[28]

Swearingen's platform had multiple facets, most of which were highlighted in the broadside pamphlet printed for his campaign and mailed to business owners in the larger towns across South Carolina. Swearingen did not try to hide his blindness; rather, he announced it in headline type on the broadside. A photograph filled the center of the page, taking up almost one-third of the document, with highlights of his life printed in banner type alongside. To the right states his educational experiences:

"Student at South Carolina College 1895–1899," and "Teacher in Cedar Springs Institute 1899–1908"; to the left, two more biographical statements: "Born January 9, 1875," and "Made Blind by the Accidental Discharge of his Gun while out Hunting January 13, 1888."[29] After several days of vote counting, Swearingen eventually won 61,379 to Stiles R. Mellichamp's 48,426, for a total of 109,805 votes cast. Swearingen defeated the only opponent to finish the race, Mellichamp, by a total of 12, 911 votes (over 11%).[30]

Proving his ability to mainstream society was one of Swearingen's early foci: once elected, he quickly established a public routine of efficiency and developed a knack for keeping his staff at ease. Using his gifted memory and his spatial skills at understanding maps/directions more prominent in the adventitiously blind than the congenitally blind Swearingen daily would walk the ten-block route from his home on Blanding Street in Columbia to his office unaccompanied. His son John explained:

> In his early days as state superintendent of education, his office was in one of those tall buildings ... he used to walk from the house to his office by himself. He knew his way around, and in those days there weren't that many cars on the street. And he was able to manage those things for himself. He did it without any problem at all.[31]

Organization governed Swearingen's professional life. His staff quickly grew used to his routine: he entered the office, had mail dictated to him, typed responses, made calls, and handled other bits of official business. Swearingen was out to prove his worth as a man without regard to his perceived disability: he hardly ever refused invitations to barbecues, picnics, family gatherings, political campaign meetings, graduation ceremonies, or school dedications. Whether it was loyalty to the state, a real sense of duty in his position, a means to prove himself, or more attempts at confounding social opinion, Swearingen traveled the state frequently. He completely muddied the waters of discussion regarding issues such as those outlined by Catherine Kudlick, including "who deserves the government's assistance and protection, what constitutes a capable citizen, and who merits the full rights of citizenship."[32] More specifically, while society of the time didn't necessarily view people who were blind as being capable citizens, Swearingen was elected to office and held it unopposed for a decade and a half.

One duty that took Swearingen out of the office regularly was inspection of new school buildings. At the outset, builders and superintendents alike doubted Swearingen's abilities in this capacity. He took great pleasure, however, in performing highly detailed inspections that caught construction errors missed by sighted colleagues. Mary Swearingen recalled a county superintendent telling her once that her husband could "find out more about a building with one trip than [the superintendent could] by watching them build it." Swearingen was methodical in his work:

> With his cane he checked the height of the ceiling and quickly stepped off the width of the room. With his sensitive perception to light, he could face the windows and remark, "I see you have your windows where you get good light." Some spectators were ready to swear he had a magic sense of some sort. He tested floor strength by his shiver-the-timber method. He would find a strategic point and suddenly bounce up and down energetically. If from two or three vantage points he could hear no rattles, he was happy. If, however, a carpenter had not braced his sills well enough, Mr. Swearingen was quick to suggest with some asperity that "these sills should be strengthened and steadied..." He would ask about the desks, the blackboards, and the heating facilities of the school building.[33]

Swearingen not only compensated for his blindness while in office, but performed all of his duties in a much more direct fashion than many of his predecessors. His efficiency and capability characterized not only the routine tasks of the office, but also Swearingen's view of his professional responsibilities. He not only wanted to maintain the public schools while he was in office, but he also aspired to affect significant change. Swearingen capitalized on the new spirit of reform that swept the nation and South Carolina through his time in office, 1909–1922. He successfully posted several significant pieces of legislation[34] and began several independent programs. Compulsory education, extended school terms and increased tax revenues to schools affected all students in the state. When the flu epidemic closed the schools and much of the state in 1919–1920, Swearingen demanded districts continue paying teachers. Most significantly, Swearingen's experiences in being treated as disabled made him particularly sensitive to those populations so labeled by mainstream society for their social as well as physical differences: he continued his supportive attitude towards hitherto educationally disenfranchised youth. He dramatically increased funding for African American students, arguing in his annual reports that public schools must consider equalizing:

> The time has come when this problem [expanding schools so all students have equal access through tenth grade] has reached the negro schools... Personally I favor the use of identical standards for all schools. If the instruction and organization of a colored high school, organized and directed by local school officers, and superintended and directed by men and women responsible to local authorities, conform to the high school standards of the state, I believe such a negro school ought to be accepted as an integral part of our high school system.[35]

Swearingen also greatly increased outreach efforts to mill workers and their children. He opened a great number of mill schools and worked with mill school advocate Wil Lou Gray to begin a program of adult education and literacy. In 1920, they began their "Midsummer Drive Against Illiteracy," coauthoring a pamphlet that detailed a plan for schools to implement evening adult literacy programs. The rear cover of the pamphlet summarized a vision of the program that tapped into South Carolinians' senses of historical appropriateness and masculine achievement: "Let South Carolina Secede from Illiteracy."[36] To accomplish his ends, Swearingen alternately cooperated and battled political and philanthropic forces on the state and national levels, including the General Education Board and Governor Coleman Blease.

## CONFLICTS: SWEARINGEN AND THE POLITICS OF SOUTH CAROLINA

While Swearingen was an advocate of vocational education, he did not support the General Education Board (GEB), one of the nation's most significant philanthropic agencies assisting, among others, African American schools. A group of private philanthropists operating out of New York City, the GEB was an organization that purportedly sought to assist Southern education; however, the GEB incorporated agents who completely subscribed to the vocational-only model of education throughout Southern universities and government agencies, such as state departments of education, in order to promote the organization's goals nationwide.[37] These agents, in turn, spread the GEB philosophy of vocational-only education throughout the South. While this can be viewed as a positive influx of money, specifically for schools serving marginalized populations, the intent was arguably pecuniary and borderline racist.

For the most part, Southerners welcomed the GEB funding of African American schools for a variety of reasons; there were, however, a few sporadic and isolated individuals who resisted GEB efforts as unwelcome intrusions of Northern philanthropy. Swearingen publicly opposed GEB intervention in South Carolina's schools: he did not appreciate the control placed over his office by an outside agency, there was a bit of post-Reconstruction resistance to another round of Northern intervention, and he certainly questioned the curriculum dictated by the GEB, recognizing the racist tendencies inherent in it. [38] While the relationship was initially collegial, starting in 1921 directors and representatives of the GEB were subjected to Swearingen's frustrated invectives. In a letter of response to Wallace Buttrick, a director with the Board, Swearingen wrote, "[y]ou have the absolute right to do as you choose with your own funds. I decline, however, to play the part of the fish dangling at the end of your line."[39]

Swearingen repeatedly expressed growing frustration and mistrust of the GEB's efforts. In April, he wrote to Abraham Flexner "[I]t is high time for a clear understanding between all parties. The use of your contributions means nothing to me individually and I cannot afford to be harassed and bedeviled by meddlesome dictation and afterthoughts."[40] In June, Swearingen wrote again to Flexner: "If you do not wish to support the work, simply keep the money … I am tired of being deviled with variations and uncertainties that will not allow me to plan definitely for the activities."[41]

Swearingen was also an outspoken critic of Governor Coleman Blease. The Governor was renowned for physically threatening opponents and promising sound thrashings to anyone who questioned or opposed him. Filled with abrasive and profane language, the state legislature frequently had to censor Blease's addresses. On one level, Blease was the logical culmination of the populist politics that had ruled the state since before the Civil War: for decades, Blease was particularly adept at tapping into the zeitgeist of the state, and elections in which he ran as a candidate had the highest voter turnout in the twentieth century. As historian Walter Edgar phrased it, "Bleaseism was a last hurrah of a dying world."[42]

In some regard it was the echoes of an unreconstructed South that led to Blease's popularity: he was a public face on racism, which directly led to his popularity among White workers. Yet, this is only a negligibly small part of the overall picture. The attitudes of White workers, mainly textile workers in the upcountry region, combined concerns about race, class, and gender. Blease was skilled at tapping into these interwoven concerns, recognizing that to the workers, independence was woven of citizenship, economic autonomy, White supremacy, and masculinity.[43]

Swearingen could not have been more different. He opposed discrimination and racism, and believed there was a place for the government in helping others. Blease and Swearingen were also polar opposites in the realm of intellectualism. Throughout his life Swearingen used his gifted mind and memory as assets. Blease was an outspoken anti-intellectual who encouraged a blatant distrust of intellectuals as part of the aristocracy. These patterns of conflict came to a head in the election of 1914.

Blease again ran for governor; this time, however, it was with the vocal opposition of one of South Carolina's most powerful politicians, Benjamin Tillman. Blease viewed Tillman as a former mentor, and Tillman was one of the most populist and popular politicians in South Carolina; Blease faced a tremendous electoral struggle in light of Tillman's opposition. In the midst of this political conflagration, in January 1914, Swearingen wrote Blease, asking the governor to explain his view on rural graded schools: "[a]t the 1913 session of the Legislature, you opposed State aid to two-teacher and three-teacher schools in the country. I understand that your position ... is still unchanged. If you care to express your views on this policy, and your attitude toward rural graded schools, I shall be glad to learn your position."[44]

Blease's response was furious, full of invective, and typical of South Carolina politics. While Swearingen's question was clearly not meant to defame the governor, Blease chose to take out the anger felt towards Tillman on Swearingen, the nephew of "Pitchfork Ben." Rather than address his policy toward state support of schools, Blease demonstrated his utter contempt for Swearingen by attacking him on a personal level: "I do not care to speak of your infirmity—but unless you have been imposed upon by reasons of your infirmity, I cannot understand this statement." Then, in spite of Swearingen's efforts to keep politics out of the office, Blease began a political attack. "I can understand why your uncle, Senator Tillman, has endeavored to injure me politically, and I presume his influence over you, being afflicted as you are, caused you to write the willful [sic] and malicious falsehood."[45]

The 1914 election was a turning point in South Carolina politics. Blease was defeated (he wouldn't be again elected until 1922), and every candidate who had aligned himself with Blease lost. Newly elected governor Richard Manning, a progressive, prepared to move into the governor's mansion. Blease was so anti-progressive that he chose to resign five days before his term ended, abandoning his responsibilities rather than turning the position over to Manning in person.[46]

Throughout his term, Swearingen was notably apolitical and honest in his office. When a book salesman threatened to campaign against Swearingen, the State Superintendent's reply was direct: "neither your bribe nor your threat makes any impression on me. When I have to sell my soul for political support, I shall gladly step out."[47] This resistance to politics was not more true than in a tragic but interesting event in Swearingen's life, that of his final campaign in 1922. After 14 years as State Superintendent of Education, Swearingen decided to run for Governor. His opponent in the Governor's race was his nemesis Cole Blease. As the politics became heated, however, Blease's attacks on Swearingen became increasingly hostile and personal. Rather than fight such a dirty campaign, Swearingen withdrew from the race and re-entered for State Superintendent.

Swearingen's son, John E. Swearingen Jr., explained that his father was told the Ku Klux Klan opposed him in the gubernatorial bid.[48] While his son did not remember the Klan ever threatening the family or making an appearance at the family's home, Mary Swearingen remembered "the night before his withdrawal, a group of men visited him. He had always considered them friends. They urged that he withdraw from the governor's race because the 'cards have been stacked against you'." Just two pages earlier in her memoir, Mary recounted Klan opposition to her husband in terms of his refusal to play politics with his position. "He never considered the political effects of his decisions," she recalled. "When the KKK accused him of giving teacher certificates to Catholics, Jews, and Negroes, he said frankly, 'Of course I do. What do you expect me to do? Break the law to suit prejudice?'"[49]

Swearingen also had a personal friendship with J.J. McSwain, a Congressman who served as Swearingen's best man and a frequent speaker at Klan rallies. If McSwain was involved, then it is safe to assume that while the Klan was serious in not supporting Swearingen, it had made no threats to him or his family. It is also safe to assume that it was McSwain who warned Swearingen of the cards being stacked against him. The Klan's bravado may have arisen as well from a weakening of progressivism: by 1922, the Civil War, Reconstruction, and the concomitant strife were well on their way to myth.

Those who joined the Klan or otherwise worked to continue discrimination in their daily lives perceived themselves as moral, enforcing traditional social order and law. They also believed that the "aristocrats" who questioned White superiority and the need for lynching were effete and socially dangerous. Cole Blease embodied this antebellum notion of Southern life: he unequivocally defended lynching because he wished to protect womanly virtues: "'whenever the constitution of my state steps between me and the defense of the virtue of a White woman … then I say to hell with the Constitution!'" Blease so relished Klan-style violence that he often celebrated their extraconstitutional means of preserving the status quo with a death dance.[50] Both McSwain and Blease were Klansmen; however, McSwain practiced what in contemporary parlance would be referred to as "kinder, gentler" racism, which Swearingen could abide.

Swearingen's withdrawal conceded the resurgence of Blease's style, but was not the end of the electoral conflict between the two men. Swearingen decided to mount a bid to remain State Superintendent, re-entering that race late. Jasper Hope, the State Superintendent candidate publicly supported by Blease, campaigned actively against Swearingen, making significant inroads among the millworkers. Tapping into anti-industrial and anti-reform sentiment, Blease offered millworkers a defense of their patriarchal privilege and White equality.[51] While Swearingen spent much of his career crusading for greater educational opportunities for mill workers, the educational gains made by mill families could not compete with Blease's rhetoric. Describing the election loss to family friend Sophie Rasor, Swearingen explained that "[t]he cotton mill vote went against me about three to one. This was the strongest element in the opposition, so far as any one class of schools or voters was concerned."[52] Swearingen never held public office again.

## CONCLUSION: SWEARINGEN'S LEGACY IN SOUTH CAROLINA

After leaving public service, Swearingen retired to a quiet life as a gentleman farmer. He took over the management of his extended family holdings, both in the upstate of South Carolina and in Florida. Neither Swearingen's wife nor son mentions him using the "talking books" (phonograph recordings of literature) that started coming out in the 1920s; however, once the Library of Congress began commissioning its holdings be reproduced in Braille, Swearingen became an avid reader once again. According to son John, Swearingen toured the State, volunteering his time at the Confederate Veterans Hospitals and speaking to groups that supported people with disabilities:

> His message always was, 'Don't give in to that handicap, don't just sit in a rocking chair waiting for somebody to take care of you. You've got to do something to justify your own existence, or work with whatever you have in the best way you know how to do it.'[53]

Plagued by headaches throughout his career as a result of the birdshot left in his head and face from the accident, Swearingen's health began to deteriorate in his later years. As early as the 1940s, his headaches began to become insufferable. Swearingen's other senses began to fail him with the onset of old age as well. First, his hearing began to suffer; son John had Swearingen fit with a hearing aid, which Swearingen wore when more than one person was visiting with him. Eventually, Braille books became too heavy for him to hold. Also, his sense of touch began to deteriorate; he commented often to his wife that Braille magazines were not printed as clearly as they used to be. Soon, he stopped his usual habits; he no longer sat on the porch, read his Braille books, listened to the radio, nor had anyone read the daily newspaper to him. After a year-long bout of invalidism, Swearingen passed away early morning September 27, 1957 at the age of 82.

Swearingen's successful career is a clear reminder that, while "[s]ociety assumes that everyone places the highest value on the 'naturally working body',"[54] such a definition is just that: a social construct with no biological basis. While it is safe to assume that Swearingen would not have chosen to be blind, once he came to accept this part of his life Swearingen led the best life he could. It is equally safe to say that Swearingen never allowed social definitions of what a blind man was capable define him; he spent his entire adult life marking success after success, disproving these definitions.

His success in improving the schools was just one example. To say he moved the schools of South Carolina into the twentieth century is not overstating the case. While transcending the values of his time, Swearingen was also very much a product of those values; however, his efforts to improve the schools of the state are vast:

- He raised awareness and funding regarding African American schools while resisting the popular vocational-only model
- He insisted on the passage of compulsory attendance laws
- He gained extensions of length of the annual school term
- He began a system of statewide accreditation of schools
- He increased public school funding for all populations, including implementing national funding efforts such as the Smith-Hughes Act
- He targeted White wage earners in the mills and their children for educational opportunity
- He honestly believed education was the best means to social empowerment.

It was his peculiar and complex understanding of social norms, and his willingness to actively work to transcend these norms, that inspired him to run for office. No more apt description exists than that provided by his wife, Mary:

> The layman of today, or even the students of educational progress in our state, can scarcely believe the school system of South Carolina was as inadequate as it was when Mr. Swearingen became State Superintendent of Education fifty years ago. But I must admit that it gives me a feeling of infinite pride to see how he grappled with the situation, determined to correct abuses, to extend opportunities, and to create a worthwhile public school program.[55]

Swearingen's legacy in terms of a career of "firsts" as a blind public figure in South Carolina was profound:

- He was the first student who was blind to be admitted to the South Carolina College
- He was the first candidate who was blind to run for office
- He was the only state superintendent who was blind in South Carolina's history.

While many people who are adventitiously blind interpret their lack of vision as "an actively repressed *memento mori*" (reminder of the mortality)[56] of their sight, Swearingen never viewed himself as disabled. In fact, as is the case with many people with disabilities, the notion that his blindness caused suffering, or diminished or devalued his life would be abhorrent.[57] Typifying his attitude is a story recounted by son John. One afternoon, during the Great Depression, Swearingen was out walking with his family when a beggar approached and asked for money. Swearingen fumbled in his pocket to find a coin. The beggar, shocked at Swearingen's blindness, apologized, saying "Oh, I'm sorry mister, I didn't realize you was afflicted." Swearingen's response was blunt and perfect: "Here, take your money. I'm not afflicted, I just can't see."[58]

Swearingen believed people who are blind are, indeed, "full-fledged members of society" that prove themselves by "desist[ing] from asking or accepting special favors" in contrast with those who viewed blindness as "so disabling a handicap that only if it were equalized through contemporary laws and regulations could blind people hope to approach parity with the sighted."[59] As recounted by wife Mary, Swearingen did everything he could to transform and transcend by example social definitions of disability:

> Mr. Swearingen himself never complained about the hardships and handicaps of blindness; his own practice and example inculcated similar attitudes in his blind friends. He urged them to participate in business and society and preached to them the therapy of work. He considered locomotion, reading, and social recognition of friends and acquaintances the most difficult problems of blindness.

Enforced idleness was not far behind, and almost equally difficult to avoid.

> Mr. Swearingen's attitude as well as his example were an inspiration not only to the blind of his generation but to the sighted as well.[60]

Swearingen should remain an example and inspiration; however, he should not only be taken as an inspiration to people with disabilities. In contemporary society, if those employed in state departments of education across the United States could emulate Swearingen's honest discourse regarding social and financial inequities facing our students that will not be cured by additional assessments the public schools of the United States would likely see great improvements. If Swearingen could remind contemporary public servants of his bravery as a politician, doing the right thing in spite of its unpopularity, imagine how many beneficial pieces of legislation could get passed. If the general public would remember his admonition to always work for the best in any situation rather than allow themselves to wallow in the cult of victimhood, imagine the progress we could make as a society. Indeed, if these "if's" were followed and we could bring his memory to the public, the United States would be a remarkably different, substantively better place.

## NOTES

1. The Smith-Hughes Act was the 1917 federal act that provided funds to public schools for the promotion of agricultural and vocational education. Cardinal Principles were the 1918 national educational report that realigned secondary education into seven curricular strands, including new categories such as vocational education and health; traditional academic subjects were classified together into one strand in the report, rather than the traditional "three r's" approach.
2. James Dreyfuss, *John Eldred Swearingen: Superintendent of Education in South Carolina 1909–1922* (Columbia: University of South Carolina College of Education, 1997), 2.
3. People who are adventitiously blind develop their blindness later in life, possibly as a result of forces such as an accident, trauma, disease, or medication. Those born blind are referred to as congenitally blind. Frances A. Koestler, *The Unseen Minority: A Social History of Blindness in America* (New York: David McKay Company, 1976), 191.
4. For a more detailed explanation of the role of physical ability/disability on biographical analysis, see Robert Gittings, *The Nature of Biography* (Seattle: University of Washington Press, 1978), 49–52.
5. Swearingen met his future wife while early in office; they married after she had begun a teaching career of her own. Mary Hough Swearingen, *A Gallant Journey: Mr. Swearingen and His Family* (Columbia: University of South Carolina Press, 1983), 98.
6. James Garraty, *The Nature of Biography* (New York: Alfred A Knopf, 1957), 4–6.
7. In actuality, not only did Swearingen's father serve, but all of his father's brothers served as well; most survived the war, but two gave their lives for the Southern cause. Mary Hough Swearingen presents a detailed accounting of the Swearingen family from their arrival in America from Holland in 1636 through her husband and children's lives in *A Gallant Journey*. Accounts of John Cloud Swearingen and Anna Tillman Swearingen are found in Swearingen, *A Gallant Journey*, 14–25.
8. Details of John Eldred Swearingen's childhood, including the hunting accident that led to his blindness, are recounted in Swearingen, *A Gallant Journey*, Chapter 3, "The Light is Spent", 26 – 38.
9. Swearingen, *A Gallant Journey*, 26 – 38. Upon his mother's passing, Swearingen wrote to friends extensively about the role his mother played in his rehabilitation and beginning of his political career, correspondence that

survives in the John E. Swearingen Papers, Box 2, Folder 60, (Columbia, SC: South Caroliniana Library).

10. Founded in 1849, Swearingen's wife refers to it as the South Carolina School for the Deaf and Blind; however, in their 1892 work Gallaudet and Bell refer to it as the "South Carolina Institute for the Deaf and Dumb and Blind." Edward Milner Gallaudet and Alexander Graham Bell, *Education of Deaf Children: Evidence of Edward Miner Gallaudet and Alexander Graham Bell* (Washington, D.C.: Volta Bureau, 1892), 72.
11. Swearingen, *A Gallant Journey*, 18–19.
12. Mary Klages, *Woeful Afflictions: Disability and Sentimentality in Victorian America* (Philadelphia: University of Pennsylvania Press, 1999), 33.
13. For an excellent, thorough comparison of the two publications, see Catherine J. Kudlick, "The outlook of *The Problem* and the problem with the *Outlook*: Two advocacy journals reinvent blind people in turn-of-the-Century America." In *The New Disability History: American Perspectives* eds. P. K. Longmore & L. Umansky (New York: New York University Press, 2001), 187–213.
14. For a more detailed discussion on Keller's impact on the blind, see Koestler, *The Unseen Minority*, 53–90.
15. "To present play in sign language: Helen Menken plans to attempt mute Portia." *The State*, April 2, 1922, 2.
16. Catherine J. Kudlick, "Disability history: why we need another 'other'." *American Historical Review* 108, (June 2003): 777. For a much more thorough discussion of the role of soldiers on perceptions of people with disabilities, see David A. Gerber, *Disabled Veterans in History* (Ann Arbor, MI: University of Michigan Press, 2000).
17. Thomas D. Cutsforth, *The Blind in School and Society* (New York: American Foundation for the Blind, 1951), 25.
18. Ibid., 222.
19. Swearingen, *A Gallant Journey*, 40.
20. Myron G. Eisenberg, "Disability as stigma." In *Disabled People as Second-Class Citizens*, eds. M. G. Eisenberg, et al. (New York: Springer Publishing Company, 1982), 4.
21. Swearingen, *A Gallant Journey*, 43–44. The grading scale at the college was broken into divisions; division I meant marks between 80–100% down the scale to division IV that meant marks less than 40%. Swearingen never was marked out of division I. Within the division, a single star meant a mark between 90–95%; double stars signified 95–100%.
22. E. Anthony Rotundo, "Boy Culture: Middle Class Boyhood in Nineteenth-Century America." In *Meanings for Manhood: Constructions of Masculinity in Victorian America*, eds. M. C. Carnes & C. Griffen, (Chicago: University of Chicago Press, 1990), 22.
23. The eldest of Swearingen's three children, John Jr. was born in 1918. After a successful career as president of Standard Oil, amongst other offices and honors, he became a fixture in the Chicago philanthropic and social circles. He died in 2007.

24. John E. Swearingen, Jr., interview by Edward Janak, July 30, 2002), Interview 1, tape 1 side 1.
25. Swearingen, *A Gallant Journey*, 50.
26. Ibid., 60.
27. Ibid., 100.
28. Both Swearingen, in his papers, and wife Mary, in her memoir recount many of the details of the first campaign; however, as an example of Southern gentility, neither recount their opponents by name. Mary simply refers to them as "prominent, respected, 'old school' gentlemen, both of whom had been closely associated with educational work in South Carolina for many years ... each resented the candidacy of the other as a sort of unwarranted intrusion." Swearingen, *A Gallant Journey*, 100. In the August 25 1908 edition of *The State* newspaper, however, primary results were tabulated for three candidates: Swearingen, Stiles R. Mellichamp, and E.C. Elmore. Mellichamp and Swearingen won their primaries and moved on to the election.
29. John E. Swearingen, "John E. Swearingen: Candidate for State Superintendent of Schools," Legal Box, John E. Swearingen Papers South Caroliniana Library, Columbia, SC.
30. "Election results" *The State*, September 13, 1908, 1. Early reports had the two candidates in a "very close" race (*The State*, September 8, 1908, p. 1 col. 6), but Swearingen was declared the winner the day after the race—on Wednesday, September 9.
31. Swearingen, interviewed by Janak, tape 1 side 1.
32. Kudlick, "Disability history": 766.
33. Swearingen, *A Gallant Journey*, 116.
34. Swearingen had been working on several pieces of educational legislation with no success until 1914, including bills for compulsory education and extensions of length of term, statewide accreditation of schools, increased public school funding for both White and African American schools, and increased personnel in his office.
35. John E. Swearingen, *Fiftieth Annual Report of the State Superintendent of Education of the State of South Carolina* (Columbia: Gonzales and Bryan State Printers, 1919), 24.
36. John E. Swearingen and Wil Lou Gray, *Midsummer Drive Against Illiteracy for White Schools* (Columbia: Office of the State Superintendent of Education, 1920), Cover.
37. Charles Biebel, "Private foundations and public policy: The case of secondary education during the Great Depression," *History of Education Quarterly* 16 (1976): 3–4. For a more detailed description of the GEB's efforts in vocational-only funding, see also Eric Anderson and Alfred A. Moss, "*Dangerous Donations: Northern Philanthropy and Southern Black Education, 1902–1930* (Columbia: University of Missouri Press, 1999), 85–107.
38. In his article on GEB funding, James Anderson describes Southern resistance to the GEB's efforts as a "series of isolated incidents"; the only specific example of this resistance Anderson presents is that of Swearingen. James Anderson, "Northern foundations and the shaping of Southern

Black rural education 1902–1935," *History of Education Quarterly* 18 (Winter 1978): 383.

39. John E. Swearingen to Wallace Buttrick, January 29, 1921, Series 1: Appropriations; Subseries 1: The Early Southern Program (Supervisor of Rural Schools—White, 1912–1927), *General Education Board Archives,* Rockefeller University, New York City, NY.
40. John E. Swearingen to Abraham Flexner, April 11, 1921, Series 1: Appropriations; Subseries 1; The Early Southern Program (State Agent for Secondary Education 1919–1926),*General Education Board Archives,* Rockefeller University, New York City, NY.
41. John E. Swearingen to Abraham Flexner, June 9, 1921, Series 1: Appropriations; Subseries 1; The Early Southern Program (Supervisor of Rural Schools—Negro, 1917–1952), *General Education Board Archives,* Rockefeller University, New York City, NY.
42. Walter Edgar, *South Carolina in the Modern Age* (Columbia: University of South Carolina Press, 1992), 34.
43. Bryant Simon, *A Fabric of Defeat: The Politics of South Carolina Millhands 1910–1948* (Chapel Hill: University of North Carolina Press, 1998), 67.
44. John E. Swearingen to Coleman Blease, January 27, 1914, Miscellaneous papers—Letters to State Officials, Box #14, Governor's Papers of Coleman Livingston Blease (1911– 1915), South Carolina Repository of History and Archives, Columbia, SC.
45. Coleman Blease to John E. Swearingen, January 29, 1914, Governor's papers of Coleman Livingston Blease (1911– 1915). Miscellaneous papers—Letters to State Officials, Box # 14, South Carolina Repository of History and Archives, Columbia, SC.
46. Walter Edgar, *South Carolina: A History* (Columbia: University of South Carolina Press, 1998), 664.
47. Swearingen, *A Gallant Journey,* 113.
48. John E. Swearingen, Jr. interviewed by Edward Janak, November 1, 2002, Interview 2, tape 1 side 1.
49. Swearingen, *A Gallant Journey,* 112–114.
50. Bryant Simon, "The appeal of Cole Blease of South Carolina: Race, class, and sex in the New South," *The Journal of Southern History* 62, (February 1996): 82–83.
51. Simon, *A Fabric of Defeat,* 34.
52. John E. Swearingen to Sophie Rasor, September 19, 1922, Box 3, Folder 90, John E. Swearingen Papers: South Caroliniana Library, Columbia, SC.
53. Swearingen, interviewed by Janak, Interview 1tape 1 side 1.
54. Rod Michalko, *The Difference that Disability Makes*. (Philadelphia: Temple University Press, 2002), 47.
55. Swearingen, *A Gallant Journey,* 107.
56. Michalko, *The Difference that Disability Makes,* 10.
57. Ibid., 50.
58. Swearingen, interviewed by Janak, Interview 1tape 1 side 1.
59. Koestler, *The Unseen Minority,* 176.
60. Swearingen, *A Gallant Journey,* 61.

CHAPTER 6

# CORRESPONDENCE STUDY AND THE "CRIME OF THE CENTURY"

## Helen Williams, Nathan Leopold, and the Stateville Correspondence School

**Von Pittman**

In late November, 1930, Helen Williams, Director of the Bureau of Correspondence Study at the State University of Iowa (SUI; now the University of Iowa), received a letter of a kind that independent study directors at American universities continue to receive today. Written in pencil on a sheet of cheap, lined paper torn from a tablet, it bore the rubber stamp mark "CENSOR." The number 9306 followed the writer's name. A convict wanted information about studying advanced mathematics by correspondence. He described his previous math work, said he would like to study "The Calculus," and asked for advice on the best courses in which to enroll.[1]

Correspondence study (now generally called "independent study") offices have long responded to such letters with a course bulletin and perhaps a form letter stipulating enrollment procedures. In this case, how-

*Life Stories: Exploring Issues in Educational History Through Biography*
pp. 107–130

ever, the Director of Correspondence Study took the time to study the request. After consulting one of SUI's math professors, Williams suggested that the convict's completion of high school algebra and his independent work in plane trigonometry while in prison should have prepared him to do satisfactory work in analytic geometry. By paying a fee of $14.00, he could enroll for three semester hours of credit as an unclassified student. [2]

On December 1, 1930, Nathan Leopold, one of the country's most notorious convicts, drew a money order from his account in the warden's office of the Illinois State Penitentiary in Joliet. He then applied for enrollment in the SUI program.[3] Leopold's enrollment in an SUI geometry course, by correspondence, marked the inauguration of a partnership between a notorious murderer and an obscure university bureaucrat that would lead to the creation and sustained operation of a rigorous, effective, and respected high school. This high school—formally named the Stateville Correspondence School (SCS)—would serve thousands of men throughout the penal systems of Illinois, then in a handful in other states, at no cost to the State of Illinois. This prisoner-run and prisoner-taught school endured until the early 1950s, when the Illinois State Penitentiary system completed the institution of a comprehensive system of state-funded prison education. It chose not to replace the Stateville Correspondence School but to integrate it into the new system. Thus, the informal, and largely accidental, partnership between Nathan Leopold and Helen Williams would have a profound impact upon prison education programs within the Illinois penal system, and—to a limited extent—beyond it.

Richard Loeb's and Nathan Leopold's murder of Bobby Franks in the Spring of 1924 has inspired numerous novels, films, and plays, the first of which—Robert Harris's play *Rope*—opened in 1929.[4] In addition to the usually sensationalized newspaper accounts from the 1920s, journalistic accounts have continued to appear in print periodicals and on Web sites. However, in spite of the wide and persisting popular interest in the "Crime of the Century," it has prompted little scholarly work. Until very recently, only Hal Higdon's *Leopold and Loeb: The Crime of the Century*, first issued in 1975, provided a comprehensive account.[5] In 2008, Simon Baatz, a professor at John Jay College and the Graduate Center of the City University of New York, published *For the Thrill of It: Leopold, Loeb, and the Murder that Shocked Jazz Age Chicago*, a scholarly book that could qualify for the "true crime" genre in bookstores.[6] It now represents the definitive account of the murder case and trial.

Material on the incarceration of Leopold and Loeb, Loeb's death, and Leopold's life after being paroled is understandably harder to obtain, although both Higdon and Baatz provided some information. Leopold's memoir, *Life Plus 99 Years*, is critical to the study of this period.[7] However, because it was a part of Leopold's strategy to obtain parole and release, it must be used cautiously, even skeptically. Not surprisingly, Leopold created a highly self-serving narrative. Reporter Gladys Erickson's *Warden Ragen of Joliet* provides useful detail on Loeb's murder and the latter stages of Leopold's incarceration.[8] With the exception of *Life Plus 99 Years*, none of these sources deal with the SCS in any detail.

Leopold and Loeb created SCS with virtually no assistance from the State of Illinois, or its penal system. Leopold's long-term friendship with Helen Williams, Director of the Bureau of Correspondence Study at SUI, provided a useful, high-quality secondary education to a population that previously had no access.

## STUDENT-CONVICT AND ADVISER

In the spring of 1924, Leopold and his friend Richard Loeb kidnapped and murdered a fourteen-year-old boy named Bobby Franks, then sent a ransom note to his father. Although Leopold and Loeb had begun planning their crime in the late fall, their choice of a victim was last minute and almost random. While highly intelligent young men, they quickly failed as criminals. Once placed under arrest, their alibis and evasions fell apart. The district attorney asked for the death penalty. Only their youth—Leopold was 19, Loeb, 18—and their families' good sense in hiring Clarence Darrow saved them from the gallows.

Helen Williams had earned her undergraduate degree at SUI in 1910. After two quarters of graduate work in history at the University of Chicago, she taught school for two years in Scranton, Pennsylvania. She returned to Iowa City to work in various capacities for the SUI Extension Division. A slight woman, her picture reveals an infectious smile. She became the first Director of University Extension's Bureau of Correspondence Study in 1920.[9] At that time, SUI had been offering correspondence courses for only four years. Williams would remain in the same position until 1949. She is now remembered as a pioneer in the field of collegiate distance education and in the delivery of college courses by radio. She was one of the few female administrators at SUI, albeit at a low rank. In 1990, the American Association for Collegiate Independent Study (AACIS) named its major prize for curriculum design "The Helen Williams Award."[10]

From the beginning of their incarceration, both Leopold and his friend and fellow felon enrolled in correspondence courses. Soon after arriving at the "Old Prison" at Joliet, Leopold began to work his way through the textbooks that William Rainey Harper, the founding president of the University of Chicago, had created for use in his Hebrew correspondence courses in the late nineteenth century. Loeb enrolled in a Latin course from Columbia University. Between them, they would enroll in numerous courses—both esoteric and practical—including Egyptian hieroglyphics, Greek comedy, Sanskrit, and business shorthand. During civil proceedings after his release from prison, Leopold would use his knowledge of Sanskrit to take notes so that he could keep them absolutely confidential.[11]

Nathan Leopold and Richard Loeb differed from the usual correspondence student in several ways. They were not only convicts, but "lifers." Nineteen at the age of the Franks murder, the short, sallow Leopold had already received his undergraduate degree from the University of Chicago and was enrolled as a first-year law student at the same university. Richard Loeb, a tall, fair, outgoing young man, had graduated from the University of Michigan at 18 and then begun graduate study in history at the University of Chicago. Both were graduates of elite private prep schools: Leopold from the Harvard School and Loeb from the University of Chicago's "U-High."

According to Leopold, while in prison, he became obsessed with learning how to calculate the area under a curve. "I got hold of a catalogue of the Home Study Department of the State University of Iowa and addressed a letter to the director. In so doing I acquired a friend who has stood by me steadfastly ever since."[12] Why Leopold chose to explore SUI courses rather than courses from the University of Chicago or some other institution is unknown. The most likely explanation is that he looked at the catalogues of several university programs—possibly shelved in the libraries at Stateville and Joliet or obtained by family members—and inquired about the courses that most interested him. Even today, convicts frequently send inquiries to every program for which they can find an address. The fact that Leopold received a personal answer from SUI, with a considered response to his question, no doubt made its program attractive. Williams' almost certain recognition of Leopold's name probably accounts for her decision to send an encouraging reply, rather than a form letter, to his inquiry.

While still working on his first SUI math correspondence course, Leopold asked to enroll in an advanced Hebrew course. This presented an embarrassing problem for Helen Williams. As often happened in correspondence/independent study programs, while the course listing appeared in the catalogue, the study guide and lesson sheets had never been written. Professor (and Rabbi) Moses Jung had agreed to write them but had never gotten around to the task.[13]

Williams contacted Professor Jung and explained the problem. "I am enclosing a letter from a person whose name I believe you will recognize at once as a prisoner in Illinois State Penitentiary at Joliet." She continued, "I am writing Mr. Leopold, telling him that I am asking for your advice, but I am not telling him that our course in Hebrew language has never been written. I believe this is the first actual request that we have ever had for it."[14] She suggested providing an "arranged" course, in which Leopold and Jung would communicate directly, outside the University's correspondence program. She would turn Leopold's entire tuition of $12 over to Jung, without taking the Correspondence Bureau's normal overhead charge. Jung assented. He not only guided Leopold through the arranged course, he worked with him one-on-one for several more years, as Leopold studied large portions of the *Talmud*, as well as medieval and contemporary Hebrew literature.[15]

Upon completing his lessons and receiving the professor's comments in Math 4C in March, 1941, Leopold asked Williams to approve John Taylor, Superintendent of Education for the Illinois State Penitentiary, to proctor his exams.[16] As has always been the practice in collegiate correspondence programs, exams had to be mailed to designated authority figures who observed the students as they took them. That approved proctor then sealed the examination, signed a statement that the student had taken it in his or her presence, then mailed it back to the university. Williams approved Taylor as the proctor and mailed Leopold's exam to him. After receiving nothing from either Taylor or Leopold for more than a month, she wrote Taylor, gently reminding him that exams should be administered and returned promptly. "It would be a good thing if Mr. Leopold could take his examination before long."[17]

Williams did not know about the violence that had broken out inside both the "Old Prison" at Joliet and the more modern facility at Stateville, five miles away. The "Old Prison" had been in a state of high tension since late February, when guards—who had been tipped off—lay in wait for an expected escape attempt, then shot and killed three prisoners as they tried to scale the wall. The next day, the convicts set fires—one with Leopold's lighter—in retaliation. The guards quickly extinguished them. A riot broke out in the kitchen. The inmates broke windows, captured a guard captain, and broke his arm. The guards on the walls ended the incident by firing down into the yard, killing another two prisoners. Immediately after regaining control, the staff "shook down" the cells. When Leopold was allowed to return to his cell, he found that all of his books, correspondence, and papers had been confiscated.[18]

Shortly after the "Old Prison" riot, a guard told Leopold that he would be moved to the new facility at Stateville, where he had temporarily been housed earlier, and which he much preferred. Just as the prison bus transporting him and 29 other prisoners pulled up to the Stateville gate, a riot broke out there. The bus returned to Joliet. A few days later, when the administration regained control, Leopold once again took the bus to the new facility.[19] Given the state of affairs, Superintendent Taylor's choice not to assign a high priority to proctoring Leopold's test is not surprising.

In late April, Taylor sent Williams two communications. In a conventional business letter, he simply said that he had not yet been able to schedule the exam. Also, he said, the textbook that Leopold had borrowed from the SUI library had been lost. He did not mention the shakedown. However, in an undated, handwritten note, Taylor told Williams that the riots had prevented him from administering the test; he hoped to be in a position to do it soon. Also, he had searched for the lost book so that Leopold could study for the exam, but had had no success. Williams used her own funds to purchase another copy of the textbook, which she mailed to Leopold so that he could prepare for the test. Finally, in late May, Taylor returned the completed exam and said that the "lost" textbook had been found and would be returned.[20]

Helen Williams became a sort of *de facto* academic adviser and advocate for Leopold, frequently working as a "go-between." In October, 1931, as Leopold was about to complete his second math course with Professor John Reilly, he asked Williams how to proceed: "I should like to work toward an understanding of the Mathematics of Relativity. I have no idea how long this would require, nor what specific courses would be necessary, and it is precisely this point which I should like to have explained."[21]

Williams took Leopold's question to Professor Reilly, who suggested SUI's second course in integral calculus as the next logical step. After that, he would consider arranging some individual courses for Leopold. While his department unfortunately had a policy against offering advanced math courses by correspondence, Reilly hoped it could be changed. However, should that not happen soon, Leopold could take courses in differential equations, analytical geometry, mechanics, and perhaps the theory of equations. Williams passed his message along to Leopold.[22]

## THE STATEVILLE CORRESPONDENCE SCHOOL (SCS)

Leopold credited Richard Loeb with raising the idea of creating a correspondence study high school inside Stateville. The sole school in the penitentiary offered only grades one through eight. It covered only the most fundamental skills. Most participants were barely literate, at least when they began. The elementary school's classification as a work assignment amounted to a disincentive. Students were not allowed to request other work assignments that offered greater status and slightly more commissary money. School assignments offered fewer privileges and a considerably lower status than jobs in the carpentry shop or kitchen, for example.

Thus, inmates with more desirable work assignments rarely chose to leave them to attend school.

Beyond elementary school, proprietary (commercial, profit-seeking) correspondence schools offered the only alternative. Most offered little beyond lists of assigned readings followed by sheets of objective questions. Few offered serious instruction. Even then, only the few inmates whose families could afford to pay for such courses had access to them. In January, 1933, when the Stateville Correspondence School opened, only three men were enrolled in proprietary correspondence courses.[23]

Loeb and Leopold decided that the greatest need for education inside Joliet and Stateville was at the high school level. They chose the correspondence teaching-learning model for several reasons. They knew that few men would participate should they be forced to give up the status and privileges of their other work assignments. With correspondence courses, they could hold onto their work assignments and do their schoolwork during cell time. Because there were no extrinsic rewards for participation, Leopold and Loeb said, only men who sincerely wanted high school-level instruction for its own sake would enroll. In a formal proposal they prepared to submit to Education Superintendent John Taylor and Warden Frank Whipp, Loeb and Leopold explained:

> The advantages of this system are obvious. It would place a high school education within the reach of any inmate industrious enough to take advantage of the privilege. To those interested in some particular subject, such as history or languages, it would offer a chance to spend their spare time pleasantly and profitably. Finally, since certificates of completion could be given, following satisfactory work in a course, the inmate would have a definite goal to strive for. A great deal of the irregular studying, at the present time done by inmates, could thus be directed into channels which would benefit them and have a direct effect on their rehabilitation as members of society.[24]

Correspondence study was not a new idea in the United States generally, or in prisons specifically. Indeed, this instructional format enjoyed great popularity in the period between the World Wars. During the 1920s, more than 2,000,000 people enrolled in correspondence courses—usually vocationally or professionally oriented—each year. As Dorothy Canfield Fisher noted, that amounted to more students enrolled in all of the postsecondary institutions in the country.[25]

Penitentiary inmates often enrolled in correspondence courses, usually at their families' expense. However, some state-funded prison education programs made correspondence courses—supplied by either outside vendors or university extension programs—available to inmates. The New Jersey State Prison had introduced correspondence courses to the American penal system in 1906. By the 1920s, California inmates could take correspondence courses free of charge from the University of California Extension program. At San Quentin, residents could take a dozen "letter box" courses that had been written and printed—and were graded—inside the prison.[26]

There is no indication that Leopold and Loeb were influenced by other prison education correspondence course programs. However, from their own experience, they were familiar with correspondence study's advantages and limitations. It did not prevent men from holding desirable work assignments. Just as importantly, if not more so, it could be offered at virtually no cost to the institution.

Loeb, who sometimes did domestic work in Warden Whipp's quarters, told Mrs. Whipp about the program. She encouraged him to take it forward. Warden Whipp eventually granted Loeb a hearing that resulted in permission to open the correspondence school. Leopold and Loeb spent the last two months of 1932 preparing course materials. Leopold told Williams that he and Loeb had modeled their school on university departments such as hers. They intended to offer as comprehensive a high school curriculum as practicable. The teachers were inmate volunteers. Superintendent of Education John Taylor would supervise the entire project, to be known as the Stateville Correspondence School (SCS).[27]

Leopold asked Williams for help. In particular, he needed lesson sheets for subjects that could be offered in the high school curriculum:

> I realize that this is a bold request, but I feel sure that in view of the very good purpose to which this material will be put, you will not consider me presumptuous in asking whether you could see your way clear to helping us in this way.[28]

He cautioned Williams to keep the information about the school to herself. He knew from experience that publicity could cause problems. Shortly after arriving at Joliet in 1924, he had begun teaching small groups of students. A story in the Chicago papers provoked an outcry about allowing a convict of his notoriety and "deficient character" to teach other men. The warden had then shut down his classes and Leopold had not taught since.[29]

Williams sent the written materials—course guides, lesson sheets, and exams—for numerous courses. The University of Chicago's high school—U-High—and its collegiate Home Study Department also contributed instructional materials. Several years later, the University of Illinois would contribute some courses. These materials proved invaluable as outlines and templates, but Loeb and Leopold decided that in order to work for their students, the materials should contain considerably more detail.

Loeb wrote a complete textbook for *English A: Seventh and Eighth Grade English*. He designed this course around his own experience with prisoners and his perception of their practical educational needs. Because the greatest need of all the men upon release would be to seek employment, he designed "English A" to emphasize business correspondence. This course consistently enrolled the highest number of students on an annual basis.[30]

In all cases, students would follow the course outlines, read assigned materials, then respond to typed lists of questions that had been edited by Loeb or Leopold and reviewed by Superintendent Taylor. Taylor would collect the students' answer sheets and deliver them to the volunteer inmate instructors for grading and commentary. Foreign language courses offered face-to-face sessions to complement correspondence work.[31]

Helen Williams enthusiastically supported the Leopold-Loeb high school project. In addition to outlines, lesson sheets, and other ancillary materials, she sent books that were out of date for her courses but potentially useful at the prison school. While incarcerated students taking SUI courses could borrow books from the campus library, as Leopold had, non-students—like SCS inmates—of course, could not. When an SCS instructor needed a book for use in writing a course, or when a student doing research wanted a book that SCS could not provide, Williams often would check it out from the SUI library in her name and pay the postage to mail it out of her own pocketbook. She did this dozens—if not hundreds—of times in the 1930s. Sometimes, she could arrange for students to borrow books from sympathetic professors, like John Reilly. When prison instructors needed assistance on fine points of the disciplines they were teaching, Williams frequently would refer their questions to SUI professors with appropriate expertise who she believed should be sympathetic to the prison students.[32]

SCS's rules and procedures were few and simple. The program was entirely voluntary. While it required that students be qualified for high school work, it did not demand elementary school credentials. It recognized that many of the men were self-educated. The school office personnel and the Superintendent of Education evaluated applicants. If students had sufficient funds in their prison accounts, they were required to purchase textbooks, which averaged about $1.00 per course in 1936, and $1.50 per course in 1938.[33]

Students were expected to work on their lessons on their own time—meaning that they could retain their prison work assignments—at their own pace. When a student turned in a lesson, it would be graded and returned within 24 hours, the school promised. Students who ran into problems that could not easily be resolved in writing could request an appointment with the instructor. Or, if the instructor spotted the problem, or if the student simply stopped turning in lessons, he could summon the student. Halfway through the course, and again at the end, the student went to the school office for a proctored exam, so that there could be no doubt about who was really doing the course work.[34]

Leopold, presumably with the assent of the SCS faculty and the various education superintendents, repeatedly published a guiding rationale in the school's annual reports. This boilerplate suggested that education could lead to better employment prospects for men who had been released, which should lead to reductions in rates of recidivism and parole violations, a proposition that Leopold would test statistically. But further,

> [the school] furnishes an adequate outlet for pent-up mental energy, which finds few other opportunities for vigorous application; it offers opportunity to keep the mental faculties alert by constant exercise; above all it furnishes an excellent distraction from the brooding and worry to which many prisoners are prone.[35]

If true, the SCS program would not only improve the mental health of the inmates, it would help make the prisons safer and more secure facilities.

Even though the new school taught felons and employed a nontraditional teaching format, it developed some conventional features. SCS offered a full high school curriculum, with the exceptions of physics and chemistry. For obvious reasons, the faculty could not find a way to overcome the lack of lab equipment and supplies, nor, presumably, the administration's concerns about security. Because so many men lacked language skills, the school offered remedial courses in English grammar and composition.[36] Its course manuals (study guides) rivaled those of the large state and private universities. This is because the bulk of the first round of courses originated at the Universities of Chicago, Iowa, and Illinois. Loeb's—and especially Leopold's—commitment to academic standards also contributed to the instructional quality of SCS course materials. SCS issued a sophisticated, comprehensive *Handbook for Teachers*.[37] Marcie McGuire, a veteran independent study curriculum editor at the University of Missouri examined this publication and described it as follows:

> [it] provides useful and interesting information about the nature and scope of teaching in the prison schools. The chapters introduce both theoretical and practical topics, including the aim of education in correctional institutions, theory of adult education, nature of curriculum and assessments, and potential problems.... It also provides practical guidelines for new teachers (e.g., descriptions of the types of students, characteristics of effective teachers, sample grading scales, lists of available tests, samples of marked papers, lesson plans).[38]

Prison regulations necessitated an indirect communications channel. Because inmates' outgoing letters were strictly regulated in number and frequency, all mail related to the high school had to be addressed to the Education Superintendent. Leopold told Williams to send letters pertaining to the school to Superintendent John Taylor, who would pass them to him.[39] Most of the letters he sent to her were mailed over the signatures of Taylor and subsequent superintendents.

SCS opened on January 11, 1933, with 22 students enrolled in four courses—Spanish, English, history, and mathematics. Sixty-four additional students had applied for admission, pending verification of their claims to have received an eighth-grade education. The Illinois State Penitentiary's administration—no doubt with a wary eye toward public reaction—stated its support for a program that "would help solve the problem of idleness."[40] Leopold and Loeb were both in Stateville at the time, but the correspondence method made it possible and convenient for men in Joliet to take courses, also. The two prisons were located only a few miles apart and operated under a single administration. Only the Spanish course demanded actual class meetings[41] and thus could not be offered outside Stateville.

The *Chicago Tribune* identified Richard Loeb as the "Head Master," a title that does not appear in any of the archival sources pertaining to SCS. Loeb and Leopold administered the program under the supervision of the Education Superintendent. At no time was there an inmate principal, superintendent, or master. The SCS faculty members were a well-educated, colorful lot. Former University of Kansas student Teddy Dillon, the "society bandit," taught English.[42] Attorney, teacher, and kidnapper Joseph Pursifull offered Latin, while forger Mark Oettinger took charge of some of the math courses. The *Tribune* did not mention Nathan Leopold, even though he took the largest role in creating the school. Hal Higdon, the author of one of the major accounts of the Leopold-Loeb crime and prison time, speculated that the prison authorities, fearing public reaction, might have structured press releases in such a way that the two men's linked names never appeared in tandem.[43]

Indeed, both Loeb and Leopold (with his prior prison teaching experience) worried that the announcement might spark a negative public reaction that could brand the school as a frivolous and misdirected exercise. Leopold said:

> We'd obviate that by seeing to it that our courses were tougher and more complete than corresponding courses outside. We'd lean over backward in setting high academic standards—higher, just because we were convicts, than would be necessary in the free world.[44]

One Illinois-based correspondence school immediately complained about the competition. In a sidebar to a 1933 article on commercial correspondence schools, *Fortune* magazine noted that "the correspondence school started at Joliet Penitentiary by Richard Loeb, of Leopold-Loeb notoriety" was responsible for a decrease in the normally robust prison enrollments of the Moody Bible Institute. Besides placing the school in the wrong prison, *Fortune* erroneously stated that the University of Chicago had created some of the school's courses.[45]

Once the program was up and running, Warden Joseph Ragen of the Illinois penal system's Menard facility asked permission for inmates there to participate. Initially, few men at Menard were prepared for high school. Over time, however, enrollments grew to several dozen a year. Later, a handful of inmates from other male units of the Illinois penal system began to enroll.[46]

Leopold and Helen Williams maintained a respectful, but always businesslike, correspondence until 1934, when Leopold was admitted to the prison hospital for minor surgery. Williams sent Leopold a personal note, wishing him a quick recovery.[47] This initiated a personal correspondence that lasted until Leopold's death in 1971.

Later the same year, Williams told Leopold that she had been in Joliet recently, visiting friends. She had considered seeking permission for a visit, "but since I felt so certain that my request would be refused I did not make the attempt."[48] Leopold was delighted:

> I was particularly touched, Miss Williams, by your desire to stop in for a little visit. I can think of nothing which would give me more pleasure and to which I would look forward more eagerly than the opportunity of meeting personally the lady who has been so extremely good to me.[49]

A year later, in preparation for a visit with the same friends, Williams applied for—and received—permission to visit Leopold. Warden Whipp allowed Leopold and Loeb to show her the school and the prison's Sociological Research Office. Williams and Leopold became fast friends. Leopold told Williams that he had "adopted" her; she was now "Aunt Helen." She began addressing him as "Babe," the nickname Leopold's family had given him as a child, and still used.[50] Although Williams had already made a major commitment of time and energy to SCS, her new friendship with Leopold strengthened the partnership that served hundreds of convicts during the 1930s.

## A PARTNERSHIP ENDED

On the morning of January 28, 1936, Leopold and Loeb were enjoying some of the privileges that had been conferred on them—directly or indirectly—for their work with SCS. Instead of going to the dining hall for breakfast, they had sweet rolls delivered to their cells. When they got to their office, they graded papers and worked on plans for a new math course. One of the chief privileges was the washroom and shower that came with the school office. Loeb decided to take a shower before lunch. While Loeb showered, a former cellmate, James Day, entered the room, carrying a straight razor that he had kept hidden in the Protestant chaplain's office. A few minutes later, Loeb staggered out of the washroom, having sustained at least 56 slashes. Day handed the weapon to a guard and said that he had been forced to defend himself against Loeb's homosexual advances. With Leopold in the room, Loeb bled out in the prison hospital in spite of the efforts of seven doctors.[51]

Day's motive has never been clearly established. Using essentially the same sources, Leopold's *Life Plus 99 Years*, and stories from Chicago newspapers, the authors of the two scholarly accounts, Hal Higdon and Simon Baatz, offered differing interpretations of the role of prison privileges—most importantly commissary goods—in provoking Day's attack. Until Joseph Ragen's arrival in 1935, inmates had enjoyed unlimited commissary privileges. They could spend as much money as they liked from their prison accounts. Prisoners whose families deposited money in their accounts therefore could supply other inmates with cigarettes, candy, and other goods. Loeb's family gave him an allowance of $50 a month. He used it to provide goods to friends and others. In addition, Leopold and Loeb's positions at the school made them "Stateville's princes of privilege."[52]

Ragen ended the largess of the more monied prisoners, who were no longer able to reward friends or control other inmates. Higdon leaned toward attributing Day's actions to his resentment over no longer receiving "perks" from Loeb. Baatz offered another interpretation: Leob had used his relative wealth and his ability to award privileges to maneuver Day into assenting to his persistent sexual advances. The respected Catholic chaplain, Father Eligius Weir, took the opposite position and said that, if anything, Day had been enraged because Loeb had rejected his sexual overtures.[53]

The state's attorney tried Day, demanding the death penalty. However, as usual, no prisoner would testify against another, particularly in a capital case. Beyond that, the foreman later described a homophobic consensus among the members of the jury. Finally, it is possible—even probable—that nobody wanted to convict the man who had killed one of the perpetrators of the "crime of the century." After less than an hour of deliberation, the jury returned a verdict of "not guilty."[54]

Warden Ragen, frustrated by the verdict, sought to avoid further trouble by removing both Day and Leopold from the general population. He sent Leopold to the mental unit, or "bug cells." Ragen told Leopold personally that this was for his own protection. Leopold never accepted this reasoning. Because of this isolation, he could not resume his SCS work assignment for a full six months.[55]

When Leopold returned to the general population, he seriously considered asking for permission to trade his work assignment, which consisted of administering SCS and teaching some of its courses, for something new. His association of the school with Loeb made it difficult to continue, he said. However, when he had a chance to review the status of the school, he became concerned. While a clerk had kept the mechanical operations moving smoothly, Leopold found that many men had just quit sending in lessons. He contacted all currently enrolled students. Many got started again, and a few dropped out. The other teachers were not as strongly committed to SCS's survival as he. Most of them who asked for other work assignments, with more privileges, had no trouble securing them. It was becoming difficult to replace instructors who were paroled. Leopold talked enough instructors into continuing to keep the school going, saying that it should be a memorial to Richard Loeb.[56]

## SCS REACHES MATURITY

Leopold continued to run the school without Loeb but with increasing support from the warden's office and from Helen Williams. SCS began to gain notice at the state and national levels. The school added a selection of college-level math and foreign language courses in 1938, then in 1939 renamed itself the Stateville Correspondence School and Junior College, a title used until the State of Illinois' consolidation of its prison education system in 1954.[57]

In 1939, a convict named Edward Farrant, who was serving a life term in Iowa's Ft. Madison Penitentiary, asked for Williams' help in finding a Spanish correspondence course. Like most convicts, Farrant was indigent. Williams referred him to a Works Progress Administration (WPA) program that provided college correspondence courses to convicts. However, the WPA's contractor had no Spanish course at the proper level. Farrant again asked Williams for help.[58]

She enlisted Leopold, who suggested that either she or the warden at Ft. Madison should ask Warden Ragen if he would allow Farrant to enroll in the Stateville program. Ft. Madison's Director of Education made the formal request on Farrant's behalf. Leopold, writing in the name of Stateville Superintendent of Education P. J. Fitzgibbon, who had replaced Taylor, relayed the word back that, "The Warden feels that for the time being, we are not in a position to extend service outside the State of Illinois."[59]

Ragen changed this policy in 1941, Leopold's last year in SCS. Williams relayed word to Farrant that Stateville now welcomed enrollments from Ft. Madison inmates. Under the new policy, students from anywhere in the United States could enroll. That year, prisoners from two Iowa institutions, New York's Attica prison, and the South Dakota Penitentiary at Sioux Falls enrolled in SCS courses. In 1958, at Leopold's final parole hearing, Williams said that by the early 1940s, students from 19 states had enrolled in SCS courses.[60]

Professional educators, particularly from the Chicago area, began to take notice of SCS. In the late 1930s, Dr. William Johnson and Dr. Don Rogers of the Chicago Board of Education administered some of the SCS tests to 500 high school students. According to Leopold, the Chicago students' highest grades were a close match to the lowest grades of SCS students. Johnson arranged to grant SCS students academic credit at any Chicago high school upon their release. The state-level educational bureaucracy also inspected SCS and adopted the same policy. When SCS added junior college-level courses to its curriculum, it changed its name to the Stateville Correspondence School and Junior College.[61]

The SCS's inmate faculty created an honorary Advisory Council of five people who had significantly assisted the school. University of Chicago Professor Ernest Burgess, Indiana University Professor Edwin Sutherland, and Northwestern University Professor Arthur Todd—all sociologists—as well as Father Elegius Weir and Helen Williams received this honor. Thereafter, every annual report, study, and other official document carried the names of this group.[62]

Leopold designed a study that compared the rates of parole violations after release by inmates who had taken courses with SCS against those who had not. He received top-drawer assistance with his research design. University of Iowa professor E. F. Lindquist, who created the Iowa Tests of Basic Skills, still used heavily across the United States, and who would later introduce the American College Testing Program (ACT), was already a world-renowned authority on testing. When Leopold told Williams that he wanted to do a study to test the worth of SCS classes, she contacted Lindquist and asked if he could help. Lindquist consented, providing advice on some of the statistical tests. Leopold released this study in 1940 and published its findings in the SCS 1941 *Annual Report*.[63]

Overall, Leopold found that when compared with nonstudents serving in the same years, only about half the number of SCS students violated parole. He conceded that other variables, such as age and intelligence, accounted for much of the difference. However, with Professor Lindquist's assistance, he controlled for such factors. "When correction is made for all these factors," he said, "students violate parole from a third to a fourth less than do comparable non-students."[64] He explained, "The chances the difference in favor of the students is due to chance are 1 in 25."[65]

This was good enough for Helen Williams. She showed the study off to several interested SUI professors. She told sociologist F. E. Haynes, "He [Leopold] has been trying to prove that the prison school is a good thing and I believe he has proved it scientifically."[66]

Between 1933, when Leopold, Loeb, and Warden Whipp opened SCS, and 1941, when Leopold applied for other work assignments (although he continued to grade some correspondence courses), students in the Joliet, Stateville, and Menard units of the Illinois penal system, plus a handful of other units, completed a total of 2,135 correspondence courses, ranging from a low of 30 in the first year to 436 in 1940. Like other correspondence schools, SCS counted enrollments in individual courses. It did not use a head count. By 1941, SCS offered a selection of 120 courses. That year, its faculty graded and returned an average of 968 lessons per month, with each student averaging 2.3 lessons completed monthly. It did not record enrollments from institutions outside Illinois in its count.[67]

By March of 1941, Leopold had long since decided that he needed to leave the school. Warden Ragen had cancelled all of the privileges that had once made it a plum assignment. It had devolved to a situation of close confinement and hard work. After asking several times for a new job and being ignored, Leopold approached new Warden J. R. Doody in the prison yard and asked him directly for a new assignment, preferably in the x-ray room of the prison hospital. After more than a month, he received notice to report to the hospital for his new assignment. Even though Leopold would never again be involved in the administration of SCS, he would continue to grade courses—including Latin—for its students until the early 1950s.[68]

The SUI's Correspondence Bureau apparently closed its file on SCS at that time. With the exception of a 1947 request to borrow a library book, the last items in the Nathan Leopold Papers at the University of Iowa are from May, 1941. There is no evidence that Helen Williams maintained any involvement with SCS after that date. SCS continued its operations until 1954, when the Illinois State Prison School System merged it into a comprehensive educational program, offering both correspondence study and residential instruction, known as Stateville Schools.[69]

## A CONVICT'S MOTIVE

Why did Leopold and Loeb invest so much time and effort in creating, then administering SCS? Why did Leopold persist in his stewardship? Did the two cons envision the school as an opportunity to provide a needed service to men they considered oppressed and in need, or did they exploit it as a means of making serving time easier, more pleasant, and, with luck, shorter? According to Leopold, Loeb advanced the idea as a way to improve the educational opportunities inside Joliet and Stateville. The educational program, such as it was, was definitely limited and lacking. He continued it out of a sense of duty to Loeb, he claimed.

Leopold presented his version of his motives in his memoir, *Life Plus 99 Years*. His chief reason for writing it was to promote and enhance his chances for parole. Opportunism was definitely a factor. However, his long correspondence with Helen Williams seems to reveal a genuine idealism. He also took obvious pride in the State of Illinois's certification of the school's effectiveness and the post-release success of some of its alumni.[70]

Administering SCS offered some immediate, tangible rewards. Once it was operational, the pay matched that of such desirable assignments as the woodworking shop and the kitchen. That had not been the case in earlier educational programs. This was enough to keep Leopold and Loeb flush in prison currency—tobacco and other commissary goods—until Warden Ragen changed the rules. In time, Warden Whipp assigned the school an office, one with its own washroom. This gave Leopold and Loeb a great degree of privacy, a rare and precious commodity in prison. They had unprecedented access to most parts of the prison. At least once, their privileged status saved them from serious disciplinary trouble. A guard captain discovered Loeb, Leopold, and two other men sharing a bottle of good whiskey. While the four were immediately sent to solitary confinement, in under an hour, both Loeb and Leopold were released to the general population.[71] However, they had not expected such privileges when they began planning the school.

Like any school, anywhere, using any teaching format, SCS experienced cheating problems. Warden Ragen initiated the practice of recording all grades in each student's "jacket" (file), so that the parole board could consider school participation when evaluating parole applications. This attracted men with no real interest in school other than beefing up their jackets. Sometimes convicts would find someone else to do their lessons. This tactic had little impact, however, because each course required two proctored exams. However, after Warden Ragen left in 1941, the school's instructors, who had been residing in a different area than the students, were moved back into common housing, and most of their privileges were withdrawn. According to Leopold, he heard "rumors" that embittered teachers were selling grades. After about a year, and Ragen's return, the teachers were moved away from most of their students and back into a separate cell house. At least according to Leopold, the selling of grades then ceased.[72]

Gene Lovitz, who would later write a biography of poet Carl Sandburg, advanced a cynical view of Leopold's motivation. Lovitz began a sentence for armed robbery at Stateville in 1948. He and Leopold became close friends and regularly talked for hours about all manner of topics. Their friendship ended when Lovitz rejected what he considered Leopold's sexual advances. Even so, he maintained the highest regard for Leopold's intelligence. He passed his reactions along to Carl Sandburg, who then began to take an interest in Leopold's parole applications. However, for all of his regard for Leopold's intellect, Lovitz believed his achievements were overrated and that "he and Loeb had established the prison school for the opportunity of getting together."[73]

While Loeb probably and Leopold certainly had self-serving motives, their school nonetheless benefited the penal system and population of Illinois. There can be no doubt that the two men made SCS a useful, effective, and respected institution. Several university educators—most importantly Helen Williams—gave them strong assistance. As mentioned earlier, formal external evaluations by Illinois and Chicago education authorities, as well as University of Chicago and Northwestern University professors, provided external validation of the school's worth.[74]

## A LASTING FRIENDSHIP

While Williams's involvement with SCS effectively ended in 1941, she maintained her correspondence and friendship with Leopold. For ten years, she travelled to Stateville to attend all of his parole and clemency hearings. In 1958, Williams was among a group of witnesses, including Carl Sandburg, who appeared to testify in what turned out to be Leopold's final parole hearing.

She recounted Leopold's personal academic achievements and his role in creating and maintaining SCS. She concluded, "My acquaintance with him has shown him to be generous, thoughtful, ready to help those who have not had his advantages. In short, following the Judeo-Christian ethics of behavior, even to the point of forgiving his enemies."[75]

Upon his release on March 13, 1958, Leopold moved to Castaner, Puerto Rico, to work as an x-ray technician in a missionary hospital operated by the Church of the Brethren. He earned a master's degree in medical social work at the University of Puerto Rico, coming in first in his class and winning election as class president. He later taught math there—in Spanish. He wrote a book, *A Checklist of the Birds of Puerto Rico and the U.S. Virgin Islands*.[76]

Leopold chafed under the terms of his parole. He frequently broke all of them, he told his attorney. "I have visited most of the better whorehouses, cheap bars, and gambling casinos in greater San Juan and like 'em fine."[77] In 1961, he received parole-board permission to marry Trudi Feldman Garcia, a widow he met at a *Seder* dinner. Upon final release from parole in March, 1963, Leopold could travel as he pleased. Among his other trips, he and Trudi visited Helen Williams in Iowa City. She later visited them in San Juan.

A collection of Leopold's letters to Helen Williams—written after his release—now held in the private collection of an owner of the Web site AmericanLegends.com, reveals that he frequently discussed with her Stateville "alumni," politicians, parole board members, and prison employees he disliked. He expressed a special degree of contempt for Joseph Ragen, even though the Warden had strongly supported his parole application.[78]

Leopold sold an option for the film rights to his story to the actor Don Murray in 1962. Aware that funding for the project was not a sure thing, he nonetheless found the prospect exciting. He told Williams to start thinking about how she would like to be portrayed. Would she want her name used, for example?[79] Perhaps she would prefer to be a lady older than Leopold, "connected with a university." However,

> Even that, I am afraid, would not veil you entirely from the folks who know you. But gosh! If I had ever done for another one-tenth of what you have done for me, I'd be so proud that I'd want the whole world to know it. Please think about it and don't make a snap judgment.[80]

When Murray wrote his "treatment," he reduced Williams to a small, elderly, unnamed woman who attends the parole hearing and "gives a moving message of faith" on Leopold's behalf.[81]

Murray let his option expire due to an inability to raise funds for the project. Leonard Rayner, a producer, bought an option that expired for the same reason in 1967. The partial treatment his writer produced did not include a character based on Williams. Another actor, Tom Bosley, expressed an interest in buying rights to Leopold's story to make a film that would not deal with his crime or trial, but would concentrate on his "good works," including SCS. Not surprisingly, Leopold liked the concept. However, when Bosley learned that an option was currently in effect and that he would have to wait until it expired, he broke off communications. Don Murray made another unsuccessful attempt to secure funding in 1971. In February of that year, just months before his death, Leopold told Williams that the film would not be made that year.[82]

Helen Williams and Nathan Leopold remained friends until his death by heart attack in San Juan on August 30, 1971. Upon Williams' death in Iowa City five years later, Trudi Feldman Leopold said,

> Nathan was not held in high esteem by most of the world. Still, this gallant little lady, despite warnings from many of her friends and acquaintances who warned her against him, chose to ignore those pleas and continued to help him in every way possible until his death.[83]

Williams's assistance to—and friendship with—Nathan Leopold dominated her brief, 26-line obituary. Her long and distinguished career in collegiate distance education received comparatively little attention.[84]

## CONCLUSION

This account of Nathan Leopold, Helen Williams, and the Stateville Correspondence School is neither a straight crime story nor an inspirational story of redemption. The principals acted from motives both ambiguous and unclear. However, this odd partnership between one of the most notorious murderers of the twentieth century and an unknown, low-status educational administrator, working on the margin of her university, resulted in the creation of a school that provided a rigorous and respected secondary education to a population that the State of Illinois had chosen to ignore. Until after World War II, it represented the only opportunity for formal education at the secondary and junior college levels in the Illinois penal system. It taught via a format being used throughout the United States, and the world, to extend access to educational opportunity to places and to populations the established educational institutions had little or no interest in reaching. When the State of Illinois finally created a comprehensive prison education system, it incorporated the SCS correspondence program as one of its four major divisions. The partnership of the notorious murderer and the low-key educator exceeded all reasonable expectations.

## NOTES

1. Nathan Leopold to Secretary, Bureau of Correspondence Study, State University of Iowa, November 20, 1930, Nathan Leopold Papers, University of Iowa Libraries (hereafter cited as Nathan Leopold Papers).
2. Helen Williams to Nathan Leopold, November 22, 1930, Nathan Leopold Papers.
3. Warden's Office Voucher, December 1, 1930, Nathan Leopold Papers.
4. Simon Baatz included an essay on the creative works inspired by, or derived from, the Leopold-Loeb case in, *For the Thrill of It: Leopold, Loeb, and the Murder that Shocked Jazz Age Chicago*, (New York: Harper, 2008), 249–251.

5. Hal Higdon, *Leopold and Loeb: The Crime of the Century* (Urbana: The University of Illinois Press, 1999).
6. Simon Baatz, *For the Thrill of It: Leopold, Loeb, and the Murder that Shocked Chicago* (New York: Harper, 2008).
7. Nathan Leopold, *Life Plus 99 Years* (Garden City, NY: Doubleday & Company, Inc., 1958).
8. Gladys A. Erickson, *Warden Ragen of Joliet* (New York: E. P. Dutton & Company, Inc., 1957).
9. Jack Edward Bass, "The History of the State University of Iowa: The Extension Division" (master's thesis, State University of Iowa, 1943), 29–30.
10. Von Pittman, "Out on the Fringe: Helen Williams and Early Correspondence Study." *American Educational History Journal* 33, no. 1 (2006).
11. Hal Higdon, *Leopold and Loeb: The Crime of the Century* (Urbana, IL: University of Illinois Press, 1990), 304, 327; "Loeb Studies Latin in Jail: Chicago Slayer Enrolled in Columbia Home Study Division," *New York Times*, November 4, 1927.
12. Leopold, *Life*, 188–189.
13. Williams to Leopold, March 16, 1931; Helen Williams to Moses Jung, March 16, 1931, Nathan Leopold Papers.
14. Ibid.
15. Ibid.; Leopold, *Life*, 117.
16. Leopold to Williams, March 2, 1931, Nathan Leopold Papers.
17. Williams to John Taylor, April 23, 1931, Nathan Leopold Papers.
18. John Bartlow Martin, "Nathan Leopold's Thirty Desperate Years: Murder on His Conscience," pt.2, *Saturday Evening Post*, April 9, 1955, 71.
19. Ibid.
20. Williams to John Taylor, April 30, 1931; Helen Williams to Nathan Leopold, May 1, 1931; John Taylor to Williams, Undated; John Taylor to Helen Williams, May 22, 1931, Nathan Leopold Papers.
21. Leopold to Williams, October 26, 1931, Nathan Leopold Papers.
22. Williams to Leopold, October 29, 1931, Nathan Leopold Papers.
23. Leopold, *Life*, 223–224; "Plan for High School Correspondence Courses Under the Direction of Professor Taylor," undated manuscript, Nathan Leopold Papers; *Stateville Correspondence School Annual Report* (1936), 2, copy from Sheldon Glueck Papers, Special Collections Department, Harvard Law School Library, Cambridge. Series XII, Subseries a, Box 55, File 4; *Stateville Correspondence School and Junior College Annual Report* (1941), 8, 13, copy from the collection of American Legends, Inc. (hereafter cited as American Legends collection).
24. "Plan for High School Correspondence Courses Under the Direction of Professor Taylor," undated manuscript, Nathan Leopold Papers.
25. Dorothy Canfield Fisher, *Why Stop Learning?* (New York: Harcourt, Brace, & Co., 1927), 23; Walton S. Bittner and Hervey F. Mallory, *University Teaching by Mail* (New York: The Macmillan Company, 1933), 31.
26. Ray Mars Simpson, "Prison Stagnation Since 1900," *Journal of Criminal Law and Criminology,"* 26, no. 6 (March 1936), 879–882; Benjamin Justice,

"A College of Morals: Educational Reform at San Quentin Prison, 1880–1920," *History of Education Quarterly*, 40, no. 3 (Fall 2000), 280–301.

27. Leopold, *Life*, 226; Leopold to Williams, December 1, 1932, Nathan Leopold Papers.
28. Ibid.
29. Leopold, *Life*, 226; Williams to John Taylor, December 6, 1932, Nathan Leopold Papers.
30. "Loeb, as Head Master, Opens Prison School," *Chicago Daily Tribune*, January 12, 1933; Williams to Edward J. Tarrant, May 2, 1941, Nathan Leopold Papers; Leopold, *Life*, 226; *SCS Annual Report* (1936), 2; *SCSJC Annual Report* (1938), copies from Sheldon Glueck Papers, Special Collections Department, Harvard Law School Library, Cambridge. Series XII, Subseries a, Box 55, file 4.
31. *SCSJC Annual Report* (1941), 8, 13, American Legends collection.
32. Leopold, *Life*, 190; Williams to Leopold, May 27, 1931; Williams to Leopold, December 21, 1932; P.J. Fitzgibbon to Williams, December 14, 1936, Nathan Leopold Papers.
33. *SCS Annual Report* (1936), 1; *SCSJC Annual Report* (1938), 1.
34. *SCS Annual Report* (1936), 1; *SCSJC Annual Report* (1941).
35. *SCSJC Annual Report* (1941), American Legends collection.
36. *SCSJC Annual Report* (1941) 5, American Legends collection.
37. Stateville Correspondence School, *A Handbook for Teachers in the Stateville Schools*, undated, Leopold and Loeb Archive, Series LXXXV (Elmer Gertz Papers), Charles Deering McCormick Library of Special Collections, Northwestern University Library (hereafter cited as Leopold and Loeb Archive).
38. Marcie McGuire to Von Pittman, July 15, 2008, in the author's possession. Marcie McGuire has served as the Head Editor of the Center for Distance and Independent Study at the University of Missouri since 1998. She is responsible for the development and editing of curricular materials for more than 150 collegiate and 200 high school level courses offered via distance education formats. Before taking this position, she wrote and edited curricular materials for the Project Construct National Center at the University of Missouri. From 1987 until 1993, McGuire wrote and tested curricular materials for the University of Missouri's Assessment Resource Center. She has taught college-level composition at the University of Missouri and Stephens College.
39. Leopold to Williams, December 1, 1932, Nathan Leopold Papers.
40. "Loeb, as Head Master, Opens Prison School" *Chicago Tribune*, January 12, 1933.
41. Ibid.
42. Higdon, *Leopold and Loeb*.
43. Ibid., Chicago Tribune, "Loeb."
44. Leopold, *Life*, 225.
45. "Smaller Fry," *Fortune*, 7, no. 6, (June 1933), 66.
46. Leopold, *Life*, 232; *SCS Annual Report*, (1941), 33, American Legends collection.

47. Leopold, *Life*, 189-190.
48. Williams to Leopold, May 22, 1934, Nathan Leopold Papers.
49. Leopold to Williams, May 28, 1934, Nathan Leopold Papers.
50. Leopold, *Life*, 189–190; P. J. Fitzgibbon to Williams, March 18, 1935; Nathan Leopold Papers.
51. Leopold, *Life*, 266. Higdon, *Leopold and Loeb*, 295–300.
52. Higdon, *Leopold and Loeb*, 292.
53. Ibid., 292–294; Baatz, *For the Thrill*, 430–431.
54. Higdon, *Leopold and Loeb*, 300.
55. Higdon, *Leopold and Loeb*, 303; Leopold, *Life*, 272.
56. Leopold, *Life*, 281–282; 293.
57. *SCSJC Annual Report* (1938), 1 American Legends collection.
58. Edward Farrant to Williams, April 8, 1940, Nathan Leopold Papers.
59. J. E. Rees to P. J. Fitzgibbon, May 15, 1940; P. J. Fitzgibbon (Leopold) to Williams, May 20, 1940, Nathan Leopold Papers.
60. Williams to Edward Farrant, May 20, 1941, Nathan Leopold Papers; *SCS Annual Report* (1941), 12, American Legends collection; Elmer Gertz, *A Handful of Clients* (Chicago: Follett Publishing, 1965), 79.
61. Leopold, *Life*, 283.
62. Leopold, *Life*, 283–284.
63. *SCS Annual Report* (1941), American Legends collection; P. J. Fitzgibbon (Leopold) to Williams, April 29, 1940, Nathan Leopold Papers.
64. P. J. Fitzgibbon (Leopold) to Williams, August 29, 1940, Nathan Leopold Papers.
65. *SCS Annual Report* (1941), 4, American Legends collection.
66. Williams to F. E. Haynes, April 30, 1940, Nathan Leopold Papers.
67. *SCS Annual Report* (1941), 5, 14–16, American Legends collection.
68. Leopold, *Life*, 293, 296, 347–348.
69. *Illinois State Prison School System, A Survey of the Stateville Schools* (1957), unpublished report, Leopold and Loeb Archive, box 14, folder 7.
70. Leopold, *Life*, 233–234.
71. Higdon, *Leopold and Loeb*, 290.
72. Leopold, *Life*, 282–283.
73. Higdon, *Leopold and Loeb*, 307–308.
74. Leopold, *Life*, 255, 283.
75. Cited in Gertz, *A Handful of Clients*, 80.
76. Nathan Leopold, *A Checklist of the Birds of Puerto Rico and the U.S. Virgin Islands*, bulletin no. 168, Agricultrual Experimental Station, Rio Piedras, Puerto Rico, 1963.
77. Leopold to Elmer Gertz, May 4, 1947, cited in Higdon, *Leopold and Loeb*, 337.
78. Leopold to Williams, March 16, 1964, American Legends collection; Gertz, *A Handful of Clients*, 146. Leopold praised Ragen's skills and fairness as an administrator in his memoirs. This was no doubt a political position, since he wrote the book as part of his campaign to obtain parole.

79. Leopold to Elmer Gertz, July 26, 1968, Leopold and Loeb Archive, box 1, folder 6; Leopold to Williams, March 2, 1964, American Legends collection.
80. Leopold to Williams, March 2, 1964, American Legends collection.
81. Don Murray, *Beyond the Night: A film Outline from Life Plus 99 Years*, undated film treatment, Leopold and Loeb Archive, box 1, folder 6.
82. Leopold to Elmer Gertz, July 26, 1968; Alfred Allen Lewis, *The Nathan Leopold Story: Outline for a screen treatment*, undated; Tom Bosley to Elmer Gertz, September 14, 1967; Leopold to Elmer Gertz, July 26, 1968, Leopold and Loeb Archive, box 1, folder 6; Leopold to Williams, February 1, 1971, American Legends collection.
83. Trudi Leopold, unpublished manuscript, Helen Williams News File, University of Iowa.
84. Obituary of Helen Williams, *Iowa City Press Citizen*, 8 January 1976.

# PART III

## EDUCATIONAL REFORM

CHAPTER 7

# THE SECOND GREAT AWAKENING AND AMERICAN EDUCATIONAL REFORM

## Insights From the Biography of John Milton Gregory

**John F. Wakefield**

School attendance in America at the beginning of the nineteenth century was undemocratic. Poor and working-class households could not afford the loss of a potential worker. Children would often work at home or be hired out. Children of slaves were not schooled at all. Further, the subjects taught in school were limited. Young boys and girls who attended the common school would learn reading, writing, spelling, and arithmetic. In some towns, nine- or ten-year-old boys could attend a grammar school, where they learned English grammar, Latin, Greek, history, geography, and mathematics. Older girls as well as older boys might attend an academy, where they could learn whatever the teacher was prepared to teach, but early academies generally limited girls to coursework in composition, music and art. A few young, privileged white men could attend college to prepare for a career in the ministry or law.

*Life Stories: Exploring Issues in Educational History Through Biography*
pp. 133–154

This picture would change dramatically by the end of the nineteenth century, when education would become more practical and increasingly, if not yet equally, accessible to all. What caused the change in practicality and access? Scholars have found that following Thomas Jefferson, many supporters of public schools argued that democracy is best assured by an educated populace,[1] but another cause of the public school movement is frequently overlooked. A religious movement known as the Second Great Awakening surged through what is now the Eastern half of the United States in the first half of the nineteenth century. The first Great Awakening 100 years earlier focused on spiritual regeneration. It strengthened evangelical denominations such as Methodists, Baptists, Congregationalists and Presbyterians. The second wave had a social impact, generating popular support for temperance, the abolition of slavery, and other social reforms, including universal education. The relationship of the Second Great Awakening to the gradual realization of universal education in America can be explored through the life of John Milton Gregory (1822–1898).[2]

## I

A disproportionate number of nineteenth century educational reformers came from the Northeast, and Gregory was no exception. His family lived in Sand Lake, New York, about ten miles east of Albany. The area was religiously "cooler" than the famously "burned-over" district to the west, but that did not mean religious beliefs were less common or less firmly held. In 1805, Protestants in Sand Lake erected a Union Meeting House (which stands today) and worshipped there. Among them was Joseph Gregory, the father of John Milton Gregory. Known locally as "Deacon Josie," Joseph was remembered as "a type of the Puritan, industrious, scrupulously honest, almost gloomily religious, his language being full of Biblical phrases."[3] His first wife, Ruth Babcock, died after the birth of their first child in 1811. His second wife, Rachel Bullock, bore nine children. Rachel's seventh child was born on July 6, 1822, and he was named after her favorite poet. Rachel Gregory died when John Milton Gregory was only four, but because he was literate from a very early age, she possibly taught him how to read.

In 1831, Joseph married a widow, Almira Foster, who had ten children of her own, and he set his large, blended family apart with a group of other believers to form the Second Baptist Church of Sand Lake. Although separate from other Protestant believers, they were not "antimission." In 1835, the "2d Sand Lake church and congregation" supported the American Baptist Home Mission Society by giving their minister a life membership.[4] It is doubtful, however, that the church would have supported united, evangelical efforts such as temperance societies, abolition societies, or interdenominational Sunday schools, all of which grew out of the Second Great Awakening.

Joseph Gregory was a subsistence farmer and a tanner who had a small shoe and harness factory. His son John attended a common school briefly when he was ten. The school was taught by 20-year-old Erasmus D. Towner, who was a "licentiate" (a person licensed to preach) under the oversight of the minister of the Sand Lake church.[5] John learned how to read Latin there. After a term, his father put him to work grinding hemlock bark to extract tannin. When he broke his arm on this machine, his 17-year-old brother Lewis told his father that "the only way John would ever be able to make a living was to give him an education and fit him to teach."[6] Persuaded, Joseph sent him to a private school taught by Dr. Joseph H. Elmore, a local physician. John Gregory studied there until he was baptized into the Sand Lake church in April, 1835. After his baptism, his father put him back to work for two years in the tannery.[7]

What led him out of this small sphere was a chance to teach. Lewis lived with his half-sister Sarah and her husband John Reed in Gilboa, about 40 miles southwest of Sand Lake. Lewis taught at a private school there, and he persuaded his father to let John join him to teach Latin as long as he returned home in the summers to work in the tannery. After a year, Lewis married and left teaching to work with John Reed, and at 16, John Gregory became the principal teacher.[8]

His next move would free him altogether from working for his father. In 1839, his brother Lewis wrote to one of his sisters that "John Milton is quite unwell this summer. Pa talks of sending him to school for he can't work."[9] His father did not have the money to pay for more education, but he did release him from summer work. For the next three years, John Gregory stayed with his sister Lois and her husband in Poughkeepsie to attend Dutchess County Academy. To pay his way, Gregory taught part time in Gilboa and part time in La Grange (10 miles east of Poughkeepsie).

Poughkeepsie was healthier for him than working at home, and it opened to him a broader view of religion than the one held by his father. His uncle Uriah was a "freighter" or shipper of goods. Unlike his brother, he was heavily involved in the temperance movement. In a letter written in 1840 and addressed to him as president of the temperance society in Poughkeepsie, the secretary of the Dover Plains chapter urged Uriah to give a lecture and "stir up" the people.[10] Uriah was a Baptist, but one characteristic of religiously "awakened" evangelicals was their willingness to unify in support of social reforms such as temperance. John Gregory increasingly turned to this uncle as his mentor.

With the support of his siblings and his uncle, he set his sights on attending Union College, the first interdenominational college in the United States. Madison College (later Colgate) was the Baptist institution of higher education in New York, but Union was the product of religious cooperation between members of the Dutch Reformed Church and the mainstream evangelical denominations. Located in Schenectady and founded in 1795, "the new Institution was open to every religion, and the name UNION was given to it, to show that all sects and all races beneath its roof were one."[11] Episcopalians were welcome, but Roman Catholics, Jews, and non-believers would have been uncomfortable in its abounding, Protestant culture. The harmony and symmetrical arrangement of the new buildings suggested the design of a religious community open to the world on one side. The students were exclusively male.

An early rule provides insight into the religious ethos of the College, which was interdenominational Protestantism:

> As it is the right of every religious denomination to enjoy their peculiar sentiments and modes of worship, it is ordered that the Officers of College, in their instruction of the students, avoid as much as possible those controverted points which have so long divided the Christian world; but, as the principles of irreligion are destructive of society and pernicious to all regular and salutary discipline in literary institutions, it is also ordered that if any student shall avow or propagate principles subversive of religion or morals he shall be liable to admonition, suspension or expulsion.[12]

This rule led to unity not through compulsion but through avoidance of controversy among Protestant sects. Controversial points—such as predestination, the timing or method of baptism, and church organization—were not to be disputed in class. From an emphasis on commonalities, the officers, faculty, and students were to create a harmonious, religious society whose members were free to develop their talents in order to improve themselves and—after they graduated—the wider society. What was not tolerated was "irreligion."

The path for students to become interdenominational, Protestant learners was defined by its president, Eliphalet Nott. The Reverend Nott, who presided over the college for an astonishing 62 years, did not assert his Presbyterian affiliation within the college walls. He did assert personal control over disciplinary practices by replacing faculty meetings to decide disciplinary matters with a personal interview with the president. The purpose was to instill self-discipline in the offending student by evoking the conscience and eventually, a penitent confession. There were many offenses because Union accepted young men who had been expelled by other colleges. Writing later, Gregory remarked that "hundreds of young men, expelled with ignominy from other institutions, were brought by their sorrowing parents to Dr. Nott as their last resort, and under the magic influence of his discipline, these young men were restored to manhood and to hope."[13] Long before Union College was described as the mother of fraternities or the mother of college presidents it had the whispered reputation of a reform school. The size of Gregory's class grew from 21 to 90 as young men in need of reform rolled in.

John Gregory entered Union College in 1842, when he was 20 years old. He later wrote that he never regretted entering it at such a late age. "I had read a great many books before I went to college, and this was a great advantage to me."[14] The advantage was both financial and psychological. His readings before college gave him enough advanced standing to wait until the third term of the freshman year to attend. Further, independent study or study with a tutor allowed him to be absent for six out of a total of 12 terms and still graduate with his class;[15] during these absences he taught school to earn enough to pay most of the costs of attending college. Paying his own way was difficult, but it allowed him to be psychologically as well as financially independent.

He wrote to his father after he turned 21 both to apprise him of his independence and to explain his increasingly liberal religious view. In a letter from Gilboa, dated March 2, 1844, he addressed his father as "the guardian and guide of my early youth":

> I am now living in the enjoyment of a good degree of the favor of my heavenly Father and I feel to thank Him that He has brought me out of darkness into the enjoyment of the light of His countenance. I begin to feel more earnest desires for the spread of the gospel, and for the happiness temporal and eternal of my fellow men. It was the absence of these desires with other things that induced me to believe that my earlier conversion was not genuine. In regard to my future course my views are also changing somewhat. I still think that I shall teach some after concluding my collegiate course, if a good opportunity offers; but I have almost determined that I will choose some profession, what one I cannot, as yet, certainly tell. I shall probably decide ere I again return home after the next summer term. In the meantime, I pray that God may direct me to choose that sphere of life in which I can do most good.[16]

Gregory had replaced his earlier religious commitment, which involved obedience to his biological father, with a commitment to his "heavenly Father" as a guide for further decisions. He questioned the authenticity of his earlier conversion experience, and he indicated his awakening to socially enlightened religious duties.[17]

Gregory was slowly developing the ideology of a Christian social reformer, as evidenced by his view of the celebration of the semi-centennial of the founding of Union College. A thousand of "the brotherhood" (as the alumni called themselves) gathered at the College on July 22nd, 1845 to praise their *alma mater.* The featured speaker of the day was Eliphalet Nott. Gregory was present for the summer term of his junior year. He remembered "that great throng of educated men, thickly sprinkled with the gray heads of the brightest and greatest names of the nation, bent reverently before the surpassingly venerable form of their great teacher."[18] At the end of his speech, Nott gave them a charge:

> Cause it to be known on earth, and told in heaven, that other Brainerds have arisen to preach the gospel, other Hales to expound the law, other Howards to cheer the prisoner in his dungeon, and other Granville Sharps to raise their voice in behalf of the down trodden slaves; nor falter in your course, nor feel that your work, as redeemed and educated men, is done, until the reign of Messiah is established, pain and sin banished from a renovated earth, and virtue and happiness rendered universal.[19]

Eliphalet Nott charged the alumni with a mission. At the end of his speech, he evoked the names of a missionary, a jurist, a philanthropist, and a social activist, none of whom was living but all of whom were Protestant social reformers. He envisaged the mission of the brotherhood as a continuance of social reform until the beginning of what was called "the millennial reign."

The spiritual impetus of the Second Great Awakening was Christian millennialism—the belief that Jesus Christ would return to reign over society for 1,000 years before the end of the world. This belief was based on a literal interpretation of a passage from the New Testament Book of Revelation that became the lynchpin for a set of beliefs linked to other biblical passages that spoke of end times. Some millenarians calculated the day when the "latter times" would begin, waited for them to arrive, and were profoundly disappointed when they did not. Other visionaries—such as Eliphalet Nott—fervently believed that their duty was to hasten "the day" by improving themselves and society. Believers like Nott were *evangelical millennialists*, Protestants who believed that their reform efforts could bring about the millennial reign.[20] Their ideology predominated during the Second Great Awakening and offered a cause with which Protestant youth could identify, including young men being schooled for the professions.

It is uncertain how many of the alumni had been awakened to evangelical millennialism through the persistent influence of Nott, but Gregory described him as a venerable Christian leader and the Union brotherhood as his reverent followers. Fifty years later, Gregory's accomplishments would be listed in the roll of alumni as State Superintendent of Public Instruction, Michigan; President, Kalamazoo College; Regent, Illinois Industrial University; and Commissioner, U.S. Civil Service.[21] The graduating class in 1846 would become 38 lawyers, 21 clergymen, seven professors, five medical doctors, five bankers, and three officers of large corporations. Among them were eight members of state legislatures, two college presidents, the Chancellor of New York (the highest judicial office in the state), and the Governor of New York. How many of them were evangelical millennialists is impossible to say, but it is certain that Nott as their ideological leader had a significant social impact through them.

## II

The career path that Gregory travelled to become an educational reformer was not straight but winding. As Gregory continued into his junior and senior years, he experimented with subjects that were not part of the traditional course of study. Beginning in 1829, Union offered a parallel "scientific" course that substituted modern languages, advanced math, and applied sciences for Greek, Hebrew, and scientific theory in the classical course. Gregory was enrolled in the classical course, but he took extra subjects in both his junior and senior years. In his junior year, he took "geodesy" (theory of surveying), which was normally required for seniors in the scientific course. In his senior year, he took French and civil engineering as extra subjects. Civil engineering was a new offering in 1845, appearing for the first time in the catalog that year. There is no record of what Gregory took in the third term of his senior year, but his coursework probably included reading law, which was in the scientific—not the classical—curriculum.[22]

His diverse interests are partly explained by his continued reliance on his uncle Uriah. In the early 1840s, Uriah's shipping business in Poughkeepsie went bankrupt, a lingering effect of the depression that followed the financial Panic of 1837. In 1843, he moved to Deposit, New York and re-established a shipping business that rafted lumber down the Delaware River to Philadelphia. Business boomed. Over the next two years, John Gregory spent winter terms (from January to April) teaching school in Deposit, even becoming a member of the First Baptist Church there in November, 1844.[23]

Due to absences more than electives, he anticipated that he would need to attend Union over the winter term of his senior year, but he had no other way to pay the costs except to borrow the money. In a letter sent on Thanksgiving Day, 1845 from Sand Lake, he reminded his uncle, "you wrote me that if life and health were spared you, you would let me have the $50 to take me through the next term."[24] He also asked for a job over the summer. "I am getting a very good knowledge of the theory of leveling and engineering but would require some practice. I wish if possible you would ascertain what can be done about it [a surveying job] before you write again."[25] He was looking for a way to graduate with his class and for a way to pay back the money that he wanted to borrow.

Sometime earlier, Gregory had decided on law as a profession. "John Reed wishes me to come to Gilboa next summer and pursue my law studies there," he continued. "He will board me and wait till I am able to pay him. But I choose rather to go at some business by which I may get the means to pay off my debt, as I shall be able to study better with a free heart. If you think I cannot get business on the R.R., I will try and get a school."[26] By his senior year, law was clearly in his sights, but he was out of money and running out of time. Gregory may have read law at the firm of Paige and Potter in Schenectady during his last term at Union, and he may have continued his law studies for a few months after he graduated, but contrary to the suggestion of his biographers, he did not study law for two years after college. He returned to Deposit to earn enough money to repay his uncle.

After Gregory graduated from Union College in July, 1846, a one-page circular appeared in Deposit to announce that a new academy would open on October 5th with "J. M. Gregory, A. B." as its principal.[27] His unmarried sister Emeline was advertised as its preceptress. Both were "well known as successful teachers." Its curriculum listed a "juvenile class" (corresponding to a common school) and a set of courses for older students that indicated a college preparatory curriculum (including French) with practical subjects (such as surveying) worked in. In addition to Uriah, the trustees included William Wheeler, a well-to-do lumber merchant and deacon in the Presbyterian Church. This modern, interdenominational academy was scheduled to meet for two, 12-week terms separated by a one-week Christmas vacation. A receipt dated March 23, 1847 from Deposit Academy for tuition paid to "JM & E Gregory" shows that the academy met, that Gregory taught there, and that he was paid. The receipt is in his handwriting.[28]

Something happened that year in Deposit to detour the path of his development as a social reformer. In a diary begun in June, 1847, after the school year was over, there is a record of "prolonged and secret prayer" and the terse entry, "Have agreed to go and reside at Hoosick Falls and preach to the people there."[29] Hoosick Falls is about 100 miles northeast of Deposit but only 20 miles from Sand Lake. His move represented the sudden decision to become a minister.

Financially supported by the Baptist Missionary Convention of the State of New York, Gregory left Deposit, preached at Hoosick Falls as a licentiate of the Sand Lake church, and was ordained a Baptist minister on December 23, 1847.[30] On July 6, 1848 (his next birthday), he wrote in the diary, "Within the year I have been solemnly and publicly ordained to the work of the ministry, have had a church organized in my field of labor, have enjoyed a revival, and have baptized 38 souls."[31] According to one account, "the Lord poured out his spirit" on the little group at Hoosick Falls that year,[32] but Gregory's sudden entry into the ministry did not represent a fulfillment of his plan to pursue law.

What happened? We probably do not know the whole story, but his daughter Allene hypothesized that Gregory regressed to fulfill the wish of his long-deceased mother that he enter the ministry. In the Puritan tradition, he began a diary to correct his faults, to record major events in his life, and to leave a record for generations to come. Snippets from his diary in 1847–48 that were published by Allene—who is the last person known to have read it in its entirety—reveal the symptoms of major depression: Difficulty concentrating, feelings of hopelessness, inappropriate feelings of guilt, disinterest in eating, and thoughts of his own death. He may have inherited this predisposition from a "gloomy" father and from a paternal grandfather who committed suicide in "a fit of despondency."[33] He preached persuasively, but he was not happy.

On September 6th, 1848 another surprising event occurred. He married his second cousin, Julia Gregory, at the Sand Lake church. As is true of many women of her time, little is known about her. Born on September 7th, 1830, she was the daughter of Dr. Charles H. and Kezia Gregory, who worshipped at the Sand Lake church for a time. John Gregory had known her since her birth. Several of Julia's letters to her youngest son Grant reveal that she was well-educated. Excerpts from his diary indicate that his mental state improved after their marriage, but his occasional bouts with depression must have been stressful to them both.[34]

John and Julia Gregory would not remain long in Hoosick Falls. His health began to fail, and his diary entries indicate that Julia was also unhappy there. After the birth of their first child, the Gregorys moved west in 1850 to a pastorate in Akron, Ohio, but the move did not improve his health or that of his wife, which began to deteriorate due to an unspecified, chronic illness. Over the next 16 years, Julia would give birth to six more children, but absences from the family for reasons of health would grow longer and longer until Grant would later recall, "I saw little of her."[35] Eventually, she would spend long absences with relatives in New York.

Their unhappiness forced him to confront his identity issue: the choice of a vocation suitable to the ambitions awakened at Union College. In a surprisingly happy diary entry for July 11, 1852, he revealed that he was engaged throughout the day in teaching. The preceding winter, "after much painful hesitation I resigned my post at Akron and the last of March came to Detroit to take charge of a high school or low college instituted for me by my brother Uriah."[36] A younger brother had started up Detroit

Commercial College, and he had invited John Gregory to direct a new literary division of it. The move proved salutary to him and at least temporarily to his wife. According to Grant, "From that time it may be said that the ruling passion of his life was to aid humanity through education."[37] His identity issues were finally resolved. He continued to preach during the rest of his life but only as a guest minister.

One of the earliest signs of the emergence of his identity as a social reformer was a series of articles that he wrote in 1853 for a Baptist newspaper while teaching in Michigan. He significantly titled them "Christian Union." The title had both a public and a private meaning. Publicly, he stated his belief that division among Christians caused "the church itself to be the fatal obstacle to the final triumphs of the Gospel."[38] More specifically, he argued that "the army of the Cross seems at last in movement for its final conquest of the world,"[39] but sectarian infighting prevented further progress toward the millennial reign. He approved the "World's Convention for the Promotion of Christian Union," which was a Protestant group that had met in London in 1846, but he felt that it had not gone far enough to be thoroughly interdenominational.

Privately, he modeled his interdenominational approach to Protestant Christianity after that of Union College (the second meaning of "Christian Union"). Gregory believed that progress toward social perfection could only be achieved by searching for common ground in principle and avoiding divisive issues in practice. This was the rule of interdenominational discipline that he had learned at college. It was evangelical in the sense that it applied to all Protestant denominations, and it was millennial in the sense that it was designed to lead to improvements in society, hastening the millennial reign. With this series of idealistic articles on Christian union, Gregory declared his readiness to engage the world as an evangelical millennialist.

By midcentury, enthusiasm for universal education had grown. Horace Mann, the champion of the common school movement in Massachusetts, surveyed eight well-known New England educators in 1847 about the effect of educating *everyone* for ten months of each year for 12 years. The curriculum would blend moral with intellectual instruction. The educators agreed that such an education would revolutionize society. Mann saw universal education as the means to pursue all other social reforms. "In universal education, every 'follower of God and friend of human kind' will find the only sure means of carrying forward that particular reform to which he was devoted."[40] Mann saw universal education as the fulcrum to leverage all social change. The reader "must borrow the language of the Paradise he would describe" to depict the outcome.[41] One could envision the result as a Golden Age, a paradise on earth—or a millennial reign. Mann was not an evangelical millennialist, but he understood how the political support of millennialists could bring about universal education. His *Eleventh Report* was an invitation to millennialists to join him and rally around the cause of universal education.

Gregory joined the newly formed Michigan State Teachers' Association (MSTA) and rose rapidly in its ranks, becoming the first editor of *The Michigan Journal of Education and Teachers' Magazine* in 1854. That year, Horace Mann gave the invited address at the MSTA annual meeting, and Gregory was elected president. He quit teaching a year later, lived off the journal's advertising revenue, and stumped Michigan to establish local teacher associations.[42]

His mission was both educational and evangelical. The introductory editorial of the journal stated that its purpose was "to promote the correct and thorough and universal education of the sons and daughters of the State of Michigan."[43] In the second year of his journal, Gregory quoted Horace Greeley, editor of *The New York Tribune*: "Universal Education! Grand, inspiring idea. And shall there come a time, when the delver in the mine and the rice-swamp, the orphans of the prodigal and the felon, the very offspring of shame, shall be truly, systematically educated? Glorious consummation! morning twilight of the millennium! Who will not joyfully labor, and court sacrifice, and suffer reproach, if he may hasten, by even so much as a day, its blessed coming?"[44] Greeley, who was a well-known advocate of the common school, left ambiguous whether the "blessed coming" was the advent of the millennium or the advent of universal education. To him, they were the same, as they were to Gregory: "In the universal spread of learning and liberty and love, the beautiful trinity of human hope, the teacher may yet witness the fitting end of his work."[45] Gregory punned on the word *end,* because he believed that the beginning of the millennium was both the goal and cessation of toil by a teacher.

There is some evidence in Gregory's articles that the MSTA was created as a parallel to other evangelical associations (such as the YMCA and the YWCA) bent on social reform. At the end of the introductory article to the January, 1857 issue, he announced that teachers were on the march and in step with other millennialists. "Let nothing then turn us aside from our work. Let no lack of public sympathy, nor poor wages drive us back. Pause not till schools worthy the high dignity and immortal destiny of the human soul shall open their doors to all the children in the land, and till a noble, intelligent, virtuous and christian [*sic*] manhood shall rise and ripen throughout a regenerated World."[46] With language reminiscent of Eliphalet Nott's charge to the Union College alumni, Gregory shared his vision of universal education with the teachers who read his magazine.

In 1857, the Michigan legislature authorized two copies of it for each township, but the Superintendent of Public Instruction cancelled the State subscriptions for 1858, at least in part because of the financial crisis that was the Panic of 1857. This decision, along with the cancellation of teachers' institutes, was unpopular. Perhaps unconsciously, it struck at the heart and the head of millennialism in public education—the teachers' institute to awaken the "spirit" of the teacher in a quasi-religious revival, and the teachers' journal to nourish its growth.[47]

One of the consequences was the Republican nomination and election of John Gregory as the new Superintendent of Public Instruction for the State of Michigan, an office that he held from January 1, 1859 until he declined a third re-nomination in 1864. One of his first acts was to re-establish teachers' institutes, and he spoke at nearly every one. One student during this period described him as "a man of small stature, compactly built, with flashing dark eyes, in his quick and forceful movement indicating the alertness of his mind, the earnestness of his purpose, and a certain intensity of nature that came prominently to view in public address."[48] His farewell as journal editor told of his plans: "We have labored ever with the single aim to promote the great interests of universal education. This aim we shall pursue with unfaltering faith."[49] He pledged that he would "keep the faith" of evangelical millennialism as he rose in office.

Gregory's religious ideology was patterned after the interdenominational leadership of Eliphalet Nott, and it was militantly expressed through his writings as Superintendent of Public Instruction. As the Civil War erupted, he believed that he was in position to put educational reforms into practice. "Our school system has in it an almost undreamed of power for good," he wrote in his superintendent's report for 1861. "What it has done and is now doing are but faint prophecies of the good it will do when worked with more skill, and to the highest pitch of its capacity."[50] During his terms in office, Gregory advocated many reforms including the elimination of the rate bill—which was a local tax on families with school children—and the organization of more "union" or public high schools to create a free alternative to private academies. Although he was unsuccessful in outlawing rate bills, the number of public high schools more than tripled from 1859 to 1864. These and other reform efforts earned him the reputation of a pioneering superintendent.[51]

As he gained confidence, he also became increasingly frank about what he meant by the cause of "universal education." In his last report to the legislature, he asserted that "education must become more religious;" he argued that Bible reading should be conducted in public schools; and he recommended a type of religious instruction that he thought would be "without offense to any but the atheist, or the heathen."[52] He implied that religious instruction in the public schools could be so formulated that no one who believed in the God of the Bible would object to it. Universal education was to include everyone in a form of religious education.

Gregory was limited in his ecumenical reach, however, by his commitment to the interdenominational form of Protestantism that he had experienced at Union College. The further he developed his idea of religious instruction in the public schools to accommodate non-Protestant believers, such as the growing Roman Catholic population in Michigan, the more reticent he became. His commitments to evangelical millennialism limited the breadth of religious practices that he wanted taught in his ideal public school. His ideological fidelity bound him to the faith of Union College.

From many northern, Protestant pulpits, the Civil War was interpreted as the Apocalypse that would precede the millennium. Julia Ward Howe's "Battle Hymn of the Republic" became a popular Union song that would echo in churches and schools for the next century or more. Gregory interpreted the war as an apocalyptic struggle between ignorance (South) and universal education (North). Beginning in 1862, thousands of teachers, many of them sponsored by missionary societies and supported by the federal government, swept south and west to spread "the light" (both school-based learning and evangelical Christianity) to hasten the millennial dawn.[53] John Gregory's younger brothers Uriah and Silas were among them. After mustering out of the army and training as a Baptist minister, Uriah went west, becoming president of a Baptist College in California and with his wife, eventually founding a school for homeless boys. Sponsored by the American Baptist Home Mission Society, Silas moved south and became president of two Baptist colleges for freed men and women.

Gregory would remain in the Midwest and serve as president of two colleges, one private and one public. In 1868, he became president of the National Teachers Association, the predecessor of the NEA. The movement toward "universal education" was well-organized and national, and Gregory became one of its leaders.

## III

Gregory did not join the army during the Civil War because of his responsibilities to his wife and family. He was asked if he wanted a regiment raised for him, but he was "convinced by his family physician and relations that this step would mean the death of his wife, who was an invalid with four small children," so he refused.[54] Rather than pursuing his agenda on the battlefield or in politics, he sought opportunities in higher education.

In November of 1863, Dr. J. A. B. Stone, the president of Kalamazoo College, resigned under pressure from the Board of Trustees. Kalamazoo was the oldest Baptist College in Michigan and had two departments (male and female) and a theological school. All were under financial pressure because of "unfortunate" fiscal management. Along with the resignation of Dr. Stone came the resignation of his wife Lucinda (or Lucy), who was principal of the female department. The situation became worse when Dr. Stone was charged with immorality by members of the First Baptist Church of Kalamazoo. A church court heard the trial; he was judged guilty of two affairs (one with a former student); and because he was unrepentant, he was "denied the hand of fellowship;"[55] in other words, he was expelled from the local church.

Gregory had been a member of the Board of Trustees since 1857. He was familiar with the controversy. When others on the Board asked him to assume the presidency, he did so on condition that the institutional debt was to be paid and that the Board name him as its president. By September, 1864 the funds had been raised, and the Board elected Gregory as the new college president and president of the Board. His inaugural address, "The Right and Duty of Christianity to Educate," was his most comprehensive statement on the role of religion in education.

Gregory argued that public schools were more limited than private schools in their mission. He believed that they were governed by public laws and could produce conformity to them, but without religion, they were imperfect because they could not adequately address issues of character. To that end, some form of Christianity was necessary. "To banish it," he said, "is to banish the only adequate agent for a full and rounded development of human souls."[56] This use of Christianity to complete the education of the individual was part of "universal education." It made no sense to Gregory to educate every child if society did not also develop his or her character "God-ward." He saw Christianity as uniquely suited to that end.

Some members of the Board of Trustees were advocates of a strongly denominational school. If they expected Gregory to please them in that regard, they were disappointed. Gregory maintained his interdenominational views throughout his presidency. His accomplishments, however, were limited. Enrollment doubled in 1865–1866, but the increase is not easily attributed to his efforts. Male enrollment increased as soldiers mustered out of service. Female enrollment increased when Lucy Stone (who became a social reformer in her own right) ended women's classes in her home. The most that can be said is that Gregory placed the college on a firm financial footing and that he opened the doors to receive back most of the students who had left.

During this period, he developed other means to pursue his millennialist mission. He helped resuscitate the Michigan teachers' journal that had ceased publication during the Civil War. At the same time, he helped launch a new "undenominational" journal for Sunday school teachers in the Midwest. He regarded them as twins. He refined "seven laws of teaching" that he had developed from long study, and he began to serial publish them in both *The Michigan Teacher* and *The Sunday School Teacher.* Their nearly simultaneous publication in journals for public school teachers and for Sunday school teachers revealed his view that public education and religious education should increasingly overlap as the millennium approached.

In February of 1867, Thomas Quick (a trustee-elect of a newly authorized university that later became the University of Illinois) contacted Gregory. A Baptist himself, Quick wished to put Gregory up for approval as regent at the first Board meeting. Gregory jumped at the chance to develop a new university for the public. "I replied favorably," Gregory wrote in his diary, "and on the day mentioned was elected Regent of the Illinois Industrial University."[57] He brought to the university his mission of universal education.

Gregory believed that all public universities should share this mission. As Superintendent of Public Instruction in Michigan, he had said, "Our State University, now so magnificent in growth, was not a success from the outset. Years of trial, and almost of entire defeat passed, before rising above the region of party and sectarian strife and personal ambitions, it breathed free in the purer atmosphere of true learning and universal education."[58] The evolution of the University of Michigan into a successful institution did not mean to Gregory that it rose above religion. With his friend from the MSTA, Erastus O. Haven, at the helm, he was confident that religion was not being neglected. Haven would go on to become the first president of Northwestern University and would end his career as a bishop with the Methodist church.

Gregory expressed his hopes for Illinois Industrial University on March 11, 1868 at the opening of the school. The inaugural ceremony was held at University Hall. The first speaker was almost certainly invited by Gregory as a substitute for his ideological mentor, Eliphalet Nott, who had died the previous year. The Reverend Charles D. Nott was a grandson of the deceased president, an alumnus (1854) of Union College, and a Presbyterian minister in Urbana, Illinois from 1866 to 1868. He had also married Sophronia H. Gregory, a relative of the new college president and his wife. Nott opened the ceremonies by reading from a Bible to a crowd that "filled the hall to overflowing."[59] What followed was spoken solemnly and publicly with interludes of religious songs and hymns by a choir. If not a religious meeting, it was close.

The first speaker that day was Dr. Newton Bateman, the Illinois State Superintendent of Public Instruction. He identified fellow Illinoisan Jonathan Baldwin Turner, the fiery advocate of industrial and agrarian education, as the father of land grant institutions. In the 1850s, Turner had sounded his own millennial theme, arguing that industrial education would prepare the way for "the millennium of labor," by which he meant such education would restore dignity and status to labor, reversing the curse of toil for the millennial reign to come.[60]

Bateman reviewed the legislation governing the mission of the land grant university and distinguished it from other institutions, including (by name) Union College. "What then is the grand distinguishing feature, purpose, hope of this University? In my view it is to form a closer alliance between Labor and Learning; between Science and the Manual Arts; between Man and Nature; between the Human Soul and God as seen in and revealed through His works."[61] Bateman charted a direction for Illinois Industrial University in both secular and religious terms. In the end, he thanked God that "monopolies of learning, by privileged classes" were a feature of the past. "Henceforth, the inscription upon the temples of highest learning, as well as the common school, is to be '*Whosoever will, let him come.*'"[62] The allusion was to the moment in an evangelical revival for sinners to come forward and make a religious commitment.

Gregory spoke next, sharing his vision for the University. Most of what he foresaw consisted of mortal obstacles ahead—conflicts and challenges that would threaten the survival of the University during its infancy. Eventually, he saw the university uniting learning with labor, elevating the status of labor, making labor more productive, developing a corps at the "West Point for the working world" to lead change, and promoting the welfare of the nation. Only towards the end of his speech did he address what he saw as "a grander and broader triumph than all these,"[63] which was universal education. "Let us but demonstrate that the highest culture is compatible with the active pursuit of industry, and that the richest learning will pay in a corn field or a carpenter's shop, and we have made not only universal education a possible possession, but a fated necessity of the race."[64] Through universal education, not just industrial education, the new school would accord with God's will for mankind.

During Gregory's presidency, the culture of Illinois Industrial University was essentially Protestant. Like Nott, Gregory did not assert his denominational affiliation, and he chose faculty from different Protestant denominations. Daily chapel and Sunday services were compulsory for students. Although a few non-Protestants undoubtedly attended, they did not make their beliefs widely known.[65] There were also significant departures from the culture of Union College. Military science was compulsory, the faculty made disciplinary decisions, and beginning in 1870, women were regularly admitted. Students labored to help support the school, keeping costs of attendance low enough that students could put themselves through school. These departures from the culture at Union did not diminish Gregory's implementation of "universal education." They enhanced it.

Illinois was not the only public university to begin with a Protestant culture. Many other land grant colleges began similarly.[66] For example, Adonijah Welch (1821–1889), the former principal of the Michigan State Normal School and Gregory's associate in MSTA days, became president of Iowa State Industrial College (later Iowa State University). He served as president from 1869 to 1883. Josiah Pickard (1824–1914), president of the University of Iowa from 1878 to 1887, knew Gregory from being state superintendent of schools in Wisconsin. His views were similar enough to those of Gregory that after Gregory resigned as president of Illinois in 1880, Pickard co-edited with him a newspaper for Midwestern educators titled *The Present Age*. As all of Gregory's projects, it had a millennial theme, but this project would last only three years.

## IV

The evangelical army that had set out to transform the world began to pass into history. A number of factors—such religious pluralism, scientific empiricism, and Darwinism—caused it to lose influence, provoking many millennialists to resign or retire. They were unable to pass their influence on to the next generation, which was at work defining a new worldview.

John Gregory's younger son, Grant, is a case in point. After finishing high school, he sold books for a year; then he entered a literary course of study at the University of Illinois. A note scrawled on the bottom of a letter from his father reads, "I seemed to believe in Darwinism in 1883."[67] Grant's original letter has not been found, but his father's reply criticized Darwin's theory from a religious point of view. He warned Grant to stay away from "shallow unbelief,"[68] but the younger Gregory may have found something useful in Darwinism. Social Darwinism gave journalists such as Mark Twain and William Dean Howells a realistic interpretation of the affluence and rampant greed of the 1880s. After Grant graduated from college in 1887, he became a reporter for the *Kansas City Star*, then a reporter and editor for newspapers in New York City.[69] Realism would have been at home in newspaper offices during what became known as the Gilded Age.

A religious idealist to the end, John Gregory found himself increasingly out of place in public education. After a tour as superintendent of Baptist missionary colleges in the South (later HBCUs), he was appointed by President Chester A. Arthur (a fellow Union graduate) as one of the first U.S. Civil Service commissioners. He helped to create a merit-based system of hiring federal employees to replace the spoils system. From

Washington, he also oversaw the simultaneous publication in 1886 of the final version of his teacher preparation textbook, *The Seven Laws of Teaching*, by the Congregational Sunday-School and Publishing Society, The (Presbyterian) Westminster Press, and The (Adventist) Review and Herald. It was a *tour de force* for an evangelical millennialist, but praise by public educators was cautious. Henry Barnard's prestigious *American Journal of Education* said that it was "a bright day when such a book is issued by a denominational publishing house."[70] The review praised *The Seven Laws of Teaching*, but it also categorized it as religious literature.

Gregory was never able to accommodate the shift in public education to a progressive ideology that was not religious. His fidelity to the principles of evangelical millennialism would not allow it. He died in Washington, D.C. on October 19, 1898 and was buried on the Illinois campus. Julia had preceded him in death (on July 6, 1877) and was buried in Kalamazoo. Gregory was survived by his second wife, Louisa, four daughters, and two sons.

Gregory's biography illustrates how the democratization of education in America—its spread to the least privileged in society—accelerated during the middle decades of the nineteenth century through the movement for universal education. Evangelical millennialists led in this movement, motivated by their desire to usher in a 1,000-year reign of Jesus Christ on earth. Looking back at Gregory's life, we can see that his religious beliefs inspired his efforts to provide what he considered a complete education for everyone. As an evangelical millennialist, Gregory was motivated by the hope that his and others' efforts to reform education would eventually transform a nation, and in a sense, they did, making education generally accessible and laying a foundation for further reforms and educational progress.

## NOTES

1. Lawrence Cremin, *The American Common School* (New York: Teachers College Press, 1951); Rush Welter, *Popular Education and Democratic Thought in America* (New York: Columbia Univ. Press, 1962); and more recently, David F. Labaree, "Public Goods, Private Goods: The American Struggle over Educational Goals," *American Educational Research Journal* 34 (Spring 1997): 39–81. Kaestle suggested a contrasting, religious hypothesis: "The pervasiveness of a semiofficial, nationalistic, nervous ideology that stressed self-discipline for insiders and cultural conversion for outsiders helps to explain the similarity and the success of school reform in different antebellum Northern states." Carl F. Kaestle, *Pillars of the Republic: Common Schools and American Society, 1780–1860* (New York: Farrar, Straus & Giroux, 1983), 95. The research presented here supports Kaestle's hypothesis.

2. Gregory's biographers are Allene Gregory, *John Milton Gregory: A Biography* (Chicago: Covici-McGee, 1923) and Harry A. Kersey, *John Milton Gregory and the University of Illinois* (Urbana: Univ. of Illinois Press, 1968).
3. Grant Gregory to Allene Gregory, 28 August 1917, Allene G. Allen Research File, 1898–1920, University of Illinois Archives, Urbana.
4. *Third Report of the Executive Committee of the American Baptist Home Mission Society* (New York: ABHMS, 1835), 5.
5. Gregory, *John Gregory*, 11. Towner attended Williams College from 1829 to 1831. He was expelled in his first year because he was alleged to have repeatedly set fire to a college out-building, but a year later, another student confessed, and the faculty voted to let Towner back in. He returned but did not graduate, choosing instead to enter the ministry by becoming a licentiate at Sand Lake. http://archives.williams.edu/timeline.php?id=108 (accessed December 9, 2010); John Peck and John Lawton, *An Historical Sketch of the Baptist Missionary Convention of the State of New York* (Utica, NY: Bennett and Bright, 1837), 166.
6. Gregory, *John Gregory*, 11.
7. Ibid, 11–12; Charles A. Richmond, "Dr. Gregory's Early Days," *Alumni Quarterly of the University of Illinois* 8 (July 1914), 148.
8. Gregory, *John Gregory*, 12.
9. Ibid.
10. Joshua H. Rodgers to Uriah Gregory, 13 January 1840, Uriah Gregory Collection, 1840–1843, Box 1, file 11, #211. Broome County Historical Society, Binghamton, New York.
11. Isaiah Townsend, 22 July 1845, In Andrew V. V. Raymond, *Union University: Its History, Influence, Characteristics and Equipment*, Vol. 1 (New York: Lewis, 1907), 8.
12. Raymond, *Union University*, 148.
13. John M. Gregory, "Dr. Nott," *Michigan Teacher* 1 (May 1866), 160.
14. John M. Gregory to Grant Gregory, 8 May 1881, In Grant to Allene Gregory, 28 August 1917, Allen Research File.
15. Merit Rolls, Class Graduating July 1846; Archives and Special Collections, Union College.
16. John M. Gregory to Joseph Gregory, 2 March 1844, in Richmond, "Early Days," 151.
17. Gregory's earlier conversion experience was a vision of Christ calling to him from Sand Lake. Gregory, *John Gregory*, 33–34; Richmond, "Early Days," 148.
18. Gregory, "Dr. Nott," 160.
19. Ibid., 161–162.
20. Ernest L. Tuveson, *Redeemer Nation: The Idea of America's Millennial Role* (Chicago: Univ. of Chicago Press, 1968), 34; Daniel W. Howe, "Pursuing the Millennium," In *What Hath God Wrought?: The Transformation of America, 1815–1848* (New York: Oxford Univ. Press, 2007): 285–327.
21. Union College, *Centennial Catalogue of the Officers and Alumni of Union College* (Troy: Troy Times, 1895), 72.

22. Merit Rolls, Class Graduating July 1846; Archives and Special Collections, Union College; Union College, *Catalogues, Sept. 1845* (Schenectady: Riggs, 1845), 28.
23. Richmond, "Early Days," 150; First Baptist Church, Deposit, Delaware County, New York http://www.dcnyhistory.org/joyce/chdeposit.html (accessed December 10, 2010).
24. John M. Gregory to Uriah Gregory, Thanksgiving Day 1845, Uriah Gregory Collection, Box 1, file 13, #259. Broome County Historical Society, Binghamton, New York.
25. Ibid.
26. Ibid.
27. "Deposit Academy," 14 September 1846, Broadsides sy 1846, no. 68, New York Historical Society, New York.
28. Receipt from Deposit Academy, 23 March 1847, Uriah Gregory Collection, Personal letters, 1847–1860, Box 1, file 3, #30. Broome County Historical Society, Binghamton, New York.
29. Gregory, *John Gregory,* 30.
30. Richmond, "Early Days," 148.
31. Gregory, *John Gregory,* 47–48.
32. Stephen Wright, *History of the Shaftsbury Baptist Association, 1781–1853* (Troy: Johnson, 1853), 275.
33. Gregory, *John Gregory,* 6–7, 27, 30; Grant to Allene Gregory, 28 August 1917, Allen Research File.
34. Charles Gregory ran an Underground Railway station (his woodshed). He separated from the Sand Lake church when it did not support abolition. None of the churches of the Hudson River Baptist Association did; a decision "bitterly denounced" by abolitionists. Grant Gregory, *Ancestors and Descendants of Henry Gregory* (Provincetown, MA: Author, n.d.), 225. Robert A. Baker, *Relations Between Northern and Southern Baptists* (New York: Arno, 1980), 48. Letters by Julia to Grant Gregory are among the Gregory Family Letters, Ross and Dorothy Lake Gregory Moffett Papers, Archives of American Art, Smithsonian Institution.
35. Grant to Allene Gregory, 28 August 1917, Allen Research File.
36. Gregory, *John Gregory,* 58.
37. Grant to Allene Gregory, 28 August 1917, Allen Research File.
38. John M. Gregory, "Christian Union," *Michigan Christian Herald* 12 (April-July 1853). Gregory Scrapbooks, Box 1, University of Illinois Archives.
39. Ibid.
40. Horace Mann, *Eleventh Annual Report of the Board of Education* (Boston: Dutton and Wentworth, 1848), 135.
41. Ibid., 133.
42. W. L. Smith, *Historical Sketches of Education in Michigan* (Lansing: George, 1880), 140; "Michigan State Teachers' Association," *Michigan Journal of Education and Teachers' Magazine* 1 (May 1854), 152.
43. "Introductory Observations," *Michigan Journal of Education and Teachers' Magazine* 1 (January 1854), 2.

44. Horace Greeley, "Universal Education," *Michigan Journal of Education and Teachers' Magazine* 2 (January 1855): 30.
45. "Where is Our Best Mind?" *Michigan Journal of Education and Teachers' Magazine* 2 (October 1855), 313.
46. "Introduction to Volume IV," *Michigan Journal of Education and Teachers' Magazine* 2 (January 1857), 2.
47. Paul H. Mattingly, "Educational Revivals in Ante-Bellum New England," *History of Education Quarterly* 11 (Spring 1971): 39–71.
48. Martin L. D'ooge, "Dr. Gregory as Superintendent of Public Instruction in Michigan," *Alumni Quarterly of the University of Illinois* 8 (July 1914), 153.
49. John M. Gregory, "Retirement Message," *Michigan Journal of Education and Teachers' Magazine* 6 (December 1858), 382.
50. John M. Gregory, *Twenty-Fifth Annual Report of the Superintendent of Public Instruction of the State of Michigan* (Lansing: Kerr, 1861), 10.
51. D'ooge, "Gregory as Superintendent:" 153–59.
52. John M. Gregory, *Twenty-Eighth Annual Report of the Superintendent of Public Instruction of the State of Michigan* (Lansing: Kerr, 1864), 51.
53. James H. Moorehead, *American Apocalypse: Yankee Protestants and the Civil War, 1860–1869* (New Haven: Yale Univ. Press, 1978); John M. Gregory, *Twenty-Seventh Annual Report of the Superintendent of Public Instruction of the State of Michigan* (Lansing: Kerr, 1863), 75.
54. Grant to Allene Gregory, 28 August 1917, Allen Research File.
55. Charles T. Goodsell and Willis F. Dunbar, *Centennial History of Kalamazoo College: 1833–1933* (Kalamazoo: Kalamazoo College, 1933), 72.
56. John M. Gregory, *The Right and Duty of Christianity to Educate* (Kalamazoo: Walden, Ames, 1865), 7.
57. Gregory, *John Gregory*, 135.
58. John M. Gregory, *Twenty-Third Annual Report of the Superintendent of Public Instruction of the State of Michigan* (Lansing: Hosmer & Kerr, 1860), 124.
59. Board of Trustees, "Inauguration of the University," *First Annual Report of the Board of Trustees of the Illinois Industrial University* (Springfield: Baker, 1868), 149.
60. Jonathan B. Turner, "The Millennium of Labor," in *Reports Made to the Nineteenth General Assembly of the State of Illinois* (Springfield: Lamphier & Walker, 1855): 595–605; Brett H. Smith, "Reversing the Curse: Agricultural Millennialism at the Illinois Industrial University," *Church History* 73 (December 2004): 759–91.
61. Board of Trustees, "Inauguration," 169.
62. Ibid., 172–173.
63. Ibid., 181.
64. Ibid., 182.
65. Winton U. Solberg, *The University of Illinois 1867–1894: An Intellectual and Cultural History* (Urbana: Univ. of Illinois Press, 1968).
66. Earle D. Rose, "Religious Influences in the Development of State Colleges and Universities," *Indiana Magazine of History* 46 (December 1950): 341–62.

67. John M. Gregory to Grant Gregory, November 24, 1881, Gregory Letters, Smithsonian.
68. John M. Gregory to Grant Gregory, January 10, 1883, Gregory Letters, Smithsonian.
69. Gregory, *Ancestors and Descendents,* 412.
70. Review of *The Seven Laws of Teaching* by John M. Gregory, *American Journal of Education* 23 (April 1886): 26.

CHAPTER 8

# MORE VALUABLE THAN EVEN RADIUM[1]

## Christine Ladd-Franklin's Perspective on Intellect and the Life of the Mind

**Andrea Walton**

"I hold out to them the good example of the University of Chicago, and I hope to make it 'work' in course of time," confided Christine Ladd-Franklin, noted color theorist and logician, to a sympathetic male colleague in 1914.[2] An unsalaried lecturer and one of the few women then offering graduate instruction at Columbia, Ladd-Franklin was critical of the gender barriers and anti-feminist biases she perceived at the Ivy League university. To Ladd's frustration, Columbia remained far more willing to admit women into its graduate departments than to hire them as faculty. This was the case despite women's achievements not only at the nation's women's colleges but also at male-dominated coeducational universities. Ever the tireless reformer and optimist, Ladd-Franklin hoped that her own example as a highly productive scholar and distinguished lecturer, together with her vigilance and continued prodding, might prick the conscience of Columbia men and help break down the barriers militating against women's advancement on campus. These barriers continued, she

*Life Stories: Exploring Issues in Educational History Through Biography*
pp. 155–175

believed, contrary to both common sense and meritocratic values. To her, the mind was neither male nor female: it was gender-neutral. Intellectual power was not to be wasted; it was to be embraced, cultivated, and enabled. From her vantage point, the intellect was, simply put, "more valuable than even radium."[3]

This essay explores how Christine Ladd-Franklin (1847-1930) conceptualized the capabilities and contributions of educated women and the meaning she attached to the life of the mind. As such, this study builds upon and contributes to a rich feminist literature aiming to integrate women's experience into historical writing on higher education, the disciplines, and the professions. In addition to recovering the research achievements of women scientists like Ladd-Franklin, historians have pointed to gender biases within academic culture, considered whether gender shapes scientific knowledge, and highlighted the strategies women adopted to fight exclusion and marginalization in male-dominated fields and institutions.[4] In making common cause with the existing literature on women academicians and scientists, this biography hopes to emphasize a dimension of scholarly women's story that albeit embedded within accounts of her pioneering achievements is too often overshadowed or muted by discussion of the hurdles she negotiated striving to build a career and achieve by male-modeled norms—and that is, what did intellect and the opportunity to pursue a life devoted to intellectual matters (traditionally held to be a masculine rather than a feminine pursuit) mean to this woman?

In order to consider this question, this essay considers the contours of one particular woman's life in depth. Biography, as Barbara Finkelstein has described eloquently, "is to history what a telescope is to the stars. It reveals the invisible, extracts detail from myriad points of light, uncovers sources of illumination, and helps us disaggregate and reconstruct large heavenly pictures." Indeed, moving well beyond mere chronology, the historical study of a life "offers a unique lens through which one can assess the relative power of political, economic, cultural, social, and generational processes on the life chances of individuals."[5]

In focusing on Christine Ladd-Franklin, this essay seeks to open a window to the social world that Ladd-Franklin and other kindred women were compelled to negotiate in the late nineteenth and early twentieth centuries. We see how Ladd-Franklin's ability to envision and, beyond that, to realize an intellectual life and solidify her identify as an intellectual woman—to embrace her heroine Mary Wollstonecraft's dictum that women's "first duty is to themselves as rational creatures"—took shape against the landscape of major growth and innovation in higher education, especially the pivotal educational advances for women and the rise of research universities in the decades from the 1860s through the Progressive Era.[6] As this essay will explore, Ladd-Franklin's career was profoundly shaped by and capitalized upon these major changes. She was an early female collegian (Vassar Class of 1869), was among the first generation of university-trained psychologists, traveled to Germany for postdoctoral training, and spearheaded efforts of the Associate of Collegiate Alumnae (ACA) and, later, the American Association of University Women (AAUW) to improve research conditions and fellowship opportunities for women. Further, although she lacked a regular academic appointment, she prized her years at two of the nation's top research centers—Johns Hopkins University and Columbia University.

These notable achievements solidified Ladd-Franklin's international reputation during her life time, and in our day have interested feminist historians of science.[7] This essay seeks to broaden our angle of vision of Ladd-Franklin's biography, to discern the pivotal moments in her life—in her girlhood, adolescence, schooling, married life, and career—that contributed to shaping her identity as an intellectual woman and helped steel her commitment to a scholarly life. The aim is to understand better how this accomplished woman—whom philosopher-settlement founder Jane Addams once described (though perhaps not entirely admiringly) as "the most intellectual woman" she had ever met—viewed the life of the mind and the connection between individual intellectual fulfillment and one's contribution to women's advancement.[8]

## FULFILLING AN INTELLECTUAL MOTHER'S EXPECTATIONS

Christine Ladd, also known as Kitty, was born in New York City on December 1, 1847, the first child born to Eliphalet and Augusta Niles Ladd. Her father, a New York City merchant, taught his daughter the value of hard work and perseverance. Her mother, a homemaker with a progressive social outlook (she was a staunch supporter of women's rights), encouraged her three children in daily prayer and avid reading. Both parents hailed from Protestant, patrician New England families that prided themselves on public service, duty, and leadership. In turn, their daughter's intellectual aspirations and the career she forged, one blending a dedication to the ideals of the academy and the rigors of intellectual life, especially to science, and support for women's intellectual and social rights, exemplified this Yankee heritage.[9]

Christine Ladd spent her early years with her family at the Niles family homestead in Windsor, Connecticut, but was sent to live with her paternal grandmother in New Hampshire in 1860, following Augusta's death from pneumonia. Ladd's diary entries from this formative period contain stylized expressions of a daughter's grief, provide insight into her family life, and shed light on Ladd's preoccupation with many of the intellectual questions, aspirations and social concerns (e.g., slavery and women's rights) that were shared widely by her generation of White, middle-class young women—particularly those who became teachers, settlements workers, and charity organizers.

The restlessness of Ladd's teenage years seems to have been tied, at least in part, to an inner struggle centering on her own spirituality and emergent identity as an intellectually ambitious young Christian woman, and by her growing sense of isolation and disillusionment with the foibles she perceived in her own character and in those around her: "I cannot make up my mind to be a Christian, although I long to be one," she wrote in the summer of 1861.[10] Ladd was also troubled by her father's remarriage. In response, Ladd tried to devote her energies to study and self-cultivation, viewing this as a period of youthful independence before assuming the conventional responsibilities of adulthood—or what she in fact described as the "trials and sorrows" of womanhood. Relishing her "educational privileges," she found her intellectual ambitions consonant with the sense of duty upheld by her extended family, but had great difficulty reconciling her ambition and cerebral bent—traits that were culturally acceptable for men—with traditional religious sentiment and the social conventions of "women's sphere."[11]

Even as a teenager, Ladd valued public achievement above all else, and impatiently berated herself for not yet making her mark upon the world. In her prayers for Thanksgiving Day, 1861, the young woman stalwartly resolved to display more "energy," "industry," "tact," and "promptitude."[12] Such traits, she believed, were the key to a "better happiness in a world to come."[13] But despite the outstanding scholastic performance her hard work produced, young Ladd's confidence was fragile and at times wavered. In such moments, she turned to her mother's memory, for Augusta had been her major role model of strength, intellect, and caring. "If only I had someone to love me ..." she agonized in her diary, but I am so "unpleasing, so disagreeable, no wonder I am despised." She continued, "Oh mother come back from the echoless shore."[14]

A turning point in young Ladd's ability to conceptualize her own future as a leader came in early 1863. As she witnessed the violence unleashed by the Civil War, questions about social justice, the nature of equality, and her own life's purpose preoccupied her heart and mind. She took a keen interest as the subject of slavery was debated at prayer meetings and in the press. Writing in her diary on the 12th of May, 1863, she described the "genius and esprit" of abolitionist Harriet Beecher Stowe, and began to contemplate her own life's course, reflecting a growing maturity and heightened social awareness.[15] What was life's purpose? What would be a suitable goal for her ambition? she mused. Her initial choice of vocation was set: she planned to study to become a literature teacher.

To Ladd's thinking, all else paled compared in significance to a consideration of the social issues facing the country and the task of settling on one's path in life. The youthful world of dance parties and flirtatious kissing games that seemingly absorbed her cousins held no attraction for her, and she found herself disaffected from many of her adult relatives.[16] She dreamed of living instead "among educated people," individuals who like herself believed that "there is nothing like intellectual labor to polish one."[17]

Even if the independent-minded Ladd at times ascribed her spiritual wavering or limitations, at least partly, to her gender, she eventually, like many women of her generation who forged public careers, would envision her gender as her strength.[18] Part of her education in this regard came from being exposed to intellectual women. Indeed, she came to understand more clearly the conservatism of her household and the oppression of women in society when she attended a lecture by the woman's rights advocate and abolitionist Anna Dickinson. Arriving at the lecture hall "fully prepared to find fault" with the speaker's views, Ladd was instead impressed by Dickinson's eloquence and by the righteousness of her social cause. Her faith in women and self-confidence restored, Ladd was determined to cast off the conventional thinking of her relatives: "So long have I been under the government of these antiquarians ... now I shake off the shackles and am once more my own master."[19]

Ladd's youthful struggle to excel and shape her own identity—to harmonize spiritual and intellectual life—led her to focus on education and to find encouragement in the advances for women she observed. "I am crying for very joy. I have been reading an account of the Vassar Female College that is to be the glorious emancipation proclamation for woman,"[20] she wrote on March 27, 1862. This "collegiate experiment" in women's liberal arts education, she believed, would build laudably upon the pioneering efforts of earlier seminary founders Catharine Beecher (Hartford Seminary, 1821) and Mary Lyon (Mt. Holyoke, 1836). In Ladd's view, women had been excluded or distanced from the institutions of male-dominated culture, by custom and law, and then ridiculed by men for their shortcomings. The opening of collegiate education to women was, she believed, a vital avenue for improving women's collective lot and a direct challenge to pseudo-scientific and anti-feminist doubts about women's intellectual capabilities.[21] Having excelled in Greek and having graduated at the head of her class at coeducational Wesleyan Academy (in Wilbraham, Massachusetts), Ladd made preparing for the Vassar entrance examination the focus of her energies; to Ladd, attending college would honor her mother's memory and uphold the qualities she most admired in Augusta: her "angel's zeal" for learning, her self-reliance, and her belief in working for the complementary goals of women's advancement and Christian goodness. Standing among Vassar's earliest graduates would satisfy the emotional imperative of embracing her mother's values and, beyond that, would enable her to contribute, on a personal level, to the process she described joyously as the "great reformation" of American "womanhood."[22]

One cannot underestimate the considerable difficulties that Ladd and other young women of her generation encountered in trying to develop their intellectual selves and their identities as scholars. Social pressures and attitudes precluded an academic career for all but the most ingenious and persevering or privileged women. "Surely woman has in her something noble, something higher than bread and butter. If ambition is right in man, is it not also right in woman?" Ladd asked. "Shall she not seek with all her strength to elevate her sex above its present degraded position, seek to attain her proper sphere …?" Her admiration for female leaders like orator Anna Dickinson led Ladd to consider her own possible niche. Her deep attachment to the notion of social progress and individual achievement reflected the pervasive Social Darwinism of her era: "The true sphere for everyone is that for which his capacity fills him, and to no other ought he to aspire. But the ages onward roll and still the world progresses … God cannot let his people continue forever in ignorance and blindness." "I am to do something, no matter how humble, for the benefit of my race," wrote Ladd, in 1863, and then added purposefully, "Let me strive to do something befitting womanhood." [23]

Christine's diary entry described her resolve to secure a Vassar education in cadences evoking what M. Carey Thomas described as the "passionate desire" of women of this generation to pursue higher education.[24] "I must be firm, perhaps I have some money … which will take me to that consummation devoutly to be wished," Ladd wrote. She vowed to "give up any and everything for knowledge.… I feel that I am born for something higher and nobler than to be married off [to] the highest bidder in the market of husbands."[25]

Her enthusiasm notwithstanding, Ladd's path to obtaining her Vassar degree in 1869 was far from smooth. In July of 1866, after weeks of trepidation, she finally gathered the courage to disclose her college aspirations to her relatives only to have her grandmother vehemently oppose her plan, warning that four years of advanced studies would seriously diminish her marriage prospects. Ladd's response, albeit self-deprecatory, proved strategically sound. "[I]t would afford me great pleasure to entangle a husband but there was no one in the place who would have me or whom I would have …" she claimed. Marshaling statistical evidence of a "great excess of males" in New England, she justified her plans not in terms of her intellectual ambition or affinity with the woman's rights crusade but as a practical matter—namely, preparation for the period of economic independence before marriage that many young women faced. Satisfied with her coup, she wrote in her diary, "[I] proved that as I was decidedly not handsome my chances were very small. Therefore since I would not find a husband to support me I must—myself ... so I needed an education. Grandma succumbed."[26]

Fortunately for Ladd, her aunt, Augusta's sister, was more receptive to the idea of a young woman attending college. Thanks largely to her aunt's emotional and financial support, Ladd was able to enroll in Vassar's second entering class. Although the college represented a noteworthy development in women's education in terms of rigor and endowment, Vassar College was by no means a seedbed of radicalism. Its curriculum and campus culture were designed to cultivate the refined, admirable qualities of educated Christian womanhood in students rather than imbue them with independence and inspire them to pursue a career. Moreover, Vassar's small faculty and daily academic affairs were dominated by men.[27]

To her disappointment, Vassar failed to measure up to the vision of a "cloistered" tower of learning that Ladd had relished as an intellectually eager school girl.[28] Perhaps, however, no mid-nineteenth-century American college, even one of the established Eastern men's institutions, could have satisfied Ladd's heightened expectations. After a year, she left Vassar temporarily, to help care for her younger siblings and to earn some money by teaching before resuming her studies. The hiatus also allowed her to consider her post-college plans. Ladd's first love was physics, yet she was pragmatic. She realized that women, regardless of their intellectual gifts and qualifications, were excluded from most universities and had great difficulty obtaining access to scientific equipment and laboratories.[29] She therefore turned to teaching, a socially acceptable and accessible form of employment and financial independence for women. Ladd wrote to her friend Dr. G.H. Sherman of Yale as she weighed the possibility of joining a small circle of her college classmates in opening a secondary school to prepare girls for Vassar, "I hate teaching, but there is nothing else for poor women to do. Meanwhile I can devote my spare time to optics which is at present the object of my dreams."[30] In the years immediately following Vassar, Ladd taught school, with the aim of financing her graduate studies, and likely studied mathematics on a non-degree basis at Harvard with W.E. Byerly and James Mill Pierce. She also began to publish, with articles appearing in *The Analyst* and *The Educational Times*.[31]

## FROM WOMEN'S COLLEGE TO UNIVERSITY: ANOTHER EXPERIMENT IN HIGHER EDUCATION

Much as she had single-mindedly pursued admission to Vassar—touted as the "best" in women's liberal arts education—Ladd aspired to the "best" in university education—Baltimore's Johns Hopkins University (JHU). Opened in 1876, JHU emphasized German-style graduate seminars, laboratory work, and original investigation. Whereas by the 1870s, state universities had generally adopted coeducation (compelled by their public mission), privately endowed JHU was able to guard its all-male admission policy.

Christine Ladd's graduate admission at Johns Hopkins (actually, the acceptance of "C. Ladd," as her application read) was advocated by the English-born and -trained JHU professor of mathematics, J.J. Sylvester, who recognized Ladd's name from her publications in the *Educational Times*.[32] Upon Sylvester's urging, JHU officials invited the young school teacher to begin her studies in 1878; and, later, provided her with a fellowship from 1879 to 1882.

Ladd was not the first woman to make special arrangements for graduate studies at JHU.[33] One of her notable predecessors was M. Carey Thomas (Cornell, A.B. 1877), who would later become president of Bryn Mawr College (1894 to 1922) and a prominent advocate for women's education as a leader in the College Entrance Examination Board and the AAUW.[34] Hailing from one of Baltimore's well-to-do Quaker families, Thomas, like Ladd, had a father who fully supported his daughter's intellectual ambitions.[35] Moreover, Thomas similarly saw her academic pursuits as part of the fight on behalf of all women—and felt both the exhilaration and anxiety of belonging to a pioneering generation of female collegians. As a young girl, she had tearfully sought her mother's reassurance after reading Dr. Edward Clarke's *Sex in Education* (1873), a popular treatise arguing that collegiate studies imperiled female reproductive health.[36]

But Thomas's admission to study Greek at JHU "without class attendance," fell far short of her childhood dreams: she had to sit behind a screen during lectures or to consult privately with professors. Dissatisfied with such dehumanizing arrangements—"a kind of living death"[37]—Thomas left JHU, traveling first to Leipzeig, Germany, where women were permitted to study but were not awarded degrees, and then to Zurich, Switzerland, where she earned her PhD in philology in 1882.

No less aware of the inequalities women faced at JHU than Thomas, Ladd opted to remain, primarily to continue her studies with William Storey and C.S. Peirce. She completed the coursework for a doctorate in mathematics in 1882, writing a well-received dissertation on "The Algebra of Logic," but Johns Hopkins officials withheld her degree.[38] At the time, few American women, even faculty at the prestigious Northeastern women's colleges, held doctorates, and JHU's status-conscious trustees were wary that any hint of formalizing coeducation might diminish the university's stature and competitive standing.[39]

The end of her doctoral studies, though, opened a new chapter in Ladd's JHU career. That August, Ladd married Fabian Franklin, a Hungarian-born mathematician somewhat her junior, who, after receiving his PhD from JHU in 1880 joined the faculty. The marriage between Christine Ladd-Franklin (she used a hyphenated surname) and Fabian Franklin was a marriage of equals, anchored in their shared commitments to intellectual life and career, family, civic reform, and social concerns. In many ways, Christine Ladd-Franklin found her guide for living—whether in personal or professional matters—in Mary Wollstonecraft's *Vindication of the Rights of Woman* (1792). Here was a well-reasoned justification for women's education and a persuasive argument for "men [to be] content with rational fellowship instead of slavish obedience" on women's part.[40]

These early years as a faculty wife at JHU found Ladd-Franklin forging a career that combined childrearing (her daughter Margaret was born in 1883), unsalaried lecturing, reform activity in Baltimore, and contributions to the *Nation* on scientific news and a host of topics relating to women: including, for instance, ethnological perspectives on female subordination, the social contributions of working-girls clubs in America, the exclusion of women from intellectual and public life in Germany, and reviews of recently published biographies of talented and unconventional women—such as author Louisa May Alcott, astronomer Maria Mitchell, and physician Elizabeth Blackwell.[41]

Given her wide range of talents and interests, perhaps no other U.S. academic institution could have offered Ladd-Franklin so stimulating an intellectual environment.[42] This was the era when JHU was home to G. Stanley Hall, Charles S. Peirce, G.S. Morris, and a cluster of talented male graduate students who would later be influential in the field of psychology, among them John Dewey, James McKeen Cattell, Joseph Jastrow, and E.C. Sanford.[43] But even if JHU was an intellectually vibrant campus, academic affairs in the department of psychology were not always calm. Department chair G. Stanley Hall alienated many of his JHU students and colleagues (on both personal and intellectual grounds). Certainly, there is little evidence to suggest, especially if the views of intellectual women Hall later published in *Adolescence*, 1904, are telling, that Hall would have been sympathetic to someone like Ladd-Franklin.[44] But the void left by Hall's resignation in 1888 created a possibility for JHU—and, eventually, for Ladd-Franklin. By 1903, JHU had recovered from the financial straits of the 1890s, and President Ira Remsen, Daniel Coit Gilman's successor, had hired Princeton's James Mark Baldwin to re-organize the Johns Hopkins psychology department. Ladd-Franklin knew Baldwin, having already served for two years as an associate editor (logic and philosophy) for his *Dictionary of Philosophy*. Under Baldwin, the department departed from Hall's German-style model and re-emphasized psychology's links to philosophy. By 1895, Fabian Franklin had resigned his JHU mathematics professorship to pursue a full-time career in journalism, accepting an editorship at the *Baltimore News*, but from 1904 to 1909, Ladd-Franklin lectured in the psychology and logic department. By this time, she had already traveled to Germany (having accompanied her husband during his sabbatical year, 1891–92), where she studied with three world renowned researchers in the study of color vision—G.E. Muller, Hermann von Helmholtz, and Arthur Konig—and had garnered attention for her own theory of color vision at the International Congress of Psychology in London.

## LADD-FRANKLIN ADVOCATES FOR WOMEN'S UNIVERSITY EDUCATION

In addition to her growing preeminence as a scientist, Ladd-Franklin also had emerged during the JHU stage of her career as a stateswoman who had a keen grasp of trends in higher education and of the intellectual and financial resources needed to cultivate female talent. From her New England youth and Vassar days, Ladd-Franklin had regarded education as a touchstone for liberating women and men from unexamined tradition and irrational patterns of thought. Why should there be "patrician" and "plebeian" education that buttresses the disparities between the educated and the uneducated, and a system that perpetuates sexual inequality? she asked. Like many other thinkers of her day, who were weaned on Social Darwinian notions, Ladd-Franklin was convinced that society's advancement would depend on broadening educational opportunities for women. She was encouraged that college attendance for women was becoming more acceptable and more financially attainable. Too many women, she believed, had internalized and, thereupon, perpetuated the very social expectations that oppressed women. "Self-sacrificing" women, Ladd-Franklin argued, must be "artificially guarded against themselves." Living in a college community helped free a young woman from the conservatism of family and home and from the "unavoidable annoyances" of housekeeping; engagement in campus life would elevate her "mental plane."[45]

If, in Ladd-Franklin's view, college was in fact an inherent part of a young woman's road to emotional maturity and intellectual independence, she also realized that the academic enterprise and the pathway to intellectual and social leadership had changed fundamentally during the span of her own career. Twenty-five years earlier, a competent individual might have advanced by "easy stages" from being a college student to a professor, but by the 1890s the growing emphasis on expertise and credentials now required candidates who aspired to leadership in scientific and scholarly professions, charity organizations, or any other public field be educated "far beyond a college course."[46]

What type of education did modern women need? Although she was the product of a woman's college and a loyal member of women's advocacy groups, such as the AAUW, throughout her adult life, Ladd-Franklin rejected gender segregation in intellectual matters. Her Johns Hopkins years gave Ladd-Franklin insight into the ways institutions routinely structure the relationship between the sexes and led her to reject separatism as outdated. Her own success lecturing at JHU strengthened Ladd-Franklin's belief that there was little "abnormal" or "improper" about women teaching men. Coeducation at the university level, she believed, as did her former JHU classmate M. Carey Thomas, was a sensible, efficient use of intellectual resources.[47] Educating men and women together recognized the contributions of both. Moreover, the presence of researchers and graduate students, regardless of sex, uplifted the tenor and rigor of undergraduate life. In short, it was imperative to equalize educational and career opportunities for women. This meant opening admission for women to the nation's premier research universities like Johns Hopkins, whose laboratory and library resources and faculty expertise could not be duplicated.[48]

Ladd-Franklin understood that it was possible to help broaden educational opportunity for women working through the power of philanthropy and voluntary action and the power of the pen.[49] Drawing upon her organizational savvy and energized by her feminist politics, Ladd-Franklin helped organize and served as chair of the Baltimore Association for the Promotion of the University Education for Women in 1897. Members of this advocacy group were disappointed that Baltimore's citizenry in terms of their engagement with the cause of women's education as a matter of civic pride, if not simple justice, lagged behind their counterparts in New York City, Cambridge, Providence—or even the centuries-old university towns of England.[50]

Ladd-Franklin, noted philanthropist Mary Garrett, and the 11 other members of the Baltimore Association petitioned the Johns Hopkins trustees to adopt graduate coeducation ("one of the most salient and unmistakable phenomena of our time"), but the Johns Hopkins Trustees rejected the proposal in polite but summary terms as "inexpedient."[51] The Association therefore set about to publicize women's plight by offering a $500 fellowship for a Maryland woman to pursue advanced studies abroad. (Ladd-Franklin chaired the first selection committee.)[52] Ladd-Franklin similarly led the ACA in establishing fellowships for U.S. women to travel to Europe for first-rate advanced training.[53] As an admiring ACA colleague put it, the fellowships were a means by which to "storm the coveted citadels of learning" and give women entry to those "sacred precincts."[54]

Ladd-Franklin was astute enough to realize that creating more equitable opportunities for women meant changing attitudes and common practices in academic culture. Why should women's opportunities be so restricted? Ladd-Franklin asked in a 1904 article for the ACA, titled "Endowed Professorships for Women." Scholarly editors, she pointed out, concerned themselves only with the caliber of one's intellectual contribution and did not ask whether an author was a man or a woman. What if trustees and presidents were to follow this same "dispassionate" method in evaluating candidates for professorships in coeducational colleges? Ladd-Franklin proposed. While believing that professorships could be decided "without regard to sex or with very little regard" there was also, in Ladd-Franklin's view, a justification for more affirmative steps on behalf of women based on sex: "whenever the woman applicant for a position is distinctly superior … she shall have the position." This was a "modest intermediate stage" toward an endowed professorship for women.[55]

Ladd-Franklin's vision of change hoped to equalize the playing field for women. By the turn of the century, when the numbers of female doctorates had risen nearly eight-fold, she identified the crucial need to provide intellectual women with career alternatives to teaching: "It is the more highly trained who are most deserving of our sympathy. It is for them that we wish to secure—by hothouse methods if necessary—not the position of the overworked teacher in the smaller colleges but rather the minor professorships in the major universities, those which offer leisure at first, and, later, opportunity for advancement."[56]

Ladd-Franklin was convinced that the principle of economy largely explained the teaching profession's openness to women, and therefore argued that money could provide an "entering wedge" for women doctorates seeking employment. "At the present time (in the East) a woman must either be very cheap or very distinguished … we propose to make her the one to enable her to become the other," she wrote in 1905.[57]

## CHANGING WORLDS: FROM JOHNS HOPKINS AND BALTIMORE TO COLUMBIA AND NEW YORK CITY

When Christine Ladd-Franklin, husband Fabian, and young daughter, Margaret, arrived in Manhattan in 1910 (Fabian had accepted an editorship), faculty at Columbia and academics nationwide still hotly debated the nature of women's intellectual achievements and the relationship between sex variability and genius.[58] Columbia's psychology department—which included such notables as department chair James McKeen Cattell, Robert Sessions Woodworth, Edward Thorndike, John Dewey, and James Hyslop—had no women faculty, though numbers of women had earned master's degrees and doctorates since the days back in 1891 when Columbia's trustees deliberated for a month before permitting the gifted Vassar graduate Margaret Floy Washburn to audit Cattell's courses.[59]

Editor of *Science* and *American Men of Science* [sic], Cattell was familiar with Ladd-Franklin's submissions to *Science* and respected her starred status in the first edition of his *American Men of Science*, which recognized 982 men and only 18 women.[60] But Cattell had angered many female academics, Ladd-Franklin included, by discounting social prejudice among university men as an explanation of women's underrepresentation in *American Men of Science* and the professoriate. A feisty, strong-willed man whose ideas reflected a striking and unusual combination of sexist and socialist politics, Cattell, like Ladd-Franklin herself, never backed away from controversy. "It is difficult to avoid the conclusion that there is an innate sexual disqualification," he wrote in 1910.[61] But, as Margaret Rossiter has discussed, Cattell's views on the subject had already begun to shift when Ladd-Franklin joined his department.[62]

For her part, Christine Ladd-Franklin, was, by all accounts, already a controversial figure in psychological circles and a familiar name to readers of the *Nation* when she arrived at Columbia. Her theoretical contributions and extensive publications by their example rebutted the views of female inferiority put forth by some influential scientific men, among them her Columbia colleague Edward Thorndike and former JHU colleague now Clark University president G. Stanley Hall. Moreover, Ladd-Franklin had achieved a confident—and in some eyes, too aggressive and disquieting—self-image as a scientist. She was outspoken when researchers or textbook editors deferentially acknowledged the early works of Helmholtz or Herring (two pillars of German psychology), but failed to cite her more recent and synthetic evolutionary theory (which she touted as a "Hegelian" contribution in an age of increasing compartmentalization). She protected her intellectual property vigorously and in the process gained a reputation as a feisty, "belligerent" proponent of her color theories.[62] Ladd-Franklin was often devastatingly brutal in her criticism of colleagues whose experimentation or scholarship she believed lacked rigor, and she was equally impatient with social views she deemed guided by prejudice rather than rationality.[63] She keenly resented any instance when she was seemingly denied an invitation to attend a scientific meeting or join a committee because of her sex. Such action was an untenable violation of the principles of science and professional ethics.[64]

In October, 1914, Ladd-Franklin approached Robert S. Woodworth, Cattell's successor as department chair, about securing a formal appointment to lecture on her specialties—color vision and logic. In support of Ladd-Franklin's case, Woodworth reminded Columbia's President Nicholas Murray Butler that "her reputation and mastery of her specialty would reflect credit on the University and be of service in the work of the department."[65] Butler, himself a Columbia-trained philosopher, had once heard Ladd-Franklin lecture at Johns Hopkins and was quite impressed, by "the originality and profundity" of her literature on Logic. He supported the idea of a lectureship for Ladd-Franklin but did not commit Columbia's financial resources toward creating a position. He recommended her to an unsalaried position in December of 1914.

The next March, armed with the legitimacy of her Columbia University title, Ladd-Franklin wrote to Cornell's E.B. Titchener, founder and head of the Experimentalists, a small professional group that refused women membership, about the group's upcoming meeting to be held on Columbia's campus. She criticized his policy of barring women, especially at her "very door," as "unconscientious, so immoral—worse than that—so unscientific!" Her criticism rested not only in Titchener's disregard for the precedence that the Philosophical and Psychological Associations admitted women, but also in the belief that the exclusion of women (or, more to the point, *her* exclusion) hindered the quality of the scientific debate: "And you need me! I particularly want to discuss for you at this meeting the present vagaries of Watson, Dunlap, and [her Columbia colleagues] Rand and Ferree—(Watson doubly)."[66]

While Ladd-Franklin generally showed the world beyond Columbia's campus only her pride in her Columbia University affiliation, her close friends knew the barriers she encountered and the frustrations she endured. Her friend Dr. Simon Flexner, a noted medical educator-researcher and supporter of women's education and opportunities in science, encouraged her. He was "delighted" that she had secured the library facilities at Columbia that she needed, which, he added, "should have been placed at your disposal long ago and without delay."[67]

Even after her formal appointment at Columbia, Ladd-Franklin's negotiations with university officers to maintain her minimal professional requirements—an office and a phone—were at times contentious. One such incident occurred late in 1917 when a Columbia official, perhaps Secretary Frank Fackenthal, became annoyed by Ladd-Franklin's complaints and reminded her that one "so unemolumented" as her should make no demands on the university. She rejoined that "Mr. B. [President Nicolas Murray Butler] is a gentleman," to which the official firmly replied, "I am not. I am an officer of the government of the university."[68]

Ladd-Franklin's ire was raised. Having confidently assessed her intellectual value to Columbia, she steeled herself to fight. How many Columbia professors lectured in four departments? How many had been among Cattell's first 500 starred scientists? Had she not been told by a German professor that she was "better fitted" for university life than any of his colleagues [all men]? Her personal notes on the incident reflected her deep sense of propriety and her indignation at what she regarded as Columbia's refusal to extend her due professional courtesy: "What letters, what appeals over his head to the trustees to be allowed to present a modest locker, bookshelf to the university and to lend it my books!" This particular situation was eventually resolved and tensions diffused when a university official assured her that Columbia had been congratulated on having the privilege of hearing her lectures on symbolic logic.[69] Ladd-Franklin was not impressed by insincere flattery but a certain deference and recognition of her preeminence as a scientist were prerequisite to any relationship with her.

Ladd-Franklin was keenly aware that not all Columbia departments and faculty members were unequivocally accepting of a woman colleague. As she wrote to a friend at all-male Princeton University in 1917, "Columbia is far too proud to permit a person of my poor sex to address it on the subject of logic! Men are "simply wonderful" in the discovery of premises!" Fittingly, she underscored the irony of her marginalization at Columbia with a syllogism, "None can be members of the faculty who are not in receipt of a salary. Dr. Ladd-Franklin is not in receipt of a salary...." Continuing, she added, "I have never definitely refused to accept one—it is that I offered, faute de mieux, to lecture for nothing, and I have been, for four years, a member of the psychology faculty."[70]

Perhaps it was the heady nature of university life and an affirming sense of intellectual if not financial reward that sustained Ladd-Franklin's Columbia career, despite the rocky times. Certainly she valued the respect she felt on President Nicholas Murray Butler's part. Her cordial relationship with President Butler was anchored in their shared intellectual standards and common disciplinary interests but also in their mutual interest in reform and civic life. Both valued the ties between university and city life. She occasionally sent him a courteously phrased, but assertive, note directing his attention to her latest lecture series. She was never reluctant to speak directly to Butler when she discerned a problem or felt slighted or wronged, as was the case, for example, when she was denied a library carrel, or when the psychology library was overcrowded, or yet another time when some Columbia College boys teased her as they crossed on the Broadway sidewalk.[71] For her part, Ladd-Franklin conceptualized the university as an arena to be guided by intellect and moral integrity. Ladd-Franklin was therefore incensed that Columbia's School of Journalism hired the behaviorist J.B. Watson, who had been fired from Johns Hopkins in 1919 for having an extra-marital affair with his graduate assistant.[72] Alarmed by what she perceived as Columbia's acquiescence in a professor's impropriety, Ladd-Franklin sent a brief note admonishing President Butler. Was Columbia "to fail to support President Goodenow [of Johns Hopkins] in this effort to keep this world good and decent?" She then added, asserting her own indignation and sense of self-importance as a Columbia affiliate and, hence, representative of the university: "I like to know, in such cases—authoritatively—just what one is to say."[73]

## FULL CIRCLE: A MOTHER'S EXAMPLE, A DAUGHTER'S CONTRIBUTIONS TO CHANGE, AND THE END OF A CAREER

Ladd-Franklin's years at Columbia brought the deep satisfaction of once again being situated at a leading university. From here, reflecting back over the years of her highly productive career, she could "[extract] detail from myriad points of light" (to borrow Finkelstein's phrase) and discern the figures and moments that saliently shaped her career.[75] Her intellectual life had taken root in antebellum New England, had been enriched by the educational experiments at Vassar and JHU, and her hard-won education applied not only in the science lab but also in her leadership in women's voluntary associations, professional groups, and civic life in Baltimore and Manhattan, but in some ways it was the women of her family who had most inspired her. In an April 1918 interview for the *Buffalo Express*, she recalled that "the first specific influence that led me toward serious intellectual pursuits was my mother's character and family circle." As she explained, "My mother was one of four sisters, all of whom were brilliant women. In spite of the fact that they were widely separated by marriage, they would return in the summers to our family home in Windsor, Connecticut, and there led a delightful intellectual life together."[76]

Much as memories of Augusta Ladd's social values had profoundly inspired her daughter, Ladd-Franklin's scientific career, her spirited civic involvement, and her work in women's organizations inspired her daughter Margaret, Bryn Mawr College, '07, to work on behalf of women's intellectual and social equality. Notably, Margaret published *The Case for Suffrage* in 1913 and in the 1920s helped galvanize support among New York City women's groups and Columbia alumni to open Columbia's Law School to women. This goal was finally achieved in 1926. Proud of her daughter's triumph (the type of satisfying work on behalf of womanhood to which young Christine Ladd had herself aspired), Ladd-Franklin's mind turned toward correcting an old injustice. She decided to petition the Johns Hopkins trustees for the doctorate she had rightfully earned in

1882, and, in fact, was adamant that the PhD be awarded for her graduate studies rather than for her professional work during the intervening 44 years. She received the doctorate in 1926, during the same week as JHU commemorated the 50th anniversary of the late Daniel Coit Gilman's inauguration as its first president. While some interpreted the bestowal as a sign of "the great change that [had] come over U.S. education in less than a century," history, including controversy in our own times over women's scientific abilities, shows that gender biases were not so easily erased.[77]

"Labor is Heaven's choicest gift," Christine Ladd had asserted in her girlhood diary.[78] What began in the 1860s as a New England school girl's crusade to win her own family's support for her plans to attend Vassar College became a young woman's venture to secure advanced scientific training, first at Johns Hopkins and later at the German universities of Gottingen and Berlin. What had been an individual goal eventually translated into a lifelong devotion to a public cause. Ladd-Franklin's last years at Columbia were busy and productive, filled with nine-hour work days, punctuated by the occasional cigarette break. Four years after belatedly receiving her PhD, Christine Ladd-Franklin died at the age of 82, after a brief case of pneumonia. "She was the youngest person on the Columbia campus," wrote her Columbia eulogist Cassius J. Keyser, Adrain Professor Emeritus of Mathematics. "It should be noted that her strenuous intellectual life was not incompatible with the possession of great feminine charm," he wrote assuredly. Hers was a "long unbroken scientific activity fashioned by a very rare union in her of analytical and logical power with intuition."[79] Keyser's remembrances while conveying his deep collegial respect nevertheless reflected the cultural tensions between intellect and femininity that confronted Ladd-Franklin throughout her career. A woman who from girlhood prided herself on living by reason, rather than by sentiment, and who committed her considerable energies not only to building her own career but also to advancing women's status in the academy, Ladd-Franklin continually pushed back. Even in death, Ladd-Franklin contributed to advancing commonly held views about scholarly womanhood. As the *New York Times'* tribute succinctly put it, her many accomplishments were something "for anti-feminists to consider."[80]

## NOTES

1. Undated memorandum on the PhD, page 2, Box 49, Christine Ladd-Franklin Papers, Rare Book and Manuscript Collection, Butler Library, Columbia University, New York; hereafter Ladd-Franklin Papers.

2. Christine Ladd-Franklin to Professor Moore, December 8, 1918, Box 18, Ladd-Franklin Papers.
3. See note 1.
4. For example, Margaret Rossiter, *Women Scientists in America: Struggles and Strategies to 1940* (Baltimore: Johns Hopkins University Press, 1982); Penina Glazer and Miriam Slater, *Unequal Colleagues: The Entrance of Women into the Professions, 1890 to 1940* (New Brunswick: Rutgers University Press, 1987); Scarborough and Furumoto, eds., *Untold Lives* (New York: Columbia University Press, 1987); Pnina G. Abir-Am and Dorinda Outram, eds., *Uneasy Careers and Intimate Lives: Women in Science, 1879–1979* (New Brunswick: Rutgers University Press, 1987), Evelyn Fox-Keller, *Feeling for the Organism: The Life and Work of Barbara McClintock* (San Francisco: W.H. Freeman, 1983); and Londa Schiebinger, *Gendered Innovations in Science and Engineering* (Palo Alto: Stanford University Press, 2008).
5. Barbara Finkelstein, "Revealing Human Agency: the Uses of Biography in the Study of Educational History," in Craig Kridel, ed., *Writing Educational Biography: Explorations in Qualitative Research* (New York: Taylor Francis, 1988), 45; 45–60.
6. M. Carey Thomas, "Present Tendencies," *Educational Review* 35 (1908): 64–85; Ladd-Franklin's review of the new edition (1891) of Mary Wollstonecraft's *A Vindication of the Rights of Women*, as cited in Furumoto, "Collegial Exclusion," 110.
7. Furumoto, "Collegial Exclusion," 109–129; Furumoto, "Joining Separate Spheres: Christine Ladd-Franklin, Woman Scientists (1847–1930), *American Psychologist* 47 (February 1992): 175–182; Andrea Walton, Chapter 4, in "Women at Columbia: A Study of Power and Empowerment in the Lives of Six Women," (Columbia University PhD dissertation, 1995), 115–168; *Notable American Women*, s.v. "Ladd-Franklin, Christine."
8. Victoria Bissell Brown, *The Education of Jane Addams* (Philadelphia: University of Pennsylvania Press, 2004), 175.
9. Ladd-Franklin's father's uncle, William Ladd, founded the American Peace Society. Her mother's uncle, John Milton Niles, served as a senator from Connecticut and was later Postmaster General. See various clippings in the Ladd-Franklin papers.
10. Christine Ladd-Franklin diaries, July 27, 1861; November 29, 1861, Vassar College Special Collections, Poughkeepsie, New York; hereafter CLF diaries.
11. CLF diaries, April 15, 1863.
12. CLF diaries, Thanksgiving, 1861.
13. CLF diaries, December 31, 1860.
14. CLF diaries, November 25, 1861 and November 29, 1961.
15. CLF diaries, March 12, 1863.
16. CLF diaries, January 2, 1863; February 25, 1863.
17. CLF diaries, January 8, 1863.
18. CLF diaries, January 22, 1863.
19. CLF diaries, n.d. p. 96; *Notable American Women*, s.v. "Dickinson, Anna."
20. CLF diaries, March 27, 1862.

21. CLF diaries, n.d. p.104. See also Christine Ladd-Franklin, "Vassar College," *Nation* (1890) 50: 483–84.
22. CLF diaries, May 1, 1863.
23. All quotes from CLF diaries, May 15, 1863.
24. Thomas, "Present Tendencies."
25. CLF diaries, March, 1863.
26. CLF diaries, July 23, 1866.
27. Frances A. Wood, *Earliest Years at Vassar: Personal Recollections* (Poughkeepsie: Vassar College Press, 1909), 6.
28. Undated manuscript, p.33, Box 12, Ladd-Franklin Papers.
29. *The Biographical Cyclopedia Of American Women* (1928), s.v. "Ladd-Franklin, Christine."
30. Ladd to Sherman, April 17, 1869, Box 22, Ladd-Franklin Papers.
31. *Women in Psychology: a Bio-Bibliographic Sourcebook* (New York: Greenwood Press, 1990), s.v. "Ladd-Franklin, Christine."
32. Fabian Franklin, *The Life of Daniel Coit Gilman* (New York: Dodd, Mead, 1890), 214.
33. See also Julia B. Morgan, "Women at The Johns Hopkins University: A History," *www.library.jhu.edu/collections/specialcollections/archives/womenshistory/index.html* (accessed December 29, 2008).
34. Andrea Walton, "Cultivating a Place for Selective All-Female Education in A Coeducational World: Women Educators and Professional Voluntary Associations, 1880–1926," in *"A Faithful Mirror"—Reflections on the College Board and Education in America*, edited by Michael Johanek, (New York: The College Board, 2001), 134–193.
35. Laurel Furumoto, "Joining Separate Spheres—Christine Ladd-Franklin, Woman-Scientist (1847–1930)," *American Psychologist* 47 (1992): 175–182.
36. Marjorie Housepian Dobkin, ed., *The Making of a Feminist: The Early Journals and Letters of M. Carey Thomas* (Kent, Ohio: Kent State University Press, 1979) 69.
37. Quoted in Edith Finch, *Carey Thomas of Bryn Mawr* (New York: Harper, 1947), 72;
38. Her alma mater, Vassar, awarded her an honorary degree, LLD, in 1887.
39. Margaret Rossiter, "Doctorates for American Women," *History of Education Quarterly* 22 (1982): 159–183.
40. Christine Ladd-Franklin, *Nation* 52 (February 19, 1891): 163.
41. See, for example, the review of Edward von Hartmann, *The Sexes Compared and Other Essays* by Ladd-Franklin in the *Nation* 61 (August 29, 1893): 154–5. Furumoto argues that Mitchell was a great inspiration to Ladd-Franklin in "Joining Separate Spheres," 177.
42. Like many scholars in the nation's new research universities, Ladd-Franklin's interests embraced several interrelated areas that had yet to delineate their boundaries and professionalize: among them, psychology, philosophy, physics, logic, and mathematics.
43. Philip J. Pauly, "G. Stanley Hall and His Successors: A History of the First Half-Century of Psychology at Johns Hopkins," in *One Hundred Years of Psychological Research in America: G. Stanley Hall and the Johns Hopkins Tradition*,

ed. Stewart H. Hulse and Bert E. Green Jr. (Baltimore: Johns Hopkins University Press, 1986), 21–51. See "The Johns Hopkins University, 1882–1884," in George Dykhuizen, *The Life and Mind of John Dewey* (Carbondale: Southern Illinois University Press, 1973), 28–43, esp. 29–32.

44. Scarborough and Furumoto (1987) note Hall's view, expressed in *Adolescence*, that intellectual women were "functionally castrated," 4.
45. See Ladd-Franklin, "College Life for Women," *Nation* 49 (October 24, 1889): 327; "Coeducation," *Nation* (January 24, 1888): 293; M. Carey Thomas, "Present Tendencies," *Educational Review* 35 (1908): 68; Barbara Cross, ed., *The Educated Woman in America* (New York: Teachers College Press, 1965), 41.
46. Ibid.
47. Thomas, "Present Tendencies."
48. Ibid, 10. See also Christine Ladd-Franklin, Undated manuscript, p. 12, Box 18, CLF & FF Papers.
49. Andrea Walton, *Women and Philanthropy in Education* (Bloomington: Indiana University Press, 2005).
50. Lilian Welsh, *Reminiscences of Thirty years in Baltimore* (Baltimore: Norman Remington, Co, 1925), 16.
51. Quoted in Welsh, 17.
52. Welsh, *Reminiscences*, 23.
53. Rossiter discusses Ladd-Franklin's efforts as part of a broader discussion of activist-minded female scientists in *American Women in Science*, 38–50. See also, Margaret Rossiter, "Doctorates for American Women,"165.
54. Bessie Bradwell Helmer to Phoebe Hearst, 1 May 1894, cited in Rossiter, *American Women Scientists*, 169. Christine Ladd-Franklin, paper presented to the ACA, 24 October 1890, Series 6, No. 20.
55. Kate Holladay [Claghorn] to Ladd-Franklin, October 14, 1898; October 25, 1898, Box 3, Ladd-Franklin Papers. See also Rossiter, *American Women Scientists*, 49–50 for Ladd-Franklin's involvement with the ACA Berliner Fellowships, which helped support women's research.
56. Christine Ladd-Franklin, "Endowed Professorships for Women," *Publications of the Association of Collegiate Alumnae*, Series III, No. 9 (1904) 53–61, p. 55.
57. Manuscript, 1905, Box 18, Ladd-Franklin Papers.
58. Cynthia Russett, *Sexual Science: The Victorian Construction of Womanhood* (Cambridge: Harvard University Press, 1991).
59. See "Margaret Floy Washburn," in vol. 2 of *History of Psychology in Autobiography*, ed. Carl Murchison (Worcester, Ma.: Clark University Press, 1932), 338; Furumoto, "A Little Hard on the Ladies," and Rosalind Rosenberg, *Beyond Separate Spheres: Intellectual Roots of Modern Feminism* (New Haven: Yale University Press), 67.
60. Cattell wrote to Ladd complimenting her: "Everything you write seems to me excellent," August 3, 1896, Cattell to Ladd, Box 10, Ladd-Franklin Papers. Both Christine Ladd-Franklin and Fabian Franklin had been starred in Cattell's original (1910) list of prominent scientists.

61. James McKeen Cattell, "Further Statistical Study of American Men of Science," *Science* 176 (1910): 110.
62. Rossiter, *American Women of Science*, 108–109.
63. Christine Ladd-Franklin, *Colour and Colour Theories*, C.K.O. preface, ed. Robert Woodworth (New York: Harcourt, Brace, and Company, 1929), vii; *Notable American Women*, s.v. "Ladd-Franklin, Christine."
64. Ladd-Franklin to Ferree, May 30, 1921; Ladd-Franklin to Professor Carr, August 16, 1925; Ladd-Franklin to Professor Hunter, January 8, 1928; Ladd-Franklin to Professor Keyners, August 3, 1927; Ladd-Franklin to Muller, April 18, 1928; Ladd-Franklin to M. Pieron, July 25, 1926; Ladd-Franklin to Titchner, August 16, 1925 all in Box 8, Ladd-Franklin Papers. Harry Helson, *Saturday Review of Literature*, 20 July 1929. My interpretation here follows along lines similar to Laurel Furumoto, "A Little Hard on the Ladies," 109–129.
65. Helson, *Saturday Review of Literature*, July 20, 1929.
66. Woodworth to Butler, October 26, 1914, Robert Sessions Woodworth Papers, Central Files Collection, Columbia University, New York City, New York; hereafter cited as Woodworth Central Files.
67. Ladd-Franklin to Titchener, n.d., Box 8, Ladd-Franklin Papers.
68. Flexner to Ladd-Franklin, November 21, 1913, Box 3, Ladd-Franklin Papers.
69. Handwritten notes dated November 12, 1917, Box 14, Ladd-Franklin Papers.
70. Ibid.
71. Christine Ladd-Franklin to Professor Moore, December 8, 1917, Box 8, Ladd-Franklin Papers.
72. Ladd-Franklin to Butler, May 11, 1920, Box 3; undated handwritten note, Box 8; Ladd-Franklin Papers. See also, Nicholas Murray Butler to Dean F.J.E. Woodbridge, February 18, 1924, Butler Central Files.
73. For Ladd-Franklin's sense of "Anglo-Saxon morality"; see Christine Ladd-Franklin, "Dangers of Paris for the American Student," *Nation* 71 (1900): 149.
74. Ladd-Franklin to Butler, n.d., Box 8, Ladd-Franklin Papers.
75. Finkelstein, "Revealing Human Agency," 55.
76. Quoted in vcencyclopedia.vassar.edu/index.php/Christine_Ladd-Franklin, (accessed May 15, 2009).
77. "At Johns Hopkins," *Time Magazine*. March 1, 1926.
78. CLF diaries, n.d., p. 74.
79. Obituary, Box 14, Ladd-Franklin Papers.
80. Obituary, New York Times, March 7, 1930.

CHAPTER 9

# LUCY SPENCE MORICE

## Working Toward a Just Society Via the Education of Citizens and Socialist Feminist Collective Action

**Lynne Trethewey**

Brought up in the free-thinking tradition of the Unitarian Church but turning to Socialism and the Anglican Church after marriage, Lucy Spence Morice (1859–1951) was actively engaged in the educative work of numerous intellectual and social reform groups in Adelaide, South Australia (SA), from 1895 onwards. Other than inclusion in Jones' research publications of the 1980s,[1] however, Morice's name and place in South Australian history is all but forgotten. This article seeks to revivify memories of Morice as an enfranchised, cultured, intellectual woman possessed of a highly developed social conscience and a wide-awake vital interest in the foremost questions of the day, whose life was devoted to the pursuit of social justice in the interests of women and children especially.

The ensuing exposition of Morice's political philosophy and contribution to the advancement of post-suffrage feminist causes in South Australian society pulls together, expands upon, and re-interprets Jones' seminal work on Morice and her associates from a feminist revisionist historical perspective. Informed by the writings of Caine, Lewis, Ryan and

*Life Stories: Exploring Issues in Educational History Through Biography*
pp. 177–196

Lake,[2] this article utilizes biographical methods and network analysis to help explain the genesis of Morice's passion for studying social problems "from all sides," and her socialist-feminist politics. It seeks also to argue that her informal but expansive social ties, plus her links to professional women and social progressives of both sexes, were central to her unpaid labour in organizations/associations which aimed to affect reforms via the education of citizens and collective, non-party political activism.

## "SURROUNDED BY FINE AND ENRICHING INFLUENCES IN HER EARLY LIFE, MRS. MORICE IS NOT A SYMPATHISER MERELY ON THE SURFACE"

Louise (Lucy) Spence Morice, daughter of Jessie (née Cumming) and John Brodie Spence (E.S. & A. Bank manager, State M.P. 1881–87), was born in Adelaide on 1 March 1859. Brought up "in the broadest possible way" in the Unitarian Church rather than the orthodox Presbyterianism of her Scottish forebears, Lucy was educated in private schools. In the summer quarter when the Spences resided at the beach suburb of Glenelg she attended "the most absurd educational establishment where the girls of the first families learnt to read, write and do sums," conducted by "an ancient Scottish lady" whose pedagogical approach involved the use of Dr. Brewer's *Guides to Knowledge*—"questions and answers to be memorized." Whilst otherwise living above the E.S. & A. Bank city branch, she appreciated the "most intelligent teaching of English and French" by the "quite unconventional" Annie Montgomery Martin at her progressive school for girls, mainly from Unitarian and other non-conformist families, in Pulteney Street, Adelaide.[3] Here, it is important to note that Unitarians like the Spences and Miss Martin, to whom Lucy owed to a great extent her love and knowledge of literature, were an intellectual elite in colonial Adelaide. Prominent in discussions of contemporary issues and at the forefront of social reform, subscribers represented every shade of political opinion for the Church's principal appeal to well-educated people of substantial means lay in its emphasis on rationality and, in the tradition of nineteenth-century liberalism, the right to individual conscience and independent conviction. A member of the Suffrage League deputation to the Premier in 1891, Martin was also active in the (short-lived) Woman's League which Morice initiated in July 1895 with a view to educating recently enfranchised South Australian women "socially and politically ... apart from all considerations of class and party, and to interest ourselves specially in questions relating to women and children."[4]

The young Lucy Spence was also surrounded by "fine and enriching" family influences. "To have had Catherine Helen Spence for my aunt," she enthused, "was indeed wonderfully good fortune, and added to that my beloved parents, John and Jessie Spence, both of them intelligent, educated, liberal and over-flowing with kindness."[5] In particular, her distinguished "Auntie Kate"—a teacher, journalist, author, Unitarian Church preacher, philanthropist, political and social reformer, and self-styled "new woman" of the late nineteenth century, was to niece Lucy a dear friend, mentor and inspirational role model. Describing her as "a wonderful personality with such a generosity of mind and such marvelous knowledge stored up," who "made no social nor cultural distinctions" Lucy considered that knowing C. H. Spence was in itself a liberal education. Further recalling her aunt's regular Sunday visits after church, armed with a sheaf of letters from world-wide correspondents to discuss with her favorite brother, Lucy averred: "I was the only one of the clan (second-generation) who cared for any of the things which so vitally interested her and my father. Socialism, Single Tax, Proportional Representation, Communism ... all phases of religious thought and philosophy ... everything for the furtherance of human happiness and well being she studied earnestly, and all schemes for betterment and reform had her attention."[6] Thus, even in her "carefree days" Lucy was "not without a sense that there were more interesting and dignified employments in life than ribbon work and gossip, and for this I was indebted to my kinswoman Catherine Helen Spence [whose] motto was 'Everything human can be improved'."[7]

As Jones summarizes, the bond between Lucy and her Auntie Kate (even stronger after John Spence's death in 1902) was based on strong family ties, their shared Unitarian faith and deep love of reading, many mutual friends, and years of co-operation in working for social justice, especially for women and children, from mid-1895 until C. H. Spence died on 3 April 1910. Morice's own niece, Anne Wainwright, claims that what Morice wrote of "Auntie Kate" is self-revealing, for she too gave freely to anyone needing practical help or understanding and was entirely without class prejudice. Always interested in women's reform efforts, she kept herself well informed on current affairs at home and abroad, had connections to "everyone who was 'doing anything' [in Adelaide]" and therefore likely to engage with her in varied forms of social service—all the while being "as devoted to new ideas as most people are to old" and studying the underlying causes of social ills from wide-ranging viewpoints.[8] Jones' description is of a woman more passionate and impulsive than her aunt, equally dedicated to righting social wrongs but whose energy for some years was directed to her family.

Lucy Spence married London-born and Bedford Grammar School-educated James Percy Morice (SA parliamentary librarian 1886–1918 and parliamentary clerk 1901–1936) at a Unitarian service in her father's home, "Fenton," Glenelg, on 20 March 1886. In 1892 she gave birth to a son and sometime later a daughter who died shortly after being delivered by a mid-wife whose unprofessional, unhygienic ways almost caused Mrs. Morice's death too. Only the intervention of her neighbor and close friend Joanna, wife of the wealthy businessman and philanthropist Robert Barr Smith, saved her life. In the broader context of early twentieth century concern about the high rate of infant mortality, this birthing experience combined with Morice's compassion for all children furnished a personal motive for her later joining the Puericulture Committee of the British Science Guild SA Branch (inaugurated July 1910), which repeatedly lobbied Parliament in the 1910s for implementation of its recommendations on infant nurture, maternal education, early notification of births and the registration of mid-wives; also to found the Adelaide School for Mothers with Dr. Helen Mayo (an Adelaide medical graduate) in 1909, and as the Institute's first president to campaign against high infant mortality rates.[9]

## MORICE'S SOCIALIST-FEMINIST POLITICS

Morice's activism in the 1890s and early twentieth century was premised largely on Fabian ideas and feminist modes of "doing politics." Her feminist politics were clearly influenced by C. H. Spence and their mutual friends in the fin de siècle women's movement in Australia—most notably Annie M. Martin and Rose Birks who both held office in the South Australian Woman's Suffrage League, and the founders of women's non-party political education associations interstate, Rose Scott in New South Wales and Vida Goldstein in Victoria. These leading women subscribed to the following tenets of organized post-suffrage feminism: non-party, non-sectarian ideal; stand together as women irrespective of class or cultural difference; emphasis on educating women socially and politically; spirit of co-operation with men in politics; key role of the state in making collective provision for the less fortunate; equal citizenship and an equal moral standard for men and women a major aim; joint action to educate the public and pressure governments. Summarizing her own strongly held beliefs, Morice declared before a 1920s' meeting of the Adelaide Archdiocesan Mothers' Union: "What is necessary for the common weal is individual conscience and collective action. ... We are citizens with duties to fulfill to the community to which we belong ... the chiefest [being] the education of the ignorant, the protection of the weak; and [since] individually power is very small we must join together with societies for doing that great work that is waiting to be accomplished."[10] Now because "knowledge without action is barren and action without knowledge is often disastrous," she added, we must first educate ourselves by studying social problems in depth, then act—constitutionally, in united fashion and undaunted by criticism, to develop public opinion in favour of whatever reforms may be required.

Her embracing of Fabianism came after the Morices read, "with illuminating effect," all of George Bernard Shaw's works and tracts produced by the Fabian Society in London (established 1884), which were regularly debated in the socio-political and intellectual circles in which they moved. Fabianism, an approach to the study of social questions based on socialist ideas, eschewed grandiose theoretical speculations and concentrated on how to implement detailed practical reforms by constitutional means. Fabians rejected the economic doctrine of laissez-faire and, putting their hopes in the "permeation" of existing institutions and the "inevitability of gradualness," stressed the need for state action to ensure greater equality and the elimination of poverty.[11] The Morices foregathered with the Shaws, the Chestertons, the Sidney Webbs and other prominent Fabians in London in 1903. They became particularly friendly with Mr. Pease, secretary of the Fabian Society, and his "extraordinarily capable" wife whom Lucy greatly admired: "She was one of those clever and charming women who somehow combined djibbahs and domesticity, cooking and intellectual conversation—a Poor Law guardian, a member of the Board of Education, and the best of wives and housekeepers. The Labor Party afterwards invited her to become a candidate for Parliament."[12] On returning to South Australia the Morices helped to found an Adelaide Fabian group together with an Anglican clergyman, for according to Lucy it was becoming a Socialist that led her into the English Church. Here she discovered anew "the simple, beautiful Socialism of the Gospels," declaring that "as a matter of fact Socialism is only this—an effort to put into practical politics the teaching of them."[13]

## "MY DEAR, I HAVE HITCHED MY WAGON TO SO MANY STARS!"

### Engaged All Her Adult Life in the Most Varied Forms of Social Service and Education

The right to vote was extended to South Australian women in January 1895. Freed by domestic help, and with husband James sharing her passion for modern literature and for delving deeply into the reason of existing social conditions, a middle-aged Lucy Morice embarked upon multifarious reform projects.

## 1. MORICE'S FIRST PUBLIC EXPERIMENT IN WOMEN'S SOCIAL AND POLITICAL EDUCATION

Morice's socialist-feminist politics, personal ideals, and preferred modus operandi are nowhere more clearly articulated than in her inaugural address to the Woman's League (WL) that she and C. H. Spence founded together in July 1895. It is therefore worth quoting at length.

> So long as we women of South Australia were unenfranchised there was much talk amongst those in favour of the extended franchise as to the effect we should have. Public life was to be moralised and politics purified, but the Bill has been passed for more than six months and what do we find? The women are either doing nothing to fit themselves for the task .... or else joining on to the existing Leagues and accepting the teachings and opinions of their leaders. Some of us, feeling that this line of action might stultify us, and could not lend to independence of thought, determined to try and rouse ourselves and other women to form a 'Woman's League'.
>
> Realizing that individually only a few of us are capable of teaching, yet the co-operative force of many earnest-minded women must be a force for good, the first object of the Woman's League is educational—To educate ourselves, politically and socially, that we may be capable of intelligently taking part in the politics of our country. To attain this end we must realize our own ignorance, and once having done that, set about diligently learning and unlearning; giving to matters of public importance conscientious and disinterested thought. With our own advancement will come as matter of course the necessity for able representatives, and our endeavours must be given to securing these men, or, if need be, women of ability and good character. The means of education that the League proposes to adopt is, first of all, a series of free elementary lectures to be given by those who have had some experience and opportunity for study on such subjects as 'Our Duties as Citizens'. We hope shortly to start a library for members, and shall be glad of gifts of books on political and social subjects.
>
> The second object, which contains in its essence, to my mind, the most important factor of all, is the assertion that we are to stand together as women, apart from all considerations of class and party.... The latter part of clause 2 comes as a natural sequence—'To interest ourselves specially in questions affecting women and children'. That means a great deal, following as it does upon a recognition of our common womanhood and consequent sisterhood. We hope that the League, formed as it is on a basis of absolute equality, will be able to so act upon public opinion that Early Closing Acts will be unnecessary and sweating work impossible.
>
> The third object—'To try by all means in our power to interest other women in this movement, and to awaken in them a sense of responsibility', is one that every League member should take to heart. If each one of us works for the cause in our own circle, quietly and earnestly, it will spread and spread, and become a real power for good in the land.[14]

By subsequently speaking out in opposition to the Woman's League joining forces with the National Defense League and Young Liberal Party Association, Morice further revealed her ideological stance. The main reason for not allying themselves with such associations, she argued, was to avoid binding WL members to vote according to the dictates of their male Executives—not only because these associations fought against extension of the franchise to women but now, seemingly intent on silencing women's voices or calling upon them to vote in the interests of the propertied and privileged classes, were acting "with unconstitutionality and unconscientiously." To have any effect on the political world, she elaborated, "we should stand clear of existing parties and make a new party to support the right and not the expedient course; a woman's party for all women where those of the classes above stand shoulder to shoulder with their sisters of the masses," each learning from the other so as to break down mutual distrust and suspicion between rich and poor, the educated and the uneducated, "which in itself would help the work along."[15] Few of us recognize the interdependence of humanity, she continued, "that if one class suffers wrong and injustice in the long run the consequences inevitably must be felt by the whole body politic." Besides, it was in their own interests to demand of the state that the people shall be decently housed, educated and employed, the weak protected, the strong curbed; and albeit "state control is stigmatised as Socialism, with our very imperfect human nature we need a system by which at least equality of opportunity can be guaranteed to the sons of men." In conclusion, Morice asked WL members to go into the question at issue for themselves: "do not be content with the shallow learning of people who only repeat parrot-like and who have never given an hour's serious study to any of the social problems confronting us." If any wished to know what socialism is, though, she would recommend the Fabian Society's publication of the same title, it being "the best exposition of our aims and ideals that has been written."[16]

Over the next year the Woman's League held meetings on a catholic range of topics: "The State Ourselves," early closing, better protection for young girls, constitutional reform, free education, the Guttenberg System, amendment of laws in respect of women and children, effective voting, official and parliamentary positions for women, property laws, "Foundations of Government," vivisection, "Individualism and Collectivism," Federation, "Lessons from the recent elections," the laws of bequest and maintenance, plus Morice's own papers on the nationalisation of health and the Fabian Society publication "Sweating, its causes and cure." Additionally, the League Committee voted to preserve any important lectures, speeches, and letters on political and social questions garnered from Adelaide's two daily newspapers, worked co-operatively with the Women's

Christian Temperance Union (WCTU) and the Working Women's Trade Union (WWTU), and publicized its open meetings, held "to discuss serious subjects for our enlightenment," in the Woman's Column of the *Weekly Herald* (Adelaide's labor newspaper).[17] To Morice's great disappointment, though, the Woman's League ended in April 1897—in her view because of the absorption of women into party politics and "Brother Man, who desired above all things to keep the world safe for [male-controlled] democracy and sound finance, and distrusted the entry into political life of mothers and wives and sisters who might be expected to bring along disturbing ideas and suggestions."[18] Irrespective of the reasons for the League's demise, as Jones points out, Morice's experience of her first public venture gave her a basis for future activities—notably in the Women's Non-Party Political Association (WNPPA) which she founded in July 1909 on the advice of Victorian feminist and long-time friend Vida Goldstein.

## 2. SOCIAL STUDY AND WOMEN'S INDUSTRIAL REFORM

In the interim and beyond, Morice engaged in a range of other intellectual pursuits as well as social and industrial reform initiatives, always for the purposes of self- and public education and based on the principle of co-operation. In sequence, there was "The Social Students" over which C.H. Spence presided: "a very small, insignificant body of no practical importance, just enquiring into things".[19] Morice was also a member of the Theosophical Society (like her aunt), held salon afternoons for "interesting persons" of different intellectual persuasions, and in 1911–12 served on the board of the Adelaide Literary Theatre. All the while she kept in touch with even the smallest sidelines of social reform throughout the globe via newspapers, her network of interstate and overseas correspondents, and the modern literature in the fields of social work, education, history and philosophy she avidly read.

Next came the Working Women's Co-operative Clothing Company (WWCCC) whose factory was opened by C. H. Spence in February 1902. Morice was a 'housewife' member, her aunt's successor as Board chairman in 1910, and liquidator in February 1913 when notices of winding up the company were issued. An idealistic enterprise designed to overcome women's economic difficulties, the Company provided exemplary working conditions in its capacious, well-lit, scrupulously clean and electric-powered two-storied factory for the mutual benefit of members. The all-female shareholders in this co-operative venture were a truly representative group, comprising those who designated themselves "lady," many "housewives," a grocer, a baker, a domestic servant, matron of a girls' club, a nurse at the Destitute Asylum, WCTU members, several school teachers, women employed in the clothing trade, the WWTU secretary, Inspector of Factories Agnes Milne, and Morice's close friend Joanna Barr Smith (née Elder, whose brother Thomas and husband Robert were partners in a leading mercantile and pastoral firm). Jones concludes from the foregoing list of shareholders' names and occupations that such widely based co-operation provided powerful evidence of the effects of informal education among women on industrial matters and opened opportunities for further influence.[20]

During this same period, as the WWCCC flourished, Morice and C. H. Spence also supported a new women's trade union, the Women Employees' Mutual Association (WEMA), whose aims were to:

1. Improve the conditions of employment in the various classes of work engaged in by its members
2. Amicably settle by conference or arbitration any dispute which may arise between employers and its members
3. Promote the welfare of its members morally, socially and intellectually
4. Co-operate with other organizations having similar objects and aims
5. Carry out the provisions of the Provident Fund.[21]

Morice joined the United Trades and Labor Council committee which collaborated with another committee from the Working Women's Trade Union to bring Labor organizer Miss Lilian Locke of Victoria to Adelaide. The goal of this endeavour was to get "all sorts" of women workers organized (not just those in the clothing trade already represented by the WWTU, formed in 1889 in response to the problems of sweated labour). Arriving in Adelaide on 16 September 1905, Locke spent the next three weeks publicizing her message of women's industrial unity and friendly co-operation at public meetings in the city and suburbs, in the homes of "lady sympathisers" like Morice, at Democratic Clubs, and at a Trades Hall social gathering over which Labor Premier Thomas Price presided. Exemplifying the links that existed in Adelaide between women from differing backgrounds who worked for common causes, Locke stayed with Morice for one week of her visit and Morice subsequently became an active honorary WEMA member. She "presided" at the piano for the opening song, "Come friends, the world wants mending," at its first meeting in January 1906 and addressed the April 23 meeting on the co-operative movement in Ghent (where, two months prior, a convention of socialist women had resolved to agitate for universal women's suffrage and the election of women socialists to public office).[22]

Shortly thereafter, Morice discontinued active participation in the WEMA due to other time-consuming commitments. Most notable among these commitments were her unpaid work in connection with the fledgling free kindergarten movement in South Australia, the Adelaide School for Mothers' Institute, and the Puericulture Committee of the British Science Guild SA Branch, plus the foundation of a new but this time practical experiment in women's political education and social reform—the Women's Non-Party Political Association (WNPPA). All this in a period when improved paediatric practices and New Education ideas had reached Australia amid concern about the education, health, and welfare of "the child as a future citizen" and post-suffrage feminists articulated the idea of Australia as an ethical, maternalist welfare state. Members of feminist organizations such as the WNPPA in Adelaide thus worked together to enhance women's independence but also addressed the realities of interdependence, calling for collective provision and state regulation as well as the appointment of women to a range of protective positions in state bureaucracies.[23]

## 3. WOMEN AND CHILD HEALTH, EDUCATION, AND WELFARE INITIATIVES

A recent article by Trethewey[24] details Morice's contribution to the cause of Kindergarten in South Australia, which, in a life dedicated to varied forms of philanthropic social service, became her dearest work. Kindergarten she regarded as "not a charity but a far-reaching educational reform ... a regenerating factor which brings love and order and beauty into the lives and homes of the people ... a spiritual force helping to build securely the future of the Commonwealth."[25] Morice played a key role within the Kindergarten Union of South Australia (KUSA) that she co-founded in September 1905 earning the appellation "mother of the kindergartens" in Adelaide. As long-serving honorary secretary of the Union and its education committee she gave KUSA's record a continuity it could not otherwise have had. As an unpaid lecturer at the Kindergarten Teachers' College she made her history of education course "a good line of hooks on which to hang her many ideas and ideals of education."[26] She was also a prime force in the first decade of the Kindergarten Graduates' Club whose program provided in-service education for kindergartners, was an important additional means of funding KUSA's activities, and strengthened bonds of friendship as well as the social service ideals that underpinned the Union's work. Lastly, as with her other reform initiatives, Morice exploited her social connections to the full in advancing the cause of Kindergarten financially, policy-wise, and practically.

Then, as a result of networking with visiting delegates at the May 1909 Interstate Congress of Workers among Dependent Children in Adelaide, and stimulated by an address on the St. Pancras School for Mothers that Englishman Mr. McDougall delivered before a small gathering of women whilst visiting his sister, Rose Birks, Morice co-founded the Adelaide School for Mothers Institute with Dr. Helen Mayo. Morice chaired the inaugural School for Mothers Committee meeting, held on 22 September 1909, at which the aim of the association was defined: "to promote the education of the Mother in all that concerns the physical, mental and moral development of herself and her offspring ... avoiding charity in any material sense" such that "when the workers of the Association meet with cases of need they shall communicate with the charitable agencies already existing."[27] The actual work and implementation of policy lay mainly with Dr. Mayo and Miss Harriet Stirling, a member of the State Children's Council along with C. H. Spence. Paid secretarial assistance was provided by social welfare activist Annie Hornabrook, daughter of Archdeacon Hornabrook whom Morice knew well through her affiliation with the Church of England. Hornabrook's brief was to attend the weekly (from 1910 fortnightly) mothers' meetings where work "of a practical and educational character" was undertaken; also all committee meetings, and to do some home visiting. Notably, all three women were foundation members of the WNPPA which Morice was similarly inspired to form by a delegate at the aforementioned child welfare conference—Vida Goldstein, representing the Women's Political Association of Victoria, who stayed with the Morices during her visit from Melbourne.

Mayo was also involved with Morice in the work of the Kindergarten Union. Illustrating the strong personal links that underpinned the complementary activities of KUSA and the Adelaide School for Mothers, she acted as both a medical officer to the kindergarten children and unpaid lecturer in hygiene at KTC until November 1910. In her role of KU Organising Secretary Morice arranged for the Mothers' School to begin as an amplification of existing KU Mothers' Clubs, meeting on Thursday afternoons at the Franklin Street Free Kindergarten where advice was given on feeding, bathing, dressing, and sewing babies' clothes in addition to the routine weighing of infants to help determine their general progress. When president of the School for Mothers Institute from September 1909 until March 1911, Morice in typical fashion also drew upon her excellent organizing skills and extensive social contacts to engage speakers for the program of lectures/demonstrations, arrange a public meeting to publicize the School's work, hold a fund-raising performance of "Prunella," and hold tea-parties for kindergarten mothers to explain plans for the next year. Meanwhile, she also encouraged Central Methodist Mission crêche workers to collaborate with the Mothers' School and she actively supported Mayo's campaign to reduce the high rate of infant and maternal deaths in South Australia. Mayo and Stirling's health care initiative thus successfully launched under Morice's presidential wing, the Adelaide School's work quickly expanded in the Institute's own premises and later at suburban and country branches.[28] Re-named the Mothers' and Babies' Health Association in 1926, the School for Mothers was credited with having been responsible for a steady fall in the State's infant mortality rate to a low 2.3% of births in 1937.

After resigning from the School for Mothers' Institute Committee, Morice pursued the work of women and child health reform through the puericulture sub-committee of the Science Guild. The Guild's modus operandi was consistent with Morice's preferred way of "doing politics." Thus, the Puericulture Committee's professional and lay members of both sexes enquired into the conditions of children's birth, rearing, and health before tabling reports in February 1914 and as issued in pamphlet form in 1916. Their recommendations were then set before the Guild "for consideration, discussion and finality, also to a practical issue." The Guild subsequently proceeded, "by joint action, to convince the people at large, the Government and political parties, by means of publications, meetings, lectures, conferences and deputations," of the necessity of applying scientific principles to all branches of human endeavour as affected the national welfare.[29] Constituted "as a distinct educational movement," the Guild in Adelaide attracted interest in its puericulture work through republication in *The Mail* from week to week "those of its reports which bear upon the physical, intellectual and moral improvement of childhood, and its development into a healthy and useful manhood and womanhood." Sometimes, though, its public advice on the management of children's health and well-being was greeted with derision. For instance, "Anti-Meddling" protested against the sanctity of the home being invaded by "the machinations of eugenicists, hygienists and all other varieties of faddists," and in the belief that mothers instinctively knew best noted that "the well-meaning busybodies who profess to be so concerned about the care of babies" were mostly child-less themselves. A Guild spokesperson tersely replied that "the control of [scientific] knowledge" was infinitely better than "the laissez-faire of ignorance."[30] On a second front, Guild deputations to the Peake and Vaughan governments in April 1914 and October 1915, both led by University of Adelaide Professor of Physics Kerr Grant and including Helen Mayo, were sympathetically heard but the various puericulture reforms they urged were not translated into legislation until much later. The Notification of Births Act (No. 1775), for example, required concerted action on the part of the National Council of

Women (representing about 40 women's organizations), at the behest of the School for Mothers, before it was finally passed in 1926.

## 4. AN EFFECTIVE EDUCATIONAL FORCE: THE WOMEN'S NON-PARTY POLITICAL ASSOCIATION

The lessons Morice had learned about the power of women's networks to effect change, and the importance of personal contacts between organizations constituted for common purposes, were put to best use in the WNPPA that she founded in July 1909. Morice personally moved in varied circles. She had connections with women unionists, professional women, and via her aunt with feminist activists everywhere. At the same time, she also attended Government House functions and was best friends with wealthy philanthropist Joanna Barr Smith. In her work for the Science Guild and KUSA she was directly involved with high-ranking politicians, medical men, and leading educationists and academics. Prominent clergy and their wives were among the steady stream of visitors that the Morices received at home. By virtue of her husband's parliamentary work and membership of the exclusive, male-only Adelaide Club she was ideally placed to gain intimate knowledge of South Australian political affairs and take advantage of his social connections with "men of influence." C. H. Spence's journalism contacts likewise proved beneficial to Morice's reformist endeavours.

Jones argues that the likes of Morice and her associates, already in the vanguard of the post-suffrage women's movement, exerted an even more powerful influence in the relatively small, close-knit Adelaide community once they were conjoined in the WNPPA (more commonly known as the Women's Non-Party (WNPA) and later re-named the League of Women Voters). Morice succeeded her aunt as president of this feminist organization which took practical and successful steps to educate citizens and thereby stimulate legislative and administrative reform in numerous areas affecting women and children. Working at grass-roots level in separate committees, this articulate, well-educated group with delegates from all other women's associations in Adelaide generated pressure on politicians for social change by means of deputations, petitions, letters and newspaper publicity, by joining forces with other social reform bodies, and by networking with feminists in other States.[31]

Growing into a more than 300-strong association by 1929, the WNPA's foundation membership included private and state school teachers and headmistresses, social welfare workers, artists, wives of clergy, WCTU members, medical graduates Dr. Violet Plummer and Helen Mayo, plus other women who had worked for feminist causes with Morice previously.

Morice organized this disparate group of like-minded women into a tight-knit, active body with specific aims: "to educate citizens to appreciate the value of non-party political and industrial action, and to protect the interests of women and children and the home under Municipal, State and National Government".[32] These objects were amplified in the platform which formed part of the constitution and in 1912 included: equal federal marriage and divorce laws, equal parental rights over children, equal pay for equal work, pure food and milk supply, education reform, protection of boys and girls to the age of 21 against the vicious and depraved, appointment of a special children's magistracy and of women to public office, stringent legislation to protect the child wage earner, reform of the liquor trade, international women's suffrage, international peace and arbitration, and proportional representation.

Members frequently discussed formal education topics at WNPA meetings, Association speakers addressed other women's societies, and the Executive sought widely for outside experts to inform the membership and the general community about subjects that were the focus of their reformist endeavours. Morice herself spoke on new education ideas and "experiments in education," the Science Guild's efforts to effect puericulture reform, Olive Schreiner's book *Women and Labour*, implications of the militant suffrage movement in England for South Australian women, and women, war and social reconstruction thereafter. Additionally, the widely read Morice was a logical choice to convene the Library Committee, responsible for circulating and recommending works on current topics dealing with women. Study and Debating Circles likewise concentrated on WNPA members' self-education, the Press and Paper Committee on educating the public by passing records of Association meetings to journalists, meanwhile sharing news of women's activities, accomplishments and their legal position and rights at home, interstate and overseas via the association's in-house monthly newsletter. (From 1922 they produced their own newspaper, *The Non-Party News*.)[33] Correspondence was also maintained with women's non-party organizations in other States: Vida Goldstein wrote from Victoria, Bessie Rischbieth from Western Australia, and Rose Scott from New South Wales. In turn, WNPA news was sent to Goldstein's journal, the *Woman Voter*, and Rischbieth's publication, *The Dawn*.

At Morice's invitation Goldstein addressed the 15 October 1913 WNPA meeting and gave a public lecture in the Co-operative Hall on October 31 on "The importance of non-party organisation." Some months earlier Morice reminisced in a press interview about her personal relations with Goldstein, their shared political views, and Goldstein's role in forming the WNPPA of South Australia. "We've been friends for years," said Morice, and on the subject of Goldstein's recent fight for the Federal seat of Kooyong: "I consider that she is the only candidate in the Commonwealth really representing women, and she's been loyally supported." As for politics: "We have a lack of education there, have we not? After the Suffrage Bill passed my first public work was to form a Woman's League for Political and Social Education—it didn't flourish very well after the first enthusiasm passed, and when Vida Goldstein came to me for a visit we turned it into the Non-Party Political Association."[34] When the WNPA celebrated its twenty-first birthday in June 1930, Goldstein and past-president Morice were invited to a public meeting where the subject for discussion was "The need for a more co-operative spirit in politics"—the mantra of both of these leading feminists in their respective States.

Such co-operation between women (or at least sisterly sympathy) extended beyond local and interstate networking to the forging of international links. The first recorded instance of this is the visit to Adelaide in May 1913 of two English teacher-suffragists, Harriet Newcomb and Margaret Hodge, who at a special WNPA meeting chaired by Morice outlined the franchise movement in England from its early nineteenth-century beginnings up to the foundation of the Women's Social and Political Union (representing 44 franchise societies and religious bodies). As ANZWVA secretary, Newcomb also spoke about the work of the Australian and New Zealand Women Voters' Association in London, and of plans to form a British Dominions Woman Suffrage Union (BDWSU) on their return to England. Following their addresses the WNPA passed a motion "expressing sympathy with our un-enfranchised sisters overseas" together with the formal resolution: "That knowing from 18 years experience the value of co-operation between men and women in political life, this meeting express[es] the desire that the principle of universal suffrage be extended all over the British Empire."[35] Morice afterwards declared that she personally was "entirely with" the English suffragettes: "They know what they are about, and one pays no heed to the lying reports that are circulated. They are grand, heroic women." When then asked, "What do you think of the attitude of our [Adelaide] women to politics and their own sex?" Morice replied: "Ah, there is a great need of an improved sense of solidarity. More than anything else women here in our country need to learn loyalty to their own sex, to stand by other women, sinking pettiness and differences out of sight when the occasion arises, for the women to stand together. We were granted the vote so easily and we had not the suffrage fight to bring out these fine qualities as it is doing in the women in England. There is so much work waiting here for women to take hold of and always the same few are pushed into it. It moves one to think what women could do in this State, in this city, if there was unity of purpose among us."[36]

Newcomb and Hodge were respectively elected secretary and press secretary of the BDWSU which was formally inaugurated in July 1914 and occupied an office in the same building as the International Women's Suffrage Alliance. In following years, Newcomb's correspondence with feminist organizations like the WNPA kept the enfranchised and non-enfranchised women of the Empire in touch with each other and informed them of developments in the international women's movement. Hodge publicized the activities of the Union and its affiliates both in England and overseas.[37] Such international links were renewed when WNPA activist Annie Hornabrook travelled to London to assist the BDWSU's war-time work, and when in 1920 she, Lucy Morice and Mrs. Elizabeth Nicholls (long-serving president of the WCTU of SA) were appointed to represent the WNPA and its West Australian counterpart, the Women's Service Guild, at women's conferences in Europe.

Meanwhile, in Adelaide, Morice assiduously worked on the WNPA subcommittee formed in 1911 "for the protection of women and children," co-operating with delegates from other women's organizations and the Social Reform Bureau on influential deputations to the Premier and Chief Secretary which requested reform of the female prison system. Specific requests included the appointment of women as jurors, justices, police matrons, and board members of government-supported institutions, a special magistrate for the Children's Court, a female probation officer attached to the Police Court, and a medical woman to have charge of all female inmates of gaols and reformatories."[38] Indeed, it was largely due to WNPA political activism that Senior Probation Officer Kate Cocks was transferred from the State Children's Department towards the end of 1915 in order to establish South Australia's Women Police Department. Her case is a prime example of how women's non-party political associations operated to win support for feminist policies, help shape legislation, and install women in public office.[39]

Morice represented the WNPA on the April 1915 deputation to Chief Secretary Styles which secured Cocks' appointment as Principal Police Matron; also on the deputation (likewise organized by the Social Reform Bureau) in November 1915 which sought alterations in the law of bequests for the benefit of widows and orphans. Several years earlier she successfully proposed a resolution, sent to Federal Members of Parliament, which initiated another (long-term) WNPA educational project: "As women of the Commonwealth are enfranchised citizens equally with men that women have equal opportunities for employment as men as well as equal pay for equal work in the Federal [public] service."[40] Intimating in a footnote that if women could not obtain justice from men the WNPA would have to take steps to send women to represent them in Parliament, Morice also kept alive C. H. Spence's campaign to institute the Hare system of proportional representation by leading a WNPA deputation to Premier Verran on "effective voting" in August 1913. Moreover, it was at her suggestion that during State elections all parliamentary candidates' views on feminist policies were canvassed by the WNPA and the responses publicized in order to better inform women's vote, which they were exhorted to use collectively and wisely. Reflecting Morice's own reform agenda, questions circulated during the 1912 and 1918 elections included: Are you in favour of equal pay for equal work? The resolutions contained in the report of the SA Branch of the British Science Guild on infant nurture? Increased government support to (a) the School for Mothers; (b) Free Kindergartens (c) children's playgrounds?

## REMEMBERING "A VERY REMARKABLE OLD LADY"

L. S. Morice, in her prime at this time, was remembered as "a plump motherly figure, determined, sure and energetic, her drive and humanity forever seeking a cause.... Her bluntness was sometimes browbeating, her impatience with those whose vision was not as great as hers sometimes tactless, but she never asked others to do what she would not do herself."[41] Her activism within the WNPA continued into the 1920s when she was in the sixth decade of her life and the Association's name changed to the League of Women Voters. In 1936, aged 77 but still a very active member of the Kindergarten Union Executive and in regular contact with League members who perpetuated her legacy, Morice's life-time of service to education and the welfare of others was recognized by the award of an M.B.E. (Member of the British Empire). At the age of 86 she was described as "a diminutive figure, retaining all the graciousness and dignity of her generation, with a pretty wit, a live interest in modern literature and philosophies, and a wide knowledge of the affairs of the day ... a very remarkable old lady whose qualities made her an inspiring leader, not only among those interested in social and educational reforms but in the intellectual life of Adelaide."[42] In the annals of this State, remarked the same journalist, "the name of Lucy Morice is worthy of a place alongside that of her distinguished kinswoman, Catherine Helen Spence." Before dying on 10 June 1951, "very weary of the frustration and ineptitude which accompanies great age" (she was 92), Morice left instructions that her body be privately cremated and that "no-one shall wear mourning for me nor send any flowers."[43] Accordingly only a brief notice (no obituary, or mention in the "Deaths" column) appeared in the Adelaide *Advertiser.* The only permanent memorial to Lucy Spence Morice is the North Adelaide kindergarten named in her honour where her M.B.E. hangs below a photograph of her taken on the occasion of this award.

## NOTES

1. Helen Jones, *Nothing seemed impossible: women's education and social change in South Australia 1875–1915* (Brisbane: University of Queensland Press, 1985); *In her own name. Women in South Australian history* (Adelaide: Wakefield Press, 1986); "Lucy Spence Morice and Catherine Helen Spence: partners in South Australian social reform", *Journal of the Historical Society of South Australia* (*JHSSA*) 11 (1983): 48–64.
2. Barbara Caine, "Feminist biography and feminist history", *Women's History Review* 2, No. 2 (1974); Jane Lewis, *Women in social action in Victorian and Edwardian England* (Aldershot: Edwin Elgar, 1990); Mary Ryan, "The power of women's networks," In *Sex and class in women's history*, ed. J. L. Newton, M. P. Ryan and J. R. Walkowitz (London: Routledge & Kegan Paul, 1983); Marilyn Lake, *Getting Equal. The history of Australian feminism* (Sydney: Allen & Unwin, 1999).
3. "Auntie Kate—Catherine Helen Spence. Reminiscences of her niece, Mrs. Lucy Spence Morice" (typescript, n.d.): 1–2, Mortlock Library of South Australiana (MLSA), PRG88/18; S. Eade, "Summary of transcript of tape recording made at Mrs. Caw's flat with Mrs. Beckwith, Mrs. Moore and Mr. Kirby re the Unitarian Christian Church and its subscribers in 1870s Adelaide," Barr Smith Library (BSL) Special Collection, Hübbe-Caw papers (1859–1988), MSS0046/47/4.
4. "Objects," Woman's League Minute Books (1895–1897), MLSA, SRG690/2.
5. "Auntie Kate": 2; "Our Adelaide Women of Interest. A chat with Mrs Morice," *Daily Herald*, 28 June 1913, Magazine section: 13.
6. Lucy Morice to Rose Scott (founder of the Women's Political Education League in NSW), 12 April 1910, Mitchell Library, Sydney, Rose Scott correspondence, A2278; L. S. Morice, "Biographical notes on C. H. Spence": 1–3, 16, MLSA, PRG88/19; "A chat with Mrs Morice".
7. "About Catherine Helen Spence. Lighter side of a leader's life. Told by Lucy Morice" (newspaper clipping, n.d.), Papers re Catherine Helen Spence, BSL, MSS0046/47/4.
8. Anne Wainwright, "A tribute to Lucy Spence Morice" (typescript: Adelaide, 1962), University of South Australia Kindergarten Teachers' College archives; "Educationist honoured," newspaper cuttings re Lucy Morice, Hübbe-Caw papers, MSS0046/47/4.
9. For details of Lucy Morice's involvement with Helen Mayo and Harriet Stirling of the State Children's Council in early twentieth century puericulture reform, see Jones, *In Her Own Name*, 166–7. Note: The birth of Lucy and James Morice's daughter was not officially recorded.
10. "Address by Mrs. Morice to the Church of England Mothers' Union, Diocese of Adelaide" (handwritten, n.d.), Hübbe-Caw papers, MSS0046/47.
11. A. Bullock and O. Stallybrass, eds., *The Fontana Dictionary of Modern Thought* (London: Fontana/Collins, 1983), 226.
12. "Kindergarten progress. Views of Mrs. J. P. Morice" (newspaper clipping, n.d.), MSS0046/47/4; "A chat with Mrs. Morice".

13. L. S. Morice, "Address to the Woman's League" (n.d.), SRG690/2/5.
14. L. S. Morice, "Condensed copy of report presented at the League's first meeting showing the aims and scope of its operations," SRG690/2.
15. Morice, "Address to the Woman's League."
16. *What Socialism Is* (Adelaide: Fabian Society, c.1890).
17. L. S. Morice, "Hon. Secretary's Report for 1896," SRG690/2/3; "The Woman's Column (by a lady contributor)," *Weekly Herald*, 31 July 1896: 5; Woman's League Minute Books, SRG690/1.
18. Morice, "Auntie Kate": 4; SRG690/2/3.
19. "Auntie Kate": 4.
20. Jones, *JHSSA* 11: 53-54.
21. "Rules of the Women Employees' Mutual Association of South Australia," MLSA, 334.7/W.
22. "Minutes of UTLC meeting, 27 November 1908", Trades and Labor Council Minutes Book (1906–1910), MLSA, SRG1/1/4: 351; "Trades and Labor Council" and "Women Employees' Mutual Association", *Daily Herald*, 3 March 1906: 5; 28 April 1906: 8; 12 May 1906: 5; 7 July 1906: 7.
23. Lake, *Getting Equal*, 11–12, 55–58.
24. Lynne Trethewey, "Lucy Spence Morice: 'mother of kindergartens' in South Australia," *History of Education Review* 37, No. 2 (2008): 14–25.
25. Kindergarten Union of South Australia, "Annual Report" (1906–07): 5; (1909–10): 3; (1911–12): 8, State Records of South Australia (SRSA), GRG69/17.
26. "Talks given by Lillian de Lissa at the Golden Jubilee of the Kindergarten Union of SA, 1955": 10, MLSA, de Lissa papers, PRG253/10.
27. "Minutes of Committee meeting, 22 September and 20 October 1909", School for Mothers Minute Book, MLSA, SRG199/1/1; Committee of the School for Mothers' Institute, Adelaide, "First Annual Report" (22 September 1909–31 July 1910), SRG199/2/1: 1.
28. Dr. Helen Mayo, "History of the Mothers' and Babies' Health Association of South Australia," MLSA, Helen Mayo papers, PRG127/6; School for Mothers Minute Book (September 1909-September 1913), SRG199/1/1 (unpaginated).
29. British Science Guild, *Objects and Constitution* (pamphlet, n.d.), State Library of South Australia (SLSA); British Science Guild, SA Branch, "Annual Report for 1914–15": 1, and 1915–16: 1–3, and 1917–18: 3–4, and *Race Building. Science Guild's great work. No. 1* (pamphlet: Adelaide, 1916), SLSA; "Care for the child. Deputation to Chief Secretary. Better legislation asked for," *Register*, 2 April 1914: 16; "Caring for infant life. Deputation to the Premier," *Register*, 5 October 1915: 8.
30. Letters to the Editor, "Care of the child," *Register*, 3 April 1914: 7 and 4 April 1914: 19.
31. Jones, *JHSSA* 11: 58–61; Lake, 13.
32. "Constitution of the Women's Non-Party Political Association of South Australia," Minutes of WNPPA meetings (July 1909–October 1922): pasted in at 1 February 1911, MLSA, SRG116/1/1; "Women's Non-Party Political Association" (objects, officers, platform), *Herald*, 11 September 1911: 4.

33. Vivienne Szekeres, "A history of the League of Women Voters in South Australia 1909–1976", B.A. Hons. thesis (University of Adelaide: 1976); Minutes of WNPPA meetings July 1909–October 1922: various pages, SRG116/1/1.
34. "A chat with Mrs Morice."
35. WNPPA, "Minutes of Special Meeting, 1 May 1913," SRG116/1/1: 73. See also Lynne Trethewey and Kay Whitehead, "Beyond centre and periphery: transnationalism in two teacher/suffragettes' work," *History of Education* 32, no. 5 (2003): 547–559.
36. *Daily Herald*, 28 June 1913.
37. K. Whitehead and L. Trethewey, "Aging and activism in the context of the British Dominions Woman Suffrage Union, 1914–1922," *Women's Studies International Forum* 31 (2008): 30–41.
38. "Social questions. Prison reform promised. Responsibilities of citizens," *Evening Journal*, 1 December 1911: 1; "Wanted—women police patrols. Strong case made out by Social Reform Bureau. Chief Secretary promises consideration," *Daily Herald*, 28 April 1915; "Women police. Request to Government", *Register*, 28 April 1915: 7; WNPPA, "Minutes of Special Meeting to consider punishments for assaults on defenseless women and children, 9 October 1911" and "Minutes of 41st WNPA meeting, 18 June 1913" and "70th meeting, 21 April 1915," SRG116/1/1: 46–7, 75, 117–8.
39. L. Trethewey, "Christian feminism in action: Kate Cocks's social welfare work in South Australia, 1900–1950," *History of Education* 36, no. 6 (2008): 715–734.
40. "Minutes of WNPA Committee meeting, 26 September 1911."
41. H. Jones, ed., *Jubilee History of the Kindergarten Union of South Australia 1905–1955* (Adelaide: KUSA, 1975), 60.
42. "The Mother of the Kindergartens," *Advertiser*, 30 October 1946.
43. Wainwright, "A tribute to Lucy Spence Morice": 10; H. Jones, "Morice, Louise (Lucy)," In Bede Nairne and Geoffrey Searle, gen. eds., *Australian Dictionary of Biography. Vol. 10* (Melbourne: Melbourne University Press, 1986), 587; "Death of Mrs Lucy Morice," *Advertiser*, 13 June 1951: 2.

CHAPTER 10

# GEORGE S. COUNTS

## Leading Social Reconstructionist

**Bruce Romanish**

### INTRODUCTION

There is probably no legacy more flattering to a scholar than to have one's ideas maintain their relevance for generations to come. That clearly is the case with George S. Counts. Some of his most impactful writings, including one of his best-known tracts, *Dare the School Build a New Social Order?*, published in 1932 at the depths of what is termed the Great Depression, were clarion calls for the nation to address its economic and social inequalities as part of its commitment to a democratic system. The parallels between then and now are striking in economic and political terms with the current Great Recession, which is described as the worst economic downturn since the 1930s.

This biography begins with a sketch that gives context to the subsequent review of Counts' educational outlook, which in turn forms the basis for his characterization as a social reconstructionist. The biography further provides an analysis of important segments of Counts' career that have received limited attention or are underdeveloped in the literature. One is his leadership and activism in forging the teacher union movement in the United States, including his tenure as President of the Ameri-

*Life Stories: Exploring Issues in Educational History Through Biography*
pp. 197–214

can Federation of Teachers during a critical and formative period, which calls attention to the recent moves to severely curtail teacher unionism across the country. Another realm is his scholarship as an expert on Soviet Education and the Soviet system, which was an important focus of his work, almost his entire career. Finally, a discussion of his FBI file, which is presented here for the first time, is included.

The paper employs an historical and descriptive approach that brings an interpretive and critical lens to the subjects at hand, particularly his position on indoctrination and imposition. In addition to using the primary sources of Counts' publications and related primary and secondary sources, it incorporates important information and perspectives garnered by the author via personal interviews with Counts' colleagues and associates who were contemporaries. These sources, and Counts' FBI file, have not been employed by other scholars. Taped interviews of Counts, housed in his collection at Southern Illinois University and not cited in the major publications about Counts, are also incorporated.

## COUNTS—A BIOGRAPHICAL BACKGROUND

Though it was a day about which Counts personally claimed to have recalled little, he was born George Sylvester Counts on December 9, 1889, on a farm in rural northeast Kansas near Baldwin.[1] This was a watershed period in U.S. history marking a shift from an agrarian, rural society to one rapidly becoming industrialized and urban. It was a time when the country moved to the city and his presence in part of the old yet part of the new society during his life, meant both shaped his outlooks.[2] But more than frontier America shaped his perspectives in his youth. His mother was a descendant of the Pilgrim leader William Bradford, signer of the Mayflower Compact and governor of the Plymouth Colony for 30 years. His family also tied him to the struggle for human freedom. When Virginia, by a margin of one vote, decided to retain the slave system, his paternal great grandmother became a "conscientious objector," sold her land, freed her slaves, and moved west to Ohio.[3]

Raised in a Methodist family, religion was an important part of Counts' life. His parents were ardent Christians, thus George and his five siblings were nurtured in the faith. At the age of six he earned a dollar from his grandfather for learning the Books of the Bible in order. Church and Sunday school were part of every Sunday. Once he reached college age his aunt was determined he become a minister, having set aside the money for a seminary interview, which she also arranged.[4]

In the end, Counts chose the podium over the pulpit by attending Baker College, a Methodist institution. But his undying commitment to the worth and dignity of each individual along with his devotion to the brotherhood of man [sic] throughout his life reflect the Judeo-Christian values rooted in frontier traditions. His almost missionary zeal for social justice no doubt reflects these influences. Though he adhered to these values to the end of his life, in time other factors caused him to reject Christian theology. The revolutionary ideas he later encountered while studying at the University of Chicago and in his estimation the convincing theory of organic evolution, which he readily adopted, caused him to embrace a new Weltanschauung.[5]

Counts graduated at the head of his class at Baker and displayed signs of future leadership as president of his class and fraternity along with other organizations and athletic associations. In 1913 he was awarded a Rhodes scholarship but in between his application and the award he married Lois Hazel Bailey. Marriage at that time was a disqualifier for Rhodes scholars. They later had two daughters, Esther and Martha.[6]

His professional life in academe began at Delaware College, now University of Delaware, where he led the Department of Education for two years. In 1918 he went to Harris Teachers College in St. Louis but after a year took a position at the University of Washington in Seattle where a year later he was lured away by Yale University for a six-year stint. He then went to the University of Chicago before settling at Teachers College Columbia University in 1927 where he remained until retirement. But retirement meant something different for him as he then taught at the University of Pittsburgh, University of Colorado, Michigan State, Northwestern, and finally Southern Illinois University in 1962. He ended his career in Carbondale in 1971 at the age of 82.[7]

## COUNTS' EDUCATIONAL OUTLOOK

For much of his career George S. Counts was a radical force in American educational thought. His ideas coupled with his oratorical skills would on occasion bring a room full of academics to their feet. A contemporary of John Dewey at Teachers College for many years, Counts was a leading voice among a cadre of scholars known as "social reconstructionists." This school of thought viewed the education of the young, in important respects, as a means to an end. That is, their education, and by extension the students themselves, was to be aimed at ameliorating societal ills as part of a democratic commitment. He wanted to see education treated as a social study in part as a counter-force to the dominance of psychology and child study.[8]

Based on his reading of human history he believed education is always a representation of a particular culture in a particular setting. According to Counts, "There have been as many educations in history as there have been societies. It is as much an integral part of a culture or civilization as an economic or political system. The very way in which education is conceived, whether its purpose is to enslave or free the mind, is an expression of the society which it serves ... of necessity education is a most intimate expression of a particular civilization."[9] Therefore, to fashion an educational ideal appropriate for American society as it existed required a careful assessment of the society in its historical and worldly setting. If this was done, he believed education in the United States would, at its base, have a desire to achieve a democratic ideal. Democracy, as a system and process, implicitly gave life to the idea that society would and could seek to better itself.

The ultimate value in a democracy was, then, the worth and dignity of the individual. Writing in 1949 he stated, as he had many times, "probably the most distinctive feature of a democracy is the value which it places on the individual human being, regardless of race, creed, family, or other social category ... in the measure that individuals are treated unequally and arbitrarily with respect to educational advantage, economic opportunity, administration of justice, enjoyment of rights and responsibilities, or access to social rewards and honors, the society involved violates this basic principle."[10]

Counts was more a social and educational theorist than he was concerned with the practical implementation of an educational outlook. The application of his ideals was manifested more by how he executed his life, than it was in any concrete educational applications. But one area of thought deserves additional attention here because it underscores his activist inclinations and how they manifested themselves in his educational outlook.

## IMPOSITION AND INDOCTRINATION

While many progressive educators of his era focused their attention primarily on instructional methods and the nature of the child, Counts directed his efforts to the social aims and purposes of schooling. His perspective reflected a belief that the future would be more collectivist in nature and therefore it was critical that it be organized with fundamental commitments to a democratic ethos.[11] In fact, he concluded that by this gauge many "progressive" educators were not progressive at all.

His critique was anchored in the proposition that education cannot be a neutral undertaking and efforts to prevent any impositions upon the life of the youngster were futile and misplaced. Rather, he called for a close examination of the forces at work in an attempt to direct them towards positive ends. This contrasted with many progressive schools which followed child-centeredness in part as a reaction against the traditional subject-centered curriculum that tended to ignore individual student interests and talents. But the focus on the child alone lacked direction and orientation, as Counts saw it, and did not reflect genuinely progressive social and political aims. In Counts' view, child-centered advocates too often lacked deep and abiding loyalties, possessed few convictions for which they would sacrifice much, would find it hard to live without their customary material comforts, were insensitive to accepted forms of social justice, were content to play the role of interested spectator in the drama of human history, rarely moved outside the pleasant circles of their social class, and, in the day of severe trial, would "follow the lead of the most powerful and respectable forces in society and at the same time find good reasons for so doing."[12] He did not disparage the idea of being child centered, per se, but rather took issue with the movement's lack of a solid social foundation. A school could not become progressive by mere resolve. He likened the difficulty of founding a progressive educational movement to that of creating a progressive political party. If it was not rooted in some profound social movement or trend, it could be but an instrument of deception.[13]

His use of the term indoctrination as a desired educational approach naturally troubled many educators who feared it would devolve into little more than blatant mind control or the inculcation of a mindless patriotism. And it was never sufficient to the case that he chose the use of the term in its historic and more literal sense. He leaned on a Webster definition, which meant to instruct in doctrines, principles, theories, or beliefs; to instruct; to teach. It derived from the Latin doctrina—to instruct. Counts was somewhat in agreement with his challengers—if they agreed on the meaning of their terms. He acknowledged that indoctrination was possibly too strong and uncompromising in its vernacular and that imposition might be a better term to use. Yet, he warned that even this term needed to carry its milder connotations. Curiously, when civic education inculcated ideas of national solidarity and patriotism, Counts' opposition did not feel indoctrination had occurred.[14] Counts held that cultural evolution or indeed its basic maintenance would be impossible if the achievements of one generation were not transmitted to the next by the process of teaching and learning.[15]

He placed the matter in proper perspective when, years later, he related an experience he had with his colleague John Dewey in 1932 in which they had a robust debate over the issue of indoctrination. Though Counts' position, again, was to reject the proposition that anything should be taught as fixed or as dogma, he defended the idea of "imposition" as a basic and inescapable aspect of the process of rearing the young in any society. A few weeks later Counts gave an address to a group of New York City teachers and Dewey was present. When it was time for Q & A, "the great philosopher rose and said he had checked the meaning of the word indoctrination in Webster's Dictionary and discovered it meant 'teaching'."[16]

During the Second World War, when pressure increased for the inculcation of patriotic values not only in schools but in public life everywhere, Counts opposed attempts to bring what he saw as despotism into public schools under the guise of teacher patriotism. Patriotism, if it was democratic by nature and concerned with the interests of the people as a whole, could be appropriate as he saw it.[17] But this would be distinguished from mindless indoctrination of the flag-waving variety. Indeed, he warned that the teaching of blind loyalties to democracy's traditional machinery would doubtless be the surest way of destroying it.[18]

But Counts cannot have it both ways. It's not possible to simultaneously avoid, yet directly engage in indoctrination, no matter how much definitional gymnastics are employed. There is a great difference between the socialization everyone receives by virtue of being born into a given culture or civilization, and the political education one receives through a formal school curriculum. Sociologists distinguish between what are termed covert and overt socialization and that in essence is what is at issue. "Think of the old cliché about the mind being an excellent servant but a terrible master."[19] Counts failed to incorporate the necessity of critical thought as part of democratic citizenship, and as something to serve as a counterbalance to socialization or imposition. This critical dimension, common to nearly all notions of autonomy, is also at the core of a democratic education.[20]

Counts was not troubled by the apparent conflict between his devotion to democracy as an end and his comfort level with viewing students as a means, despite an axiom of democratic theory that democratic ends are tied to democratic means. I find it too easy for him to argue that some forms of imposition on the young are inevitable, unavoidable, and to a degree necessary if not desirable, and then to use that as a basis to support direct, overt imposition or indoctrination. It is one thing to assert that culture by definition socializes its members. It's another huge step to then categorize certain other forms of socialization as necessary.

By viewing the young predominantly as a means to an end, laudable though it may appear in serving democratic goals, Counts was curiously much closer to the forms of education used in political systems he would characterize as authoritarian. Moreover, his view stands alongside the passionate and deeply committed forces of all political stripes whether they are religious fundamentalists around the world, or ultra right-wing groups, or radical leftists, who have a blue print for how the whole of society should be organized. These groups don't quibble about indoctrination or imposition as an educational tool—they accept and embrace the concept. For them, true believers all, the fight is over "what" needs to be implanted in young minds not whether such means are problematic. It is on this point that Counts' educational position is most deserving of critique, in my judgment.

Yet Counts never abandoned his view that the young needed to be given a vision, a future to embrace, to identify with, and to engage in ways that would make it realized. Writing during the same time frame, Walter Lippmann lent support to Counts' perspective with his own when he wrote, "If a civilization is to be coherent and confident it must be known in that civilization what its ideals are. There must exist in the form of clearly available ideas an understanding of what the fulfillment of the promise of that civilization might mean, an imaginative conception of the good at which it might, and, if it is to flourish, at which it must aim."[21] In this statement Lippmann set forth the very essence of Counts' position. Only through an adequate vision anchored to democratic values could the young find their place in the world and at the same time improve upon it. Counts clearly favored the development of inquiring and independent minds among the young, but hastened to note that even this worthy aim implied a form of imposition since possessing a critical mind is not a characteristic at birth.

## AMERICAN FEDERATION OF TEACHERS

From his earliest days as an educator Counts was supportive of teachers and their professional rights. He favored an elevation of their status and believed that if the school was to be an agency on behalf of social betterment, teachers would be the vanguard. For this mission to be realized, however, teachers would have to struggle to achieve it. In order for teachers to be in a position of school and social transformation, they would need to be organized to gain adequate compensation, to have a voice in the formulation of educational policies, and to obtain tenure. If the ancient doctrine of academic freedom were to be upheld, teachers would have to do it.[22] Teachers would have to break away from the nineteenth century tradition that held a genteel view of the teacher and expected him or her to be quiet, moral, apolitical, and penniless.[23]

This meant the progressive minded teachers of the nation would have to unite in a powerful organization, militantly devoted to the building of a better social order and to the fulfillment, under the conditions of industrial civilization, of the democratic aspirations of the American people. This organization would need the material resources, the legal talent, and the trained intelligence necessary to wage successful campaigns in the press, the courts, and legislative chambers across the country. It would have to defend its members against the ignorance of the masses and the malevolence of the privileged.[24] Because private and special interests pressured the public schools with regularity, teachers' organizations would have to safeguard intellectual freedom against external encroachments. Counts' perspective, in the words of Lawrence Cremin, was that "in the absence of a powerful profession, the most representative control in the world could not save the schools from the demoralizing buffeting of partisan popular passions."[25]

So committed was Counts to the teacher union movement that he accepted the challenge of seeking the Presidency of the AFT, and prevailed. While John Dewey was issued card #1 in the AFT and coined the slogan of its masthead "Education for Democracy and Democracy in Education," it was Counts who was called upon to rescue the union during one of its darkest hours.

The importance of Counts to the AFT story can be summarized as a battle to save the union from communist influence. During the depression, and especially during the 1930s, enmity towards capitalism rose significantly. In many circles growing numbers of Americans became increasingly intrigued by and drawn to socialist ideas, and considerable numbers developed a genuine curiosity concerning theoretical communism. Still others became actively involved with the Communist Party whose fortunes were tied largely to the dictates of Moscow. The trade union movement became fertile ground for communist advances and this extended to the AFT as well. In addition to infiltrating the teachers' union movement, communism found an ideological appeal among some members of the intellectual class.

New York City was a source of great strength to the AFT since the organized teachers were employed in the nation's largest public school system. Within the New York local there was a College Section of university faculty that had become fairly radicalized. The vocal attacks on free enterprise by some caused a split within the group. Some viewed these assaults as unwarranted and unnecessary and soon many leading academics withdrew their membership from the AFT, including John Dewey. Their dissatisfaction with communist control and the growing tendency to place party line above the interests of the public schools as they saw it, left them no choice but to depart. One of the few who remained among those considered to be social reconstructionists was George S. Counts.

William Green, President of the American Federation of Labor, and his organization, had actually lost control of the New York Local No. 5 by the mid 1930s. And communists held sway in the Cleveland union and Madison, Wisconsin as well. The issue was further complicated by efforts within the labor movement to join the CIO with the AFL and where advocates stood in relation to their overall political persuasions was critical in many cases. Increasingly, the AFL was concerned that the AFT was not only giving the labor movement a tarnished reputation, the growing fear was it would join a different labor movement.

By this time, Counts himself had completed his own metamorphosis regarding the promise of the Soviet Union. As with many others during the depths of the depression, Counts, who was far more knowledgeable than most on the subject, saw the Soviet experiment as providing some answers to the inability of American capitalism to deal with its economic crisis. In the 1920s he was hopeful the dictatorship would disappear in the Soviet Union. During his visit there in 1927 Soviet educational leaders told him that by his next visit they would have freedom, causing him to be somewhat sanguine about their future.[26] But after Stalin began his infamous purges and consolidated his power, Counts lost faith that the Soviet people would soon have freedom.[27]

Despite the view of some (including the FBI)[28] that Counts harbored communist sympathies or worse during this period, his record of private and public actions support the contrary.[29] Nonetheless, as a matter of principle and a commitment to democratic civil liberties he opposed mass expulsions from the AFT even though he recognized the level of communist involvement in various locals and as importantly, the harm they were doing to the teacher union movement.

After losing an election to lead the College Teachers Union, and with the support and cajoling by others, he was persuaded to stand for election in 1939 as President of the American Federation of Teachers. In an extremely close outcome decided by two dozen votes Counts emerged victorious.[30] He would fulfill the role from 1939 to 1942. In retrospect, the choice was a good one from the standpoint of the union. In addition to being a long time member of the Federation, he was certainly a nationally prominent educational figure and his position at Teachers College made him keenly aware of the circumstances in New York. Finally, while many of his colleagues, and some very close friends, had abandoned the union earlier, his enduring commitment was a significant credential.

It's difficult to determine how important this AFT election was for the future of the teaching profession and indeed the labor movement itself. But it is clear that William Green was concerned about communist developments within the labor union and announced to the press in 1939 that the AFT should not permit itself to remain "a breeding ground for communists."[31] There was speculation Green issued an ultimatum to the AFT that gave it three months to clean itself up. Counts' rise to President gave the AFT someone with the courage and intellectual heft to withstand the continuing challenges within the AFT, because by 1940 the opposition mounted a challenge to his re-election. When the ballots were counted he defeated John DeBoer of the University of Illinois.[32]

Following the election, Counts set in motion the machinery to oust all the Communist-dominated locals in the AFT. The AFL favored the revocation of their charters and the re-establishment of new bona fide local unions of teachers. The effort by Counts to remove the Communists was not precedent-setting within the labor movement; recognizing the tactic of "bore-from-within" the AFL had refused, for example, to seat a Communist delegation from Butte, Montana, at its 1923 convention.[33]

Counts and the AFT pursued a very open process that provided ample opportunity for both sides to make their case via hearings, through discussions in the AFT journal, through newspapers, etc. As a result of the due process provided in the AFT Constitution, in the spring of 1941 the AFT Executive Council moved to expel Locals No. 5, No. 537 (College Teachers in NY), and Philadelphia Local No. 192. The final vote to remove was by a referendum of the entire membership that prevailed by a very slim 5 to 4 margin.[34] As satisfying as this victory was to Counts and the AFT leadership on certain levels, it came at a heavy cost. The total membership was reduced by a third and there was ample repair work to be done. But in 1941 Counts was once again nominated for the Presidency and this time he was unopposed. When the 524 ballots in his support were counted and announced (8 others were cast as blanks), the convention rose and gave a thunderous applause with cheers.[35]

Counts extended his political activism launched by his AFT Presidency by going on to found the Liberal Party in New York in 1944, a result of a split with the Labor Party owing in part to its communist and far left influences.[36] He was then recruited to be the Liberal Party's candidate for U.S. Senate in 1952. The split among the field of candidates on the left enabled Irving Ives to retain his seat as New York's Republican U.S. Senator, with Counts garnering just under a half million votes.

## COUNTS THE SOVIET EXPERT

During much of Counts' career he was one of the leading American experts on the Soviet Union, its schools, and its society. Because his politics were on the left coupled with his political activism, his scholarly pursuits as a Soviet expert lent grist to the mill of those reactionaries who unreflectively connected the dots to support their suspicions of his communist pedigree. His gravitational interest in the Soviet Union was far more innocent and originated when, in 1927, he joined Teachers College, Columbia University as Assistant Director of the International Institute and discovered that no one at the Institute had made the Soviet Union their topical focus. Counts visited the U.S.S.R. as part of a labor delegation prior to his appointment at Columbia and since he needed his own part of the globe as a specialty the Soviet Union was a logical choice.[37] He visited the Soviet Union again in 1929 when he drove a new Ford over 6,000 miles throughout the country and published the account in, *A Ford Crosses Soviet Russia*.[38] During this period, little more than a decade after the Bolshevik revolution, there was a sense of optimism in the U.S.S.R. and Counts saw in person what was termed "socialism with a human face" and he was generally impressed by what they were trying to achieve in their schools.[39]

But the greatest appeal to Counts was the Soviet effort to plan and control their economy. It was an enigma to him that the technological and industrial power of the United States was rendered powerless while great human suffering was mounting due to the very lack of ability to move the machinery of the economy. The context was the depression and Counts believed if their experiment would fail it would not be due to its system of planning and economic coordination.[40]

Counts wrote about the Soviet Union and its education system for over three decades until 1959. He spoke fluent Russian and read *Pravda* daily throughout his career until his "final" retirement from Southern Illinois University. Though he was somewhat infatuated with the Soviet experiment, he never sought to import its ideas. By the latter part of the mid-1930s he understood the true nature of their goals and became disenchanted.[41] He concluded the new giant posed a great danger to the free world.

Counts believed the Soviet challenge to the west and to the United States in particular came not from the Red Army or the Communist International but rather from the State Planning Commission and the system of Soviet education. In a conversation with the famous historian H.G. Wells, Joseph Stalin revealed something vital to keep in mind about Soviet education at the time. He said: "Education is a weapon whose effect depends on who holds it in his hands and at whom it is aimed."[42] As a result the Central Committee devoted significant time and energy not only to the broad philosophical and ideological aspects of education, but also to textbook preparation, teaching methods, classroom organization, etc. Nothing was too small or insignificant to engage the Committee's attention, right down to the number and length of the recess periods in primary schools.[43]

Behind the power of the Kremlin could be seen the power of Soviet education, something to be seen as the key to understanding Soviet strength. It was the first great state in history, according to Counts, to employ the full force of organized education to achieve a distant apocalyptic goal.[44] All educational agencies were placed under the auspices of the state. It was a comprehensive system, which included practically all of the cultural and formative influences of society, save the church and family—both of which had their influence reduced. Education was connected to major divisions of the press, other media, literature, art, libraries, museums, institutions tied to family and community, youth groups, party organizations; movies, theater, even the circus, were all part of the apparatus.[45]

As unsettling as this comprehensive marshaling of forces to shape the human mind is to most of us, it reveals the elevated status of education within the Soviet framework. But without the development of its educational system, Counts was convinced the Soviet Union would have remained a backward nation, incapable of challenging the rest of the world. And their accomplishments were almost without parallel in some respects. In 1917 when they began, illiteracy was at 60%. In a short span of years they could boast of "eradicating" illiteracy.[46] And in educational terms their pedagogy was in the early years progressive and experimental. Later, in 1957 when Sputnik was launched and sent terror throughout the United States, delegations were sent to observe what the Soviets were doing in their schools to accomplish such scientific prowess. But as with the philosophical saw that a foot cannot be dipped in the same stream twice, the Soviet schools of the 1950s were not the ones their space scientists attended. Many of them were products of the earlier period of progressive educational reform.

No heresy or dissent was tolerated in any form. The acceptance of the faith had to be absolute. The entire apparatus of the state and society was employed to prevent outside ideas from entering. In the end it is easy to see the inherent contradictions. Any society seeking to capitalize on the intellectual potential of its people cannot at the same time corral the human mind. Obviously short-term aims may be achieved such as building basic literacy and generating allegiance to a system, but the mind doesn't achieve boundless potential in a bounded setting. And while Counts saw the danger and the problems with this scenario, he credited their design as a remarkable effort in size and scope given the lofty aspirations of the regime.

Counts explained by example the level of monolithic control over education that developed. In 1934, at the behest of Stalin himself, at a meeting of the Central Executive Committee of the Communist Party (CEC), they decided to re-write the history books. Outlines for new books were developed by scholars, which were referred back to the CEC. It in turn sharply criticized the outlines and appointed a review committee to go over them and make corrections. The committee was composed of the three most powerful men in the Soviet Union: Stalin, Kirov, and Zhdanov. Kirov was second in command to Stalin and later became the first victim of the Great Purge that began in 1936. Zhdanov was an important member of the politburo.[47] These powerful men examined and criticized the outlines of textbooks for teaching history in the schools. Their "Remarks and Outlines" were published and served as guiding directives for the writing of history textbooks used in Soviet schools.[48]

## COUNTS AND THE FBI

Owing to Counts' left-leaning ideology, his career interest in and his travel to the Soviet Union, and his political activism, the U.S. paranoia of the "red menace" made him a prime prospect for FBI tracking and investigation. Based on my examination of Counts' FBI File obtained through a Freedom of Information request, the work of the FBI reflects more on the way U.S. Citizens were investigated than it does on Counts' actions. By that, I mean the ease by which accusers could smear someone, without the target of the smear having any knowledge of the claims, and the readiness of the FBI to assume credibility on the part of accusers, represent a sad chapter in the history of a great nation. I'll discuss two events housed in the file that illustrate the point.[49]

One summary by the FBI dated October 20, 1942, which includes a thorough biography of Counts' academic and personal life, after years of inquiry and investigation that proceeded from assumptions of guilt regarding Counts' membership and support of communism, concludes with this statement: "In view of the results of the above reported preliminary investigation, it would appear that subject is not sympathetic to the Communist cause. For this reason, no further investigation is being contemplated in this office, and this case is considered closed."[50] Yet further portions of the file reveal that FBI file activity continued through the 1950s and 1960s in part reflecting the increased intensity of the "red scare" in the post war United States, but also resulting from the efforts of groups such as the American Council of Christian Churches and The General Federation of Women's Clubs, which appear in multiple portions of the file.

One episode, reported to the Director, J. Edgar Hoover, in 1951, involved a Mr. Louis Gibarti, who was a former Comintern agent who operated in the United States between 1928 and 1938 and was himself a communist in Hungary. He was interviewed in Paris by the FBI in 1951. The document asserts, "Informant believed to be reliable who has furnished accurate information in the past" yet a hand written insertion on the same page dated June 3, 1955 states his "credibility is not known since he has in the past furnished both reliable and unreliable information." Nonetheless, he identified Counts as being a "member at large" of the

Communist Party, which meant he wasn't linked to any nucleus because those members had to carry out additional duties, such as recruitment, which required divulging their identity as party members. Instead, the postulate went: "at large" members would engage in other organizations and advance the communists' interests without having to reveal their true sympathies. So, they were secret members and were subject to Party discipline but would not be known as Communist. Gibarti then adds credibility to his claim by adding in 1934 Counts told Gibarti personally he was a Communist Party member.[51]

In a separate memo dated December 3, 1951, however, following a subsequent interview with Gibarti in France, Gibarti then was more circumspect in his ability to identify Counts and said he could not identify Counts any further. He was in fact unable to verify a picture of Counts as the person he previously claimed was the person who spoke to him personally about his communist activities.[52]

A second portion of the file I want to address focuses on Counts' writings and public speaking. Two books that received the most attention were *Dare the School Build a New Social Order?* and *New Russia's Primer*.[53] At points Counts is held accountable for statements in the Primer when in fact he was merely a translator. Had Counts' other writing on the Soviet Union been consulted, the record would reveal a perspective that warned about the threats posed by Soviet Education and the Soviet system rather than a voice championing communism and its virtues. There were also newspaper articles or clippings of some his public lectures that also attributed things to him which were inaccurate regarding his stance towards the Soviets. But no citations were ever provided from the books or newspaper pieces or by other detractors leaving the audiences to take things at face value or to take it upon themselves to read Counts' books in their entirety.

The FBI was very thorough in assembling a full dossier of Counts' organizational memberships and related involvement as well as his political activities. It also thoroughly catalogued all his scholarly work. It is obvious Counts was a person of interest whose life and activities were tracked for several decades by the FBI.

## SUMMARY

The legacy of George S. Counts has many layers. A towering educational scholar known internationally; a progressive voice for American society, American education, and American democracy; an activist and politician who lived out by example the clarion call he made for teachers to move to the vanguard of political and social change; and a leading expert on Soviet society and education; these are categories that best capture and describe his life and career. He was a pioneer in advancing the sociology of education. Several of his seminal works represent some of the first attempts to analyze the effects of social class on the nation's schools, including *The Selective Character of American Secondary Education* (1922), *The Senior High School Curriculum* (1926), *The Social Composition of Boards of Education: A Study in the Social Control of Public Education* (1927), and *Secondary Education and Industrialism* (1929). Yet, with all his accomplishments and successes, he remains best known for the 52-page tract, *Dare the School Build a New Social Order?* (1932).

According to those who knew him well, he was a magnificent teacher. Lawrence A. Cremin knew Counts as a lecturer, a seminar leader, a dissertation advisor, and "later as a mentor, faculty colleague, and treasured friend. He was extraordinary in every one of these roles..."[54] According to Cremin, students at Teachers College respected him profoundly. "He was no saint to be venerated but rather a wise, learned, and dedicated teacher, who professed in the field of education superbly. His example remains lively in my mind even today."[55]

While he lost his early hope that the Soviet Union would provide a model for using central planning as a way to moderate the vicissitudes of economic boom and bust, Counts remained convinced that some degree of centralized economic management was sound. Though he was a Norman Thomas supporter for President in 1932, he voted for FDR in the next three elections as a more pragmatic path. He can safely be termed a democratic socialist for much of his career but only if the term is applied in its historic rather than contemporary American mistaken vernacular.[56] But, in the main, he falls within the tradition of American progressivism and populism.

During the 1930s and 1940s Counts was considered by many to be the leading intellectual figure at Teachers College, Columbia University, following the departures of John Dewey and Edward L. Thorndike.[57] He edited the *Social Frontier* during its most influential years and was its first editor.[58] For reasons not understood or known, he burned most of his papers when he left Teachers College in 1955. The only remnants of his work at Teachers College available to me were in an old filing cabinet stuck in the back of a secluded storage room that contained mostly early hand written drafts of various articles, program proposals for Teachers College, and other later publications.

As President of the American Federation of Teachers he gave the teachers' union movement a social purpose and social conscience and he believed fervently that the school could not rise much above the level of the teachers. Though not the language of his era, he was one of the earliest proponents of teacher empowerment and championed teacher rights and voice.

His progressive politics coupled with his interest in the Soviet Union garnered the attention of the FBI. Friends and neighbors were interviewed, phone calls were accessed, etc.[59] In the end, FBI investigations and surveillance yielded no evidence that he was ever a communist or a sympathizer. But that was insufficient to eliminate FBI suspicions.

## NOTES

1. George S. Counts, "A Humble Autobiography," NSSE 70th Yearbook (1971): 151–154.
2. George S. Counts, Recorded Interview No. 13, Southern Illinois University-Carbondale(1966). In the Counts papers, Morris Library Special Collections.
3. John L. Childs, *American Pragmatism and Education* (New York: Henry Holt and Company, 1956), 212.
4. Counts, Recorded Interview, No. 13.
5. Ibid.
6. Counts, "A Humble Autobiography."
7. Childs, *American Pragmatism and Education,* 215.
8. Ellen Condliffe Lagemann, "Prophecy or Profession? George S. Counts and the Social Study of Education" *American Journal of Education,* 100 (1992): 137.
9. George S. Counts, "A Rational Faith in Education," *Teachers College Record* 60 (1958): 257.
10. George S. Counts, "Educate for Democracy," *Phi Delta Kappan* 30 (1949): 194.
11. Gerald L. Gutek, *The Educational Theory of George S. Counts* (Columbus: Ohio State University Press, 1970).
12. Counts, *Dare the School Build a New Social order*? 6.
13. George S. Counts, Secondary Education and Industrialism (Cambridge: Harvard University Press, 1929).
14. Gutek, 1970, 117.
15. George S. Counts, *The Social Foundations of Education* (New York: Charles Scribner's Sons, 1934), 536.
16. George S. Counts, "Should the Teacher Always Be Neutral?" P*hi Delta Kappan* 51 (1969), 186.
17. George S. Counts, "The Teaching of Patriotism," *American Teacher* 24 (1940), 7.
18. George S. Counts, "The Prospect of American Democracy," *NEA Addresses and Proceedings*, 1937.
19. David F. Wallace, *This Is Water* (New York: Little, Brown, and Co. 2009), 53.
20. Claudia Bloser, Aron Schopf, and Marcus Willaschek, "Autonomy, Experience, and Reflection. On a Neglected Aspect of Personal Autonomy." *Ethical Theory and Moral Practice* 13 (2010):239–253; and Judith Herb, "Report of Student Success Rate According to Licensure Programs for Required

Social Foundations of Education Course," Submitted for NCATE Accreditation Reporting, Ohio: University of Toledo, 2007.

21. Walter Lippmann, *A Preface To Morals* (New York: Macmillan, Co., 1929), 322.
22. *A Call to the Teachers of the Nation, by the Committee of the Progressive Education Association on Social and Economic Problems* (New York: John Day Company, 1938).
23. Marshall O. Donley, *Power To The Teacher* (Bloomington: Indiana University Press, 1976).
24. *A Call to the Teachers of the Nation.*
25. Lawrence A. Cremin, *The Transformation of the School* (New York: Vintage books, 1961), 226.
26. Robert W. Iverson, *The Communist and the Schools* (New York: Harcourt, Brace, and Company, 1959).
27. George S. Counts, Recorded Interview #94, N.D., Southern Illinois University-Carbondale, In the Counts papers, Morris Library Special Collections.
28. FBI File of George S. Counts, obtained through the Freedom of Information Act.
29. Gutek, *The Educational Theory of George S. Counts* 84.
30. Convention Proceedings, 23rd Annual American Federation of Teachers Convention, August 21–25, 1939, 725.
31. William E. Eaton, *The American Federation of Teachers*, 1916–1961 (Carbondale: Southern Illinois University Press, 1975), 99–102.
32. Convention Proceedings, 24th Annual AFT Convention, 19–23 August, 1940, 416.
33. Eaton, 85.
34. Carl J. Megel, "A.F.T. Action on Communism," *American Teacher* 4 (1953), 20.
35. Convention Proceedings, 25th Annual American Federation of Teachers Convention, August 22–26, 1941, 505.
36. John E. Vargo, "End of the Line for the New York Liberal Party?" http://www.liberalparty.org/vargoarticlep1.htm (1997–2011).
37. Personal Interview with William H.E. Johnson, March 8, 1980. Johnson was then Professor Emeritus at the University of Pittsburgh, was a Soviet scholar himself, and knew Counts well.
38. George S. Counts, *A Ford Crosses Soviet Russia* (Boston: The Stratford Company, 1930).
39. Personal Interview with William H.E. Johnson, March 8, 1980.
40. George S. Counts, *The Soviet Challenge to America* (New York: John Day Company, 1931).
41. Personal Interview with William H.E. Johnson, March 8, 1980.
42. George S. Counts, "Soviet Education and the Democratic Ideal in Education," *American Teacher* 6 (1951), 18.
43. George S. Counts, *The Country of the Blind* (Boston: Houghton Mifflin Company, 1949), 259.

44. George S. Counts, "The Real Challenge of Soviet Education," *Educational Forum* 23 (1959), 263.
45. Counts, "Soviet Education and the Democratic Ideal," 18; *The Country of the Blind*, 245.
46. George S. Counts, *Khruschev and the Central Committee Speak on Education* (Pittsburgh: University of Pittsburgh Press, 1959).
47. Sydney Harcave, *Russia a History* (Philadelphia: J.B. Lippincott Company, 1964).
48. George S. Counts, "Some Recent Tendencies in Soviet Education," *American Teacher* 32 (1947), 17.
49. The FBI File is not arranged by any pagination except for selected pieces within the file. It is a compilation of separate segments and correspondence. I've cited each in this paper by descriptions and other identifiers and included page numbers where available. The contents of the file, minus deletions, were de-classified in 1981. It totals 201 pages with several redundancies, albeit different time periods.
50. Counts FBI File, "Memorandum for Mr. Mumford," 6.
51. Confidential Letter to the FBI Director, March 29, 1951, 3.
52. Memo to the FBI Director, December 3, 1951.
53. M. Ilin, *New Russia's Primer* (New York: Houghton Mifflin Company, 1931). Translated by Nucia Lodge and George. S. Counts.
54. Craig Kridel, Robert V. Bullough, Jr., and Paul Shaker, *Teachers and Mentors: Profiles of Distinguished Twentieth-Century Professors of Education* (New York: Garland Publishing, 1996), 237.
55. Ibid., 243.
56. Personal Interview with Ben Davidson, January 4, 1980. Davidson was a Labor Party and Liberal Party member, and a close friend of Counts.
57. Interview with Teachers College President Lawrence A. Cremin in his office, Sept. 25, 1979.
58. Ellen Condliffe Lagemann, "Prophecy or Profession? George S. Counts and the Social Study of Education," *American Journal of Education* 100 (1992): 137.
59. Personal Interview with Counts's daughter, Martha L. Counts, January 5, 1980.

# PART IV

## INTERPRETING EDUCATORS' LIVES

CHAPTER 11

# BEYOND LIFE WRITING

## Reflections on Biography and Historiography

**A. J. Angulo**

In May 2001, I attended a conference on "The Craft of Biography" hosted by Harvard University's Charles Warren Center for Studies in American History. At the conference, historian Bernard Bailyn discussed the challenges of writing *The Ordeal of Thomas Hutchinson*. He concluded his talk with a surprising and memorable comment: there are really only three reasons why anyone should bother writing a biography. One reason, he argued, was that the subject must have influenced the course of history. Lives in this category have left an imprint on a branch of history—whether political, intellectual, economic, religious, and so forth—in some significant way. Second, if not a significant participant in recorded history, the figure must give special insight into the experiences and interests of large numbers of people. In this case, the life becomes a means through which we can improve our understanding of broader social movements and realities. Third, if neither of the first two applies, the life must have been witness to a significant historical event. By this standard, the selection of the subject is almost wholly dependent on the extent and quality of records the subject left behind.[1]

At the time, I was conducting research for what became *William Barton Rogers and the Idea of MIT*. What struck me right away about Bailyn's rea-

*Life Stories: Exploring Issues in Educational History Through Biography*
pp. 217–232

sons was how each of them applied to Rogers. I'd learned enough about Rogers by this point to know that his life had historiographical value well beyond his most oft-cited claim to distinction—that he was the conceptual founder of the Massachusetts Institute of Technology. He was also a nineteenth century scientist—a geologist and physicist—who spent half of his career at William and Mary and the University of Virginia, who directed the Virginia Geological Survey, who was active in the professionalization of science, and who later left the South as the Civil War approached, began anew in Massachusetts, and went on to establish MIT. What drew me to this subject was the way in which his life intersected with broader concerns (and even heated debates) in the historiography.[2]

This essay will consider three of these intersections and how they align with Bailyn's heuristic. First, there's the traditional interpretation of MIT's origins. I suggest below that our understanding of this contribution to educational history has been wedded unnecessarily to macro-level developments in mid-nineteenth century America; in essence, scholars have ignored a critical, biographical perspective—the life experiences and intellectual history of the founder—that offers a much more satisfactory explanation for why and how the institution came into being. Second, Rogers participated in a broad-based movement to bring about the professionalization of science. His approach to scientific inquiry sidestepped well-established categories created by historians of science, providing an alternative glimpse into the lives of scientists of the era. Finally, Rogers' life as an educator and researcher in Virginia engages a longstanding debate in southern history. Some scholars have viewed the Old South as romantic and unscientific, perhaps even hostile to science; others vehemently reject this view; very few have made much use of biography to engage either side. Rogers served as a crucial witness to the development of southern science and higher education in the years leading up to the Civil War, and his letters and papers offer a new dimension to this historiographical controversy.

## A LIFE IN EDUCATION

Rogers' idea of MIT was a hotly contested and, yet, highly influential model in higher education history. It was controversial to classicists and scientists alike, but influential in shaping the discourse and, at many institutions, the practice of science and scientific instruction. The forces and principles that brought this institution into existence, however, have largely been misunderstood in the literature.[3]

Historians of higher education have long dubbed MIT as a product of mid-nineteenth century American utilitarianism. This claim is present in classic as well as recent histories of American colleges and universities. According to classic works by Frederick Rudolph (*The American College and University: A History* and *Curriculum: A History of the Undergraduate Course of Study Since 1636*), the Institute emerged as a result of the Land-Grant Act of 1862. MIT, argues Rudolph, came into existence because "state legislatures were supporting higher education of a more popular nature than the old time college with its religious orientation and adherence to the classical course of study." More recent work by Roger Geiger extends this interpretation. Geiger suggests that MIT's origins are linked to an antebellum technical education movement and the ultra-utilitarian ideals the movement represented. The Institute, rooted in the "useful knowledge tradition," had a "technical" mission that "secured sponsorship from among the industrial and intellectual elite of Boston" and, thus, secured "public support as Massachusetts's land-grant engineering school." This story reappears in John Thelin's *A History of American Higher Education*. Thelin reminds us of the "useful education" and the "practical education" that was promoted by Justin Morrill's act through institutions like MIT.[4]

While the literature has focused on the populist, technical, land-grant aspects of the Institute's origins, scholars have overlooked the life of its founder and the founding documents he produced. The absence of a biographical study on Rogers (and, until recently, a substantive institutional history of MIT) has left the principal agent in the story silent and invisible.[5]

A cursory review of Rogers' early career as an educator is sufficient to illustrate that the land grant movement was virtually irrelevant to the origins of MIT. The idea of the Institute came about long before any talk of granting western lands for the benefit of east coast colleges. Its origins can be traced back to Rogers' first faculty appointment at the Maryland Institute in 1827. After having studied science under his father at William and Mary, he became an instructor at the Maryland Institute in Baltimore where he taught courses on mathematics, physics, chemistry, and astronomy. The Institute was a short-lived experiment that offered popular scientific lectures to the general community, but its impact on Rogers had great staying power. It launched his thinking about the need for an institution that promoted "scientific information" without the typical trappings of the classical college and its curriculum centered on Latin and Greek. Without question, his experiences in Baltimore were formative.[6]

His stint at the Maryland Institute sparked a lifelong passion for educational reform out of which a series of proposals for the establishment of his own "polytechnic" institute were developed. Each of these proposals emphasized the need to teach practical and theoretical sciences for the preparation of the next generation of scientists. He drafted his first formal plan in 1837 for the Franklin Institute in Pennsylvania. By this time,

Rogers was a professor of science at the University of Virginia, an institution that provided great freedom to teach and conduct research in the sciences—more so than almost any other antebellum college. Nevertheless, he believed that a distinct institution was necessary for the kind of studies he envisioned. In this "School of Arts" proposal for the Franklin Institute, he wanted to offer future scientists, engineers, mechanics, and others a professional scientific education. The proposal faded into the mist of a financial panic that hit the state and the country, but he refined the ideas and built on them for a second proposal: "Plan for a Polytechnic School in Boston (1846)." Rogers sent the plan to John A. Lowell of the Lowell Institute and redoubled his efforts to promote a professional scientific education. Although Lowell gave it a cool reception, a very similar program was established at Harvard as the Lawrence Scientific School in 1847. It's highly probable that Lowell shared the plans with Abbott Lawrence, a close business associate of Lowell's, who then pressed the idea, accompanied by a generous endowment, in Cambridge. Rogers closely monitored developments at Lawrence and noted how its most dominant member, Louis Agassiz, had recast the school in his own image. Agassiz pushed for basic research and science and thwarted the mission of offering a broad professional scientific education. This gave Rogers a final opening in 1860 to propose a third and final three-part plan (e.g., research, teaching, and service) for a Massachusetts Institute of Technology, a plan that was approved by the state legislature and chartered the following year.[7]

The original program of study offered by the Institute reflected Rogers' dual approach to scientific inquiry based on theory and practice. His objective, put simply, was to offer more breadth and depth in scientific training than any other institution in America. That meant more practical and more theoretical work than any course of study taught elsewhere. He laid out this vision in two documents, now known as the *Objects and Plan* (1860) and the *Scope and Plan* (1864). MIT's Bachelor's of Science, he explained, would be a four-year degree program. The first two years of formal study focused on general scientific theories, followed by another two years of specialized course work in either applied or basic science. Rogers described it as a plan that began with "fundamental principles" and led to a "systematic training in applied sciences" or "advanced" studies. Students could specialize in one of several areas: chemistry, geology, architecture, two kinds of engineering (civil and topographical; mechanical), and "general science and literature," a theory-oriented degree concentration.[8]

Rogers' early career and reform efforts provide an important corrective to the two main impressions that have been well-established in the historiography of American higher education: that MIT is inextricably linked to the land-grant movement and that MIT was essentially fitted for practical, utilitarian studies. Neither assertion can be reconciled with Rogers' life in education. He began proposing educational reforms in the 1830s and continued this line of work until the founding of MIT in 1861 (a year before the Morrill Act). What's more, it would be a mistake to characterize the work at the Institute as applied or utilitarian. Rogers approached scientific instruction through a combination of both theory and practice. In his last speech at MIT in 1882, he reminded listeners that "formerly a wide separation existed between theory and practice. Now in every fabric that is made, every structure that is reared, they are closely united into one interlocking system—the practical is based on the scientific, and the scientific is solidly built upon the practical." He saw MIT playing a central role in bringing together these branches of science. The founding seal he'd created for the institution many years earlier (and still in use today) captured his belief in the need for both theory and practice.[9]

Rogers' dual aims for the Institute, as portrayed in his life's work and represented in the seal, complicates traditional interpretations in the historiography. Biography, in this case, highlights this complexity and informs our understanding of the experiences that led to the idea of the Institute. This is significant, according to Bailyn's first rationale, largely because Rogers' idea had long-term consequences for the scope and development of American higher education.

## A LIFE IN SCIENCE

While Rogers' life refashions our understanding of MIT's origins, his participation in the professionalization of American science engages two basic claims made by historians of science: one intellectual, the other social. His life intersects with an important intellectual claim about how scientists of the early to mid-nineteenth century thought about science. His approach to research as well as statements about the synergy between the instrumental and the theoretical have direct implications for established categories in the literature. The social claim has to do with the process of professionalization. Rogers took part in profession-building activities, and this dimension of his life adds nuance and texture to the historiography.

Historians of science have written extensively on an intellectual divide that existed in early nineteenth century American science between Baconians and Humboldtians. Followers of Francis Bacon generally focused on fact-collecting, as opposed to theory-building. Baconians tended to shy away from grand speculation and preferred instead to gather data, specimens, observations, and so on, as if to create a storehouse of knowledge for later generations. Their view, in short, was that scientists should refrain from constructing theories in such areas as zoology or botany until all the facts were in. Great museums and collections were built around this tendency. Consider, for instance, the storied Museum of Comparative Zoology and Botanical Gardens at Harvard. These became leading repositories of facts. In the case of the MCZ, this meant thousands of jars containing all manner of animal specimens at different stages of development. In the case of the Gardens, it meant bundles of grasses, drawers bristling with flowers, envelopes brimming with seeds. An inductive approach to science carried the day in these repositories. At the same time, those who followed Alexander von Humboldt, the German naturalist and explorer, found the Baconian project wanting. As early as 1805, Humboldt chided those concerned "exclusively with the descriptive science and collecting." Instead, he aimed for a "terrestrial physics" to discover "the great and constant laws of nature." What good was a rock found in the Andes, wondered Humboldtians, without an understanding of the many forces and phenomena surrounding the rock and its environs? The real task of the scientist, they argued, was to develop a theoretical understanding, something generalizable or at least something with the potential for generalization.[10]

Rogers doesn't fit neatly into either dominant category discussed by historians of science. His approach to science gives rise to an alternative perspective identified in *William Barton Rogers and the Idea of MIT* as the "useful arts." The useful arts, to his mind, meant an appreciation for the advancement of practical *as well as* theoretical knowledge. He viewed these bodies of knowledge as separate and distinct, both of which were essential for the full understanding of natural phenomena and the improvement of the human condition. The useful arts also stood for the belief that the exploration of practical and theoretical scientific knowledge as separate fields of inquiry would naturally yield insights into the interrelationship between the two. Theory could inform practice and practice could inform theory. On these matters, Rogers was no systematic philosopher of science and, therefore, the concepts of theory and practice aren't defined with precision in his personal and professional papers. But when he talked in terms of theory, he often referred to "general laws" and "principles" of science. He viewed his own theories as reaching beyond fact-gathering and into the realm of generalization. When discussing practice, Rogers described "practical lessons" or the "applications" of knowledge for practical purposes. He believed that the everyday practical concerns of nineteenth century Americans, from farmers to engineers, could be improved by the deliberate exploration and refinement of practical knowledge. These were the convictions that stood at the center of what Rogers meant by the useful arts.[11]

His scientific activities in geology and natural philosophy were firmly rooted in the useful arts tradition. His geological research on the Survey of Virginia, an internal improvements project of the antebellum period, offers a good illustration of this approach. As director of the Survey, Rogers explicitly aimed for the advancement of practical and theoretical knowledge. The practical knowledge produced by the project had implications for agriculturists, miners, builders, and architects. Those working in agriculture, for instance, stood to benefit from Rogers' soil analyses and stratigraphic studies that dispelled certain myths about farming prevalent in the early to mid nineteenth century. At the same time, he was engaged in a separate and distinct process of constructing a theory about mountain chain formation. As the survey moved from east to west, from farmland to the Appalachian Mountains, Rogers turned his attention to the theoretical debates in geology then occurring in Europe. With one of his three brothers, he produced a "wave theory" that generalized about the formation of all mountain chains across the globe.[12]

The historiographical significance of Rogers' research is that it gives insight into a circle of scientists who moved beyond the Baconian-Humboldtian divide. This circle generally understood the useful arts as having to do with the application of knowledge for practical purposes. Some emphasized knowledge in the definition, such as the concepts, theories, and ideas of science. Others emphasized the practical applications, as in the tools, methods, and machinery that science was perceived to produce. Still others, like physicist Joseph Henry, understood the useful arts to represent a balance between theory and practice that approximated Rogers' own use of the phrase. As Henry put it, "We have practical men in great numbers without theory and theoretic men without practice. Now, it is evidently the union of these two in the same individual from whom we must expect the greatest and most successful efforts of art." Rogers, Henry, and other adherents of the useful arts persuasion developed patterns and values that tended to blend mainline Baconian-Humboldtian approaches.[13]

This useful arts approach to science clearly distinguished Rogers from a number of well-studied scientists of his generation, such as Louis Agassiz and Jacob Bigelow. On the one hand, Agassiz, a zoologist and natural historian, can be accurately described as representing the nineteenth century impulses for basic research. Little in his scientific thought aimed at producing knowledge that was applied in nature. In the 1840s, when he accepted a position at Harvard's Lawrence School of Science, Agassiz steered the program toward basic and theoretical interests. Jacob Bigelow, on the other hand, was a physician and professor of medicine at Harvard who advocated an ultra-utilitarian approach to science. He believed scientists should work on "ameliorating the condition of the human race, from the want of any solid and sustaining basis of practical utility." Rogers' useful arts ideal was not merely a median point between Agassiz and Bigelow, but, rather, a composite of the two. Eschewing the partisan rhetoric of both, Rogers displayed across his career an interest in the goals of basic, theoretical research as well as practical knowledge.[14]

As with his scientific activities, the useful arts came to define Rogers' approach to the professionalization of science. Historians have long considered profession-building as "the most significant development of nineteenth century American science." Rogers helped organize and lead the American Association for Geologists and Naturalists, American Association for the Advancement of Science, the National Academy of Sciences, and other local, national, and international organizations. Across most of his career, however, his useful arts ideals clashed with the values held by the self-proclaimed Lazzaroni, a group of elite American scientists. The Lazzaroni, headed by Alexander Dallas Bache, Superintendent of the United States Coast Survey, were influential in national-level science. In their effort to distinguish American scientists from "charlatans" and to mirror the attention given to theory in European science, Bache and his cohort privileged theoreticians (at the expense of practitioners) in American science organizations. Rogers offered an alternate vision, one based on the useful arts. While also concerned with the prevalence of charlatans in America and the state of science in Europe, he viewed practical scientists as essential to the comprehensive exploration of scientific knowledge. He valued the interactions between theoreticians and practitioners as much as he valued the interactions between theoretical and practical ideas in his own research. Rogers' experiences with the professionalization of science reveal the role played by the useful arts as an organizing theme in the American scientific community. They illustrate the conflicting values, aims, and ambitions of this generation of scientists.[15]

Rogers' clashes with the Lazzaroni add to the historiographical discourse over whether the elite group existed at all. Historians March Beach and Robert V. Bruce, for example, have separately examined the characteristics of this cohort and have reached differing conclusions. Beach's still-provocative analysis argues that no such cabal ever existed. His work points to evidence that suggests that the Lazzaroni rarely met as a group and rarely agreed on matters concerning education, control of the American Association for the Advancement of Science, the establishment of the Dudley Observatory, and the founding of the National Academy of Sciences. Based on this lack of cohesiveness and internal consistency, Beach concludes that these scientists wielded less power as a group than historians have previously attributed to them. Bruce's research, however, paints a different picture. In his response to Beach, Bruce claims that members of the Lazzaroni "did see one or another of the group often, they had close professional ties, they corresponded voluminously, and—what is most telling—they consciously saw themselves as a brotherhood, united in promoting the scientific enterprise in America along organized, European lines." While the Lazzaroni can't be said to have been monolithic on every concern, Rogers' conflicts with them indicate that they closed ranks when they were opposed, particularly when faced with a useful arts proponent such as Rogers. While there were many minor clashes, the most prominent involved a "constitutional crisis" at the American Association for the Advancement of Science in the 1850s and the founding and membership of the National Academy of Sciences in the 1860s. Rogers' emphasis on both theory and practice challenged the Lazzaroni's European-styled ambitions for organizing the science community and established a useful arts undercurrent in nineteenth century professionalization.[16]

## A LIFE IN THE OLD SOUTH

As with the history of education and history of science, Rogers' life adds a valuable perspective to our understanding of southern history. In this case, scholars have for decades debated a central point: Was antebellum southern culture anti-intellectual and, more specifically, inimical to science and educational reform?

On the one hand, a solid line of scholarship states emphatically that slavery impeded the development of science and education in the Old South. Samuel Eliot Morrison and Thomas Cary Johnson touched off the scholarly quarrel in the early twentieth century. Johnson took personally Morrison's interpretation that conditions in antebellum southern states worked against creative and scientific thought. In response, Johnson wrote *Scientific Interests in the Old South* to defend the region's achievements. His study sought to uncover "the fact" that in the 60 years before the Civil War "those people of the Southern States … were intensely interested in the exploration and mystery of the forces of nature." Mid-twentieth century scholarship followed Morrison's interpretation with Clement Eaton's depiction of the southern mind as largely romantic and unscientific. In his *Freedom-of-thought Struggle in the Old South* and *The Mind of the Old South*, science languished under the medieval imagination of plantation communities. His influential works defined the problem in terms of the demise of liberal philosophy. Southern political culture of the late eighteenth century, he argued, commonly identified with Enlightenment beliefs centered on reason, tolerance, and cosmopolitanism. Yet, by the early nineteenth century, the values had transformed into a form of "benightedness" centered on emotionalism, hyper-sensitivity, and provincialism. The transformation, he noted, loomed large for scientists in slaveholding societies who encountered isolation or even blatant opposition, such as intimidation and violence, to their teaching and research. Other writers of Eaton's period emphasized the way the Old South's sensitivity to northern criticism on the slavery issue extended to other areas of thought. "From the taboo on criticism of slavery," argued journalist and historian Wilbur Cash, "it was but an easy step to interpreting every criticism of the South on whatever score as disloyalty—to making such criticisms so dangerous that none but a madman would risk it." Conformity and consensus, described Cash, came to dominate southern life. In such an environment, scientists struggled to advance interests that required free inquiry and debate. Later studies by historians like George H. Daniels (1968), Drew Faust (1977), John McCardell (1979), John C. Green (1984), and Robert V. Bruce (1987) continued the line of scholarship that emphasized the lack of science in the Old South.[17]

Recent scholarship has returned to the debate by probing more deeply into the lives of the Joseph LeContes, John Bachmans, and other scientists of note from the antebellum period. As Ronald and Janet Numbers have argued, the accomplishments of these scientists show "there are few historical or logical reasons for suspecting that slavery per se inhibits science." In their reappraisal of science in the Old South, Numbers and Numbers assert that science developed firm roots in the region. Lester D. Stephens' more recent assessment takes their idea one step further, declaring that "only three other cities in the United States ... exceeded Charleston in natural history studies." According to Stephens, historians have overlooked the productive circle of naturalists in Charleston that included Edmund Ravenel, John Edwards Holbrook, Lewis Gibbes, Francis Holmes, John McGrady, and John Bachman. Admitting to a comparatively lower output of scientific research in the Old South, Stephens nevertheless maintained that "factors other than slavery" were at fault.[18]

Rogers' exposure to southern civilization makes him a special witness to events leading up to the Civil War. He studied at the College of William and Mary (1819–1821), assumed a science professorship at the same institution (1828–1835), and moved to a natural philosophy professorship at the University of Virginia (1835–1853) before leaving for Massachusetts where he lived until his death in 1882. This means that he lived, worked, taught, and conducted research for almost 34 years in the Old South.[19]

He came away from his southern experience with the belief that the culture of slavery significantly impeded the development of education and science. It detracted from education for the same reason Thomas Jefferson believed that slavery had a negative impact on the cultural development of the South. Jefferson once said that "The whole commerce between master and slave is a perpetual exercise of the most boisterous passions, the most unremitting despotism on the one part, and degrading submissions on the other." For him, the impropriety of slavery was not the injustice to African Americans. Jefferson owned slaves and, although he had misgivings about the institution, didn't free them. Rather, the problem was that "Our children see this, and learn to imitate it ... puts on the same airs ... [and] gives loose to his worst passions." Rogers discovered exactly this problem in southern higher education as it related to the slave society's code of honor. Southern students, he observed, often lost control of their passions if a professor failed to treat these individuals as sons of a master class. The institution of slavery had made them terribly sensitive to any commands made by faculty. If a student viewed an order or command as a breech in the code of honor, faculty would expect a fierce response.[20]

His first discovery of student "passions" that detracted from the learning environment was during his student years. One of his peers, John A. Dabney, was reprimanded by Rogers' father, Patrick Kerr, for whispering in class. As soon as the student was reprimanded, Dabney began to demand "satisfaction." His honor challenged, Dabney looked to settle the matter after class where he waved a menacing stick and shouted that "his gray hairs only, protected him from the Punishment which his Conduct merited." A scuffle followed.[21]

Witnessing his father in a brawl with a student gave Rogers (and gives us) insight into the problem of slavery and antebellum higher education, but it probably didn't prepare him for his own encounters with student "passions." After replacing his father at William and Mary, Rogers experienced first hand surprisingly violent manifestations of slave culture. On one occasion, he found himself at the receiving end of a loaded pistol. The confrontation began when student Charles Byrd had been disciplined for riding a horse inside a campus building. Rogers described the enraged student as having a stick in one hand and a pistol in the other, addressing the professor in "the rudest and most insulting language" and "demanding satisfaction" from Rogers for injuring his honor. Byrd stated that he "had a mind to cowhide" Rogers, an allusion to the punishment typically given to slaves. The professor fled to his apartment on campus; the student followed, and, while slamming against the professor's door, Byrd promised to shoot Rogers. In the end, the faculty voted to submit the case for legal prosecution, but it began wearing Rogers' patience thin. So too did the events he witnessed in Charlottesville. During his tenure at the University of Virginia, he saw eminent professors like mathematician James Joseph Sylvester driven away because of student "passions." He battled the Virginia Assembly's attempts to cut funding for the university—and even permanently shutter Jefferson's experiment—because of rioting and disturbances on the campus. He grieved over the fatal shooting of the institution's president (then called chairman) John A. G. Davis during another student rebellion.[22]

Rogers' experiences indicate that the slave-related cultural problem faced in the Old South may have been a far larger and stronger force than recent scholars suggest. It affected campus life, as witnessed by Rogers and his father, but it also affected scientific research. As Director of the state's Geological Survey, Rogers faced annual funding problems by a legislature embroiled in sectional matters. Much of the difficulty had to do with the view that his research represented "Yankee" science, especially his exploration of coal in the western part of the state. Virginia leaders lost interest in the project as North-South tensions escalated. Comparing his survey to those being conducted in New England around the same time, he stated "But how sad the contrast experienced here.... I feel that I am but half-alive here, and am more than ever resolved, when able, to quit the scene for one more congenial to my tastes and more likely to promote my happiness." The Survey became another casualty in the culture war on the way to the Civil War when the Virginia Assembly cancelled its funding, denying Rogers the opportunity to finish the research, final analysis, and written report.[23]

To Rogers, these were problems emanating from slaveholding civilization not found to the same degree elsewhere in the nation. The intellectual energies, he believed, "have been *misapplied*. They have not been directed to the investigation of the best modes of elevating the *moral nature* of our citizens, of dispensing *truth* in all its purifying and en[n]obling influences." Rather, slavery had defeated attempts at "establishing that foundation of knowledge upon which every *permanently good* superstructure in government must be raised." The problem, in short, is that the South's defense of slavery had "devoted with all the energy of selfish passions, to the most futile energies to balancing and counterbalancing local interests and local prejudices." With these observations, Rogers concluded that the violence, intolerance, and anti-intellectualism of southern culture couldn't be reconciled with his personal goals as a scientist and as an educational reformer. So he left for Boston in 1853.[24]

Rogers' life enters the historiographical debate about the Old South by illustrating that a plan on the scale of MIT couldn't have been established in the region at that time. The culture of slavery—with its code of honor, violence, and lack of state interest in non-slavery related pursuits—made MIT, for Rogers, an impossibility. "Ever since I have known something of the knowledge-seeking spirit, and the intellectual capacities of the community in and around Boston," he sighed, "I have felt persuaded that of all places in the world it was the most certain to derive the highest benefits from a Polytechnic Institution." He was hardly alone. Other professors experienced similar struggles and gave similar reasons for leaving southern institutions of higher education before the Civil War. F.A.P. Barnard, John and Joseph LeConte, William T. Sherman and Francis Lieber all left before, during, or immediately after the Civil War. This scientific and educational "brain drain" can be described as the Southern Sieve, a movement of intellectuals out of the region that's well-documented by Rogers and has direct implications for historiographical debates about the Old South.[25]

## CONCLUSION

It would be difficult to overstate the significance of biography in relation to historiography in a case like William Barton Rogers. His life informs our understanding of history of education, history of science, and history of the Old South. His life experiences tell us something new about how MIT emerged, what scientists thought about science and professionalization, and how slavery affected science and education in the South before the Civil War. Rogers, as a biographical subject, also confirms the usefulness of Bailyn's three-part heuristic. That Rogers contributed to higher education history is clear with the establishment of MIT. His scientific research and professional activities illuminate the lives of other scientists who typically fall outside the dominant interpretive framework established by historians of science. And his observations about antebellum Virginia offer an unmistakable volley in the on-going debates over slavery, science, and education in the region.

What all this may suggest to those interested in either biography or historiography is that both biographers and historians should be alert to the ways in which these kinds of interrelationships exist. Without an adequate reading of the many bodies of historical scholarship that relate to a particular life, it's unlikely that biographers will have the breadth necessary to see how a subject challenges or reinforces traditional interpretations in the literature. It's more than an academic exercise; it's critical to why we should bother writing our biographies in the first place, as Bailyn explains it. What's more, the historiographical literature is too often guilty of making sweeping claims that don't align with the experiences of specific individuals. Biographies offer an essential counterpoint. They are vital to understanding whether a general interpretive framework from the historiography can withstand scrutiny at the individual level.

## NOTES

1. Bernard Bailyn, *The Ordeal of Thomas Hutchinson* (Cambridge: Belknap Press of Harvard University Press, 1974).
2. A. J. Angulo, *William Barton Rogers and the Idea of MIT* (Baltimore: Johns Hopkins University Press, 2009).
3. On MIT as a controversial and influential force in American higher education history, see A. J. Angulo, "The Initial Reception of MIT, 1861–1882," *Perspectives on the History of Higher Education* [formerly, *History of Higher Education Annual*] 26 (2007): 1–28. See also, Julius A. Stratton and Loretta Mannix, *Mind and Hand: The Birth of MIT* (Cambridge: MIT Press, 2005).
4. Frederick Rudolph, *The American College and University: A History* (New York: Alfred A. Knopf, 1962), 188; Frederick Rudolph, *Curriculum: A History of the American Undergraduate Course of Study Since 1636* (San Francisco, 1977); Roger Geiger, "The Rise and Fall of Useful Knowledge: Higher Education for Science, Agriculture, and the Mechanic Arts, 1850–1875," in *The American College in the Nineteenth Century*, ed., Geiger. (Nashville: Vanderbilt University Press, 2000), 154–155, 160; John R. Thelin, *A History of American Higher Education* (Baltimore: Johns Hopkins University Press, 2004), 77, 123. Most of the literature that bears directly on MIT has approached the Institute from an internalist perspective; see, for example, Samuel Prescott, *When MIT was Boston Tech* (Cambridge: MIT Press, 1954); Richard Rakes Shrock, *Geology at MIT, 1865–1965: A History of the First Hundred Years of Geology at Massachusetts Institute of Technology* (2 vols., Cambridge: MIT Press, 1977–1982); Silas W. Holman, "Massachusetts Institute of Technology," in *History of Higher Education in Massachusetts*, ed., George Gary Bush. (Washington, D.C.: G.P.O., 1891): 280–319; James P. Munroe, "The Beginning of the Massachusetts Institute of Technology," *Technology Quarterly* 1 (May 1888): 285–297.
5. For the most recent institutional history of MIT, see Stratton and Mannix, *Mind and Hand*.
6. Angulo, *Rogers and the Idea*, 1–2, 13–16.
7. Ibid., 71–85, 89–100.
8. Ibid., 89–100, 117–123.
9. Ibid., ix.
10. Nicholas Jardine, James A. Secord, and Emma C. Spary, eds., *Cultures of Natural History* (New York: Cambridge University Press, 1996) includes a cultural survey of approaches to nineteenth century natural history; Michael Dettelbach, "Humboldtian Science," in *Natural History*, eds., Jardine, et. al., 288–289. For a sampling of the literature on Baconianism in America, see George H. Daniels, *American Science in the Age of Jackson* (New York: Columbia University Press, 1968); John C. Greene, *American Science in the Age of Jefferson* (Ames: Iowa State University Press, 1984); Robert V. Bruce, *The Launching of Modern American Science* (New York: Knopf, 1987); Theodore Dwight Bozeman, *Protestants in an Age of Science: The Baconian Ideal and Antebellum Religious Thought* (Chapel Hill: University of North

Carolina Press, 1977); and Herbert Hovencamp, *Science and Religion in America, 1800–1860* (Philadelphia: University of Pennsylvania 1978).

11. For examples of Rogers' views on theory and practice, see the following: *Memorial for the Establishment of a School of Arts* (Philadelphia: J. Crissy, 1837), 8–9; "A Plan for a Polytechnic School in Boston [1846]," in *Life and Letters of William Barton Rogers*, ed., E. Savage. (2 vols., Boston: Houghton Mifflin and Co., 1898), I, 420 (cited hereafter as *LL*); *First Annual Catalogue of the Officers and Students and Programme of the Course of Instructions of the School of the Massachusetts Institute of Technology, 1865–6* (Boston: John Wilson and Sons, 1865), 23.
12. Angulo, *Rogers and the Idea*, 32–56.
13. Joseph Henry cited in Arthur P. Molella and Nathan Reingold, "Theorists and Ingenious Mechanics: Joseph Henry Defines Science," *Science Studies* 3 (October 1973): 333. Hugo Meier, "Technology and Democracy, 1800–1860," *The Mississippi Valley Historical Review* 43 (1957): 618; David Noble, *America by Design: Science, Technology, and the Rise of Corporate Capitalism* (New York: Knopf, 1977); Bibi Zorina Khan, "`The Progress of Science and the Useful Arts': Inventive Activity in the Antebellum Period" (PhD diss., UCLA, 1991); Joseph Kett, *The Pursuit of Knowledge Under Difficulties: From Self-Improvement to Adult Education in America, 1750–1990* (Stanford: Stanford University Press, 1994), 104; Geiger, ed., *The American College in the Nineteenth Century*, 154–155.
14. Edward Lurie, *Louis Agassiz: A Life in Science* (Baltimore: Johns Hopkins University Press, 1988); Clark A. Elliot and Margaret W. Rossiter, eds., *Science at Harvard University: Historical Perspectives* (Bethlehem: Lehigh University Press, 1992); Jacob Bigelow, "On Classical and Utilitarian Studies. Read Before the American Academy of Arts and Sciences, December 20, 1866," reprinted in *Modern Inquiries: Classical, Professional, and Miscellaneous*, ed., Bigelow. (Boston: Little, Brown, and Company, 1867), 46.
15. George H. Daniels, "The Process of Professionalization in American Science: The Emergent Period, 1820–1860," in *Science in America Since 1820*, ed., N. Reingold. (New York: Science History Publications, 1976), 63; Thomas L. Haskell, *The Emergence of Professional Social Science: The American Social Science Association and the Nineteenth Century Crisis of Authority* (Urbana: University of Illinois Press, 1977), 68–74; Sally Kohlstedt, *The Formation of the American Scientific Community: The American Association for the Advancement of Science, 1846–1860* (Urbana: University of Illinois Press, 1976), 156; Lilian B. Miller, in *The Lazzaroni: Science and Scientists in Mid-Nineteenth Century America* (Washington, D.C.: Smithsonian Institution Press, 1972).
16. March Beach, "Was There a Scientific Lazzaroni" in *Nineteenth Century American Science: A Reappraisal*, ed., George H. Daniels. (Evanston: Northwestern University Press, 1972), 115–132; Robert V. Bruce, *The Launching of Modern American Science* (New York: Knopf, 1987), 263–266.
17. Samuel Eliot Morrison, *The Oxford History of the United States* (Oxford: University Press, 1927); Thomas Cary Johnson, *Scientific Interests in the Old South* (New York: Appleton-Century, 1936), 10; Clement Eaton, *The Free-*

*dom-of-thought Struggle in the Old South* (New York: Harper & Row, 1964) and *The Mind of the Old South* (Baton Rouge: Louisiana State University Press, 1976); W. J. Cash, *The Mind of the South* (New York: Random House, 1941), 90; George H. Daniels, *American Science in the Age of Jackson* (New York: Columbia University Press, 1968); Drew Gilpin Faust, *A Sacred Circle: The Dilemma of the Intellectual in the Old South, 1840–1860* (Baltimore: Johns Hopkins University Press, 1977); John McCardell, *The Idea of a Southern Nation: Southern Nationalists and Southern Nationalism, 1830–1860* (New York: Norton, 1979); John C. Greene, *American Science in the Age of Jefferson* (Ames: Iowa State University Press, 1984); and Robert V. Bruce, *The Launching of Modern American Science* (New York: Knopf, 1987).

18. Lester D. Stephens, *Joseph LeConte: Gentle Prophet of Evolution* (Baton Rouge: Louisiana State University Press, 1982); Ronald L. Numbers and Janet S. Numbers, "Science in the Old South: A Reappraisal," *Journal of Southern History* 48 (1982): 184; Lester D. Stephens, *Science, Race, and Religion in the American South: John Bachman and the Charleston Circle of Naturalists, 1815–1895* (Chapel Hill: University of North Carolina Press, 2000), 2, 266.
19. Angulo, "Tenure in the Tumult," in *Rogers and the Idea*, 17–31.
20. A. J. Angulo, "William Barton Rogers and the Southern Sieve: Revisiting Science, Slavery, and Higher Learning in the Old South." *History of Education Quarterly* 45 (March 2005): 21.
21. Ibid.
22. Ibid., 22, 30–32.
23. Angulo, *Rogers and the Idea*, 22–26.
24. Ibid., 20–21.
25. William Barton Rogers to Henry Darwin Rogers, March 13, 1846, *LL I*, 259; William J. Chute, *Damn Yankee!: The First Career of Frederick A. P. Barnard, Educator, Scientist, Idealist* (Port Washington: Kennikat Press, 1978); E. Merton Coulter, "Why John and Joseph LeConte Left the University of Georgia, 1855–1856." *Georgia Historical Quarterly* 53 (1969): 18–40; Stanley P. Hirshson, *The White Tecumseh: A Biography of General William T. Sherman* (New York: J. Wiley, 1997); Charles R. Mack and Henry H. Lesesne, eds., *Francis Lieber and the Culture of the Mind* (Columbia: University of South Carolina Press, 2005).

CHAPTER 12

# CONTEXTUALIZING AND CONTESTING NATIONAL IDENTITIES

## Lillian de Lissa, 1885–1967

**Kay Whitehead**

When Lillian de Lissa retired as Principal of Gipsy Hill Training College in England in January 1947, her colleagues presented her with a testimonial, which read in part:

> We recognize with pride her magnificent work of helping to create in this country a demand for nursery schools, and of founding a College for teachers of young children. We remember that Gipsy Hill Training College was a pioneer college and suffered periods of great stress... We also remember Miss de Lissa's contribution to international understanding, especially in the field of education.[1]

Constructing a biography to encompass de Lissa's national and international influence, however, is a complex process. She was born in colonial New South Wales in 1885. By the time her career began, White women were counted as citizens in the newly federated Australia. She was a British subject by virtue of Australia's membership of the British Empire, and

*Life Stories: Exploring Issues in Educational History Through Biography*
pp. 233–252

she lived in England from 1917 until her death in 1967. Additionally, her personal and professional networks transcended both national and imperial borders. Interpretations of de Lissa's life and work varied over time and according to the country in which they were produced. American, Australian and British sources, for example, constructed de Lissa's national and international influence from different standpoints. It is thus difficult to define de Lissa "in terms of an identity, especially a national identity."[2]

De Lissa was one of a growing number of middle class women, among them many educators, whose careers crossed national boundaries in the early twentieth century. These women established webs of influence that linked independent White settler societies such as Australia and the United States as well as the "so-called [imperial] center." A transnational rather than a comparative or an international methodology is needed to encapsulate these complex links.[3] Transnational history is defined by Curthoys and Lake as "the study of the ways in which past lives and events have been shaped by processes and relationships that have transcended the borders of nation states."[4] This paper will use a transnational framework to explore the interconstitutive connections between various people and places that came within the ambit of Lillian de Lissa's life and work.

Julia and Montague de Lissa (a wine and spirit merchant) married in 1874 and brought up their family in Sydney, the capital city of the British colony of New South Wales, in the last quarter of the nineteenth century. Julia de Lissa had seven children, four of whom survived into adulthood. Lillian Daphne was born on 25th October 1885 and grew up with her older brother and sister, Osbourne and Ethel, and younger brother, Gerald in Woollahra, a suburb which "housed the 'select of the elite'."[5] Family members traveled back and forth between England and Australia, thereby indicating their wealth and their attachment to the imperial center. Remote White settler societies such as New South Wales were considered low in the imperial hierarchy, but there was an emerging colonial nationalism among the locally born White population. Matthews argues that Sydney's elite was "proud to be British and saw England and Australia as parts of a single empire."[6] This was the context in which Lillian spent her childhood and youth.

The de Lissas were portrayed as "an English family for generations interested in educational matters."[7] English families often "saw themselves as improving rough colonial society with their superior values and social standing."[8] At the same time, parents were concerned that "girls here are apt to grow up what they call Colonial, but in other words vulgar," so their exposure to such influences was carefully controlled.[9] Lillian and Ethel were educated at Riviere College, Woollahra, a private school for young ladies. Ethel's education continued at Sydney University and

Lillian enrolled at the Sydney Kindergarten Training College (also known as Froebel House), thereby beginning a life-long interest in early childhood education.[10]

Lillian trained with 28 students, seven of whom lived in Froebel House. The Principal, Frances Newton, had been recruited from the United States in 1902, an indication of the interest in American progressivism among reforming members of Sydney's elite. A graduate of the "Free Kindergarten Training School of Chicago" in 1890, she had also been much influenced by Dewey's work at the Chicago Laboratory School and his reinterpretation of Froebel's ideas to effect social reform.[11] She was a seminal influence on Lillian who graduated with distinction after two years and was "put in charge of" Ashfield free kindergarten for 18 months. This was followed by a "course of training preparing me to train teachers."[12]

There are several explanations of de Lissa's childhood and youth, not necessarily congruent, and her decision to enter the field of early childhood education. These retrospective accounts are embedded in the discourses of the era as well as the place in which they were constructed. There is also "interplay between what people are able to tell about their lives and what they perceive to be of interest to their audience."[13] As this paper will show, de Lissa had a keen sense of her audience and was ever diplomatic when it came to representing national identities.

In an interview with the *Daily Herald* in 1913, de Lissa stated that her "original plan was music as a career ... but I worked so hard it did not turn out well for my health. The kindergarten was pushed into notice as a sort of counter irritant; it became an absorbing interest."[14] The *Lone Hand* added, "It was with some consternation that her people realized that the 'balancer' had entirely tipped the scale."[15] Here, de Lissa is portrayed as thinking independently of her parents in the manner of an "Australian girl." The following issue of the *Lone Hand* argued that the "Australian girl" was modern, vivacious and self-possessed but also displayed "a quick warm sympathy" for others, whereas the "English girl" was said to be "plain, commonplace" and "more or less tainted with the appalling English superciliousness."[16] De Lissa integrated these understandings when she responded to the question why she "took up this work":

> To be very candid I was rather lordly about it. I thought it would be a nice way to do things for the poor little children, and I started the thing in a very snobbish sort of way. I went down to Woolloomooloo [free kindergarten] with the attitude of a Lady Bountiful. My mother had sent me to take up the work because I was specializing too much in music and she wanted me to have some other interest. Needless to say when I got close to the suffering of the people and realized all the hardships of their lives, my attitude soon

> changed.... Such suffering as kindergartners see makes one want to do and give all possible to make conditions better and happier for the people. What kindergarten work has meant to me is more than I can put into words. It has altered the outlook of my whole life. It has made all things different. It is rather a difficult thing to discuss.[17]

Her initial reason was located in the British tradition of middle class women's philanthropy but she re-positioned herself as a modern, progressive social reformer and "kindergartener," by which she meant a kindergarten teacher. By the 1930s, however, philanthropy had been professionalized and the focus of reform had shifted to the individual child. Thus, an Australian newspaper stated that de Lissa "first became interested in the problem of the pre-school child in industrial areas, when as a young girl, she used to teach and play with the children in the Woolloomooloo district."[18] Then in 1943 while on a lecture tour of the United States, American newspapers proposed that de Lissa had experienced an "idyllic girlhood 'down under'" and drew on contemporary preoccupations with modern youth and the generation gap to portray her as a rebellious Australian girl. "Miss de Lissa started out to be a Sydney Society girl. But one year while her well-to-do parents were 'back home' in England on holiday she enrolled in a training school for teachers there."[19] The *Oakland Tribune* stated that "lacking funds for fees, she earned her way as a pianist for the college and by teaching fellow students." De Lissa added that her American principal "encouraged me in every way and fortified me for the storm I anticipated with the return of my parents."[20] Writing for an English audience in 1957, however, de Lissa represented her girlhood as "English" though located in Australia.

> My parents were apprehensive of my undertaking professionally what they had previously indulged as a hobby; and they were soon more so at the prospect of my going to live in a city a thousand miles from home unchaperoned. Up to that time I had not been shopping or even to the kindergarten without a chaperone, as was customary in those days among English residents, who like my mother, strongly resisted the free-and-easy ways of Australians and clung tenaciously to English traditions.[21]

The city to which de Lissa referred was Adelaide, the capital city of South Australia. In September 1905 she and Newton were invited to Adelaide by Bertram Hawker to demonstrate kindergarten methods and generate interest among progressive educators, social reformers and philanthropists. The Kindergarten Union of South Australia (KUSA) was formed at a well-attended public meeting and 20-year old de Lissa was then employed to establish the first free kindergarten in the city. She took up her position as Director of the Franklin Street free kindergarten in January 1906.[22]

The free kindergarten movement in Australia, as elsewhere, was at the nexus of social and educational reform, and thus attracted many feminists. In Adelaide, de Lissa worked closely with KUSA secretary and leading feminist, Lucy Morice, so much so that she subsequently portrayed Morice as her "guide, philosopher and friend." Kindergartens were part of Morice's reform agenda and when she established the Women's Non-Party Political Association in 1909 and the School for Mothers in 1910, de Lissa served on their executive committees.[23] Nevertheless, the core of de Lissa's activism was educational reform which she believed led to social reform. With the benefit of hindsight in 1962, she wrote to an Australian friend,

> I do remember my enthusiasm for education and my unquenchable confidence in the possibility inherent in it in bringing about a new social order … I still believe that the education of the whole man is the only sound way of making for social wellbeing—slow as it inevitably is.[24]

De Lissa taught at the Franklin Street free kindergarten for only one year. For the following decade her role was two-fold. Firstly, she was General Director of KUSA and supervised the establishment of kindergartens. She was a passionate advocate of Froebelian methods and traveled widely in Australia to both learn and proselytize. In 1911, Western Australia's leading feminist, Bessie Rischbieth, invited her to Perth to demonstrate kindergarten methods. At a public meeting to consider the formation of a Kindergarten Union, "Miss de Lissa delivered an interesting discourse on the kindergarten, the training of teachers for the work, and the enormous benefits, social and national, which were to be derived from the teaching of young children under the Froebelian system."[25] In turn, in the wake of Australian federation in 1901, de Lissa's work was constructed as "vital to the wellbeing of any nation."[26] Her visit to Western Australia prompted one commentator to "wish she could be traveling Australia—with her power of inspiring enthusiasm—as a Federal Kindergartner."[27]

De Lissa's capacity to engage and inspire was already well honed by 1911 and lasted throughout her life. She was widely read, not only in educational matters, well-prepared, and often used humor (sometimes self-deprecating) at the beginning of her speeches to engage her audience. As the *Daily News* reported in 1911, "The lady who has a charming manner, also—unlike many whose paths lie in the direction of philanthropy—has a decided sense of the humorous."[28] De Lissa gave countless speeches, preferring a live audience over the new medium of radio. "When I can see my audience and the degree of the response, or boredom, or opposite, it helps me to know how to go on developing what I want to say and what changes to make."[29] These skills served de Lissa well in the second aspect of her work in Adelaide; that is Principal of the Kindergarten Training College (KTC).

The KTC was established on the same principles as the Sydney KTC and de Lissa always acknowledged her debt to Newton. She focused on the holistic development of the kindergartner; that is her head, heart and hands. Theory and practice were integrated in general and professional studies as well as practical teaching in the kindergartens. Indeed, teaching methods simulated those advocated in kindergartens. De Lissa's reports were peppered with quotations from American educators, especially Dewey, and her students also recalled the influence of American progressivism.[30] Her vision was that young women would graduate from the KTC with "a clear vision, a well-stocked and balanced mind, rich in culture, alert and interested, and eager in its search for truth, and ... a spirit of devotion to their country."[31] Kindergartners, therefore, would be both educational and social reformers.

Notwithstanding her enthusiasm, the first decade of de Lissa's work as a teacher educator was difficult. Some influential members of KUSA proposed that the KTC be amalgamated with the state training college, thereby depriving de Lissa of her position as Principal. At the annual general meeting in 1910, the 25 year old de Lissa was pitted against leading men, including the professorate of the University of Adelaide. Her uncharacteristically intemperate speech triggered questions in parliament the next day, but Morice, the consummate strategist, had deployed her feminist networks to attend and defeat the motion for amalgamation.[32]

In 1914, de Lissa was sponsored by Bertram Hawker to spend the year in Europe and the United States. She studied with Montessori in Rome and narrowly avoided being caught up in the hostilities at the outbreak of World War One when traveling to England to speak at the first Montessori conference. There, she replaced the keynote speaker, Edmond Holmes, at short notice. Some of England's leading progressive educators formed the New Ideals group at this conference, included de Lissa (and subsequently recruited her to establish the Gipsy Hill Training College in 1917). Unfortunately, de Lissa became ill in England, abandoned her plans to travel to the United States, and returned to Australia by mid-1915.[33]

Following her studies abroad, de Lissa determined to meld Froebelian and Montessorian methods in the kindergartens. In the midst of World War One she told kindergartners, all women of course, "that with us lies the work of bettering the country, building and safeguarding from within our nation that is costing so many lives to defend from without."[34] Yet, de Lissa decided to leave Australia for more remunerative work in England. Given national and imperial sensitivities, her career choice required careful justification. There was a widespread perception that there were fewer opportunities for highly skilled people in Australia so when asked whether she was "sorry" to leave, de Lissa responded "Yes… I would rather have worked in my own country had that been possible. But I am happy in the thought of my new sphere."[35] However, choosing an Australian to establish a British training college was deemed "proof that we are well up-to-date here."[36] Thus, by conceptualizing de Lissa's national identity as Australian, her future achievements could demonstrate that Australia was a modern, progressive nation. KUSA's annual report praised de Lissa's work in Adelaide generously and went a step further, positioning her as "one of the Empire Builders in Education."[37] For a new nation seeking power within the British Empire, de Lissa's projected influence could be simultaneously national and imperial. From an Australian perspective, de Lissa would be at the center of a web of influence, taking Australian ideas to Britain and many more countries besides.

In 1917 de Lissa traveled to England via the United States, making a point of visiting Hull House, Chicago, and meeting Jane Addams. Unlike many Australians who encountered prejudice on account of their colonial origins, the New Idealists embraced de Lissa and some such as Holmes served on GHTC's governing body. As a White woman with powerful networks de Lissa could thus move easily in English society. Belle Rennie, the founder of GHTC, joined Newton and Morice as one of de Lissa's confidantes.[38] When Rennie applied to the Board of Education for GHTC to be recognized as a training college, she cited de Lissa's KTC experience, her studies with Montessori, and subsequent report to the South Australian government as confirmation of "Miss de Lissa's status in the Commonwealth."[39] The new principal's Australian origins and Montessori Diploma were acknowledged at the opening ceremony and on GHTC's letterhead until about 1920.[40] Rarely thereafter, did de Lissa or others in England claim her national identity as Australian and, indeed, she returned to Australia only once in 1955.

After a brief courtship, de Lissa married Harold Turner Thompson, a Captain in the RAF and a sales manager in civilian life in December 1918. An Australian newspaper pointed out that the bride "was better known as Miss de Lissa" and, indeed, she retained her surname.[41] One of the College residences was re-organized to accommodate the newlyweds but there is no further public mention of Thompson's presence in de Lissa's life.[42] Given the rising postwar divorce rates, to which this couple contributed, it might be assumed that some wartime marriages "united men and women who were ill-matched."[43]

By 1924 de Lissa had purchased the "Old Cottage" at Oxshott and was spending her weekends and vacations there, indulging her passion for gardening. This "replica of an Old English Cottage … combined the picturesqueness of the past with the hygienic conveniences of the present."[44] According to Gipsy Hill students, the Old Cottage was "a real dream house made from 500-year-old oak beams and bricks. We thought Miss de Lissa's pictures, brass bowls and other treasures showed to advantage at [Gipsy Hill] but here, as the Americans say, they really 'Belong'."[45] These reports constructed de Lissa as a modern middle class woman and as English in her cultural and national identity.

Whereas marriage signaled the termination of paid employment for most middle class women, de Lissa's work as GHTC's Principal proceeded apace. The Board of Education regulated "voluntary" (private) training colleges such as GHTC. As the first college to cater specifically for nursery school and infant teachers, GHTC was granted "provisional" status and accorded considerable autonomy over curriculum content and examinations. The Board and external assessors moderated the results.

From the outset, GHTC was portrayed as "breaking new ground" in its focus on a mixture of progressive educational ideas that would bring about "the educational revival in England."[46] Initially, de Lissa drew on Froebel, Montessori, and Dewey in much the same manner as the KTC, and students had ongoing practical experience in the application of Froebelian and Montessorian methods at Rommany Nursery School which was attached to the College. Although students studied the same subjects as other training colleges, the rationale and content differed, especially in Biology and Hygiene. Biology's purpose was to develop the scientific skills and attitudes to study children in the manner advocated by Montessori, and Hygiene was conceptualized as a social science course that dealt with social conditions, wages, social services and so on.[47] Rennie later stated that the Board of Education "accepted and blessed various rather unconventional departures from ordinary training college procedures ... to bring out and foster personal qualities of independence, thoughtfulness and initiative to a greater degree than in ordinary institutional training."[48] Chief among these was the College Council, where students and lecturers shared equally in the general management of the College. GHTC was a democratic community.

Gipsy Hill's reputation as a pioneer college was thus established but its financial position was precarious. Rennie had originally acquired two Victorian mansions on the outskirts of London and with increasing student numbers, three more properties were leased. By 1921, debts had mounted to £10,000. A bequest and Rennie's donation of the balance saved the College but the leases were non-renewable after 1942. GHTC depended entirely on Board of Education grants and student fees, and was never able to accumulate the capital required to buy permanent premises. De Lissa (and Rennie as the College Treasurer) carried this burden for thirty years.[49]

The year 1927 brought permanent recognition by the Board of Education, which de Lissa identified as "our first big landmark." Shortly afterwards the Joint Education Board was formed and GHTC came under the University of London's jurisdiction. Thus Gipsy Hill was incorporated into mainstream British teacher education, and its examinations were more closely aligned with other training colleges. From de Lissa's perspective, the College was seminal to the "extension and development" of nursery education and much of what was "revolutionary" in GHTC's curriculum and pedagogy became "generally accepted" in the 1930s. However, democratic governance remained as a special feature of this institution.[50]

For de Lissa, 1927 was a landmark in her personal life as well as her work. She took advantage of the 1923 reforms to English divorce laws and in March 1927 filed for divorce, citing her husband's adultery at a hotel "on/about February 15/16 1927."[51] Thompson did not contest the case. Stone argues that

> By allowing a wife to divorce a husband because of a single act of adultery, Parliament had in practice made it easy for the rich to divorce by mutual consent. The way it was done was for the husband to provide his wife with the evidence of his adultery by a procedure known as a "hotel bill case."[52]

The reasons why de Lissa chose to end the marriage officially in 1927 are open to conjecture and neither she nor Thompson is known to have entered into long-term intimate relationships. Given the social stigma surrounding divorce, which intensified with the King's abdication to marry an American divorcee in 1936, the silence about this aspect of de Lissa's life is not surprising.[53]

Although her marital status was not common knowledge, de Lissa's empire-building work was reported privately among Australian friends and publicly in the press. In 1923, for example, Morice passed on "excellent news of Miss de Lissa" to Adelaide's daily newspaper: "At the great Imperial Conference on Education lately held in London, she was the only woman chosen to give an address, and her speech was printed verbatim in the *Times Educational Supplement*."[54] De Lissa articulated her long-held view that nursery schools made valuable contributions to "national life" and specially trained teachers were the keys to their success. She also described GHTC's innovative approach to teacher education.[55] In May 1924 de Lissa chaired a "propaganda meeting" at the British Empire Exhibition at Wembley.[56] These exhibitions were "designed as spectacular tourist attractions that would educate Britons and colonials alike on the extent, power and possibilities of the empire."[57] De Lissa was not speaking as an Australian, but under the auspices of the new Nursery School Association (NSA) whose object was to secure "the effective working of the [1918] Education Act as regards nursery schools."[58] Her "magnificent work of helping to create in this country a demand for nursery schools" would be carried out through this organization.

De Lissa was a key member of the NSA from its foundation in 1923. Besides presenting at its twice-yearly conferences, she participated in publicity campaigns, deputations to government departments and inquiries, and negotiations with other organizations. The NSA published three of her speeches as pamphlets, thereby indicating the alignment of their ideals.[59] Both focused on the education of the pre-school child (rather than infant care), advocated a range of methodologies, and believed that all children, not just poor children, should attend nursery school. The NSA thus resisted the National Society for Day Nurseries and the Froebel Society's requests for mergers. De Lissa was at the center of both discussions.[60] She became Chairman of the NSA in 1929 and was soon embroiled in a dispute with the NSA President, Margaret McMillan, which resulted in the latter's resignation. McMillan claimed that she was being treated as a "figurehead" by de Lissa and others, and that the NSA was doing "excellent work in well-to-do areas and also for teachers," but neglecting poor children.[61] Nevertheless, de Lissa and the NSA were active in the 1933–34 slum clearance campaign and lobbying for nursery schools on new housing estates.[62] When she resigned as Chairman in 1938, she was eulogized as "a most effective speaker on the Nursery School platform" and "a most competent Chairman."[63]

De Lissa's contribution to international understanding began with her students. Having long held the view that "teachers are not merely makers of men, but makers of society," in 1926 she added that they also needed "to have wide sympathies and to think internationally in terms of human brotherhood."[64] Like many, de Lissa feared another war and her anxieties escalated in 1931 when she took a year's sick leave and spent time in Europe. From Heidelberg she told her students, "Europe is more armed today than in 1914 ... nothing can save Europe from this catastrophe except education."[65] Gipsy Hill students soon responded by forming a League of Nations Union.[66]

A handful of "students from abroad" gave GHTC an international profile. Among the first was Bek Keng Chui from China. A reference to her as "our little Chinese student," however, is indicative that an imperial hierarchy was embedded in international understanding.[67] As Woollacott points out, White women's interactions with non-White people "underscored for them that being White meant being part of the imperial ruling elite."[68] Students from Canada, Denmark, Estonia, and Turkey, some sponsored by their governments, attended GHTC. Additionally, some British graduates "carried Gipsy Hill to the ends of the earth."[69] For example, much was made of a GHTC teacher's recruitment by Edna Noble White to set up the first Merrill-Palmer Nursery School in Detroit, and in 1926 the

College newsletter proudly announced that "still more Gipsy Hill students have 'Gone West', two of them to The Dalton School" in New York.[70] Although international students and graduates who worked abroad were a minute proportion of the cohort, they featured repeatedly in GHTC publicity and correspondence, including de Lissa's discussions with the Board of Education over the College's future. With the building leases due to expire in 1942, the College Governors launched a public appeal for £50,000 in March 1938. In order to support the appeal, the College's twenty-first birthday was a grand occasion. GHTC was constructed as a unique institution, "the first of its kind to prepare teachers for the nursery school movement" as well as making national and international contributions as suggested above.[71] The Duchess of Kent's presence implied that GHTC was important to the British Empire and Queen Mary's visit to the College in 1939 reinforced these connections.[72] News of the Duchess of Kent's visit reached Australia and gave rise to an article on de Lissa, entitled, "Nursery School expert in England: Sydney woman's work in establishing movement." This piece constructed de Lissa as an "Australian woman" who was now prominent in English national education and culture, the latter signified by her "charming home." The article also noted that de Lissa was about to publish a book on nursery schools.[73]

*Life in the Nursery School* was published in July 1939.[74] According to the Reader's Report, this "book by an English teacher on English schools and methods would be more popular than a translated account of similar books" in French and German.[75] There were many reviews in British, Australian, and American newspapers and journals, some of which acknowledged the author's Australian origins. The book was praised for its capacity to engage both mothers and teachers, and also for the breadth and balance that came from de Lissa's wide reading. Although she focused on the whole child, her scholarship indicated the increasing influence of psychology in the interwar years. The book sold well and its royalties were added to the Building Fund.[76] However, the outbreak of World War Two dashed all hope of a successful appeal.

Like many other training colleges, GHTC had to evacuate its buildings, which were subsequently destroyed in air raids. After some dislocation, de Lissa leased a mansion in Yorkshire for the remainder of the war years. As well as re-establishing GHTC, she was involved in organizing the mass evacuation of children from London and the emergency provision of wartime nursery schools.[77] Such was her national profile that she was invited to contribute to a series of articles on post war education in the *Times Educational Supplement* in 1942.[78] Then in March 1943 she traveled to the United States with the head of the women's section of the British Information Service, having been invited by the Child Study Association, Progressive Education Association and other groups.[79] De Lissa's three-month lecture tour was extended by popular demand to six months, and she spoke at mixed and women's gatherings across the country. In Detroit where she visited with her friend, Edna Noble White, her major public meeting was advertised as "War-time care of children—Britain answers our questions." In addition to the emergency provision of wartime nurseries, the flyer posed questions about women's war work, juvenile delinquency, the role of labor unions.[80] This tour was indicative not only of de Lissa's national profile but also her international standing.

As with de Lissa's departure from Australia in 1917, her 1943 lecture tour necessitated careful negotiation of national and imperial sensitivities. Goodman argues that "there remained among most Americans a visceral distrust of British motives" in World War Two.[81] De Lissa experienced this at the end of a meeting of 600–700 women in Pasadena, California, when two of them accused England of starting the war. They yelled loudly "We just won't go on being Santa Claus to England. Stop your wars yourself."[82] This incident was not reported in the American press and de Lissa did not take it to heart. She later commented to an Australian friend "There are such silly prejudices—both sides of the Atlantic."[83] Reports of her speeches in American newspapers were very positive and several identified her as "Australian-born" and "British."[84] These references to de Lissa's dual identity positioned her as an international authority rather than wholly British, and thus diluted the potential for British imperialism. They also implied a shared heritage between Australia and the United States as independent White settler societies.[85] As previously mentioned, her independent girlhood in Australia and her connections with American Frances Newton were emphasized in some newspapers. According to the *Oak Leaves*, "one guest said as Miss de Lissa left, 'If all ambassadors could kindle such friendly feelings for their countries as Miss de Lissa inspires in an hour's talk, it would be easy to achieve that neighborly international community'."[86] From an American perspective there was no evidence of English superiority in de Lissa's presentations, but from her British friend's viewpoint her English charm had conquered American brashness.

> I have thought of you such a lot being rushed about all over the States and always I have felt glad that it was you, with all your keenness and gracious personality, who had been chosen to represent us. They have plenty of keenness in the States, but I doubt if they have much of the other.[87]

Her lecture tour was represented by GHTC students as "the outstanding event of the year", and her diary and newspaper clippings were preserved by the College.[88] In Australia the *Sydney Morning Herald* made sure that its readers knew that de Lissa had formed her ideas in Australia before becoming "one of the leading authorities" in Britain, and that she was now passing them on to the Americans.[89]

De Lissa "nearly wept with joy" to see "the beauty of England" after the grueling tour.[90] She was 58 years old, thought that "a younger woman was needed to build up the work" at GHTC, and longed to retire. But the College was literally homeless. The Board of Education was keen that the College continue because of its "very good reputation." De Lissa and Rennie were faced with the options of either amalgamating with another training college or persuading a County Council to take over Gipsy Hill. The first option was rejected because it would compromise GHTC's distinctive curriculum and democratic governance. After fruitless discussions with two County Councils, de Lissa and Rennie decided that GHTC would have to close. However, with the support of the Board of Education, they eventually negotiated with the Surrey County Council to take over GHTC from mid-1946. De Lissa supervised its relocation from Yorkshire to Kingston Hill, a suburb of London, inducted her successor, Frances Batstone, and retired at the beginning of 1947.[91]

Although de Lissa ceased paid employment she did not sever her connections with the field of education. Ever concerned to support international understanding, she was involved in a British/American exchange teaching program under the auspices of the Ministry of Education and the English Speaking Union.[92] She continued committee work and chaired a National Union of Teachers (NUT) enquiry into early childhood education. In 1947, she predicted that she would have to write the report as the committee had "too poor a secretary for this."[93] She also mentioned that she was revising a draft for her forthcoming book. The 1944 Education Act had incorporated nursery schools into the national education system and both the NUT report and *Life in the Nursery School and Early Babyhood* focused on postwar reconstruction. De Lissa articulated views she had held from the beginning of her career, namely that "education and social progress must go hand in hand … The contribution men and women are able to make towards the enrichment of national and international life depends on the nature of the education they have received." Of course, teachers were the key to "building a future of national and international significance."[94]

De Lissa's commitments to GHTC graduates and students were also maintained throughout her retirement. Their parting gift was £50 to restock her garden which had been neglected during the war. Along with an invitation to inspect the new garden in 1948, graduates were forewarned that de Lissa …

> had already traced our likenesses in specific flowers. We feel we should go prepared to have some of our cherished personal illusions shattered. All

> flowers may be charming but if one thought one was a tulip, it would be so disheartening to be pointed out as a diminutive item in a rock garden.[95]

There is no record of illusions shattered or confirmed, and de Lissa maintained contact with some GHTC graduates personally, as well as the Old Students Association, which she chaired jointly with Batstone.[96] It was her intention to be a "guide, philosopher and friend" to Batstone and their relationship became one of mutual respect.[97]

Between 1947 and 1967 GHTC's Principal and former Principal cooperated in representing its past to students and graduates. De Lissa gave talks on the College's history to current students, checking beforehand "what, from the point of audience would be interesting points to include and what to omit."[98] She also wrote brief historical essays in College newsletters. In most accounts GHTC's raison d'etre was to "change the educational system" and its intellectual traditions were constructed as European. Montessori was always acknowledged and sometimes Holmes, but Froebelian influences were downplayed in the wake of World War Two. Although de Lissa's Australian origins were usually acknowledged, there was no indication that she had drawn on these experiences or on American progressivism. GHTC's curriculum was portrayed as innovative as was its democratic governance, but little was included about its influence internationally.[99] To have highlighted graduates who were employed abroad rather than in Britain would have seemed like a waste of scarce resources in an era of postwar teacher shortages.

In 1953, "old students and many other friends of the College" commissioned Gilbert Spencer to paint de Lissa's portrait, to be hung in the College hall. At the presentation ceremony, her progressive theory and practice, and her international profile were highlighted: Her name "was known in many lands"; she had received "a wonderful reception in the United States" and she had also "been invited to return to Australia next year." De Lissa's response began with characteristic humor, thanking Spencer for his "kindness" but "perhaps chiefly, for his great tact in deciding what to leave out."[100] She was equally tactful in this speech for she later wrote "nearly everyone thinks the portrait not only very unflattering, but that it misses the real 'me'! So, if the majority opinion is a true one, the future generations will not know what the maker of the College looked like!"[101] Perhaps she had this issue in mind when she commissioned a photographic portrait and presented it to KUSA at their Golden Jubilee celebrations in Adelaide in September 1955.

De Lissa was guest of honor at the KUSA celebrations and a picture book commemorating her as the maker of kindergartens (assisted by Morice and Hawker) was presented to every kindergarten child. Alas, upon meeting her, one little boy could not reconcile her "with the lady in the book … because as he said, 'YOU wear proper clothes'."[102] As this paper has shown, identity is always contextualized and contested, not the least by de Lissa. She had traveled to Australia on a British passport and is recorded as widowed in the shipping register.

The *Advertiser* re-introduced de Lissa to South Australians as "a woman who played an important part in the establishment of pre-school education in this state, and whose name is distinguished among educationists in the UK and the US."[103] She spent two very busy months in Adelaide, attending the opening of Lillian de Lissa House at the KTC, celebrating her seventieth birthday at a Garden Party, and delivering seven major speeches. Addressing professional women at the Lyceum Club, de Lissa claimed to be an Australian who was not simply abreast of ideas that were circulating within and across national borders but one from whom many ideas radiated during her career. She told of visitors from America and students from "China, Turkey, India, Denmark, Estonia and Canada" who studied at Gipsy Hill "so Australian influence traveled to these lands too." Graduates taught in Canada and the United States, and "a little bit of Australia" was left in Poland as a result of her "educational mission" after World War One. She concluded "it has been a wonderful privilege for me to have been able to take and spread abroad some of the inspiration I received here in Australia and the educational ideas and ideals that took shape during my professional work in this city of Adelaide."[104] Upon returning to England, however, de Lissa published an essay about her early work in Adelaide, (eliding the amalgamation dispute of 1909/10), along with an account of the jubilee celebrations. In contrast to her speech to the Lyceum Club, she simply stated that "Gipsy Hill students will be interested to know that their college is, in a sense, descended from the Adelaide one."[105]

De Lissa's pace of life slowed considerably after she returned from Australia. Her great joy was her garden and 1957 saw "the loveliest of lovely spring … never have I had so many primroses (carpets of them) or bluebells (great pools of blue)."[106] She entertained a steady stream of visitors including family members from Australia, GHTC graduates and even the adult children of KTC graduates. She had always been an avid reader, pronouncing in 1950 that "Churchill's second volume" was "splendid."[107] By 1960 she had resigned from most committees so "had far more leisure," but "life is duller for the lack of contacts the work brought me." She enjoyed the wireless and the new medium of television. However, she was "starving for someone who is interested in ideas and not only things!"[108] Increasingly frail and with prolonged bouts of illness, she employed a gardener and a housekeeper, but spent the last months of her life in a nursing home.

In 1966 Batstone lobbied unsuccessfully to have Lillian de Lissa included in the British New Years Honors list.[109] When she died on 16th October 1967, shortly before her eighty-second birthday, Batstone spoke at her funeral and a eulogy was published in the GHTC newsletter.[110] The NSA established a Lillian de Lissa Memorial fund and donated £500 to the new Lillian de Lissa Nursery School in Birmingham in 1972. Although those who decided the New Years Honors recipients must have contested de Lissa's national influence, the *Birmingham Post* proclaimed her as "one of Britain's greatest educational pioneers."[111] However, this paper has demonstrated that de Lissa's national identity was never fixed, but constructed in context. Her death was reported in Australia under the heading "World Pioneer in Nursery Education." The first sentence claimed that she "was distinguished among educators in the United Kingdom and United States as well as Australia." Entries claiming her as a significant Australian have subsequently appeared in the *Australian Dictionary of Biography, 200 Australian Women: A Redress Anthology* and books on Australian women pioneers in early childhood education.[112] Such are the transnational connections between people and places that marked de Lissa's life and work.

## NOTES

1. Tribute to Lillian de Lissa, De Lissa Graduates Association files, Curriculum Centre, University of South Australia, Magill Campus.
2. J. Matthews, "Modern Nomads and National Film History: The Multi-Continental Career of J. D. Williams," In *Connected Worlds: History in Transnational Perspective,* ed. A. Curthoys and M. Lake. (Canberra: Australian National University E Press, 2005): 167.
3. J. Goodman, "'Their Market Value Must be Greater for the Experience They had Gained': Secondary School Headmistresses and Empire, 1897–1914," In *Gender, Colonialism and Education: The Politics of Experience,* ed. J. Goodman and J. Martin. (London: Woburn Press, 2002): 188; See also A. Woollacott, *To Try Her Fortune in London: Australian Women, Colonialism and Modernity* (Oxford: Oxford University Press, 2001).
4. A. Curthoys and M. Lake, "Introduction," in Curthoys and Lake, *Connected Worlds,* 5.
5. New South Wales Registry of Births, Deaths and Marriages, available from http://www.bdm.nsw.gov.au/cgi-bin/IndexSearch?form=Indexing-Search&SessionID+98 INTERNET; J. Matthews, *Dance Hall & Picture Palace: Sydney's Romance with Modernity* (Sydney: Currency Press, 2005):193.
6. Matthews, *Dance Hall & Picture Palace,* 200; Woollacott, *To Try Her Fortune in London,* 16.
7. *Daily Herald* (Adelaide), 4 January, 1913: 13.

8. P. Russell, *A Wish of Distinction: Colonial Gentility and Femininity* (Melbourne: Melbourne University Press, 1994): 7.
9. Nora Young, quoted in K. Whitehead, "Women's Life-Work: Teachers in South Australia, 1836–1906," PhD Thesis, University of Adelaide, 1996: 62.
10. H. Jones, "The Acceptable Crusader: Lillian de Lissa and Pre-School Education in South Australia," In *Melbourne Studies in Education 1975, ed.* S. Murray-Smith. (Melbourne: Melbourne University Press, 1975): 126–129.
11. E. Russell, "What is the Kindergarten? Teaching the Froebel System in Australia." *New Idea,* 6 May, 1903: 794–795; see also Matthews, *Dance Hall & Picture Palace*, 202.
12. "Final Report of the Royal Commission on Education Together with Minutes of Proceedings, Evidence and Appendices," *South Australian Parliamentary Papers 1913*, No. 75: 122.
13. P. Summerfield, *Reconstructing Women's Wartime Lives: Discourse and Subjectivity in Oral Histories of the Second World War* (Manchester: Manchester University Press, 1998): 20.
14. *Daily Herald* (Adelaide), 4 January, 1913: 13.
15. *Lone Hand* (Adelaide), 1 February, 1913: xxxvi.
16. *Lone Hand* (Adelaide), 1 May, 1913: 54–55.
17. "Final Report of the Royal Commission on Education," 129.
18. Undated newspaper clipping, Edith Hubbe (Cook) and Marjorie Caw (Hubbe) Papers 1859–1988, MSS 0046/47/2, Barr Smith Library (BSL) Special Collection, University of Adelaide (hereafter Hubbe-Caw Papers, BSL).
19. *Daily Times* (Chicago), 21 April, 1943: 30.
20. *Oakland Tribune,* 21 June, 1943.
21. *Gipsy Hill Training College Newsletter,* June 1957: 2.
22. Jones, "The Acceptable Crusader," 127–137.
23. L. Trethewey, "Lucy Spence Morice: 'Mother of Kindergartens' in South Australia," *History of Education Review* 37, No. 2 (2008): 14–25.
24. L. de Lissa to Mrs Finniss, 4 June 1962, De Lissa Graduates Association files, Curriculum Centre, University of South Australia, Magill Campus.
25. *West Australian* (Perth), 16 September, 1911: 11.
26. *Lone Hand* (Adelaide), 1 February, 1913: xxxvi.
27. *Australian Kindergarten Magazine,* 11, no. 2 (1911): 5.
28. *Daily News* (Perth), 15 September, 1911: 8.
29. L. de Lissa to Miss Trevan-Hawke, undated, Gipsy Hill Training College Box 26, Kingston University Archives and Special Collections (hereafter GHTC Box 26).
30. K. Whitehead, "The Construction of Early Childhood Teachers' Professional Identities, Then and Now," *Australian Journal of Early Childhood* 33, No. 3 (2008): 35–36.
31. Kindergarten Union of South Australia Annual Report 1915/16: 8, State Library of South Australia (hereafter SLSA).
32. K. Whitehead, "'A Decided Disadvantage for the Kindergarten Students to Mix with the State Teachers'," *Paedagogica Historica* (in press).

33. Whitehead, "The Construction of Early Childhood Teachers' Professional Identities," 37.
34. L. de Lissa to Chairman of Kindergarten Union, 1 September 1915, Kindergarten Association of Western Australia, MN 525 Acc 2308A/159, J. S. Battye Library of West Australian History.
35. *Observer* (Adelaide), 24 February, 1917: 27; Woollacott, *To Try Her Fortune in London,* 6.
36. *Observer* (Adelaide), 24 February, 1917: 27.
37. Kindergarten Union of South Australia Annual Report 1916/17: 2, SLSA.
38. *Gipsy Hill Training College Newsletter,* June 1957: 2; See also Woollacott, *To Try Her Fortune in London,* 14, 34, 48.
39. B. Rennie to Secretary, Board of Education, 29 March 1917, 14 May 1917, GHTC Box 15.
40. *Times Educational Supplement,* 18 October, 1917: 400.
41. *Observer* (Adelaide), 12 April, 1919: 42.
42. *Gipsy Trail* no. 1, 1921–22: 12–14.
43. R. Phillips, *Putting Asunder: A History of Divorce in Western Society* (Cambridge: Cambridge University Press, 1988): 519.
44. Undated newspaper clipping, MSS 0046/47/2, Hubbe-Caw Papers, BSL.
45. *Wraggle-Taggles, One and All,* June 1925.
46. *Times Educational Supplement,* 18 October, 1917: 400.
47. Whitehead, "The Construction of Early Childhood Teachers' Professional Identities," 37–39.
48. B. Rennie to E. Wilkinson, 1 October 1945, Gipsy Hill Training College—General Correspondence 1946, ED 78/376, The National Archives of the United Kingdom (hereafter TNA).
49. Whitehead, "The Construction of Early Childhood Teachers' Professional Identities," 37–38.
50. *Gipsy Hill Training College Newsletter,* June 1958: 5–6.
51. Divorce Petition, Thompson, Lillian Daphne V Thompson Harold Turner, J77/2391, TNA.
52. L. Stone, *Road to Divorce: England 1530–1987* (Oxford: Oxford University Press, 1990): 397.
53. Phillips, *Putting Asunder,* 528.
54. Undated newspaper clipping, MSS 0046/47/4, Hubbe-Caw Papers, BSL.
55. *Times Educational Supplement,* 30 June, 1923: 305–306.
56. Nursery School Association First Annual Report, 1924:1, British Association of Early Childhood Education 22/1, London School of Economics (hereafter BAECE 22/1, LSE).
57. Woollacott, *To Try Her Fortune in London,* 149.
58. G. Owen, *Nursery School Education,* 3rd Edition (New York: E. P. Dutton and Co., 1928): 6.
59. See minutes 16 October 1936 and 22 January 1937, NSA Publications Committee Minutes 1936–1938, BAECE 21/6, LSE.
60. K. Nawrotzki, "'Froebel is Dead; Long Live Froebel!' The National Froebel Foundation and English Education," *History of Education* 35, No. 2 (2006): 214–215.

61. M. McMillan to L. de Lissa, 8 May 1929, 18 May 1929, Margaret McMillan correspondence 1927–1930 BAECE13/8, LSE.
62. *The Times*, 17 October, 1933: 10; Nursery School Association Twelfth Annual Report, 1935: 12, BAECE 22/3, LSE.
63. NSA Fifteenth Annual Report 1938: 1, BAECE 22/4, LSE.
64. *Gipsy Trail* no. 5, 1925–26: 2.
65. *Wraggle-Taggles, One and All,* November 1931, GHTC Box 3.
66. University of London. Training Colleges Delegacy, Visitation of Gipsy Hill Training College for Teachers of Young Children, 21 February 1933, ED 78/39, TNA; *Gipsy Trail* No. 14, 1934–35: 1.
67. *Gipsy Trail* No. 4, 1924–25:10–11.
68. Woollacott, *To Try Her Fortune in London,* 14.
69. *Gipsy Trail* No. 18, 1938–39: 3.
70. *Wraggle-Taggles, One and All,* May 1926, November 1926, GHTC Box 3.
71. *The Times,* 2 April, 1938: 8;11 November, 1938: 11; *Gipsy Trail* No. 18, 1938–39: 3.
72. *Gipsy Trail* No. 18, 1938–39: 2.
73. Undated newspaper clipping, MSS 0046/47/2, Hubbe-Caw Papers, BSL.
74. L. de Lissa, *Life in the Nursery School* (London: Longmans Green and Co.,1939).
75. "Extract from Reader's Report," GHTC Box 26.
76. Mr. Higham to L. de Lissa, 8 February 1940, and 11 November 1944 and also Newspaper Clippings Book, GHTC Box 26.
77. *Wraggle-Taggles, One and All,* Summer 1943, GHTC Box 3; *Gipsy Trail* no. 19, 1947–48: 3.
78. *Times Educational Supplement,* 24 January, 1942: 41; 31 January, 1942: 53.
79. *Washington Post,* 27 March, 1943: 1B.
80. See flyer in Merrill-Palmer Institute: Edna Noble White Collection Acc. 1066, Box 58, Folder 12, Archives of Labor and Urban Affairs, Wayne State University (hereafter Edna Noble White Papers, WSU).
81. D. Goodman, "Loving and Hating Britain: Rereading the Isolationist Debate in the USA," In *Britishness Abroad: Transnational Movements and Imperial Cultures,* ed. K. Darian-Smith, P. Grimshaw and S. Macintyre. (Melbourne: Melbourne University Press, 2007): 193.
82. L. de Lissa to M. Gutteridge, 9 June 1943, Box 58, Folder 14, Edna Noble White Papers, WSU.
83. L. de Lissa to M. Gutteridge, 19 November 1944, Box 58, Folder 13, Edna Noble White Papers, WSU.
84. See for example *Pasadena Star Times,* 6 July, 1943; *Los Angeles Times*, 4 June 1943: A5; *Chicago Daily Tribune*, 26 April, 1943: 22; *New York Times,* 11 March, 1943 in Newspaper Clippings Book, GHTC Box 26.
85. Curthoys and Lake, "Introduction," 10.
86. *Oak Leaves,* 6 May, 1943.
87. J. Boyce to L. de Lissa, 20 October 1943, GHTC Box 26.
88. *Wraggle-Taggles, One and All*, Summer 1943, GHTC Box 3; 'Diary of American Tour', GHTC Box 9; Newspaper Clippings Book, GHTC Box 26.
89. *Sydney Morning Herald,* undated, GHTC Box 9.

90. L. de Lissa to Mr Ayrton, 23 September 1943, GHTC Box 16.
91. L. de Lissa to Mr Woodhead, 26 May 1945, GHTC Box 16; Gipsy Hill Training College correspondence 1937–1945 ED 78/124, TNA; *Gipsy Trail* No. 19, 1947: 4.
92. *Advertiser,* 9 September, 1955: 10; L. de Lissa to M. Caw, 1 July 1956, MSS 0046/47/1, Hubbe-Caw Papers, BSL.
93. L. de Lissa to M. Caw, 17 December 1947, MSS 0046/47/1, Hubbe-Caw Papers, BSL.
94. L. de Lissa, *Life in the Nursery School and in Early Babyhood* (London: Longmans Green and Co.,1949): x; National Union of Teachers, *Nursery-Infant Education: Report of the Consultative Committee Appointed by the Executive of the National Union of Teachers* (London: Evans Bros Ltd, 1949).
95. *Wraggle-Taggles, One and All,* May 1948.
96. L. de Lissa to Old Students, undated, GHTC Box 3.
97. See correspondence in GHTC Box 10.
98. L. de Lissa to F. Batstone, undated, GHTC Box 10.
99. *Gipsy Hill Training College Newsletter,* June 1958: 2–8.
100. B. Rennie to Miss Trevan-Hawke, 27 October 1953, GHTC Box 3; *Presentation of the Portrait of Miss Lillian de Lissa, First Principal 1917–1947 by Gilbert Spencer, ARA* (Mayfield: The Mayfield Press, 1953): 1–6, GHTC Box 3.
101. L. de Lissa to F. Batstone, 23 June 1954, GHTC Box 10.
102. *Gipsy Hill Training College Newsletter,* June 1957: 4.
103. *Advertiser,* 9 September, 1955: 10.
104. *Talks Given by Lillian de Lissa at the Golden Jubilee of the Kindergarten Union of South Australia 1955* (Adelaide: Kindergarten Union of South Australia, 1975): 3–6.
105. *Gipsy Hill Training College Newsletter,* June 1957: 4.
106. L. de Lissa to M. Caw, 27 April 1957, MSS 0046/47/1, Hubbe-Caw Papers, BSL.
107. L. de Lissa to M. Caw, 19 March 1950, MSS 0046/47/1, Hubbe-Caw Papers, BSL.
108. L. de Lissa to K. Mellor and D. Hughes, 1 November 1960, and 24 February 1962, De Lissa Graduates Association files, Curriculum Centre, University of South Australia, Magill Campus.
109. See draft of application, 12 October 1966, GHTC Box 3.
110. *Gipsy Hill Training College Newsletter,* 1968: 5.
111. *Birmingham Post*, 26 April, 1972.
112. *Australian Dictionary of Biography,* Vol. 8 (Melbourne: Melbourne University Press): 273–274; H. Radi, *200 Australian Women: A Redress Anthology* (Sydney: Women's Redress Press Inc, 1988): 146; J. Waters, *With Passion, Perseverance and Practicality: 100 Women Who Influenced Australian Children's Services, 1841–2001* (Melbourne: OEMP Australia, 2002): 62–63.

CHAPTER 13

# NECESSARY BETRAYALS

## Reflections on Biographical Work on a Racist Ancestor

**Lucy E. Bailey**

*I sometimes feel like I'm betraying her*
*One hundred and fifty years after she wrote that first book.*

*"Julia" I call her,*
*though she usually signed her name "Author."*

*"Read with sympathy," she wrote in 1879 ...*
*though I've spent years doing the opposite:*

*pointing out her racist characters—her fear of immigrants—the white, always white kids in her stories who triumph over evil—her nature stories where even the ants become slaves.*

*How ironic, I've said, that all her books on how to clean house, how to be a proper woman, how to raise children were all written behind closed doors while her own children wandered on New England beaches, slid down hill-sides—and waited—for her to put down her pen.*

*Life Stories: Exploring Issues in Educational History Through Biography*
pp. 253–272

*Latch key kids before latch keys.*

*These are the kinds of things I say about this woman, this ancestor, this writer—dozens of books—2 children—fifty years behind closed doors.*

*And yet, I know,*
*as I sift through her pages and think about those years,*
*that every single word and every racist character she crafted*
*paved the way*
*for me*
*to write now-*

*paved the way*
*for me*
*to betray her.*

*I wonder who might read my writing one hundred and fifty years from now and what they will need to say.*

*Some betrayals are necessary.*

## INTRODUCTION

> Learn all you can about the authors whose books you read … read with sympathy. Throw yourself into the age and race of which you read, make the past present, and the distant near. [1]

The impetus for this methodological paper lies in my interests in qualitative, historical, and biographical scholarship and my belief in the value of theorizing the complex connections between researcher and subject for the conduct and representation of research. Although biographers have explored such connections in a variety of ways, including the motivational power of researchers' emotional bonds with their subjects, the limits of such affinities, and the complexity of researching and representing diverse subjects across time and place, I consider here the contours of a particular kind of researcher-subject relationship—ancestral connections—for approaching, analyzing and representing research.[2] I draw from Michelle Fine's useful construct, "working the hyphen" and reflections on my ongoing analysis of the life and writing of a nineteenth century ancestor to work various aspects of what I call the "genealogical hyphen" in interpretive work.[3] To Fine, the hyphen between researcher-subject symbolizes the enduring if sometimes imperceptible ways researchers are linked with those they study. Some researchers romanticize the complex links and affinities they perceive between researcher and subject; some leave such relationships under-theorized; others wrestle with the methodological possibilities and interpretive minefields such relationships present for the conduct of inquiry. I suggest that family relationships between researcher-subject present particular opportunities to consider how we as researchers speak "of" and "for" our fore fathers/mothers and when we must speak "through" them for other purposes.

In this paper, I consider methodological aspects of ancestral connections for the conduct of inquiry. Working the genealogical hyphen involves considering the cultural tendency to romanticize bloodlines, the particular purpose of the research enterprise, the type of "relationship" between researcher and subject, and the implications of familial representations. As part of this effort, I use Jean Patterson and Joseph Rayle's reflections on ancestral racism and descendent accountability to consider analysis of an ancestor's writing as a necessary anti-racist act.[4] This is a particular methodological choice, what might be considered a necessary betrayal of a woman immersed in a particular racial episteme, one of thousands seizing pens, who, arguably, paved the way for my own work today.[5] This focus might be considered a "betrayal" because this writer committed years of her life to forging a writing voice against a historical backdrop of gendered silencing. She took writing for women seriously, asking readers to "read with sympathy" and to throw themselves into the "age and race" of which they read.[6]

What might be considered an additional betrayal is that what seemed dear to this writer's identity—her family relationships and the values she espoused—hold little interest for me. I have always seen "her" work as a productive site to explore questions about the nineteenth century educational imagination, including how White women's writing constructed race. Indeed, my conviction is that our cultural tendency to romanticize bloodlines may undermine productive critical questions in inquiries that happen to involve family members. This point may be particularly important to consider in historical research on foremothers/fathers whose lives do not map on to conventional narratives of heroism and success. The purpose of a given study, the particular "relationship" between biographer-subject, and the methodological import of that aspect of subjectivity must determine the significance of a given relationship for the researcher endeavor.

In what follows, I begin by contextualizing my ancestor's work in White women's nineteenth century writing patterns, the racist elements of such texts, and the importance of highlighting our forefathers/mothers' racist legacies. I then describe the process of learning about this writer and what this memory reveals about the inherent silences and near misses that can occur in historical and biographical research. In the remainder of the paper, I work the genealogical hyphen, considering different ways of thinking about research on/with ancestors. I include brief excerpts from different genres of this writer's work to provide a glimpse of her writing. I conclude with the argument that researchers should remain vigilant in analyzing their investments so they can choose narrations that fit their research purpose and the life under study. As Michael Quinn Patton argues, purpose guides the research enterprise.[7] Romanticized constructions of subjects, particularly family members, may interfere with the general mission of the biographical enterprise: to narrate a life.

## WOMEN'S WRITING, RACE, AND REPRESENTATION

> Why pet, you cannot get the black from my skin … but God made my soul White, and I'm trying to keep it so. I do not want a black heart, I can tell you.[8]

This excerpt from a brief temperance lesson for children published in 1883 depicts a Black nurse speaking to an Anglo-Saxon child of her struggle to remain pure of heart. It provides an example of the way my ancestor constructed and mobilized race to serve pedagogical ends. In the tale, a mystified child attempts to scrub his nurse's Black skin free of its color and she gently responds, "why pet, you cannot get the Black from my skin." The author uses the nurse's Black body and White "heart" and "soul" as a springboard to aid White children in understanding differences between good and evil, Blackness and Whiteness, drinking and sobriety, nature and choice. The nurse in the tale is simply object and prop, frozen in servitude to a young White male citizen-in-the-making.[9] The author of this little lesson, who I refer to as Julia, was an educator (1840–1902) born and raised in New York state. During her 62 years of life, she received a private education, married a Presbyterian minister and professor, taught briefly in a women's college, and raised two children. She wrote an array of didactic novels, tracts, textbooks, and manuals of interest to women and children across a 46 year span, a period in which American women published in unprecedented numbers.[10]

Julia's writing, like that of other nineteenth century female authors, offers fraught contributions to women's history. On one hand, women's staggering educational and literary production during this century reflects changing educational fortunes and expanding professional opportunities for women worth noting and celebrating. Occupational opportunities such as authorship became increasingly available to primarily White[11] middle-class women throughout the century as literacy rates grew, the publishing industry expanded, the women's rights movement gained momentum, and the written word accrued value as a symbol of middle-class civility. Some women viewed authorship as a respectable alternative to teaching and an avenue to earn a modest income from the comfort and safety of their homes. The impossibility of pursuing higher education for the majority of American women heightened the value of printed texts, periodicals, and literary societies for women readers.[12] The public demanded texts and the publishing industry responded with zeal. The massive production of women's writing—novels, textbooks, histories, journal articles, children's books, didactic fiction, tracts—thus represents remarkable achievements for middle-class White women denied formal educational opportunities for centuries. It also represents meaningful opportunities for them to read, create, gain a public voice, and forge professional identities that had been unavailable to them previously.

Yet, White women's writing production during these years, however laudable a place it holds in American women's history, also perpetuated racist and xenophobic sentiment constitutive of an era of manifest destiny, slavery, and mass immigration. Texts that championed the domestic sphere and contributed to advancing White women's status in the nineteenth century were also riddled with racist constructions, ethnic caricatures, and assimilative imperatives.[13] Julia's work was no exception. As the excerpt of the Black nurse struggling to "keep her soul White" demonstrates, Julia often used flat and one-dimensional characters of color as springboards for lessons in sin and salvation for Anglo-Saxon characters. The mobilization of Black bodies as pedagogical tools seemed an unremarkable undertaking in her writing world, a tool no different from the insect collections, spelling words, and poetry another educator might use to facilitate White children's learning. Scholars argue that such belittling constructions of immigrants and people of color and the raceless construction of Whites in literature functioned in part to maintain Anglo-Saxon privilege in an age of anxiety and rapid change.[14]

This anxiety is certainly legible in Julia's texts. "I sing an old song," she writes in a school book preface in 1888, "when I say we are a nervous race and our children are more intensely nervous than their parents."[15] Her text is part of a broader social effort to extol nature as a tonic for rapid industrialization and demographic change. Similarly, in a work of religious fiction published in 1897 a character expresses, "it's a riddle ... a riddle, this nineteenth century life with its bad and its good, its boasting and failing. A riddle."[16] Her anxious characters often puzzle over how best to stem an increasing flow of alcoholic spirits, the exploitation of women factory workers, or the steady stream of worshippers abandoning their church pews for the lure of materialism. Other texts present earnest

Anglo-Protestants in "superior" moral and social vantage points working to spur the spiritual and social "uplift" of people of color. These paternalistic "top down" approaches to benevolence reflect the discourses of moral suasion and social reform that gripped many middle-class citizens during this century.[17]

Yet, as Vron Ware argues in her study of feminism's development within racist societies, even progressive social movements cannot escape the White supremacy that shapes their cultural context. Racist beliefs and judgments of the "worthy" and "unworthy" poor affect reformers' benevolent impulses.[18] However well-intentioned, the work of moral reformers and educators inevitably reflects the Colonialist, Imperialist and/or racist context in which it is embedded.[19] Read through this lens, Julia's educational texts and those of her contemporaries are fraught contributions to nineteenth century women's history and my own "narrative inheritance."[20]

This inheritance has possible implications for my analytic work on Julia's life and writing. In a reflective and partially autobiographical essay on Whiteness, Patterson and Rayle urge Whites to interrogate how they/we are all implicated in the history of American racism. Their essay emerged from their experiences in a doctoral session at a southern university in which an African American colleague challenged her White classmates to consider and take responsibility for their own southern ancestors' complicity in racist practices historically, in particular, American slavery. Patterson and Rayle explore their ancestors' involvement in the system of slavery that dominated southern culture and economics for centuries and thereby render visible their own connections to America's racist history. They write, "as Whites become aware of the atrocities committed by their forebears in some distant and ... nightmarish social habitus, they must begin the process of exploring and owning their personal connections to both the past and present realities of race."[21] In this view, the past "realities of race" are constitutive of our own experiences and identities in present day and the refusal to consider the possibility or actuality of our ancestors' contributions to this history is an act that displaces responsibility on to a vague Other called "racism" that remains nameless, faceless, disembodied. Theorist Donna Haraway might consider this displacement a version of a "god trick," a construction in which knowledge, action, science seems to emerge "from nowhere" rather than a situated and embodied historical subject.[22]

Approaching biographical and historical scholarship as an anti-racist act subjects The Past to the concerns of The Present, or perhaps unfairly, in Voltaire's words, "plays tricks on the dead." "Reading with sympathy," we can recognize that our foremothers and fathers were products of their time as we are of ours. Indeed, part of the biographical and historical enterprise is to explore and situate the lives under study in the context in which they lived, including in this case, the authorial shifts and racialized discourses that shaped Julia's experiences and nourished her authorial imagination. She was born and raised in an episteme in which race became a meaningful category through which to view, sort, and rank the world's inhabitants. Her conviction that America was among the "most highly civilized nations" and that "slow," "materialistic," and wicked Alaskan tribes would benefit from Protestant benevolence reflect common colonialist views in the late nineteenth century.[23] These views clearly informed her life and writing and are among many key trajectories to follow in narrating her past.

Yet, emphasizing dominant racial discourses that inevitably informed her writing and the audience needs she imagined may render invisible how she as a flesh-and-blood-being contributed to those discourses. Emphasizing discourse rather than individual acts might be read as a potentially distancing approach, a "god trick," that constructs the history of racism as something "that happened" rather than something that individual human beings did-created-perpetuated, acts which have cast long shadows into the present. Holroyd usefully reminds us that the biographical genre demands casting individuals into relief against the "remoteness of history."[24] And Julia, who lived primarily in White middle-class communities or small rural towns throughout her life, championed Whiteness and wrote into being a string of racist characters that reflect her active paternalistic and racial imaginary.

## A TURN IN A STAIRWELL

> Come ... we expect to be packed full of learning which will benefit our descendants at least to the fourth generation. Begin, Cousin Ann, time is not tarrying....[25]

A character in one of Julia's domestic manuals delivers this beckoning line in 1879, calling to a family member to join their reading discussion and thus be "packed full of learning" to benefit descendants "to the fourth generation." I began my analytic work on Julia four generations after she wrote that line and after learning of her existence through a happenstance disclosure on my mother's part.[26] While touring the Mormon leader Brigham Young's historic home in downtown Salt Lake City, my mother and I paused in a stairway alcove, waiting for the seemingly endless line of tourists in front of us to ascend the stairs. A worn brown text with gilded lettering—several inches wide on the bookshelf—caught my mother's attention. Startled, she said, "why, my ancestor wrote that book!" I remember feeling disconcerted as we stood side by side, two generations, staring through the glass-pane on an antique bookshelf, not only because I knew of no such writer in my family history but because of the rather surreal circumstances of learning this during a chance tourist excursion in the home of a patriarchal church leader and polygamist.[27] I knew a little of the Scottish cheese-makers in my family line, the narcissistic philanderer, and the cerebral soul who collected so many books his home needed special supports. I also knew of the young man who died mysteriously, tragically, leaving his family haunted with unanswered questions. Other names are etched into the family Bible, representing lives and loves that are now simply fading traces on paper. But I knew nothing of Julia; and my mother, who has little interest in romanticizing ancestry or tarrying unproductively in the past, had little more to say on the subject. The book in question turned out to be Julia's 500-something page best seller, *The Complete Home* (1879), a compendium of tips to aid White women with the staggering responsibilities of maintaining their nineteenth century households—a fitting tool, perhaps, for Brigham Young's polygamous household with over 50 children.

My thoughts have returned to that curious turn in a stairwell many times—a moment that crystallizes for me the near misses that can occur in historical work and the erratic gaps and silences that constitute any family history.[28] It has also left me with a painful and lingering picture of the unjust ways society has sifted and sorted women historically: Brigham Young's many wives huddling to consult Julia's manual from the confines of their kitchens, while Julia, thousands of miles away on a New England beach front, was writing feverishly to glorify the household so she could forge a professional identity beyond those domestic walls. Her children, so the story goes, were left to entertain themselves while whatever servants she could employ were left to mop up the breakfast crumbs. Indeed, however much Julia glorified the domestic sphere in her written work, one descendent recalled that every time Julia's "hired girl" quit, she took to her bed until another was found.[29]

As Julia continued to write from within those walls, perhaps she felt deeply the words one of her characters expressed in 1895,

> In all these questions of social life, it is the woman who has most at stake and whose voice is least heard; her opinion is ruled out of politics, even out of her church affairs, and frequently the battle is waged to rule her out of the household destinies where the fortunes of the children, whom she represents, are to be made or marred.[30]

This passage, written nearly 50 years after American women's rights activists launched the movement in Seneca Falls, seems intended to laud the work of women and protest their circumscribed economic, social, and legal status. Women's voices, Julia suggests, are those "least heard." Yet, her texts protested only the cultural silencing of White women; the African American figurations that appear nursing, farming, and fiddling in her texts often seem content with their lot. However much gender compromised Julia's legal rights and life choices, her access to the very tools through which she decried gender inequity and contributed to racist discourse—quill and ink, publishing, literacy—resulted from her class, race, and citizenship privilege. Married privilege helped as well; her husband often took responsibility for corresponding with her male publishers, perhaps so she might avoid the suggestion of impropriety sometimes associated with the act of exchanging letters with men.[31] Race and class privilege thus saturates the material form of the few artifacts that survive from any of my ancestors. Quilts stitched, songs sung, babies held, tears shed leave few material traces for the biographer's consideration.

The access to literacy and publishing these material artifacts represent provide an example of the sometimes invisible threads with which we might link The Past to The Present and the enduring legacies of privilege and racism to which Rayne and Patterson refer. The specific content of Julia's texts also casts into sharp relief her racial imaginings. The "time blurred" caricatures of people of color and ethnic minorities legible in her texts are numbingly predictable and painful to consider today: a photograph of an African American child smiling and clutching a watermelon with the caption "happy thief" written below; a grizzled Black character with a racialized dialect and expertise in opossums; Blackened and sinister Irish clergy who vie with the Protestant church for the allegiance of innocent White maidens; "uncivilized" Native Americans awaiting redemption from White missionaries; and heavily masculinized or nurturing African American female characters who serve as servants of White children. Julia's racial imaginary creates one-dimensional and formulaic characters of color and erases the subjectivity and agency of all but Anglo Protestants.[32]

## RESEARCHER/SUBJECT RELATIONSHIPS: WORKING THE GENEALOGICAL HYPHEN

> There is no thought more beautiful and far-reaching than this of the solidarity or oneness of the Family ... the individual is solitary, but God setteth the solitary in families. The stream of time is crowded with the ships of households, parents and children, youth and infancy, age with its memories.[33]

Cultural investments in bloodlines, in the "oneness of the Family," raise concrete methodological and representational issues with which biographers must grapple in the conduct of inquiry. In her notable essay, "Working the Hyphen" (1994) educational scholar Michelle Fine argues that researchers must work what she called the Self-Other hyphen in research, considering the ways various "relations between" researcher-subject limit and shape the inquiry process. Like others working within critical and interpretive paradigms, Fine refuses the conventional research stance that researchers are transparent vessels who objectively collect data from "out there" and deliver it to others without mediation or distortion. Dismissing the possibility of researcher neutrality, she argues that traditional research practices are "long on texts that inscribe some Others, preserve other Others from scrutiny, and seek to hide the researcher/writer under a veil of neutrality or objectivity."[34] She suggests that however researchers and subjects are linked, considering their attachments in the research enterprise is an important aspect of qualitative work.

Indeed, interrogating such attachments might be particularly important in biography given some scholars' conviction that bonds between a biographer and his/her subject—however partial, however constructed—are useful, if not imperative, aspects of biographical labor. Identification with A Subject, either still living or long departed, may inspire the biographer, personalize inquiry, and thicken the rendering of a human life in substantial and perhaps irreplaceable ways.[35] One feminist biographer's reflections offer a glimpse of the inspirational potential of this connection: "Emily has always been with me, invading my research and pulling at my heartstrings. I finally gave into her last year and agreed to research and write her story."[36] Similarly, for Blanche Wiesen Cook, "personal involvement [with the subject] is central ... if it fails to emerge in the course of research, I change subjects."[37] She converses with her subjects, disagrees with them, and dreams about them, and such interactions facilitate her ability to narrate their lives with sensitivity and depth.

Such identification may particularly inspire a researcher recording for posterity the life of a related individual. Bloodlines are deeply romanticized in culture, in American law, in family lore—indeed, the countless hours descendents spend sifting through attic trunks, dusty archives, and faded microfilm for traces of the past indicate their relevance for many in making sense of self, family, and heritage. The researcher's "relationship" with his/her ancestral subject may become threaded with family lore, shame and pride, the trope of bloodlines, and significantly, the identity work of the researcher. As Foucault suggests in his essay, "What is an Author?" "...I believe that it is better to try to understand that someone who is a writer is not simply doing his work in his books ... but that his major work is, in the end, *himself* in the process of writing his books."[38] Many biographers agree. Alpern suggests feminist biographical initiatives inspire deep "attachment" and "identification" with the Subject because "any biography uneasily shelters an autobiography within it." Read through these lenses, biographers "writing" their relatives may, in part, be "writing" themselves.[39]

But what do the biographers yearning for such affinity as a springboard for their research do when their subjects embody more troubling aspects of humanity, however they might define it—war criminals, war deserters, terrorists, slave owners, convicted sex offenders? Might one be more willing to explore the contributions of and develop biographical affinity for a Kennedy, an Albert Einstein, or a Martin Luther King? Are family connections with some notoriety more comfortable to admit and appealing to explore, however fraught personally—the Mommie Dearests, the Elvises, the J.D. Salingers—than those which link our bloodlines too closely with human beings who have committed deplorable acts against humanity? Cook affirms that identifying with her subject is imperative for her work: "most biographers choose to write about people they care about and can identify with."[40] These questions remind me of an acquaintance's quest to trace his family lineage in Oklahoma that ended abruptly, after discovering his ancestor had served a life sentence for murder. The association so troubled him that he refused to explore his lineage further, wary of what else he might discover, wary of what other secrets might lurk in his family history, and what the crimes of The Past might mean for his own sense of identity in The Present.

Such abruptly truncated searches speak to the power of family lineage and bloodlines in culture, discourse, and identity. They speak to the ways we all may choose to look away from some ancestors and toward, for example, the Civil War heroes or the industrious settlers that risked life and limb to help forge our nation. They speak to the ways constructions of The Present and The Past can inform each other. And also, significantly, they speak to the ways silences, inherent selectivity in family attachment, and the erratic nature of ancestral knowledge to begin with—what if I had taken that turn in Brigham Young's hallway more quickly?—fundamentally shape the biographical and historical enterprise.

Another aspect of the genealogical hyphen that merits consideration is the potential for family connections to enrich and complicate qualitative work. From a pragmatic perspective, relatives may have access to letters, photographs, and other biographical traces unavailable to those outside the family circle. Margaret Salinger relied on the confidences of her aunt and mother to write about her reclusive novelist father, J.D., as well as a crucial directive he offered years before: "the biographical facts you want are in my stories, in one form or another."[41] Although anyone could shuffle the pages of a Salinger novel searching for revealing biographical gems, only intimates might recognize the significance of a turn of phrase or a fleeting event for the man behind the novel. Similarly, outsiders to

Maori culture would be hard pressed to entice Maori women to tell their tales as some would entrust their stories only to daughters and granddaughters.[42] Shared epistemologies, cultural allegiances, as well as the ethnocentric history of Western anthropology may account in part for such protective impulses, but many recognize that family members, partners, and spouses might have unique access to anecdotes and experiences essential for crafting a full sense of the subject.

Cultural investments in bloodlines raise challenging methodological issues for researchers. In the case of biographers crafting narratives on foremothers/fathers, researchers and interviewees intrigued with ancestral linkages might easily slip into glorifying their subjects' accomplishments at the expense of critical questions. Or, others relying on interviews with family members as a data source might find themselves treading carefully in their representational choices so as not to offend the very informants that make the biographical enterprise possible. I have heard scholars relate varied struggles concerning which family secrets to include in their work (the affairs, the legal tussles, the alcoholism?), how to negotiate such decisions with family members, and, in the end, how to bear the ethical dilemma of championing particular aspects of a life and remaining silent on others that present the subject in a richer, more human, and yet, less favorable light. Researchers in such circumstances might yearn for bloodlines to carry far less symbolic weight.

Among the angles of the genealogical hyphen to consider is that focusing too heavily on contours of the researcher-subject relationships might interfere with the research enterprise. As additional theoretical frameworks "emerge to ... situate" biographical subjects, thinking beyond preconceived ideas about researchers' investments might serve biographical labor.[43] Indeed, scholars invested in narrating the lives of Others have cautioned that the trend toward researcher reflexivity in the "post-experimental" moment has at times tipped the balance between what feminist historian Marjorie Theobald calls "the imperative of the authorial voice" and the need to "empower the [historical] subject."[44] Researchers, busy wrestling with methodological dilemmas and reflecting on their research investments may overshadow, in the case of biographical work, the humanist subject that inspired their quest to begin with and leave that subject to fade back into the dust of history waiting to catch another researcher's eye. As Theobald's comments suggest, such wrestling might interrupt the biographical enterprise of narrating lives. And there are many lives to narrate.

Historians Kathleen Weiler and Sue Middleton also caution researchers of the dangers of considering too vigorously the ways they are "implicated in the choice of what is represented" in that the researcher may "write more about herself than she does about that outside of herself which she is trying to know."[45] Similarly, feminist methodologist Patti Lather reminds us in her criticism of anthropologist Ruth Behar's intensely reflexive scholarship, a fine—but crucial—line exists between acknowledging the inevitable presence of The Self in the work and shifting undue attention from The Work (however conceived) to The Self.[46] These remarks indicate the delicate balance researchers must strike between theorizing their investments and the potential erasure of the subject or the clear hyphen between researcher-subject such reflexivity might inspire. The relevance of such theorizing does not mean researcher or subject merit equal, similar, or unilateral attention at the onset of research. Theoretical investments and project purpose shape the conduct and representation of research.

## INVESTMENTS AND IMAGINARIES

> Shame to you, to turn against your own kith[!] [47]

In this line from a temperance tract published in 1879, a middle-aged domestic expresses outrage when she learns the uncle of a recently orphaned child refuses to support his own kith and kin. "Shame on ye!" she cries to the man who dislikes children, refuses to care for the child, and resents the child's father for dying in the first place. Julia's stories are full of such betrayals: drunken fathers who abandon their families, Protestants who join the Catholic Church, men and women who turn away from their "kith" to pursue their own interests. What might be considered a productive betrayal in my own analytical work is that Julia as an ancestral essence, living more than a century ago among a bevy of other ancestors, holds little interest for me. Even as I work slowly to reconstruct her life, even as I feel gratitude to have remnants of her writing labor, I subject "her" to my own interests and preoccupations. I have always seen her texts as productive analytic sites for exploring a number of methodological and historical trajectories: forms of American racism, shifts in women's lives in the nineteenth century, the emergence of female authorship, the complexities of female subjectivity, the possibilities of feminist biography, the discursive construction of gendered Whiteness through the racializing of textual Others, and the boundaries of contemporary methodological imperatives.

In a moment of fancy, I might imagine a connection to the flesh-and-blood being who was Julia when she writes to women readers in 1879,

> Take the trouble to compare, to criticize, to generalize, feel when you are reading anything *that you are your own steward*, and that you will call yourself

> to account some day for these precious things that you are putting to trust.[48]

I love this line, this call to women to read actively, passionately, to become agents in their intellectual lives. I can easily pluck these words from their nineteenth century context and use them to serve my twenty-first century projects, to claim a kind of license to be my own steward through the pages of her work, to interpret it as I may, even if such stewardship tramples on her original intent. I am equally intrigued when I stumble across descriptions of Julia charging down nature paths on a beautiful spring day with "butterflies swimming in the air." When I read such lines I hope that any woman might experience this pleasure in nature, this mobility, this freedom to pursue that which enlivens her mind. Such images inspire for me the questions Rose believes the work of life history is intended to inspire in readers: "have I lived that way? Do I want to live that way? Could I make myself live that way if I wanted to?"[49]

Where this fleeting and constructed affinity falters for me, and one of many reasons I argue that we must critically analyze the contours of researcher-subject relationships to determine which aspects are and are not significant for our research purposes, is in, for example, Julia's venomous constructions of Irish Catholic priests or her paternalistic and racialized caricatures of people of color. For instance, in the final text Julia published (1902), she creates a Black female character named Fiddlin' Jim who is "the most saucy, lazy, untidy, no account darkey alive."[50] Jim plays a fiddle, lives in squalor, and wears garish clothes more fitting for a minstrel show than a lady's parlor. A Protestant-owned press published this text to promote benevolence toward social unfortunates who reformers might have deemed at first glance as beyond redemption. Accordingly, the story depicts an articulate, respectable White woman sweeping into Jim's life with petticoats swirling and Bible in hand to transform the saucy, fiddle-playing ne'er do well into a tidy, religious and industrious soul. There is little in this tale to glorify here.

Equally troubling are the Black hired hands and immigrants that appear in the texts simply to advance plotlines. For example, in the lesson introduced earlier featuring the character of the Black nurse, the nurse bears the White child's attempt to scrub her skin clean of its color and insists, "god made my soul White and I'm trying to keep it so."[51] Utilizing the enduring tropes of Whiteness and Blackness to symbolize purity and evil, Julia mobilizes a character who tolerates scrubbing and prodding to serve the spiritual education of a young White boy. And Julia seemed to hold high hopes for the socializing power of such educational texts. As a character in a domestic manual expresses, "And we shall find when all the years are told, that nothing has so moulded and fashioned our inner lives—so made us what in the end we shall be—as reading"[52] These sobering textual constructions are part of women's history, part of my history.

Leon Edel reminds us of the need to remain vigilant to which investments and imaginaries drive our biographical choices. He writes, "in a world full of subjects—centuries crowded with notables and dunces—we may ask why a modern biographer fixes his attention on certain faces and turns his back on others."[53] Families are comprised of any number of notables and dunces upon which to focus. Considering this point in relation to my ongoing work on this ancestor's writing, one might argue that my "relationship" to this author would unquestionably influence how I interpret her work—my project, in fact, being a form of "homework" in Elizabeth St. Pierre's sense of the term: studying something potentially significant for the researcher, such as a hometown or a group to which he/she belongs.[54] If interpreting a text is a "dialectical process resulting from the interface of the variable interpretive resources people bring to bear on the text"[55] my own position as descendent of this educator (as woman) stands to be an interpretive resource influential for my approach to and analysis of her life and writing (as extensions of that woman).

These reflections bring me to a key aspect of working the genealogical hyphen: I want to speak against a discourse that romanticizes too readily the messy cultural and psychological investments in ancestry. Although organizations such as the Daughters of the American Revolution are founded on cross-generational devotion and genealogical research is a deeply meaningful enterprise for many, it is important to remember that these "discourses of affiliation"[56] are constructed affiliations, constructed investments, constructed ways of making sense of Self and Other. They are fraught, selective, partial, and riddled with cultural beliefs about identity, lineage, and what constitutes a valuable life. Like approaching a research enterprise with the conviction that sexuality, race, class, sex (or any number of other analytics) have equal significance for varied inquiry projects, the assumption that "ancestry matters" mobilizes too liberally at the outset the significance of an element that can only be determined through considering the specific research purpose. Fine reminds us that working these messy details and nuances of the hyphen is the key to exploring and understanding our own investments.

The idea that this writer as an ancestral essence matters more to me than my methodological interests, my feminism, or any number of other personal and professional allegiances constructs a romanticized vision of bloodlines that seems forced at best across 100 years, multiple generations, and the specific purposes of my research. Working the genealogical hyphen through Patterson and Rayle's reflections on ancestral racism produces different analytical possibilities than Theobald, Weiler, and Middleton's reminder that researchers' reflections sometimes obscure the subjects they seek to explore. As I continue to slowly sketch a portrait of Julia, consider her work, and seek ways to understand the struggles of nineteenth century female educators within their historical context, I also continue to work the hyphen differently.

My broader methodological contention is that researchers must consider the particular implications of research projects with, on, or for ancestors and family members so they can make analytical and representational choices that fit their project purpose and personal investments. And they must do so with the awareness that broader cultural investments in "family oneness" can shape their choices of subject, the tales they choose to tell, how they choose to tell them, and how audiences interpret them. The biographical genre welcomes subjects cast in a romantic glow. Readers and authors are often intrigued with heroic narratives of great lives, origin stories, and family connections. Yet, our connections to the past are constructed, complex, and fraught with darkness as well as light, and these complexities merit exploration and representation, and at times, betrayals. I do not know how Julia would interpret the "tricks" I have played on her—the critical questions I have asked about family connections, her work, or her life. Yet, Alice Wexler's struggle to represent Emma Goldman in all her complexity—in her case, to criticize a heroic figure—underscores my conviction that necessary tales are not always romantic ones.[57]

## NOTES

1. Julia Wright, *The Complete Home* (Philadelphia: J.C. McCurdy and Co, 1879), 211.
2. See, for example, Blanche Weisen Cook, "The Issue of Subject: A Critical Connection" and Lynda Anderson Smith, "The Biographer's Relationship with Her Subject" in *Writing Educational Biography: Explorations in Qualitative Research,* ed. Craig Kridel. (New York: Garland Publishing, 1998); Michael Holroyd, *Works on Paper: The Craft of Biography and Autobiography* (Washington, D.C.: Counterpoint, 2002).
3. Michelle Fine, "Working the Hyphen: Reinventing Self and Other in Qualitative Research." In *The Handbook of Qualitative Research*, eds. N. K. Denzin & Y. S. Lincoln, (Thousand Oaks, CA: Sage, 2004), 77–82.
4. Jean A. Patterson and Joseph M. Rayle, "De-Centering Whiteness: Personal Narratives of Race," in *Postcritical Ethnography: Reinscribing Critique,* eds. G. Noblit, S. Flores, and E. Murillo, (Creskill, New Jersey: Hampton Press, 2004).
5. See Lucy E. Bailey, "The Absent Presence of Whiteness," Unpublished Doctoral Dissertation (Ohio State University, 2002) for initial methodolog-

ical reflections on the issue of ancestral connections between researcher and subject, including my concern that cultural romanticizing of bloodlines and genealogy may—at the expense of the analytical project—preoccupy readers and researchers intrigued with such links. I suggest the importance of considering when and under what circumstances imagined connections between researcher and subject potentially interrupt analytic work and run counter to project purpose. At times, resisting the romanticizing of bloodlines and engaging in what I call a "genealogical refusal" that focuses on project rather than researcher-subject "relationship," may be a methodological necessity.

6. As Marjory Wolf argues, analytic approaches produce different interpretations, and I have interpreted Julia's work differently elsewhere. See *A Thrice Told Tale: Feminism, Postmodernism, and Ethnographic Responsibility* (Stanford: Stanford University Press, 1992).
7. Michael Quinn Patton, *Qualitative Research and Evaluation Methods, Third Edition* (Thousand Oaks: Sage Publications, 2002).
8. Wright, *The Temperance Second Reader for Families and Schools* (New York: National Temperance Society and Publication House, 1883), 53.
9. I draw examples from her texts to serve methodological reflections on the biographical project; for detailed racial analysis, see Bailey, "Absent Presence," and "Wright-ing White: The Construction of Race in Women's nineteenth Century Didactic Texts," *Journal of Thought* 41.4 (2006): 65–81; I draw ideas and language from these documents throughout this essay.
10. For information on nineteenth century women writers and their varied work see Nina Baym, *American Women Writers and the Work of History,* 1790–1860 (New Brunswick, N.J, 1995), *Woman's Fiction: A Guide to Novels by and About Women in America, 1820–1870* (Ithaca: Cornell UP, 1993 [1978]) and Susan Coultrap-McQuin, *Doing Literary Business* (North Carolina: Chapel Hill, 1990); For information on this author, see Bailey, "'A Plain Woman's Story,'" Unpublished Master's Thesis (Ohio State University, 1997). I use Julia's first name because it personalizes racism and conveys familiarity as a biographical subject.
11. I use the term "White" and "Anglo-Saxon" interchangeably here, recognizing their socially constructed, fluctuating meanings and reflecting Toni Morrison's critique of the absent presence of Whiteness in canonical literature. See *Playing in the Dark: Whiteness and the Literary Imagination* (New York: Vintage Press, 1992).
12. For a history of nineteenth century women's literary societies, see Theodora Penny Martin, *The Sound of our Own Voices* (Beacon Press, 1989).
13. See Donnarae MacCann, *White Supremacy in Children's Literature: Characterizations of African Americans,* 1830–1900 (New York: Garland Publishing, 1998).
14. See MacCann, *White Supremacy,* and Morrison, *Playing in the Dark.*
15. Wright, *Sea Side and the Way Side, Book Three* (Boston: D.C. Heath and Company, 1888).
16. Wright, *The Cardiff Estate* (New York: American Tract Society, 1897), 347.

17. Helen Damon-Moore, "The History of Women and Service in the United States: A Rich and Complex Heritage," in *The Practice of Change: Concepts and Models for Service-Learning in Women's Studies*, B. J. Balliet and K. Hefferman, eds. (Washington D.C.: American association for Higher Education, 2000), esp. 48–49.
18. Damon-Moore, "The History of Women and Service," 48–49.
19. Vron Ware, *Beyond the Pale: White Women, Racism and History* (London: Verso, 1992), esp. 119.
20. According to H. L. Goodall, narrative inheritance "refers to stories given to children by and about family members." See, "Narrative Inheritance: A Nuclear Family with Toxic Secrets," *Qualitative Inquiry* 11.4 (2005): 492–513.
21. Patterson and Rayle, "De-Centering Whiteness," 249.
22. Donna Haraway, *Simians, Cyborgs and Women: The Reinvention of Nature* (New York: Routledge, 1991), 188 and 191.
23. Wright, *Among the Alaskans* (Philadelphia: Presbyterian Board of Publication, 1883), 19–35.
24. Michael Holroyd, *Works on Paper: the Craft of Biography and Autobiography* (Washington, D.C.: Counterpoint, 2002).
25. Wright, *Complete Home*, 130.
26. This section is developed from initial reflections on that turn in Bailey, 2002.
27. Brigham Young was a key early leader in the Church of Jesus Christ of Latter Day Saints who helped settle the Salt Lake Valley during the nineteenth century. Polygamy was a normative practice in the church's early years but the contemporary LDS Church forbids it.
28. See Goodall, "Narrative Inheritance," for more on gaps and silences.
29. The texts in the bookcase were likely props selected during restoration. The "narrative inheritance" is a construction that emerges from family papers and mythology.
30. Wright, *Priest and Nun*, 1895.
31. See Susan Coultrap-McQuin, *Doing Literary Business* (Chapel Hill: University of North Carolina Press, 1990); for a discussion of women authors' efforts to navigate gendered social propriety with the demands of doing business; See Sally L. Kitch, *This Strange Society of Women: Reading the Letters and Lives of the Woman's Commonwealth*, (Columbus: Ohio State Press, 1993), for a discussion of the letter as a gendered literary form laden with symbolism.
32. Grace Elizabeth Hale uses "time blurred" in *Making Whiteness: The Culture of Segregation in the South, 1890–1940* (New York: Pantheon, 1998); Bailey, "Wright-ing White," 2006.
33. Wright, *The Complete Home*, 4.
34. Fine, "Working the Hyphen," 73.
35. See Louis Smith, "The Biographer's Relationship with Her Subject" and Linda C. Wagner-Martin, "The Issue of Gender," in *Writing Educational Biography: Explorations in Qualitative Research*, ed. C. Kridel (New York: Garland Publishing, 1998).

36. K. R. Mehaffey, "They Called her Captain: The Amazing Life of Emily Virginia Mason," *The Journal of Women's Civil War History* 2 (2001): 74–85.
37. Cook, "The Issue of Subject," 81.
38. Quoted in David Schaafsma, "Performing the Self: Constructing Written and Curricular Fictions," In *Foucault's Challenge: Discourse, Knowledge and Power in Education*, ed. T. Popkewitz (New York: Columbia University Press, 1998), 255–277.
39. Sara Alpern, Joyce Antler, Elisabeth Israels Perry and Ingrid Winther Scobie, *The Challenge of Feminist Biography: Writing the Lives of Modern American Women* (Urbana: University of Illinois Press, 1998), 10–11.
40. Cook, "The Issue of Subject," 80.
41. Margaret Salinger, *Dream Catcher: A Memoir* (Washington Square Press, 2000), xiii.
42. Linda Tuhiwai-Smith, "Connecting Pieces: Finding the Indigenous Presence in the History of Women's Education," In *Telling Women's Lives: Narrative Inquiries in the History of Women's Education*, eds. K. Weiler and S. Middleton (Buckingham: Open University Press, 1999), 64; also see Tuhiwai-Smith, *Decolonizing Methodologies: Research and Indigenous Peoples*, (London: Zed Books, 1999).
43. Alice Wexler, "Emma Goldman and the Anxiety of Biography," in *The Challenge of Feminist Biography: Writing the Lives of Modern American Women*, eds. S. Alpern, J. Antler, E. Israels Perry, and I. Winther Scobie (Urbana: University of Illinois Press, 1992), 47.
44. Marjorie Theobald, "Teachers, Memory and Oral History," In *Telling Women's Lives*, 15.
45. Weiler and Middleton, *Telling Women's Lives*, 3. Similarly, Craig Kridel expresses frustration with qualitative researchers' "endless" methodological discussions even as he advocates for greater attention to method in the field of educational biography. See "Biographical Meanderings: Reflections and Reminiscences on *Writing Educational Biography*," *Vitae Scholasticae* (2008): 5–16.
46. Patti Lather, "A Response to Doug Foley," (Unpublished Manuscript, 1997), 1.
47. Wright, *Firebrands*, 11.
48. Wright, *Complete Home*, 212.
49. Phyllis Rose, *Parallel Lives* (New York: Knopf, 1984), 5.
50. Wright, "Fiddlin' Jim" *Stories in Hearts*, (New York: American Tract Society, 1902), 134.
51. Wright, *Second Reader*, 53.
52. Wright, *Complete Home*, 199.
53. Leon Edel, *Writing Lives: Principia Biographica* (New York: Norton, 1984), 60.
54. Elizabeth St. Pierre and Wanda Pillow, Eds. *Working the Ruins: Feminist Poststructural Theory and Methods in Education*, (New York: Routledge, 2000); Bailey, 2002.

55. Norman Fairclough, "The Technologisation of Discourse." In *Texts and Practices: Readings in Critical Discourse Analysis*, eds. Carmen Rosa Caldas-Coulthard and Malcolm Coulthard (New York: Routledge, 1996), 71–84.
56. Shawn Michelle Smith discusses the historical exclusion of African Americans from the Daughters of the American Revolution, see *American Archives: Gender, Race, Class in Visual Culture* (New Jersey: Princeton University Press, 1999); for "discourses of affiliation," see Jo Anne Pagano, *Exiles and Communities: Teaching in the Patriarchal Wilderness*. (Albany, NY: State University of New York Press, 1990), 11.
57. Wexler, "Emma Goldman," 48.

# ABOUT THE EDITORS/AUTHORS

## ABOUT THE EDITORS

**Linda C. Morice** is an associate professor in the Department of Educational Leadership at Southern Illinois University Edwardsville. She is the editor of *Vitae Scholasticae: The Journal of Educational Biography.* Her research focuses on the history of educational leadership.

**Laurel Puchner** is a professor in the Department of Educational Leadership at Southern Illinois University Edwardsville. She is assistant editor of *Vitae Scholasticae: The Journal of Educational Biography.* Her research focuses on teacher education for social justice.

## ABOUT THE AUTHORS

**A. J. Angulo,** EdD, is the Elizabeth Singleton Endowed Professor of Social Foundations at Winthrop University in Rock Hill, SC.

**Lucy E. Bailey**, PhD, is an associate professor of social foundations and the director of Gender and Women's Studies at Oklahoma State University in Stillwater, OK.

**Carol B. Conaway**, PhD, is an associate professor of women's studies and affiliate associate professor of communication at the University of New Hampshire in Durham, NH.

**Bart Dredge**, PhD, is a professor and chair of the Sociology and Anthropology Department at Austin College in Sherman, TX.

**Edward A. Janak**, PhD, is an associate professor in the Department of Educational Studies at the University of Wyoming in Laramie, WY.

**Von Pittman**, PhD, is the retired director of the Center for Distance and Independent Study at the University of Missouri in Columbia, MO.

**Bruce Romanish,** EdD, is a professor emeritus in the College of Education at Washington State University in Vancouver, WA.

**Jared R. Stallones**, PhD, is a professor of education and coordinator of the Secondary Teaching Credential Program at California State University, Long Beach, CA.

**Cayce Tabor**, BA, is a student at Texas A&M University School of Law in Fort Worth, TX.

**Lynne Trethewey**, PhD, is a former adjunct senior research fellow in the School of Education, University of South Australia, Magill Campus.

**John F. Wakefield**, PhD, is a professor of education at the University of North Alabama at Florence, AL.

**Andrea Walton**, PhD, is an associate professor of education at Indiana University in Bloomington, IN.

**Kay Whitehead**, PhD, is a professor and deputy dean in the School of Education at Flinders University in Adelaide, South Australia.

CPSIA information can be obtained at www.ICGtesting.com
Printed in the USA
LVOW10s0126110214

373116LV00004B/54/P

9 781623 964900